I was signed by manager Walter Galbraith who I feel was never given due credit for bringing several great players to the club such as Willie Hamilton, John Parke and Pat Quinn, and in giving many promising youngsters their chance. I knew I was joining a big side although they had slipped somewhat in recent years, but the arrival of Jock Stein changed things. Stein was a fantastic manager with great presence, and the big disappointment was that we failed to win either the Scottish Cup or the League as the side was certainly good enough. Under Stein the crowds started to return in numbers, one cup game against Rangers attracting over 44,000. These were great days at Easter Road, with a great atmosphere and more importantly, some great players.
NEIL MARTIN

It was not only a pleasure but a privilege to play alongside so many great players at Easter Road during the '60s and '70s. People talk about the Turnbull's Tornadoes but to my mind the team of the mid-'60s was every bit as good. I was fortunate to have played under several very good managers who all improved my game, but it was made much easier by playing alongside players of the calibre of Willie Hamilton, Alex Edwards and John Brownlie to name but a few. PAT STANTON

To play for Hibs during the time of the Turnbull's Tornadoes was a truly fantastic experience. As a Hibs supporter it was a joy to line up alongside so many great players. I made my debut a short while before Eddie Turnbull joined the club in 1971, but he made me a player, and I owe everything I achieved in the game to him. ALEX CROPLEY

I enjoyed playing for Hibs in the 1970s under a fantastic coach in Eddie Turnbull. The style of football the team played was incredible – fast free flowing attacking football admired by all, and I am extremely proud to have played behind such a good team. JIM MCARTHUR

Hibernian
From Joe Baker to Turnbull's Tornadoes

TOM WRIGHT

Luath Press Limited

EDINBURGH

www.luath.co.uk

First published 2011

ISBN: 978-1-908373-09-0

The paper used in this book is sourced from renewable forestry and is FSC credited material.

The author's right to be identified as authors of this book under the Copyright, Designs and Patents Act 1988 has been asserted.

Printed and bound in the UK by MPG Books Ltd, Cornwall

Typeset in 10.5 point Sabon

To my wife Liz and my daughters Caroline and Alison

Contents

Acknowledgements

I have my good friend Phil Thomson to thank for his constant support and encouragement in making this book possible. Thanks must also go to the staff at the National Library of Scotland in Edinburgh for their endless patience and assistance, to John Fraser and Pat Stanton for their help, and also to Alex Cropley, Neil Martin and Jim McArthur. My main sources have been the *Edinburgh Evening News*, *The Scotsman*, the *Sunday Mail*, the *Daily Record* and the *Evening Times*. Also *The Scottish Football Book*, *100 Years of Hibs* (Thomson & Docherty), *The Hibees*, and *Hibernian: The Complete Story*, both by John MacKay, Hibernian FC official programmes 1960–80 and many other publications far too numerous to mention. Most of the images in this book are from my own personal collection. I am indebted to the family of the late Peter Carruthers for the use of several of his photographs. Where necessary, every effort has made to locate image copyright holders.

Foreword by Pat Stanton

Watching Hibs as a young boy was a great thrill, never dreaming that one day I would go on to play for the club.

Looking back through the different eras, the deeds of the Famous Five need no elaboration, although as Lawrie Reilly keeps reminding me, that side also had defenders, but some people tend to forget the great Hibs team of the 1960s and the fantastic players such as Willie Hamilton, Neil Martin, Eric Stevenson and Peter Cormack, to name but a few.

I was immensely proud not only to play for, but to captain the great Hibs side of the early '70s, but without doubt it was a great privilege to play for the club during both periods.

Although scores might sometimes be forgotten, many individual incidents remain firmly imprinted on my mind. I can still vividly remember standing on the terracing watching Bobby Kinloch score the famous penalty against Barcelona in 1961. Again, there is the magnificent strike by Bobby Duncan that started the ball rolling in the fantastic victory against Napoli in 1967. Yet another incident that remains clearly in mind is a goal scored by Ally MacLeod in the mid-'70s. Collecting the ball near the halfway line, Ally proceeded to beat several defenders before passing the ball past the goalkeeper and into the net. The goal itself looked quite straightforward, but it was the confidence and technical ability of an exceptional player that made it so special.

The '60s and '70s hold many special memories for me, and this book allows all of us, whether old or young, to share them.

Pat Stanton
Hibernian and Scotland

Introduction

THE GOLDEN POST-WAR YEARS of the late '40s and early '50s were perhaps the finest period of the Scottish game. During that time Hibernian burst to the fore displaying a brand of football that thrilled supporters throughout the land. Fronted by the incomparable Famous Five forward line of Smith, Johnstone, Reilly, Turnbull and Ormond, then widely recognised as the best forward line ever produced by a Scottish side, Hibs won three League Championships inside a five-year period. The team was therefore the most successful side in the long and distinguished history of the club. During the war years the general public had been starved of football and the post-war clamour for the game saw matches being watched by record-breaking crowds. There was no greater excitement to be found at a football ground than at Easter Road.

As other Scottish clubs at this time made summer tours to the Highlands or England, Hibs elected to make regular trips to European countries where they usually faced first-class sides. It was the reputation earned on the continent during this time that saw Hibs invited into the inaugural European Cup in 1955. By then, however, although they reached the semi-final, it was obvious that the great side was past its best. Bobby Johnstone had joined Manchester City earlier in the year and soon the legendary centre forward Lawrie Reilly would retire because of injury. Later Smith joined Hearts and Turnbull retired as a player to take over as trainer, leaving Ormond as the last remaining on-field member of the magical quintet.

Reilly's loss was made easier to accept by the emergence of the dynamic Joe Baker, who burst onto the scene with spectacular impact in 1957. At that time, however, Hearts had taken over the mantle not only as the top side in the city, but the entire country. The arrival of the energetic Baker would give Hibs supporters initial optimism that the great days would soon return to Easter Road. But except for a few isolated highs such as the 4-3 Scottish Cup victory against Hearts in 1958, the record-breaking 11-1 victory over Airdrie the following year and a famous Fairs Cup success against Barcelona, the following few seasons would be barren.

By then the huge post-war crowds were no more than a memory. The Hibs support, who had grown accustomed to success, had come to accept that the earlier high standards set by the side were no longer achievable. Although they were not to know it at the time, better days lay not too far ahead.

The start of the 1960s heralded not only the end of an era at Easter Road, the most successful in the club's 86-year history, but the promise of a new dawn for the game. A wind of change was sweeping through the sport. The archaic retain-and-transfer system that could – and often did – tie a player to the tenure of a club for as long as it desired, would soon be abolished, but it would take a bitter court case between the Newcastle United player George Eastham and the club to finally resolve the matter.

England Under-23 international Eastham had been in dispute with Newcastle for sometime and was keen on a move to Arsenal, who were eager to secure his services at Highbury. Newcastle United had no desire to lose a player of Eastham's capabilities, and this proved the major stumbling block. After a lengthy and acrimonious dispute, Newcastle United eventually succumbed and Eastham joined Arsenal for a reported £47,500 fee. Even then the player refused to let the matter rest. Citing a restriction of trade, the matter was referred to a court of law. Ultimately, in 1963 the decision of the court would decide in favour of the player, and the retain-and-transfer system crumbled to be replaced by the much fairer option-clause contract, which worked more in the interest of the players.

The maximum wage agreement, long a source of great contention in England, was found to be illegal and after a threatened strike by the players, it too was abolished at the start of the '60s, allowing Johnny Haynes of Fulham to become the first £100-a-week footballer. With very few exceptions, particularly during wartime, a maximum wage restriction had never been in force in Scotland, only a minimum, but top wages had usually been on par with what could be earned south of the Border. The abolition of the maximum wage in England would do Scottish clubs no favours. The greatly improved English wage structure threatened the stability of football in Scotland. Top earners in England could expect to be paid between £25 and £100 per week, compared to around £20 paid to top performers in Scotland, making the temptation of a move south extremely attractive for many of Scotland's better players.

Despite initial reluctance in some quarters, games under floodlight had become an almost universally accepted practice and with the growth of competitive European competition, everyone had woken up to the potential big money that could be made from the game.

The perceived threat from the television cameras refused to go away. During an end-of-season meeting in England, league clubs voted overwhelmingly against live televised football the following season, except for the Cup Final, international matches and European games, and only if the latter took place in midweek. However, those with a vested interest in televising live football would not be diverted from their aims, and although the change would occur slowly, it would certainly come about.

North of the Border, attempts were made to bring the game out of the shadows of the dark ages. During the summer of 1961 the football authorities had recommended new contract terms and conditions. It was suggested that from the start of the coming season, players would not be allowed to demand a transfer within the tenure of their yearly agreement, but only at the end of each season, so hopefully avoiding situations such as the long-running Joe Baker saga of the previous campaign and the disruption caused to the

Easter Road side during that time. Transfers would still be allowed during the season, but only if agreed by the selling and the buying club. Contracts that had previously expired at the end of July would now terminate on 30 June. More importantly, players who had been placed on the open-to-transfer list would now have to be paid, as opposed to the previous system that allowed clubs to terminate a player's wages the moment he asked to be placed on the list. It was also recommended that players should receive a larger slice of any transfer fee in a move authorised by the club. Clubs were to benefit by the abolition of the league levy on gate receipts. Only some of those recommendations were implemented, but at least it was a step in the right direction. This then was the situation facing Hibernian at the start of the decade.

The club's serious decline brought it to the brink of relegation in 1963, but in fact it was on the threshold of a truly defining period, when an exciting mixture of younger players would emerge from the shadows. They, along with several inspirational signings and an ambitious and innovative young manager, Jock Stein, saw Hibernian again challenging for honours, only missing out on the coveted league and cup double in the final weeks of the 1964–65 season.

The early '70s saw the emergence of yet another great side, possibly the club's greatest ever squad. Under the leadership of the former Famous Five legend Eddie Turnbull, Hibs would win the League Cup, two Drybrough Cups and also record a historic victory over near neighbours Hearts at Tynecastle on New Year's Day 1973. The following few seasons would be more than satisfactory, including yet another League Cup Final in 1974, before a slow and painful slide to relegation in 1980.

Hibernian: From Joe Baker to Turnbull's Tornadoes is the first book to examine this crucial period in such detail. From Joe Baker's transfer to Arsenal in 1961 to Eddie Turnbull's resignation in 1980 it is all here – the great players, the magnificent games (both European and domestic), the financial disputes, the transfers, all the important and sometimes the less important but no less interesting off-field happenings, and much more.

Because of Hibs' reputation on the continent I have covered all of the European games in detail (see page 19 for the pages on which these descriptions commence) and I have listed only the Hibs line-up except when they were playing against English sides. Unfortunately, I have experienced great difficulty in tracing a definitive list of substitutes for many of these matches. For Cup Finals I have included the team line-up for both teams. Appendix 1 lists, as far as possible, every player's first-team debut (my apologies for any I may have missed) and also the arrivals and departures of Hibs managers, 1961–80. With so many individual players appearing in match after match, I have opted not to include an unwieldy index and hope that any reader seeking details of particular seasons, players or landmark matches will find the chronological order and highlighted games to be adequate pointers.

The period covered in this book was one when players played for the jersey;

games usually took place on a Saturday afternoon; match-day hospitality consisted of a cold pie and a cup of lukewarm Bovril; an agent was someone who collected your pools coupon; and European football was a bonus rather than an obsession. I really wonder if the game is any better today.

Tom Wright
October 2011

Hibernian FC Timeline 1961–1980

1961 Joe Baker transferred to Torino, Johnny McLeod to Arsenal.

Willie Ormond joins Falkirk.

Manager Hugh Shaw resigns and is replaced by Walter Galbraith.

1963 Hibs narrowly avoid relegation with victory against Raith Rovers at Kirkcaldy on final day of the season.

1964 Jock Stein becomes manager at Easter Road.

Hibs win the Summer Cup, beating Aberdeen after a third game play-off. The final game is postponed until the following season after an outbreak of typhoid in the Grampian city.

Chairman Harry Swan plans to expand the Easter Road Stadium to accommodate the Commonwealth Games.

Famous 2-0 victory over Real Madrid in friendly match at Easter Road.

1965 Bob Shankly replaces Jock Stein as manager.

Record home win against Hamilton.

1966 Covered enclosure behind the Albion Road End opens on 1 January 1966.

1967 Italian side Napoli, including the great Dino Zoff, are beaten 5-0 at Easter Road in the second leg of the Fairs Cup.

Hibs lose 4-1 in the first leg in Naples making the return game a mere formality... or so they think.

1968 Colin Stein becomes Scotland's first £100,000 transfer.

1969 Hibs lose 6-2 to Celtic in the 1968–69 season League Cup Final.

Bob Shankly resigns as Hibs manager and is replaced by Willie Macfarlane.

1971 Macfarlane sacked and replaced by Dave Ewing.

Former favourite Eddie Turnbull returns to Easter Road as manager after a successful spell as the manager of Aberdeen.

1972 Hibs lose 6-1 to Celtic in a disastrous Scottish Cup Final.

Bench style seating installed in the 'Shed' at the Albion Road end of Easter Road Stadium.

Birth of 'Turnbull's Tornadoes' as Hibs defeat Celtic the following season in both the Drybrough and League Cup Finals.

1973 Hibs defeat Hearts 7-0 in the New Year's Day game at Tynecastle.

Hibs win the Drybrough Cup for a second time, defeating Celtic 1-0 after extra time.

Both ends of the main terracing at Easter Road Stadium are fenced off on the advice of the police to prevent trouble occurring when opposing fans traditionally changed ends.

1974 Hibs are defeated on penalties by Leeds United after no-scoring tie at Easter Road in the UEFA Cup.

Hibs lose 6-3 to Celtic in League Cup Final in which Joe Harper scores a hat-trick and still ends up on the losing side.

1975 Hibernian centenary year.

Hearts are defeated 1-0 at Easter Road, the goal scored by Joe Harper in Hibs' first ever Premier League game.

1977 Hibs become the first British side to wear shirt advertising.

1979 The Scottish Cup Final against Rangers goes to three games. After two 0-0 draws, Hibs lose 3-2 after extra time in third game.

George Best signed.

1980 Eddie Turnbull sacked as Hibs manager and is replaced by former teammate Willie Ormond.

Hibs relegated for only the second time in the club's history.

Hibernian FC European Record 1961–1980

In the scoreline the home leg and Hibs' score are shown first. Page numbers indicate where the text relating to each game commences, starting with the first leg of each round.

PAGES	DATE	COMPETITION	OPPONENT	H	A	
24, 26	1961–62	Fairs Cup	Belenenses	3-3	3-1	
28, 33			Red Star Belgrade	0-1	0-4	
45, 48	1962–63	Fairs Cup	Copenhagen	4-0	3-2	
50, 51			Utrecht	2-1	1-0	
56, 58			Valencia	2-1	0-5	
89, 95, 99	1965–66	Fairs Cup	Valencia	2-0	0-2	0-3
				(lose 3rd game play-off)		
124, 125	1967–68	Fairs Cup	Porto	3-0	1-3	
128, 130			Napoli	5-0	1-4	
133, 135			Leeds United	1-1	0-1	
143, 146	1968–69	Fairs Cup	Olympia	2-1	3-0	
151, 152			Lokomotive	3-1	1-0	
154, 156			Hamburg	2-1	0-1	
				(lost away goals)		
174, 177	1970–71	Fairs Cup	Malmö	6-0	3-2	
178, 179			Guimares	2-0	1-2	
182, 186			Liverpool	0-1	0-2	
214, 218	1972–73	Cup Winners'	Sporting Lisbon	6-1	1-2	
220, 223			FC Besa	7-1	1-1	
233, 237			Hajduk Split	4-2	0-3	
245, 247	1973–74	Fairs Cup	Keflavik	2-0	1-1	
248, 251			Leeds United	0-0	0-0	
				(lose 4–5 penalties)		
264, 266	1974–75	UEFA Cup	Rosenberg	9-1	3-2	
268, 270			Juventus	2-4	0-4	
280, 282	1975–76	UEFA Cup	Liverpool	1-0	1-3	
295, 296	1976–77	UEFA Cup	Sochaux	1-0	0-0	
300, 302			Oesters	2-0	1-4	
327, 329	1978–79	UEFA Cup	Norrkoping	3-2	0-0	
331, 333			Strasbourg	0-2	1-0	

Hibernian Cup and League Finishes 1961–1980

Season	League Division	Position	Scottish Cup	League Cup
1961–62	I	8th	Round 1	Group
1962–63	I	16th	Round 3	Group
1963–64	I	10th	Round 2	Semi
1964–65	I	4th	Semi	Group
1965–66	I	6th	Round 2	Semi
1966–67	I	5th	Quarter	Group
1967–68	I	3rd	Round 2	Group
1968–69	I	12th	Round 1	Final
1969–70	I	3rd	Round 1	Group
1970–71	I	12th	Semi	Quarter
1971–72	I	4th	Final	Quarter
1972–73	I	3rd	Round 4	Winners
1973–74	I	2nd	Quarter	Quarter
1974–75	I	2nd	Round 3	Final
1975–76	Premier	3rd	Quarter	Quarter
1976–77	Premier	6th	Round 4	Group
1977–78	Premier	4th	Round 4	Round 3
1978–79	Premier	5th	Final	Semi
1979–80	Premier	10th	Semi	Round 3

A New Dawn for the Game
and the End of an Era at Easter Road
1961–62

BY THE START of the 1960s it was fairly obvious that Hibernian were in serious decline. Long gone were the halcyon days of the Famous Five during the late '40s and early '50s when the club had won three League Championships, lost another only on goal average and yet another by a solitary point, all inside a six-year period. Even the euphoria of securing a famous Fairs Cup victory in March 1961 to reach the semi-finals of the tournament by defeating Barcelona – considered to be one of the best teams in the world – had subsided by the autumn. During the summer Hibs had lost the immensely popular goalscoring phenomenon Joe Baker to Italian club Torino, finally bringing to an end the almost daily disruption of enquiries regarding the player's future from a host of major clubs, both in England and abroad. In just under four seasons at Easter Road, Baker had scored 162 goals in all games, reaching the century mark before he was 21 years of age, a truly incredible statistic. It was painfully obvious that his goalscoring talents would be badly missed in the seasons ahead.

Still reeling from the disappointment of losing cult hero Baker, the Hibs fans were stunned to learn at the start of the 1961–62 season that a bid in the region of £40,000 from Arsenal for the rapidly improving Johnny McLeod had been successful. As the Easter Road players prepared for the coming season, McLeod travelled south to join his new colleagues at Highbury. McLeod, the only ever-present during the previous season, had improved out of all recognition as the campaign progressed. Winning his first full cap in the Wembley debacle against England in April when Scotland were humiliated 9-3, still the highest ever scoring game between the two sides, he had kept his place for the games against the Republic of Ireland at Hampden and Dublin, and Czechoslovakia in Bratislava. After leaving Easter Road, McLeod would not feature in the full international set-up again.

By now, Willie Ormond, the last remaining on-field member of the illustrious Famous Five, was also determined to leave Easter Road, rejecting several attempts to re-sign him for the following season, his 16th in a green and white jersey. The player's continued refusal meant that the club had now lost three influential figures almost in one fell swoop, leaving the side severely weakened, a fact not lost on the remaining players and the fans.

Sporting stylish blue tracksuits acquired during the summer trip to Italy, the players, minus transfer rebel Ormond, arrived for pre-season training in mid-July to be faced with the traditional opening day run around Arthur's Seat. Apart from Ormond, international full back John Grant was the only other regular yet to sign a new contract – he would put pen to paper later in the week. Recent additions to the staff included Tom McCreadie from Port Glasgow, Tony McGlynn from Edinburgh Thistle, Brian Marjoribanks from Airth Castle Rovers, and provisional signings Alex Cameron and Bobby Duncan, both from Edinburgh Juvenile side St Bernard's.

Rumours had been circulating that Hibs were interested in signing former Third Lanark player Ally MacLeod from Blackburn Rovers, possibly as a replacement for Ormond. Although this had been vigorously denied by the club, now, only a few days before the start of the new season, the intense newspaper speculation was over. The future Scottish international manager was signed from the English First Division side for a fee of around £6,000, just in time for the 1960 FA Cup finalist to join his new colleagues for the remainder of the pre-season training. MacLeod had been one of the first victims of the recently abolished maximum wage agreement. One of nearly 200 players who had threatened strike action unless the new wage structure was implemented, the player had been reassured by earlier public statements from manager Jack Marshall that MacLeod was such an important member of the Blackburn staff that he would have absolutely no hesitation in doubling his £20-per-week wage if ever the restrictions were lifted. MacLeod was furious to discover that England internationals Ronnie Clayton and Brian Douglas were being offered £40 per week and another two players £35, while his wage had been increased to only £25. A heated meeting with the manager ended in MacLeod being placed on the transfer list. Several Scottish clubs indicated an interest in signing the player. MacLeod himself was keen to join part-time Airdrie but wanted to remain full-time, and decided to accept Hibs' offer of £28 per week. A late, improved offer of £35 per week to stay at Blackburn was rejected by the player who had already agreed to join Hibs and commendably refused to go back on his word. In his autobiography, MacLeod revealed that he had also been contacted by the Stoke City manager Tony Waddington who wanted him to supplement a secret big-name signing he was about to make, MacLeod on one flank and the mystery player on the other. The skilful but often ungainly MacLeod confessed that he couldn't quite visualise himself on one wing with the great Stanley Matthews gracing the other.

As usual the Edinburgh Select charity match heralded the start of the new season. Burnley, who would finish the season in second place to Alf Ramsay's runaway First Division leaders Ipswich Town and runners-up in the FA Cup, were the visitors to Easter Road. The star-studded English side included future Scottish international goalkeeper Adam Blacklaw, Welsh cap Alec Elder, veteran Jimmy Adamson, the up-and-coming England prospect centre forward Ray Pointer and 1966 England World Cup squad member John Connelly. Before the game the charities selection committee was faced with an unusual dilemma in choosing a centre forward. In the past it had normally been a straight choice between Lawrie Reilly or Willie Bauld, and more recently Joe Baker or Alec Young. Reilly had now retired and Baker and Young had moved on. With no obvious candidate, the selectors plumped for the veteran Bauld, then a far from automatic first choice for Hearts. The days of the fixture attracting crowds of over 40,000 were now well in the past and half that number watched Burnley stage an impressive comeback to win 7-4 after trailing two goals to four at the interval.

On the Monday evening at Easter Road the public trial match between the first and second teams gave the fans an early opportunity to assess the players who would perhaps be in contention to replace MacLeod and Baker. Both Jim Scott and Malcolm Bogie, who had lined up alongside Baker in the Scottish Schoolboy side that had faced England at Goodison in 1954, were the obvious candidates to replace MacLeod. Bobby Kinloch, who had famously scored the winning goal against Barcelona only a few months before, but had otherwise made only occasional appearances in the first team, seemed the most likely candidate to lead the line.

It was around this time that Scottish international Willie Ormond finally ended a distinguished 15-year career at Easter Road. Ormond was allowed to join hometown side Falkirk, then in the Second Division, on a free transfer, leaving trainer Eddie Turnbull as the last surviving member of the celebrated Famous Five still at the club. The outside left, who had won three League Championship medals and six full caps during his time in Edinburgh, had been the only one of the magical five to cost the club a transfer fee when he was signed from Stenhousemuir in 1946, and as a reward for his loyal service, he was granted a free transfer which would allow him to gain financially from the move.

In the League Cup, a section comprising St Johnstone, Celtic, Partick Thistle and Hibs, was surprisingly won by the Perth side managed by former Rangers goalkeeper Bobby Brown. Joe Baker, back home on a short visit from Italy, watched the Easter Road game against Celtic from the trainers' bench and saw his replacement Bobby Kinloch score twice to give his former teammates a share of the spoils. However, two victories, two defeats and two draws, with a 3-0 reverse at Ibrox in a league match, were early indications that it would again be a long, hard season at Easter Road. At least there was the anticipation of European competition.

During the summer the Easter Road directors had been hopeful that Hibs would again be invited to take part in the Fairs Cup, but they, like the fans, were well aware that the 6-0 humiliation by Roma in the previous year's semi-final play-off would do little to enhance their prospects. On the other hand, city rivals Hearts, now free of European Cup commitments, felt that they had a good case for inclusion in place of Hibs, who had already represented the city in the tournament. Earlier, the Fairs Cup committee had requested that each member association recommend the sides to be included in that year's competition, but the SFA steadfastly refused to become involved, leaving each club to make its own application. Both Edinburgh sides were accepted. Competitive European football was gathering momentum, and Barcelona were now joined by both Valencia and Español as the Spanish representatives for the forthcoming tournament. Until then, in Spain, only Real Madrid and Barcelona had seen the merits of European competition, but now a fresh wave of enthusiasm for inter-country football was sweeping through the entire continent.

Hibs chairman Harry Swan's reputation as an extremely competent legislator was firmly established, not only in this country but much further afield, and no sooner had he arrived in Basle for the Fairs Cup draw, than he found himself co-opted onto the organising committee as the third British member on the panel alongside Sir Stanley Rous and Birmingham City chairman Robert Dare. Hibs, in Group C, were drawn against Portuguese side Belenenses in the opening round. Hearts, in Group D, would face St Gilloise from Belgium. After the draw, Swan was pleasantly surprised to be approached by representatives from Barcelona who promised, by way of apology for the disgraceful actions of some of their players in the earlier Fairs Cup match at Easter Road which had ended amid scenes of utter mayhem, that home and away friendly fixtures could be played at the expense of the Spanish club. The suggestion was welcomed by the Hibs chairman, a firm believer in the benefits of European football, but the Catalan club's heavy fixture commitments made it difficult to arrange dates.

Little was known about Belenenses but there was little doubt that they would provide a serious challenge. Portuguese football was on the ascendancy, with the 'unknown' Benfica sweeping aside all challengers, including Hearts, to lift the European Cup at Wembley the previous March by defeating Hibs' Fairs Cup opponents Barcelona 3-2 in the final. The blue-shirted Belenenses shared the city of Lisbon with Benfica and Sporting, and had an impressive record against their more famous neighbours.

Making their first ever visit to Britain, Belenenses arrived in Edinburgh the day before the match and held a brief training session at the ground that evening. It was noticeable that several of the players, particularly the four black stars, were not overly impressed with the cold and blustery Scottish weather.

As before, the rules of the tournament allowed the use of a substitute goalkeeper in the case of injury, but again Hibs would be handicapped by the SFA regulations that foolishly still refused to recognise such a move. The Easter Road side appealed for the ban to be lifted but the appeal fell on deaf ears.

Because the Portuguese season had not yet started, it was felt that Belenenses would almost certainly be well behind the fitness level and match practice of the Scots, but this notion was quickly dispelled when the visitors raced to a well deserved three-goal lead inside the opening 26 minutes of the match.

The far from happy Hibs fans were not slow to show their displeasure and soon jeers began to echo around the ground. Somehow, the home side managed to pull themselves together and up till the interval the Portuguese goal was put under ever-increasing pressure, but without a breakthrough. Goalkeeper Pereira, who would later play against England in the 1966 World Cup semi-finals, had been called upon to produce near miracles to defy Hibs on several occasions, and in the final few minutes of the first half surpassed himself by making at least seven stops, three in the incredible class, to defy the marauding green-shirted attackers.

Whatever manager Hugh Shaw had to say to his players during the break, it certainly worked and in the second half they displayed a resolution and conviction that had been sadly lacking in the opening 30 minutes of the game. A Hibs defence that had earlier looked unsteady and unsure was now in a dominant and uncompromising mood, winning every ball and tackle. With Hibs resorting to the time-honoured Scottish punt up the park, the uncomfortable Belenenses defenders found themselves under severe and constant pressure and it was no surprise when Fraser glanced home a header from a Stevenson cross a few minutes after the restart.

Within a quarter of an hour the scores drew level when Fraser scored his second of the night with another header, before captain Sammy Baird scored one of the cheekiest penalties ever seen at Easter Road. Eric Stevenson, even this early in his career displaying an obvious talent for winning penalties, was brought down inside the box by full back Castro. Then, on his run up to the ball, Baird suddenly checked his run, allowing the keeper to commit himself fully before gently rolling the ball into the other side of the goal, leaving Pereira completely stranded.

From then until the final whistle, Hibs might well have scored more as their powerful play at times threatened to swamp the Portuguese side, but desperate defending allowed the visitors to hold out and there was no more scoring.

Three goals behind at the interval and seemingly beaten, Hibs had climbed off the ropes to record a credible, or incredible draw at the end of the 90 minutes, cheered on by a vocal 20,000 crowd who encouraged their favourites to a quite amazing comeback. An exceptional display had compensated for a dreadful start. In the second half every Hibs man had been a hero, working tirelessly to make such a fantastic recovery possible, and even after the equalising goal the Edinburgh side could well have scored more. Johnny McLeod, back in Edinburgh to recover from a leg injury received while playing for Arsenal the previous Saturday, watched the game from the stand. It had not been a particularly happy time for both of the recently transferred big-money signings. Apart from the injury to McLeod, only the previous day Joe Baker had been sent off late in the match after scoring twice against Lanerossi.

FINAL SCORE: HIBERNIAN 3. BELENENSES 3.

FAIRS CUP 1ST ROUND (1ST LEG), MONDAY 4 SEPTEMBER 1961, EASTER ROAD.

HIBERNIAN: SIMPSON, HUGHES, MCCLELLAND, BAXTER, GRANT, BAIRD, SCOTT, STEVENSON, FRASER, GIBSON, MACLEOD.

Although the season was only a few weeks old, the impressive form of right back John Grant had again caught the eye of the selectors and the defender was included in the Scottish League side that faced the League of Ireland in a scrappy 1-1 draw at Hampden the following week. Scottish centre half Billy McNeill of Celtic had endured yet another particularly depressing 90 minutes, the latest in a number of poor performances in the dark blue of Scotland, leaving one newspaper reporter to comment, 'The selectors had been patient in persisting with the young centre half with an eye to the future.' It was a loyalty rarely granted to a player outside either half of the Old Firm.

During the next few weeks Tony McGlynn and Brian Marjoribanks, both called up only at the beginning of the season, made their first-team debuts, in Marjoribanks' case a scoring start in a 4-2 defeat by Hearts. It was the Gorgie side's first home win over their Edinburgh rivals for four years, but enough to relegate the Easter Road side to 16th in the table – third-bottom. Hardly ideal preparation for the forthcoming trip to Portugal!

Hibs' heavy defeat at Tynecastle by their bitter rivals did little to inspire Scottish confidence in the task ahead, particularly on learning that Belenenses had defeated Barreiro 5-1 in a league match on the Sunday.

For the Fairs Cup tie, manager Shaw gambled on a packed defensive formation that relied heavily on the counter-attack to see them through to the next round and the tactics paid off handsomely. Scott and Fraser were both in magnificent form, their swift breaks repeatedly troubling the home defence, but in John Baxter, Hibs had the game's outstanding player. Taking advantage of the numerous long clearances from defence, Baxter proved a constant menace. Scoring his side's opening two goals, the inside left was desperately unlucky not to score more, only tremendous goalkeeping by Pereira preventing him from adding to his tally. At no time did Belenenses promise to recapture the form of the first half-hour in Edinburgh, and their weary attack ran out of steam early in the second half, after repeatedly failing to breach Hibs' defensive cover.

The scores were level at the break, but with 29 minutes remaining Baxter took advantage of a mistake by Pereira to shoot into the empty net, and from then on, it was all Hibs. Stevenson scored a third with a neat header after 74 minutes and from then until the end, goalkeeper Pereira had again to be at his best to prevent his side from conceding even more goals.

The Portuguese press were generous in praise of the Edinburgh side. Lisbon's *Diáro de Noticias* thought Hibs 'had played like a single unit from goalkeeper to left wing, with special credit given to Baird, Scott, Fraser and Baxter'. The report ended by underlining that 'the local team had lacked the stamina of the visitors, whose play had furnished exuberant proof of the value of speed'.

FINAL SCORE: BELENENSES 1. HIBERNIAN 3.

FAIRS CUP 1ST ROUND (2ND LEG), WEDNESDAY 27 SEPTEMBER 1961, RESTELLO STADIUM.
HIBERNIAN: SIMPSON, GRANT, MCCLELLAND, DAVIN, EASTON, BAIRD, SCOTT, STEVENSON, FRASER, BAXTER, MACLEOD.

Despite the exciting win in Portugal Hibs were still languishing at the wrong end of the table, and a 4-0 defeat on the Saturday by Dundee United, promoted from the Second Division only two seasons before, did little to change the situation. The Tannadice grandstand was undergoing renovations, with the players changing away from the ground and arriving ready to play, but in no way could this be used as an excuse for the heavy defeat.

The following Saturday, Willie Ormond was given a rapturous reception by the Hibs fans on the veteran's first appearance back at Easter Road since his transfer. The supporters were not so appreciative 90 minutes later, however, after two goals by the outside left gave Falkirk a well deserved point in the 2-2 draw. Also in the Bairns line-up that day were former Hibs player Alex Duchart, and Jimmy Murray who had recently been signed from Hearts. Hibs right back John Fraser, who had played alongside Ormond many times in the past, found the tricky outside left an extremely difficult opponent on the day, but had too much respect for his former teammate to resort to any questionable tactics.

As part of the Joe Baker transfer deal during the summer, Torino had agreed to play a friendly match in Edinburgh. The opportunity to see both Baker, who was made captain for the evening, and Scottish international Dennis Law, a £100,000 signing from Manchester City, drew a crowd of 26,000 to Easter Road on Monday 16 October 1961. Only a few days earlier, Torino had faced Law's former side Manchester City at Maine Road losing 4-3. Baker had scored all three Torino goals and had greatly impressed the watching Manchester United manager Matt Busby. Brother Gerry, who would soon join Hibs, scored City's winning goal.

At Easter Road, even the genius of Law was not enough to prevent Hibs from running out deserved 2-0 winners in a game that was a welcome relief from the frustrations of a dismal league campaign. Unfortunately for the supporters, who were keen to see their former hero in action, Baker proved a huge disappointment. Unable to shake off the attentions of Easton throughout the entire 90 minutes, there was little sign of the skills of old, the only flash of fire from the Englishman coming when he briefly faced up to Easton after he had been fouled, before walking away with a broad smile on his face.

In an unsuccessful attempt to improve the side's dismal league form, Shaw made five changes for a home game against Third Lanark, including the introduction of the diminutive Ian Cuthbert who was making his first start for the league side. The youngster, signed the previous season from Edina Hearts, soon demonstrated a big heart with his tireless running. He also packed a good right-foot shot, but it was asking far too much of the confident teenager to make a difference all on his own. As it was, two uncharacteristic mistakes by the normally reliable goalkeeper Ronnie Simpson, who had earlier made several tremendous saves, allowed Thirds to leave Edinburgh with both points after a 3-1 win. The frustration of the Hibs fans, disgruntled at the team's poor league results and performances, came to the surface and there was almost constant barracking and slow handclapping, aimed in particular towards Kinloch and Preston who seemed genuinely unsettled by the abuse.

In his Monday column in the *Evening News*, 'Outlook' was of the opinion that:

> Hibs could well do without the rounds of slow handclapping that accompanied the defeat by Third Lanark. No doubt the people responsible will pass themselves off as Hibs supporters, but the team can well do without this type of support.

A great number of fans took exception to the article, and several letters were received defending the behaviour. A fan, using the nom de plume 'one of these types', responded:

> The writer forgets that 'these types', as he calls them, the sort of fan who supports the club through hail, rain and shine, are bitter now, as they watch the ghost of a once great side playing such doleful stuff week after week.

Many others defended their actions, one suggesting that the Hibs management should also receive the slow handclap for their team selection each week.

At the draw for the second round of the Fairs Cup in Switzerland, Hibs had been paired against Red Star Belgrade, at that time the most successful side in the former Yugoslavia. Founded by students in 1945 during the dying days of the war, Red Star had since won the League Championship six times, the cup five times, and were the best supported side in the country. Continental competition certainly held no fears for the Iron Curtain team, which had taken part in the European Cup several times, only just failing to qualify for that year's competition.

Before the game there was an almighty boost for Hibs when it was announced that four of the Yugoslav side's top players had been transferred almost in one fell swoop. The legendary Vladimar Beara, and Branco Zebel, who had won 125 Yugoslavian caps between them, had been transferred to German side Aachen, with the 29-times capped Kostics transferred to Lanerossi in Italy. Yet another player had joined an Austrian side. Even without these players, Red Star remained formidable opponents. Because of the strict Yugoslavian immigration regulations then in force, Hibs had applied for more entry visas than were actually needed in case of a late injury to one or more of the players, and there was to be disappointment for Jim Scott when he became the unlucky player to be excluded from the party that made its way to Belgrade. Thirteen players, including, as usual, only one goalkeeper – a situation that would be thought ludicrous nowadays – left from Edinburgh on the first leg of the journey to Yugoslavia.

As they set out early on the Monday morning from Easter Road, there was no indication of the ordeal that lay ahead. However, at Turnhouse Airport the party discovered that the flight had been delayed for several hours on account of the thick fog that was enveloping the London area. This was only the first in a series of postponements that would see the team arrive at their destination more than 36 hours later. Approaching Watford, the plane was required to circle the airport until the fog had cleared sufficiently to allow a landing, but on arriving at the terminal there was even more disappointment for the team when they were informed that all continental flights had been delayed indefinitely, including their flight to Zurich. After yet another interminable wait they were finally allowed to depart, but conditions over Switzerland made it impossible to proceed any further that evening and the party were taken by coach to a luxury hotel ten miles from the airport. No sooner had the players bedded down for the evening than they were informed that their flight had been rearranged for early morning, which meant a 4.30am rise. The players thought this must be a practical joke but by then most failed to see the funny side. The early morning Trans-Europe express from Zurich took them to Basle where they caught a flight to Vienna. After a further six-hour wait in the Austrian capital, the weary party set off on the final leg of the journey, finally arriving in Belgrade more than a day and a half after setting out.

Ronnie Simpson had been selected as the reserve goalkeeper for the Scottish League side who were due to play the Italian League at Hampden while the Easter Road side were in Yugoslavia, but all appeals by Hibs to secure the goalkeeper's release for the important European tie had fallen on deaf ears. Consequently, Willie Muirhead took Simpson's place in Belgrade, and Pat Hughes replaced Sammy Baird who took ill shortly after arriving.

At the state-owned stadium Red Star shared with neighbours Partizan while their own new ground was being constructed on the outskirts of the city, Hibs encountered a side at the very top of their form and were comprehensively defeated. In front of almost 30,000 exuberant home fans the young communist team, which comprised mainly of students, performed like veterans on the day. More alert and sharper than their Scottish counterparts, Belgrade used the ball intelligently, their speedy inter-passing creating constant danger in the Hibs penalty area. Too often, the Edinburgh side relied on individual skill and typical Scottish industry which was no match for the trickery and imagination of their opponents.

Maravic opened the scoring early on with a tremendous 20-yard drive that literally screamed past Muirhead. Midway through the first 45 minutes, a sloppy throw out by the goalkeeper was intercepted by centre forward Melic who had the greatest of ease in putting his side two goals ahead. Three minutes before the interval Sekularac, the best performer afield, threaded a lovely through pass to Melic who gave the Yugoslavs an unassailable three-goal lead. Hibs managed to break out of defence only rarely, but during these sporadic raids into their opponents' penalty area they twice struck the woodwork, and had Stevenson scored instead of rifling his shot against the post when the score stood at 1-0, the outcome may well have been different.

Just minutes after the restart, Maravic scored his own second and his side's fourth to put the game beyond doubt, and in all likelihood make the return leg at Easter Road in a fortnight's time a mere formality.

Although the game had been played mainly in a sporting fashion, with five minutes left to play, Jim Easton innocuously tackled inside left Sekularac and to the amazement of the Hibs players the Yugoslav reacted by kicking and punching the centre half to the ground. Before the incident could get further out of hand the referee astounded Easton and his teammates by ordering the Scottish player from the field. Easton, who had never even been booked before in his professional career, at first refused to leave the field, only doing so when persuaded by Sammy Baird, who was watching from the sidelines. Both players were pelted with oranges and various other missiles as they made their way to the tunnel. The highly talented Sekularac, who had played for Red Star against Manchester United only a few hours before the Old Trafford side perished at Munich in 1958, was guilty of dishing out rough treatment all afternoon, most of it ignored by the referee, and Easton had particular cause to feel aggrieved at being denied the expected protection of the Austrian official.

Although Hibs had been outplayed for almost the entire 90 minutes, they could perhaps count themselves unfortunate to be trailing by four goals, three of them due to bad goalkeeping blunders. After the game the local press were complimentary to Hibs, always an easy matter after victory. The editor of *Politika* thought the Scottish side had impressed the Yugoslav fans:

> They played well, their passes were precise, and they created several excellent attacks. This was Red Star's best performance for some time, and the Scots were unlucky to come up against opponents who played with more flair, imagination, combination, and liveliness.

Before leaving Belgrade manager Hugh Shaw somewhat optimistically stated, 'The score flattered Red Star, with the game hinging on some poor goalkeeping situations. This is not the end. Remember, the next time we will be playing in front of our own fans.'

For goalkeeper Willie Muirhead it *was* the end, at least at Easter Road. He would not play for the first team again, and would soon be on his way to Canadian side Toronto.

FINAL SCORE: RED STAR 4. HIBERNIAN 0.

FAIRS CUP 2ND ROUND (1ST LEG), WEDNESDAY 1 NOVEMBER 1961, JNA BELGRADE.
HIBERNIAN: MUIRHEAD, FRASER, MCCLELLAND, DAVIN, EASTON, HUGHES, STEVENSON, GIBSON BAXTER, PRESTON, MACLEOD.

On the Saturday a goal after only four minutes by Ally MacLeod was not enough to ensure victory against Aberdeen, the 1-1 draw leaving Hibs hovering dangerously near the relegation trapdoor. Less than happy at the repeated poor form of the side, the Hibs fans were demanding that some of the £100,000 that had been received from the sale of Baker and McLeod be spent on new players. Chairman Swan countered these demands, saying: 'If anyone can show me where these players are then I will sign them.' Even so, it was evident that something had to be done.

On Tuesday 7 November 1961, Hugh Shaw resigned as manager of Hibs, ending an association with the club that stretched back to 1918. Swan announced the bombshell news to the supporters, but no other information was forthcoming from either party except that the manager had offered his resignation at a heated board meeting the previous evening, and that it had been accepted.

For the Easter Road players, however, Shaw's resignation had not come as a complete surprise. For some time the manager had become increasingly detached from on-field matters, often leaving that side of things to trainer Eddie Turnbull. After 13 years as manager, Shaw was perhaps finding it difficult to sustain his personal motivation, and was not helped by the fact that the great post-war days at Easter Road were now clearly a thing of the past.

Born in Islay, Shaw had joined Hibs from Clydebank Juniors during the closing months of the Great War, quickly establishing himself in the first team. Originally a centre forward, he found his best position as left half in the great side that had contested the 1923 and 1924 Scottish Cup Finals, before joining Rangers in 1926 after a dispute with the club. Moving on to Hearts, East Fife and Leith Athletic, he finally ended his playing days as player-coach at Highland League side Elgin City. Persuaded to return to Easter Road as assistant trainer to Johnny Halligan in 1934, Shaw succeeded Halligan as first-team trainer in 1936, and had been manager at Easter Road since the untimely death of Willie McCartney in 1948. Hugely respected in the game, his abilities had been recognised by the SFA and he had been selected as trainer to several international sides including the Great Britain team that defeated the Rest of the World at Hampden in 1947. In his time as trainer at Easter Road the determined Shaw had studied physiotherapy and modern training techniques, and had used this knowledge wisely after succeeding Willie McCartney in 1948, guiding Hibs to three League Championship wins in five seasons, becoming in the process the most successful manager in the club's 86-year history.

At Easter Road Hugh Shaw had introduced the then novel practice of encouraging the players to discuss the forthcoming game after they had finished their pre-match meal. Tommy Preston recalls that as an inexperienced newcomer to the first team he was, not surprisingly, reluctant to venture an opinion. Egged on by several of the senior players, he eventually plucked up the courage to have his say, only to be met by the response from some of his teammates: 'Oh, so you think you are a football player now, do you?'

In the days immediately following Shaw's shock resignation, Swan took over the manager's duties but was quick to dispel any notion of taking over on a permanent basis, a statement no doubt welcomed both by players and fans. Determined that the club should have a new manager as soon as possible, Swan insisted that the man selected would be experienced and that the post would not be advertised, a broad hint according to many, that the candidate might already be at Easter Road in the shape of trainer Eddie Turnbull.

Meanwhile, *Evening News* columnist 'Outlook' paid generous tribute to the former manager:

> The quiet man has left Easter Road after 40 years and must not be allowed to leave the Edinburgh soccer scene without a tribute from one of the many sports writers who found it a pleasure to work with him. As a manager he was always approachable, and accepted press criticism in his stride. Quite apart from the many great players spotted and signed by him during his reign, Shaw can claim an unsurpassed knowledge among Scottish managers of the European game. An era has ended at Easter Road, and Shaw can claim, although he would be the last to do so, that he made a notable contribution to the game.

Praise indeed!

Hugh Shaw remained a well respected figure in the game. Popular with all the players who served under him, he is still mentioned with great affection to this day.

One former player recollects a humorous story involving the 'Boss' that clearly took place in more innocent times. After a midweek afternoon match at Pittodrie in the early '50s, the player concerned decided not to travel back with the official party by train as was the normal practice in those days. Instead he went to a local hostelry for a couple of bottles of stout and was not long in the premises when he was joined by Bobby Johnstone and Willie Ormond, who had also decided to spend a few hours in Aberdeen. There was no riotous drinking session, just a few beers before catching the milk train home.

On arriving at Easter Road for training the following morning he was informed by trainer Jimmy McColl that his presence was required 'upstairs', where he was confronted by an angry manager and informed that he was being held responsible for leading the two younger players astray. It was made clear that such irresponsible behaviour could not, and would not, be tolerated by the club and that he was to be severely punished. After a period of silence lasting several seconds, the by now very concerned miscreant was notified that the manager was 'writing to his mother to tell her just what her son had been up to'. It is worth mentioning that Eddie Turnbull had served for several years on the Russian convoys during the war! Shaw could also show his steel when required and often after a particularly bad defeat on the

Saturday, the players would be made to pay with a punishing training session on the Monday.

Shaw would not be lost to the game for long. Within days of leaving Easter Road he accepted a two-year contract to take over as manager of Raith Rovers, renewing contact with former Hibs trainer Bill Hunter who had returned to Starks Park a few years before.

Back at Easter Road, several team changes were made for the next match, including the return of John Grant from injury. This, however, did little to improve matters as goalkeeper Simpson conceded seven goals at Motherwell. Fortunately only five of them counted but the 5-1 scoreline meant that Hibs had now slumped to 17th place in an 18-team league, and even deeper into relegation danger. Worse still, unsettled by the recent poor form of the side both Davie Gibson and Jim Scott had requested to be placed on the open-to-transfer list.

For the return leg against Red Star at Easter Road, the acting manager made several changes to the side that had surrendered so dismally at Fir Park, but perhaps the most surprising addition was the inclusion of young Ian Cuthbert, who would be taking part in his first ever European tie after only one first team outing. As perhaps could be expected, managerless Hibs found the first leg deficit impossible to overcome and they departed the tournament almost without a whimper in front of just 9,000 hardy souls who braved the biting winter cold in the hope of seeing their favourites staging a spectacular fight back against all the odds. Instead, they witnessed a performance that highlighted the fact that the fervour and talent that had characterised Hibs' play throughout the years had gone. A desperately needed early goal never looked likely to be forthcoming and throughout the 90 minutes it was obvious that the home side had fielded too many inexperienced youngsters to trouble a team with the capabilities of Red Star.

Apart from an opening burst, Hibs were seldom an attacking force, and many supporters had already left the ground when Palincevic scored the only goal of the game with 13 minutes remaining. Bursting free down the stand side touchline, the inside forward left two defenders sprawling in his wake before placing the ball past the advancing Simpson, a signal for the remainder of the dwindling crowd to begin making their way to the exits. It was an evening of double disappointment for Edinburgh. Hearts, who had overcome Belgian side Union St Gilloise in the first round, were beaten 4-0 by Inter Milan in Italy after a 1-0 defeat at Tynecastle. After his initial earlier promise against Third Lanark, after just one league game and a place in the line-up against Red Star, young Ian Cuthbert would not play for the first team again and would soon be on his way out of Easter Road.

FINAL SCORE: HIBERNIAN 0. RED STAR 1.

FAIRS CUP 2ND ROUND (2ND LEG), WEDNESDAY 15 NOVEMBER 1961, EASTER ROAD.
HIBERNIAN: SIMPSON, FRASER, MCCLELLAND, GRANT, EASTON, DAVIN, STEVENSON, CUTHBERT, PRESTON, GIBSON, MACLEOD.

Hibs' precarious league position now made it imperative that a new manager was installed as soon as possible. As far as the press were concerned there was only one candidate: Jock Stein. The Dunfermline manager, who had produced near miracles at East End Park in such a short time, remained the clear favourite, but Harry Swan saw former Rangers goalkeeper Bobby Brown, then manager at St Johnstone, as the ideal man for the job. A statement released from Easter Road that Brown was only one of several candidates under consideration and had not actually been offered the position was later found to be untrue. Brown, who was then in the process of building a promising squad at Muirton since promotion to the First Division a little over a year before, had indeed been offered the vacant Easter Road post but had decided to remain in Perth for the time being. It was only then that Hibs turned their attentions to Fife.

Former Celtic centre half Jock Stein had been a revelation at Dunfermline since taking over in 1959. Inheriting a struggling side that seemed destined for relegation, against all the odds he had miraculously arrested the slide to secure the Pars' First Division survival. Before Stein's arrival they had managed to win only six of their 28 league matches but unbelievably all six of their remaining games under the new manager were won, including victories over both Stein's former club, Celtic, and second-placed Kilmarnock. It was the beginning of what would turn out to be a legendary career in management. Making steady progress during the next few seasons, Dunfermline had gone on to defeat Celtic in the 1961 Scottish Cup Final, their first ever national success, and were in the process of establishing a formidable European pedigree, reaching the quarter-finals of the Cup Winners' Cup that season. Stein had already been approached unofficially by the Hibs directors and was said to have been extremely keen to take over at Easter Road, but to his disappointment the Dunfermline directors refused to release him from his five-year contract and Hibs were left to look elsewhere for Shaw's replacement.

Without a win in their last nine matches, the restless fans were still demanding that new faces be brought in to help steer Hibs to safety. Swan had insisted that no new players would be bought until a new manager was in place, but probably losing his nerve at the perilous league position, Hibs swooped to sign former Motherwell and St Mirren centre forward Gerry Baker, then at Manchester City, for a 'substantial' fee believed to be in the region of £25,000.

American-born Gerry, brother of former Hibs favourite Joe, went straight into the side to face St Johnstone at Muirton Park in mid-November. Although failing to score himself, his speed and enterprise brought renewed confidence to the forward line as Hibs recorded an important 2-0 win, their first victory in competitive football for almost two months. Ironically, Joe Baker and Johnny McLeod had now been replaced in the side by Gerry Baker and Ally MacLeod.

Baker made his home debut against league leaders Dundee a week later. In front of a 15,000 crowd the home side put up a spirited performance and it was not until former Hibs legend Gordon Smith, who had joined the Angus side from Hearts at the beginning of the season, scored the third goal 15 minutes from the end that the visitors could feel assured of both points.

On Monday 27 November 1961, Walter Galbraith, a surprise choice to say the least, was announced as the new manager of Hibs. Many, including the former player himself, were of the opinion that Turnbull had been the ideal candidate to replace Shaw. Galbraith, the former Queen's Park, Clyde, New Brighton, and Accrington Stanley full back, who had been one of Bill Shankly's first signings as manager of Grimsby Town in 1951, was believed to have been offered a salary in the region of £3,000 per annum as Hibs new boss. He had enjoyed a fairly successful managerial career in England, although it has to be said, with clubs in the lower divisions. Asking for time to steer his current side, Tranmere Rovers, through the following Saturday's fixture, Galbraith, who resembled film star Douglas Fairbanks Jnr in looks, agreed to take over at Easter Road the following week. Perhaps as a portent of things to come, as Hibs were defeating St Mirren 3-2 on the Saturday – Gerry Baker opening his Easter Road account by scoring the winner against his former teammates – Tranmere Rovers were losing 1-0 to Rochdale. Galbraith's other managerial sides had also fared poorly that afternoon: Accrington Stanley were beaten 5-1 at Gillingham, while Bradford Park Avenue could only manage a home draw against Watford. Tranmere Rovers would end the season in 15th place in the English Fourth Division, while bottom-placed Accrington Stanley would resign completely from the league.

The new manager's first game was against Partick Thistle at Firhill, on 13 December 1962. A double from Baker gave Hibs a credible 2-2 draw in an unusually early Scottish Cup first-round tie. As often happens when a new manager is installed, the players put up a more determined and spirited performance than of late and came within minutes of winning the match.

The traditional New Year's Day fixture against Hearts at Easter Road was cancelled due to the severe weather that was then affecting the entire country, and when the continuing climatic conditions caused several other games to be postponed during the same period, somewhat predictably there had again been calls for a mid-season break. Dunfermline even went as far as taking a poll of their fans on the option of a winter shutdown, but overall there was little support for a motion that would raise its head many times during the intervening years; it would be almost four decades before the scheme would temporarily come into operation.

Several decent results including a no-score draw against Rangers in Edinburgh early in the New Year lifted Hibs into 11th place in the table and finally banished any lingering relegation worries. Defender Duncan Falconer, who had been pushed into the attack by Galbraith, scoring four goals in five games, sustained a head injury in the match against Rangers. Although he managed to finish the game after treatment from Eddie Turnbull, after the game, the player complained of having no recollection of the match, then collapsed on the dressing room floor. An X-ray found nothing seriously wrong but Falconer had to spend the following five days in hospital.

Hugh Shaw had found the going tough since his move to Fife. With relegation threatening Raith Rovers after a run of poor results, desperate to bolster his forward line, he was rumoured to have made a bid for Barcelona goal hero Bobby Kinloch, who was currently out of favour at Easter Road. It had not been a great time for the former Forres Mechanics player in recent months. Since scoring the winner from the penalty spot in Hibs' famous victory over the Spanish giants in 1961, Kinloch had struggled to hold down a regular first-team place and had scored only once that season in the league, again perhaps predictably from the penalty spot, in a 3-1 home defeat by Third Lanark in October.

Joe Baker, meanwhile, was finding life in Italy even worse. Sent off on Christmas Eve for the second time since leaving Hibs, he had been fined the equivalent of £250 by the club for internal disciplinary problems. Clearly all was not well in Turin. Writing in *Sports World* magazine, Brian Glanville, then widely recognised as Britain's leading authority on Italian football, was convinced that Joe Baker had made a serious error of judgement in joining Torino, 'a middle-of-the-road team constantly living in the shadow of near neighbours Juventus'. His view was that 'Baker would have been better off joining Fiorentina'.

History would prove that Baker should never have entertained the thought of playing in Italy at all, irrespective of the club.

The twice-postponed Scottish Cup tie against Partick Thistle ended in disappointment for the new manager as Hibs blundered and stumbled to defeat at Easter Road. Two goals behind thanks to defensive errors, John Fraser scored twice as Hibs staged a late comeback to level the game before Thistle scored the winner in the dying seconds, courtesy of yet another defensive lapse. The long wait for Scottish Cup success continued. Incredibly, it was now exactly 60 years since the famous old trophy had adorned the mantelpiece at Easter Road.

In the rearranged New Year's Day game against Hearts at Easter Road, a vintage performance by Willie Bauld helped set up a 4-1 victory for the visitors. The veteran Bauld, by this time failing to command a regular place in the Maroons first XI, set up his side's first three goals before scoring the fourth himself. It would be Bauld's last ever goal against his arch rivals. Scoring twice on his 'derby debut' for Hearts that afternoon was a 17-year-old Heriot's schoolboy named Alan Gordon who was destined to score many more goals at Easter Road in the future, but wearing the green and white of Hibs.

Meanwhile the unsettled Davie Gibson had agreed to join Leicester City in a £25,000 deal. The talented Gibson had been unhappy at Easter Road for some time and was desperate to try his luck in England. His new club would have to do without his services for several weeks while the National Service soldier completed a stint in Aden. Including the sale of Joe Baker and Johnny McLeod the previous summer, Gibson's transfer had now seen Hibs collect almost £130,000 in transfer transactions, a colossal sum at the time, with only a comparatively modest outlay in the acquisition of Gerry Baker and Ally MacLeod. Sensing the dissatisfaction among the support, the astute Harry Swan emphasised the need for calm and revealed that the manager had plans to bring in at least three expensive signings in the near future. Although he was well aware of the criticism regarding both the recent results and the sale of Gibson, the chairman remained convinced that this attitude would change once the fans discovered the calibre of player that the club had been in negotiations with during the past few weeks. One target was a homesick lad from Stirlingshire who was then playing for English Second Division side Leeds United. Wishing to return to his native Scotland, 19-year-old Billy Bremner had requested a transfer earlier in the season. Leeds had already turned down a bid from Hibs for the player, and the recent transfer request resulted in manager Don Revie accusing Bremner of having been 'tapped' by the Scottish club. Although the player himself denied any approach, and lacking proof, Revie felt that the player's recent attitude both on and off the field suggested that he was not far wide of the mark. The fee of £25,000 initially demanded was agreed by Hibs, but this was immediately increased to £50,000, a figure well out of the reach of Hibs, or of any Scottish club for that matter. Bremner would remain at Elland Road for the majority of his career, captaining Leeds United during the most successful period in the club's history before carving out a deserved reputation as one of the best players ever to wear the dark blue of Scotland.

At that time attendances on both sides of the border were in steady decline which was proving of great concern to the authorities, and at the end of January all 37 Scottish League clubs were invited to a meeting with the SFA and Scottish League to discuss any positive action that might go some way in arresting the shortfall. At this meeting it was revealed that Hibs had recently mailed a bombshell letter to the SFA outlining radical proposals to reduce the number of clubs in the First Division. Among these proposals was the suggestion that the guarantee for visiting First Division sides be raised to £1,000 per game, or alternatively that the home club keep all the gate money. Swan also proposed that there should be no automatic relegation from, or promotion to, the top division. Entry would be by invitation only, with provision made for financial assistance for the smaller clubs if necessary. A recommendation that an independent enquiry into the proposals be arranged was agreed. Another suggestion from Hibs was that a new end-of-season tournament should be organised which, in time, could be expanded to include clubs from England and abroad. Rangers and Celtic showed little enthusiasm for the idea, which came as no surprise as they had failed to show any initial interest in the European Cup, the Friendship Cup, or for that matter the Floodlight League, and in the end these innovative proposals came to nothing.

By now Joe Baker's stay in Italy was nearing its end. At the beginning of February both he and Dennis Law were involved in a late night car crash in Turin as Baker tested a newly acquired sports car. Failing to negotiate a roundabout, the car careered into a statue leaving Baker with a broken nose and palate and severe internal injuries, resulting in a lengthy spell in hospital. On top of this, Torino hinted that he would receive no more cash that season as a punishment for his late night indiscretion, and appealed to the Italian FA to ratify the decision. A few days later the Italian club made it known that they would welcome any transfer interest in Baker from an English side, with the proviso that the repayment of the equivalent of £1,750, which had already been advanced to the player for this and the following season, would be included in any transfer fee. As if things weren't bad enough, Baker was discharged from hospital to discover that roommate Law had already signed for Manchester United. Joe himself would soon bring his unhappy stay in Italy to an end when he became manager Billy Wright's first signing at Arsenal for a reputed £70,000 fee.

For the elder Baker brother back in Edinburgh things were going well. Since signing from Manchester City in mid-November, Gerry Baker had brought new life into a lacklustre attack, scoring four goals in ten starts from the centre forward position. Galbraith moved him to inside right. This new position allowed him more space to demonstrate his phenomenal acceleration and ball control and he had scored six goals from his last six appearances as Hibs rose to a respectable ninth place in the table.

At the beginning of March, two youngsters who were destined to play a big part in the Easter Road story were in the news. A newspaper article revealed that Celtic were interested in signing Scottish schoolboy cap Jimmy O'Rourke, who had played in every school international that season. The Holy Cross boy, who had also represented Edinburgh Schools, travelled through to Glasgow to meet the Celtic management, but despite comments from the Parkhead representatives that the player's surname suggested that he should join Celtic, O'Rourke's heart lay elsewhere, and he would shortly sign for his beloved Hibs.

The early exit from the Scottish Cup at the hands of Partick Thistle had left Hibs with a blank Saturday, and a friendly match against Everton at Easter Road had been hastily arranged. As part of the pre-match entertainment, a Scottish Youth XI faced an Edinburgh Juvenile Select side that included 15-year-old Peter Cormack of Tynecastle Boys Club in the line-up. As with O'Rourke, Hibs had been among a dozen or so clubs chasing the signature of Cormack but at the end of the season the player would join Hearts, to become in the process the first Tynecastle ground staff signing since the great Tommy Walker in the 1930s.

While first-team performances and results had been somewhat unfavourable, to say the least, the second team, under the watchful eye of Jimmy McColl, were enjoying an unbeaten 14-game run. Although the club now acknowledged that they were active in the transfer market, they still continued to pin their hopes on the future development of the youngsters then playing regularly for the second team such as Willie Wilson, Joe Davin,

Bobby Nicol, Malcolm Bogie, Tony McGlynn, Harvey McCreadie, Alec Cameron and Jim Scott.

In the middle of March at East End Park, Jock Stein's Dunfermline inflicted Hibs' heaviest league defeat of the season. Fifteen-year-old Alex Edwards, making his first team debut on the left wing, starred for the Pars in the 4-0 win. Edwards was the second youngest player to make a Scottish League debut, and he almost made it a scoring start to his senior career, when with just six minutes of the match remaining a shot from the talented youngster was only just clawed around the post by keeper Ronnie Simpson. Coincidentally goalkeeper Simpson had become Scotland's youngest ever player when he made his debut for Queen's Park aged 14 in a Summer Cup tie against Clyde in 1945 while still at school. He became the youngest ever player to take part in an official league game when he faced Hibs at the start of the 1946–47 season, aged 15. Like Simpson, Edwards would also go on to play for Hibs in the coming years.

From then until the end of the season, both Gerry Baker and Duncan Falconer would feature regularly on the scoresheet as Hibs would more often than not, win one then lose one, finally finishing the season, considering their poor start, in a more than respectable eighth position, one place lower than the previous year. Fifty-eight goals had been scored in the process, but disappointingly, a huge total of 72 had been conceded.

Baker had featured in just over half of the fixtures since his mid-season transfer but had still managed to score ten league goals, two behind top scorer Falconer. Ally MacLeod alone had featured in every match, with goalkeeper Simpson missing only the game against Red Star in Belgrade, while several of the promising youngsters, such as Cuthbert, Davin, Marjoribanks, and McGlynn had been blooded during the season.

On the day of the Scottish Cup semi-finals Hibs met Hearts at Tynecastle, but unfortunately only in an East of Scotland Shield tie. As St Mirren were defeating Celtic 3-1 to reach a final they would eventually lose 2-0 to Rangers, a disappointingly low crowd of well under 8,000 watched Hearts win 3-1, Eric Stevenson scoring Hibs' solitary counter.

Ambitious Dunfermline now put forward proposals for the reinstatement of the Summer Cup which would be played at the end of the coming season. Although the SFA council had approved the suggestion there was little interest among the bigger clubs, including Hibs, which was something of a surprise considering that Harry Swan had proposed a similar competition at the meeting of the representatives only a few months before. It goes without saying that neither Rangers nor Celtic were interested either. The idea was scrapped, at least for the time being.

At the end of the season 12 players were freed, including goalkeeper Willie Muirhead, who had not featured since the Red Star game, the versatile Bobby Nicol and utility man John Young. Sammy Baird and Bobby Kinloch were retained, but had been informed that the club would not be hard to deal with in the event of an enquiry. Almost immediately, Muirhead, Nicol and

Young, were signed on a three-month contract by Eastern Canadian League side Toronto, who were then managed by the former Hibs and Scotland goalkeeper Tommy Younger.

After what had been a trying season, both Edinburgh sides embarked on a post-season tour. As Hearts made their way by coach to the Scottish Highlands, Hibs were making their first trip to Czechoslovakia since 1946. As the players gathered at the Scotia Hotel in Great King Street on the Sunday prior to departure, Walter Galbraith was confined to bed with gastric flu and unable to travel. The only problem was that the manager had failed to notify the team of his impending absence, and only frantic last-minute telephone calls to his home cleared up the misunderstanding, leaving the party barely enough time to catch the flight after a dash to the airport. Even then their troubles were not over. On their arrival in Prague it was discovered that some items of luggage, including the strips and boots, had been misplaced en route. Enquiries revealed that they had not been loaded onto the plane during the transfer in Brussels and they arrived safely the following morning.

The tour of Czechoslovakia opened with a win. As Hearts were beating Peterhead 5-0 in the north of Scotland, Hibs overcame Spartak Pilsen 3-2 in the picturesque spa town of Karlovy Vary in a game that was shown live on Czech television. The tour proved a great success, with Hibs enhancing not only their own reputation but that of Scotland. Eddie Turnbull led the side to three wins and two draws. It was generally acknowledged that the temporary manager completely outsmarted the Czechs as far as tactics were concerned, a talent he would put to great advantage in the coming years. The opening match against Spartak Pilsen was brought to an unexpected end when the referee was instructed to call time six minutes early to enable an important bicycle race to take place, cycling being a sport that was tremendously popular in the country at the time. Another match was abruptly interrupted, this time when a parachutist landed on the pitch while the game was in progress. The match against Vitkovic, which Hibs won 2-0 and which was also shown live on television, was delayed 20 minutes to allow another bicycle race to take place and was brought to a dramatic end after 67 minutes when engineers entered the playing area to erect an electronic timing device in the centre of the pitch for yet another major bicycle race. Incredibly the referee had instructed the players to play around the giant structure but even he soon realised the absurdity of the situation and called a premature halt to the game.

Goals by Baker and Falconer gave Hibs a 2-0 victory over Spartak Usti in the penultimate game of the trip in what was the home side's first defeat by foreign opposition for six years, and the tour wound up with a credible 2-2 draw against Sokolovo. One drawback of what had otherwise been an enjoyable trip was the generally poor standard of refereeing, which had not improved since Willie McCartney saw fit to criticise the officials during Hibs' first visit to the country just after the war. Infringements that would have been penalised in Scotland were consistently allowed to go unpunished. In one bizarre incident during the match against Sokolovo, the referee stamped on

Tommy Preston's toes after the wing half challenged yet another of his absurd decisions. Prior to the game, Eddie Turnbull and *Evening News* reporter Stewart Brown had travelled to watch Sokolovo training. Unfortunately the players were training elsewhere, but their journey was not a complete waste of time: the pair were shown round the trophy room at the Spartak Stadium and amongst the memorabilia on display were artefacts from Hibs tours of Czechoslovakia in 1946 and 1954.

2

Walter Galbraith, a Freak Winter and a Flirt with Relegation

1962–63

IF THE EASTER ROAD SUPPORT had been disappointed at the club's poor form during the previous season with only 14 of the 34 league games ending in victory, early exits made from both domestic cup competitions, and humiliation in Europe, then things were about to get much worse. Only a dramatic improvement during the final few weeks of the 1962–63 season would avoid a return to the Second Division for the first time since the dark days of the early 1930s.

During the summer Walter Galbraith had returned to Tranmere Rovers to sign inside forward Johnny Byrne. Outside right Doug Logan was signed from Queen's Park and utility man Morris Stevenson joined on a free transfer from Motherwell. Other newcomers were Derek Oates from Ross County, Duncan McLeod from Brora Rangers and centre half John Blair from another of Galbraith's former teams, Bradford Park Avenue. With the exception of Byrne and Stevenson, none of the newcomers would make an impact on the struggling side.

Over at the other side of the city it had not taken Peter Cormack long to realise that cleaning toilets and the multitude of other mundane tasks that are usually associated with a job on the ground staff of a senior club were not for him. Just prior to the start of the new season the youngster had walked out of Tynecastle. Alerted by Eddie Turnbull, who had been aware of Cormack's unrest for some time, Galbraith moved quickly to sign the 16-year-old, who was only too happy to take up a similar position at Easter Road. It was a move that would be of enormous benefit to Hibs in the coming years.

Galbraith had shown that he was not afraid to give inexperienced youngsters their chance when he had selected Scot Ian Gibson for a first-team debut at Bradford just a few days after the player's 15th birthday. At the time Gibson was the youngest ever player to play in the English League. This would no doubt be of great encouragement to Cormack, the highly rated Jimmy O'Rourke, Bobby Duncan and several of the other promising youngsters on the books at Easter Road, all hoping to make a quick breakthrough into the first team.

In the usual break from pre-season training, the annual Hibs versus Franklin cricket match was still proving popular with players and fans alike. A reasonably large crowd gathered at Leith Links to enjoy a relaxing evening of cricket in the warm summer sunshine with the skill level of the players in the footballer's side ranging from the moderate to the incompetent. Not so popular, however, was the Edinburgh Select Charities match. For the second year in succession Burnley were the opponents, this time at Tynecastle, and a dull game played out under the brilliant summer sun saw the English side again running out deserved winners.

The annual charities match was now beginning to generate only moderate interest among the Edinburgh public. With gates generally in decline throughout the country, the 20,000 crowd could still be considered a reasonable attendance but it fell far short of the over 40,000 the fixture had often attracted during the previous decade, and there was little reaction from the fans when the selectors announced that changes were planned. The decision had been brought about by the direct intervention of Harry Swan who realised that with interest in competitive European football on the increase, the charity game had now lost its appeal. After expenses had been deducted, the proceeds were often so poor that it would be better if both clubs simply gave a charitable donation instead. The charity selection committee suggested that perhaps Hearts could contest the fixture one year and Hibs the next, but the Edinburgh Select had played its last game, for the time being at least. For the record, Edinburgh had won seven of the 18 games played since its inception in 1944, drawing five and losing six, scoring 49 goals and conceding 54 in the process.

At the end of the previous season both Edinburgh clubs had once again been all but promised entry into the Fairs Cup competition, but while Hibs were in Czechoslovakia during the summer, unexpected developments had taken place. It emerged that several other Scottish clubs were also keen to take part and the SFA, previously reluctant to become involved, now recommended that allocation should be based solely on merit. Champions Dundee, including the evergreen Gordon Smith, would be contesting the European Cup, and Rangers the Cup Winners' Cup. As far as the SFA were concerned, third-placed Celtic and fourth-placed Dunfermline should be nominated for the Fairs Cup. The cup organising committee, probably influenced by Harry Swan, insisted that Hibs and Celtic should represent Scotland, and although disappointed that their preferred criterion had not been used, the SFA had no option but to agree.

In England the issue had become far more complicated. There, as many as 25 sides were now keen to enter the competition but the cup organisers ultimately decided that Everton, Birmingham and Sheffield Wednesday should be invited as English representatives. The FA disagreed, suggesting instead Everton, Burnley and Sheffield United. The dispute raged fiercely, the arguments reaching such a pitch that one club threatened legal action. But, just as they had done a short while before when two Greek sides had become embroiled in a similar lengthy dispute that resulted in both being excluded from the competition, the organisers refused Birmingham, Burnley and the two Sheffield sides from taking part, leaving Everton as the sole

English representative in the first-round draw. The earlier squabble between the Greek sides had been of immediate benefit to Scotland, when Jock Stein's Dunfermline replaced the committee's first choice, Solonika, to become the third Scottish team to enter the competition. As far as the Fairs Cup committee were concerned, the individual authorities had every right to prohibit teams from that country from participating, but stressed that these authorities could not insist which teams would take part; it had always been an invitation tournament and it would remain just that. As a matter of interest, the West German FA based their recommendations for entry to the Fairs Cup both on crowd-pulling potential and the financial ability to commit fully to the tournament.

Although only in its seventh year, the Fairs Cup had already operated under four different formats and there was to be yet another change for the coming season. An extra four sides was added to make a total of 32 teams arranged in eight groups of four on a mini-knockout format, the winners of each section progressing to the quarter-finals.

Back at Easter Road Hibs had failed to qualify from a League Cup section that included Rangers, Third Lanark and St Mirren, but only just, finishing one point behind the eventual leaders, Rangers. Some things never change. In the opening game against the Light Blues at Easter Road the referee seemed intent on punishing Hibs' every move while ignoring similar indiscretions by the visitors. There could be no complaint at the result, the home side suffering a heavy 4-1 defeat, but one journalist wondered 'why the referee seemed intent in trying not to upset the large contingent that had travelled through from Glasgow for the match'.

In the Easter Road boardroom, after a 2-1 victory over St Mirren a few days later, 83-year-old Tom Hartland was presented with a silver salver to commemorate his 30 years' service as a director of the club. Born in Bristol in 1880 only five years after the formation of Hibs, Hartland had started work for a leading insurance company based in Liverpool and had been a keen fan of the Anfield side for many years. Transferred to the Edinburgh office at the outbreak of the Great War, like Harry Swan, he at first shared his football viewing between both capital clubs, but it was not long before he found himself with a leaning towards Hibs. Forming a deep friendship with the long-serving player Bobby Templeton, he started to travel with the team to the away games. In the early 1920s, along with Swan and others, he had purchased debenture shares in the club. Elected to the board in 1932, the same year that Swan had first resigned as a director, both men had since built up a wonderful working relationship which had been of inestimable value to the club. Paying his own personal tribute to Hartland, Swan reminded the invited guests of just what had been achieved at Easter Road: 'When Hartland had first joined Hibs, the stadium was capable of holding no more than 17,000 supporters, now the ground can hold more than three times that number.'

In the final League Cup section game against Third Lanark, played at

Hampden, a crowd of just under 5,000 inside a stadium designed to hold almost 150,000 failed to generate an atmosphere conducive to good football but this did not prevent Gerry Baker from scoring his first hat-trick in Hibs colours in a 4-1 victory. It was the first treble by a Hibs player since his brother Joe had notched his triple hat-trick against Peebles Rovers in the Scottish Cup 19 months before.

As usual the first Edinburgh derby of the season was eagerly awaited, but Hearts, who had earlier qualified for the League Cup quarter-finals, enjoyed a comfortable 4-0 victory. It was now 11 years since Hibs had beaten their city rivals in a league match at Easter Road. With little to choose between the sides, the main difference was in attack. Inside forward Danny Paton helped himself to a hat-trick and, ably prompted by Willie Hamilton, a recent signing from Sheffield United, Hearts were the more dangerous outfit and fully deserved their victory.

In a 2-2 draw with Motherwell a week later, goals by Baker and Byrne, both set up by new signing Harvey McCreadie, a 19-year-old from English non-league side Mosley, seemed to have secured the points, but an uncharacteristic late mistake by goalkeeper Simpson, then displaying some of the best form of his career, allowed the Steelmen to equalise. McCready, who had served under Galbraith at Accrington Stanley, had been somewhat optimistically described as being better than the great English centre forward Tommy Lawton by the manager, who remained a keen admirer. McCready scored his first goal in Hibs colours seven days later at Easter Road but it was little consolation against the five scored by Rangers. The following week another five scored by Dundee United at Tannadice, this time without reply, saw Hibs plummet to the foot of the table, level on points with Raith Rovers. After the United debacle, the disillusioned Hibs supporters demonstrated outside the main entrance only to be moved on by the police. Rumours of an impending bid for the unsettled Rangers wing half Billy Stevenson were denied by Swan who, refusing to be intimidated by the mood of the fans, remained adamant that Hibs would not be buying themselves out of trouble. In any case the £25,000 asking price was well beyond even the chairman's ambitions for the club and Stevenson would soon join Liverpool.

Although things were far from ideal on the playing side, the development of the stadium was still proceeding and the resurfacing of the car park that lay between the main terracing and the railway halt had now been completed, with new turnstiles and toilets in operation behind the terracing.

On the transfer front, Bobby Kinloch, who had recently been unable to reclaim a first team place, joined Morton, who were also said to be interested in the transfer-listed outside right Jim Scott. Former captain Sammy Baird, who was also finding it difficult to command a regular first-team place owing to the consistency of Ally MacLeod at wing half, was a target for Berwick Rangers.

In the Fairs Cup, Hibs had been drawn against Copenhagen Staevnet, a select side from Denmark. It was explained to the Danes that the dates suggested for both ties would prove difficult for Hibs to accommodate if they were to progress to the later stages of the League Cup for the first time in nine years, but as we have already seen, there had been little cause for concern regarding that particular issue.

On the eve of the game there was some good news for Hibs when they were informed that the Danish side would be without the services of Denmark's top goalscorer, Jorgen Ravn, and the immensely popular Ole Sorensen. The absence of both players would be a huge loss to the visitors, but Staevnet could still call on the services of nine full caps in their line-up. On paper, they represented a formidable challenge. Just prior to the kick-off at Easter Road there was a further bonus for the home side, when Clausen, one of Denmark's brightest youngsters, became the third Danish player to withdraw because of injury.

This was the first time that Hibs had faced a select side in the competition. Staevnet, officially known as the Copenhagen International Football Combination, selected their team from eight sides. They had been in existence for over 60 years and had previously opposed the likes of Celtic, Rangers, Hibs, and many other Scottish teams in challenge matches. Unlike the Edinburgh Select, who played only once a year, Copenhagen, one of the original members of the inaugural Fairs Cup in 1955, played regularly throughout the season and had only recently lost 5-4 to European champions Benfica, and drawn 1-1 with Arsenal.

In the first round at Easter Road, goals by Byrne, Baker and Morris Stevenson, all inside an eight-minute spell in the first half, provided the tonic so desperately needed at Easter Road, and a fortunate fourth when the Danish full back Ronnow deflected a shot into his own net gave the home side a commanding 4-0 half-time lead. There was no more scoring after the interval but the final scoreline would surely be enough to guarantee Hibs' advancement into the next round and a game against either Dutch side Utrecht or Tasmania from Berlin.

FINAL SCORE: HIBERNIAN 4. COPENHAGEN STAEVNET 0.

FAIRS CUP 1ST ROUND (1ST LEG), WEDNESDAY 3 OCTOBER 1962, EASTER ROAD.
HIBERNIAN: SIMPSON, FRASER, MCCLELLAND, GRANT, HUGHES, MACLEOD, SCOTT, BYRNE, BAKER, (M) STEVENSON, (E) STEVENSON.

Probably because of the injury crisis, Copenhagen had fielded several Second Division players and the Danish side was considered one of the poorest in the competition. There was gathering concern over the poor level of competence being displayed by some of the other entrants, as evidenced by Inter Milan's crushing 14-3 win against Hanover over two legs, and Copenhagen's earlier 11-4 aggregate win against Basle. Yet another example was Lausanne, Hibs' would-be first-round opponents the previous year, who had scratched from the competition giving the Edinburgh side a walkover. The obvious lack of preparation by the Swiss side had been a major embarrassment, not only to themselves but to the competition. It had long been anticipated that UEFA would make an attempt to take over the running of the tournament, and had this occurred then the new organising body would almost certainly have insisted that participation be based entirely on league position. The expected takeover failed to materialise although a change of authority would probably have been painless, with FA representative Stanley Rous and Hibs chairman Harry Swan almost certain to have remained as part of any new administration.

Three days after the victory over Copenhagen, the Hibs players collected their first league win bonus of the season after a narrow 1-0 victory over fellow relegation strugglers Raith Rovers at Easter Road in front of a poor crowd of 8,000. An Eric Stevenson penalty in the first half, only his second goal of the season and his first ever from the spot in senior football, was enough to lift the home side into 16th place. The game had started with two balls on the field and one ironic scribe reported that perhaps this was just what both goal-shy sides needed.

At the corresponding reserve match at Starks Park that same afternoon, Harry Swan suffered a severe nose haemorrhage that might well have had more serious consequences for the 67-year-old chairman. Doctors had initially been unable to quell the massive flow of blood and he was taken from the ground during the game and rushed to Kirkcaldy hospital, but was eventually allowed home. Unfortunately, the heavy bleeding restarted and he was forced to spend a few days in hospital as a precautionary measure.

The Hibs chairman was not alone in having his troubles to seek at Kirkcaldy. For former manager Hugh Shaw and Hibs relegation opponents Raith Rovers, things were going from bad to worse. In an attempt to lift the Fife side from the foot of the table, Shaw signed former Hibs player Andy Aitken from Falkirk. Unfortunately the new signing could do little to prevent a 10-0 defeat by Aberdeen the following week, the final scoreline only just failing to beat the Fife side's record 11-1 defeat by Morton in the 1935–36 season.

At Easter Road, encouraging back-to-back draws against Dundee and St Mirren was just the tonic needed. The results saw Hibs climb two places to 14th place in the table as they prepared to fly to Denmark for the return game against Copenhagen. Both Eric Stevenson, who had broken his leg against St Mirren three days before, and the injured Jim Easton would miss the game. Desperate efforts to get the centre half fit received unexpected, but nevertheless welcome, assistance from their opponents, who laid on the use of their medical room. Unfortunately it was to no avail and Easton would watch the match from the sidelines.

It had been planned to show the game live on Danish television, but a dispute between the television company and the Danish football authorities, who had demanded double the usual broadcasting fees, resulted in the coverage being called off at the last minute, with only brief highlights shown later in the evening.

On Tuesday 23 October 1962, the world awoke to the threat of nuclear war. As civilisation held its breath over the ultimatum delivered that morning to Russian leader Nikita Khrushchev by American President John F. Kennedy, demanding that the Soviet Union remove its atomic missiles from Cuba and asserting that the US would turn back any Cuba-bound Russian ships, Hibs took the field at the modern Idraetspark Stadium in Copenhagen for the first game under the recently improved floodlights. Khrushchev would eventually capitulate to Kennedy at the very last minute, as would Copenhagen to Hibs, but only after an initial struggle.

While far from convincing, the visitors were still way too good for the Danish opponents who at their best were only honest tryers. A large crowd had turned out in the hope of witnessing a stirring comeback by a home side that had confounded their critics by defeating the potential Danish international side 6-0 in a trial match only days before, but except for a brief period when inside right Dyremose celebrated his debut with a goal, this confidence proved groundless.

After dominating the opening period of the match, Hibs were shocked when Dyremose struck a first-time volley past Simpson after a corner on the right. The home side had the opportunity to further extend their lead when Fraser was called upon to clear after another corner, but it was Hibs who scored shortly after to level the tie on the night when Byrne stroked the ball past the partially unsighted keeper.

Only four minutes into the second half, Morris Stevenson put Hibs ahead from close range and with just over an hour of the game played their superiority was emphatically underlined when Stevenson scored his second of the night to complete a workmanlike performance by the visitors. The home side scored again four minutes later, but with the scoreline 7-2 on aggregate the goal was academic and Hibs could now look forward to a meeting with Dutch side Utrecht in the next round.

FULL TIME: COPENHAGEN 2. HIBERNIAN 3.

FAIRS CUP 1ST ROUND (2ND LEG), TUESDAY 23 OCTOBER 1962, IDRAETSPARK STADIUM.
HIBERNIAN: SIMPSON, FRASER, MCCLELLAND, GRANT, HUGHES, MACLEOD, SCOTT, FALCONER, BAKER, (M) STEVENSON; BYRNE.
REFEREE: L. RAVENS (HOLLAND).

On the Saturday a 3-0 victory over Queen of the South at Easter Road seemed certain to have dispelled any lingering fears of relegation for the home side. Lining up for Queen's were former Hibs players George Farm and Johnny Frye, but it was the impressive form of their lanky centre forward that caught the eye. Signed only the previous season from Alloa, the 22-year-old was already earning rave reviews, both for his intelligent displays and goalscoring capabilities, particularly his lethal prowess in the air. Although he had failed to register on the scoresheet, it would not be the last we would hear of Neil Martin at Easter Road.

A 4-1 away victory against Third Lanark a week later gave Hibs their first back-to-back league wins of the season. The result enabled them to climb to the dizzy heights of ninth place in the table, the highest position they would attain all season. From then on it was all downhill. Three minutes before half time Jim Scott scored the best goal of the game by far with a truly tremendous solo effort. Collecting a throw in on the half way line, the outside right proceeded to beat man after man including the goalkeeper, before tapping the ball into the net, turning to receive the rapturous acclaim of his teammates and both sets of supporters.

Losing his place after the heavy 5-0 defeat by Dundee United in September, wing half John Baxter, like Sammy Baird, was now finding difficulty in re-establishing himself in the first team owing to the fine form of Ally MacLeod and he was placed on the transfer list at his own request. It had been reported that Leeds United, who had money to spend after the recent sale of the legendary John Charles to Juventus, were interested, but despite the newspaper headlines, no contact was ever made with Easter Road.

In mid-November a fine run of seven games without defeat came to an end at Pittodrie when an uncharacteristic mistake by Simpson shortly after the restart gave the home side the lead, eventually running out easy 3-0 winners. Seven days later, despite Hibs giving one of their best displays of the season, a 2-0 home defeat by Kilmarnock sent the Edinburgh side plunging back into the relegation dogfight.

True to the promise made several months before, Barcelona arrived in Edinburgh on 21 November 1962 to play a friendly match arranged by way of an apology for the disgraceful antics of some of their players in the Fairs Cup game nearly two years before. This time there would be no repeat of the scandalous behaviour of the visitors. Many of the Spanish players who had taken part in that infamous match were still in the side, but several new faces were on display. The Spanish giants had embarked on a massive shopping spree during the close season in an attempt to become an even bigger force in the European game. In the past 12 months most of the promising youngsters in Spain had been snapped up at knock-down prices by Barcelona, thereby achieving the twin aim of improving their own side and weakening their opponents, a practice not unknown to Rangers and Celtic in Scotland.

Goalkeeper Simpson, Fraser, McClelland, Easton, Baxter and Scott, still remained in the Hibs line-up from that February evening in 1961, but this time there would be no controversy. A disappointingly small crowd of fewer than 10,000 watched Hibs deservedly beaten 3-1 by a Barcelona side well ahead in all departments of a team in the middle of transformation. Level at the break, the home side had more than matched the visitors in the opening stages of the game and could well have taken the lead just before half time, but after the interval it was a totally different story. After a lacklustre and goalless first 60 minutes, with the obviously well warned visiting players apologising profusely after every foul, all the action was contained in the final half hour. Barcelona opened the scoring before Scott equalised from a great Baker through pass, but it was all too easy for the visitors, who scored twice more, the second from the penalty spot after Kocsis had been brought down by Morris Stevenson.

Meanwhile 16-year-old Peter Cormack had been earning rave reviews in the reserves, making it extremely difficult for the manager to ignore the swift progress of the talented teenager, and on Saturday 24 November he made his first team debut on the right wing against Airdrie at Broomfield. It had been an unexpectedly quick promotion for a youngster who had only been at the club a few months and was as yet still too young to sign full professional terms. The Broomfield encounter ended in yet another disappointing display by a team totally lacking in confidence, and the home side were allowed to register a comfortable 2-1 win which saw Hibs drop yet another place in the table. The only crumb of comfort for manager Galbraith was a headed goal by debutant Cormack in the second half.

The youngster's impressive debut earned him a place in the Hibs party that made its way to Utrecht for the second round of the Fairs Cup, his first ever trip abroad. Like Copenhagen, Utrecht were also a composite side made up of players from three sides, Velox, Elinkwijk and DOS, who were the current leaders of the Division of Honour. The Netherlands Football Association had previously shown little interest in the Fairs Cup and had allowed the first four competitions to pass without representation. Now Utrecht would become the first Dutch side to take part in the tournament. All the Utrecht players were semi-professional and had done extremely well to overcome the champions of Berlin on a 5-3 aggregate, surprisingly winning the away game in the divided German city by a 2-1 scoreline.

Still deprived of the services of both the injured Stevenson and Easton, Hibs faced a side that were expected to provide a much tougher proposition than Copenhagen in the previous round.

Playing with only two forwards, the visitors fought a classic rearguard system that relied heavily on the quick break. It took them only 11 minutes to open the scoring when Falconer took full advantage of a terrible mistake by goalkeeper Van Zoghel. Thereafter it was mostly all Hibs, who deserved to be further ahead. The experienced Preston, lining up in the then unusual position of centre forward but playing in a deep lying role, was Hibs' top man as he repeatedly drew the centre half out of position before shrewdly setting up moves for his teammates. Unfortunately, the Hibs players were unable to take advantage of Preston's precision passing.

As would be expected, the home side came out fighting after the break and Hibs enjoyed a touch of luck on several occasions as Utrecht, encouraged by a fervent partisan support, reinforced their efforts to secure an equalising goal. With a little over an hour played, Joe McClelland handled the ball just prior to Morelissen forcing the ball into the net, but fortunately for Hibs, the Belgian referee had already blown for a penalty kick, much to the fury of the 15,000 Utrecht fans who thought, probably correctly, that the advantage should have been played. As the crowd hushed in expectancy, goalkeeper Simpson, often the scourge of penalty takers, threw himself to his left to smother the ball at the foot of the post before clearing upfield, and Hibs breathed again.

There was no more scoring, although luck was once again on the side of the visitors when Geurtsen hit the bar in the very last minute. It had not been the best of nights for centre forward Geurtsen. His under-par performance could probably be explained by him still feeling shaky after being involved in a collision with a car before the game as he cycled to the stadium after work. With his bicycle beyond repair he was forced to rely on the services of a passing motorist to take him to the ground. Changed days indeed!

FULL TIME: UTRECHT 0. HIBERNIAN 1.

FAIRS CUP 2ND ROUND (1ST LEG), TUESDAY 27 NOVEMBER 1962, GALGENWAARD STADIUM, UTRECHT.
HIBERNIAN: SIMPSON, FRASER, MCCLELLAND, GRANT, HUGHES, MACLEOD, SCOTT, FALCONER, PRESTON, BYRNE, (M) STEVENSON.

The recent poor run of league results had had a major impact on attendances, and therefore on gate receipts. The alarming decline in attendances on both sides of the Border, was a worrying trend and a recipe for financial disaster for many of the smaller clubs, as illustrated by the plight of Raith Rovers. It was estimated that £900 was required each fortnight to meet running costs and the visiting club's guarantee; average gate receipts at Starks Park were around £300 for each match. These were alarming statistics.

Back at Easter Road, Gerry Baker, who had missed several games because of injury, returned to the side that would face Utrecht in Edinburgh. There was also a surprise inclusion in the line-up in the shape of 16-year-old Jimmy O'Rourke, making his first team debut only a matter of months after being called up to Easter Road. Like Cormack, O'Rourke had been earning rave reviews in the reserves and might well have made his first team debut earlier, but Walter Galbraith had held him back because of the side's poor league form. Surprised to be called away from work at an electrical warehouse to take part in the pre-match training session, O'Rourke would become the youngest ever player to take part in any of the three competitive European competitions at that time.

Although they were finding domestic games a struggle, European games did not seem to be a problem for Hibs and they progressed into the third round of the Fairs Cup with a convincing 3-1 aggregate victory over the Dutch side. The win gave them a 100 per cent record in the tournament so far, and barring a miracle by Jock Stein's Dunfermline, trailing 4-0 from the first leg in Spain, they would be facing holders Valencia in the next round.

In a victory that owed more to effort than skilful football, Hibs eventually progressed through to the next round against often uncompromising opponents, with O'Rourke playing his part. There was an early scare for the home side when Van Der Linden beat Hibs' offside trap in the first minute, only to shoot narrowly past. Completely lacking in rhythm in the early stages, the unsettled Hibs were even more unsettled when Utrecht took the lead midway through the first half to put the Dutch side level on aggregate. Utrecht's lead lasted barely two minutes. Twenty-four minutes into the first half, a terrific burst of speed by Baker left his marker completely stranded as the centre forward first timed a cross ball on the run to crash an unstoppable shot high into the roof of the net past the helpless Van Zoghel. It was Baker's first European goal for the club, and it helped to lift the spirits of the disappointingly small crowd of under 6,000.

Using his phenomenal pace to great advantage, Baker repeatedly tore through the Utrecht defensive system as he took the game to his opponents, either through the middle or down the flanks. Other top men for Hibs were the prodigious and hard-working John Grant and young O'Rourke, who was desperately unlucky not to score a debut goal when his lobbed header from a Utrecht clearance beat the goalkeeper, only to shave the wrong side of the crossbar. O'Rourke displayed the heart of a lion throughout and despite being repeatedly fouled by Dacsev, he refused to be intimidated, constantly coming back for more punishment.

Shortly after the restart the game was all but over when Morris Stevenson scored a second for Hibs. As in the first game, once they sensed that defeat was inevitable, the tackling of the Utrecht players degenerated to a level that was harsh and unacceptable. Had the visitors played to the rules, Hibs undoubtedly would have added to their tally. It was just a pity that what appeared to be a revival of form should be denied its reward by the negative play of the visitors and by a weak official who should have stamped out the illegal tactics from the start.

On the final whistle, Dacsev in particular was jeered from the field by a Hibs support disgusted at the harsh and cynical treatment dished out to Baker and O'Rourke. O'Rourke, who had displayed some neat distribution throughout the 90 minutes, understandably tired near the end but he had done more than enough to suggest he had a great future in the game.

FULL TIME: HIBERNIAN 2. UTRECHT 1.

FAIRS CUP 2ND ROUND (2ND LEG), WEDNESDAY 12 DECEMBER 1962, EASTER ROAD.
HIBERNIAN: SIMPSON, FRASER, MCCLELLAND, GRANT, MUIR, MACLEOD, SCOTT, FALCONER, BAKER, O'ROURKE, (M) STEVENSON.

Hibs would have to wait to learn who they would face in the next round. It had been expected that cup holders Valencia, who held a 4-0 lead over Dunfermline from the first leg in Spain, would be their third round opponents, but a magnificent fighting performance by Jock Stein's men at East End Park that same evening gave the Pars a tremendous 6-2 victory to level the tie overall and force a third game play-off in Valencia.

In between the European games there was another unusually early round of the Scottish Cup. Unlike the previous year when they had made an exit at the first time of asking, this time Hibs had no difficulty in progressing into the next round, mainly because they had received a bye in the first.

After his impressive debut performance against Utrecht, O'Rourke kept his place in the side to face fellow European challengers Dunfermline at East End Park on the Saturday. Before the game there had been a small ceremony to officially open the Fifers' new Centre Stand. Hibs made their own contribution to the celebrations when they presented Dunfermline with a gift goal shortly before half time after Grant had been woefully short with a pass back. Near the end, Jimmy O'Rourke scored his first goal for the club when he swept a Byrne pass past future Hibs goalkeeper Jim Herriot to make it 2-2. The Edinburgh celebrations were short-lived. Dunfermline scored what was to prove the winning goal two minutes later, a result that saw Hibs dropping to fourth bottom of the table.

A few days before the turn of the year Hibs' home game against Clyde only managed to receive the go-ahead from the referee 20 minutes before the kick-off. A heavy fall of snow just before the game had discouraged all but the brave or the foolhardy, and at the kick-off there were only a few hundred hardy souls inside the ground. The entire sporting card had been heavily hit by cancellations because of the weather and in the end Hibs might well have wished that their game had also fallen by the wayside, after a strike by Harry Hood and an own goal by Pat Hughes gave the 'Bully Wee', an important 'relegation zone' victory. Ally MacLeod scored the Hibs goal from the penalty spot, but the wing half missed another in the second half which was to prove costly for the home side, which now dropped into the bottom three of the table, only one point ahead of second bottom Airdrie.

After the latest in a series of dismal performances the players left the field to a torrent of jeers from the fans who had bothered to stay to the end. Their reaction prompted the forthright Harry Swan to release a heated statement. The highly critical Swan blasted:

The supporters involved just cannot take defeat, and we can well do without them! Naturally I am as disappointed as any other supporter at the current situation, but the latest storm is nonsensical. It is not new at Easter Road, we have had it in the past as have every club. We faced it last season when things were sticky and fought ourselves free from the situation. This small coterie cannot take defeat and if that is the case they may as well stay away from Easter Road as they are no use to us if they behave like that every time they are beaten. They pay their 3/- (15p) and if they do not see what is best, then they are entitled to be annoyed, but they are doing the club, the players, and themselves no good by demonstrating. No club can afford to let spectators dictate to them. The supporters want us to sign players, but you do not find top class players easily these days. We have the potential of a good side in the reserves, but it takes time. Fans should be encouraging the players, not labouring their efforts.

Brave words. The chairman was perhaps beginning to show signs that the pressure was getting to him. Now only days short of his 67th birthday, he had been at the helm at Easter Road for nearly 30 years. Some, perhaps forgetting just what had been achieved during his tenure at Easter Road, were of the opinion that it was time for a change.

And still the snow continued to fall. The New Year's Day game against Hearts became an immediate casualty of the atrocious conditions, with eight inches of snow covering the Tynecastle pitch, as was the home game against Motherwell the following day. But this was only the start. The conditions eventually became so severe that Hibs, and almost every other side in the country, would not play another league match for nearly three months. The situation was unprecedented, breaking all records for postponed or abandoned matches. The big freeze of 1947 had been the worst since records began, but although many parts of the country had been brought to a complete standstill from mid-January to the beginning of March, relatively few football matches had been cancelled. Hibs had missed only two games during this period. The situation became so bad that two extensions were required at the end of the season to ease the fixture backlog.

Many different methods of protecting pitches from the ravages of winter had been tried, including covering the playing surface with straw, the use of braziers, and more recently a plastic sheet covering the entire pitch that could be inflated by hot air – but none had proved particularly effective. Envious eyes were cast in the direction of Murrayfield, where the underground electric blanket allowed rugby matches to proceed undisturbed by the conditions. Many thought this system was a method worth considering for football. Almost 20 years would elapse before its introduction into the Scottish game, with Hibs destined to play a prominent part in the innovation when it did arrive.

Because of results elsewhere when the very occasional game managed to escape the stranglehold of the weather, Hibs dropped another league place without even playing a game and found themselves second-bottom of the table. The situation was now critical.

In mid-January Scottish Cup winner Tommy Leishman, a former teammate of Gerry Baker at St Mirren, was signed from Liverpool for a fee believed to be around £10,000. Leishman had been one of the last signings made by the Anfield club before the legendary Bill Shankly took over as manager. A fast, powerful defender who was popular with the supporters, he was thought to be out of his depth after the club had won promotion to the top league the previous season. Because of the freak weather conditions, Leishman would make a debut of sorts on Portobello beach in a full-scale practice match as the club struggled to find training facilities that had managed to escape the grip of winter. Hibs had travelled as far as Dunbar to find a suitable training surface and as well as an offer to use the well equipped gymnasium at the Pleasance Boys Club, both Edinburgh clubs had been invited to use Powderhall Stadium where possible. The arctic conditions had obviously also affected the Scottish Cup competition, and several attempts were made to play Hibs' second round tie against Second Division Brechin City at Glebe Park. After several postponements, a request was made to the SFA for permission to play the game at nearby Arbroath, whose pitch had escaped the worst effects of the weather, presumably because of the salty sea air. A breach of the competition rules, this request was initially refused but with the situation worsening, the SFA eventually reversed the decision. By that time, however, it was too late as travel arrangements had already been made to play the game at the original venue. Before the game Brechin announced that they had acquired a 'revolutionary' new special anti-freeze mixture, which the manufacturers had claimed would soften the soil sufficiently to allow play to proceed. Whether this mixture was indeed used is uncertain, but the 2,380 robust fans who braved the elements, paying a grand total of £341 for the privilege, watched 22 players slip and slide on what one member of the press described as a 'porridge pitch that was quite clearly unplayable'. Hibs eventually managed to overcome both their stuffy opponents and the playing surface to win 2-0 in their first game for almost four weeks. At a meeting of all 37 clubs around this time, St Johnstone had proposed a six-week mid-season shutdown to start the following season. The suggestion was considered unrealistic by Harry Swan as was another proposal for summer football. According to the Hibs chairman the unpredictable Scottish weather made a winter shutdown unpractical with bad weather likely to appear outside of the anticipated period.

One proposal that was adopted was the introduction of the Pools Panel. Without football for a lengthy period, many clubs – in particular the smaller ones – were now in desperate need of a financial injection, and with the pools companies also facing extreme financial hardship due to the cancellation of the fixture lists, an emergency scheme was introduced that would see a panel of experts predict the results of the abandoned games. To come into operation only when 30 or more games in both Scotland and England had been called off, the panel consisting of Tom Finney, Tommy Lawton, Ted Drake, Arthur Ellis and Scotland's own George Young, presided over by Lord Brabazon, each receiving the then not inconsiderable sum of £100 per week, first sat on Saturday 26 January 1963, the very day that Hibs' match against Brechin had managed to escape the extreme conditions. The novelty was not universally popular, with many supporters baffled by some of the panels predictions, particularly when a Hibs side that had won only once in the league since the beginning of November were credited with an away draw against a Dundee side ten places above them in the table. The panel, however, were not so wide of the mark. When the game did eventually take place a couple of months later, a Gerry Baker hat-trick was enough to earn the away side a comfortable 3-1 victory. People soon got used to the idea of the panel, and although initially intended only as an emergency measure to tide over the bad winter, the scheme was eventually extended and is still in use today.

A reserve fixture between Hibs and Queen of the South at Easter Road on 2 March became the city's first senior game of 1963. Both sides took the opportunity to field a virtually full strength first team which gave a first competitive outing in Hibs colours for Tommy Leishman. Teenagers Jim O'Rourke and Peter Cormack featured prominently in the game and between them engineered the Hibs goal in a 2-1 defeat. Reserve team coach Jimmy McColl was less than happy with the result. His second string had been unbeaten for the previous 15 games and he joked that it was ironic that defeat should come when the team was packed with first team regulars.

By 9 March the weather had finally eased, allowing Hibs to fit in a league game, their first in nearly three months, before travelling to Spain to face Valencia in the Fairs Cup. In front of a sparse crowd of under 5,000, the home side could only manage a 1-1 draw in a drab encounter against a Third Lanark side that included former Hibs skipper Sammy Baird, who had been transferred to Cathkin a few months before. Eight weeks after his move from Liverpool, defender Tommy Leishman had finally made his first-team debut.

In the meantime, Edinburgh had been selected to host the 1970 Commonwealth Games. A major drawback for the organisers was the lack of a purpose-built sports arena in the city. Never slow to anticipate anything that could be of benefit to the football club, Harry Swan, with the backing of a local councillor, came up with the idea that an entirely rebuilt Easter Road would be an option worth considering. His ambitious plan entailed turning the pitch at a complete right angle to run from east to west and the construction of an all-covered stadium; the local authority would finance the entire project, leasing the stadium back to the football club for a minimum of 35 weeks a year. The proposal was put forward as an alternative to siting the Commonwealth Stadium at Meadowbank. One major drawback to Swan's blueprint was the likely need to erect an indoor arena, warm-up area, velodrome and swimming pool in the area, although these could possibly have been built in nearby Lochend Park. On the plus side, Edinburgh Corporation would be guaranteed an income from the football club for the better part of the year. To Swan's disappointment, the site at Meadowbank was selected, although he remained convinced that the city fathers had missed a great opportunity.

A party of 14 players, including the transfer-listed Jim Scott and John Baxter, flew from Turnhouse for the first leg of the Fairs Cup game against Valencia, the cup holders after beating Barcelona 7-3 on aggregate in the 1962 final. By a bizarre twist of fate, all of their Fairs Cup opponents so far that season had been from Scotland. In the first round Celtic, taking part in their first ever competitive European outing, had been disposed of by a 6-4 overall aggregate. In the next round Dunfermline had lost only narrowly by a 7-6 aggregate after a third game play-off in Portugal. Apparently, bad weather in Portugal had kept the neutral crowd down to under 2,000, and after the Portuguese Football Association had taken their cut and the match expenses deducted, both Dunfermline and Valencia were left to share the remaining £7.

On the eve of the match Hibs were dealt a major psychological blow when they were informed that Valencia's prolific goalscorer, Waldo, who had been expected to miss the game because of injury, had been passed fit to play.

Galbraith's intention had been to play a rearguard formation with the recalled Tommy Preston's slower style used to supply ammunition from midfield, but the defensive frailties that had been so obvious in recent months were exposed at the Mestalla Stadium as Hibs were ruthlessly torn apart and defeated 5-0. The home side, exhibiting a high pressure display of modern football, scientifically dissected the Scottish team, whose interest in the competition was already all but over. It was now imperative that Swan release the purse strings to purchase a midfield general, something desperately needed since the departure of Bobby Johnstone.

Goalkeeper Simpson, so often the saviour of Hibs, had a bad night and his indecision helped to set up several of the Valencia goals. There could have been no complaint from the visitors had the final tally run into double figures as Valencia ran riot, hitting the woodwork on three occasions, with three more cleared off the line. To say Hibs played badly would be wrong – they were never in the game long enough to play badly.

FINAL SCORE: VALENCIA 5. HIBERNIAN 0.

FAIRS CUP QUARTER-FINAL (1ST LEG), WEDNESDAY MARCH 13 1963, CAMPO DE MESTELLA STADIUM, VALENCIA.
HIBERNIAN: SIMPSON, GRANT, MCCLELLAND, LEISHMAN, HUGHES, BAXTER, SCOTT, BAKER, PRESTON, O'ROURKE, MACLEOD.

After his poor performance in Spain, Simpson was replaced by Willie Wilson for the game against Aberdeen at Easter Road, but this failed to stem the tide of league defeats as the Dons squeezed home 3-2 despite a gallant late attempt by Hibs to save the game. Hearts did their near neighbours a huge favour by defeating third-bottom Clyde 6-0 at Shawfield on the same day, meaning that Hibs' fellow strugglers had now taken 13 points from 23 games, compared to Hibs' 11 points from 19. Games in hand are one thing but sides in the relegation zone generally encounter great difficulty in winning them.

There was a brief respite from these frustrations when Hibs faced Dundee at Dens Park in the third round of the Scottish Cup. In fighting form, Hibs shook the league champions who were glad to scrape home by a first-half Alan Gilzean goal. A superb display by Willie Wilson in goal inspired his colleagues and it took a supreme effort by the Dark Blues to hold on to their lead to the final whistle.

After training on the morning of 20 March 1963, Eddie Turnbull dropped a bombshell when he suddenly announced his resignation, not only stunning the players, but taking Harry Swan and the rest of the directors completely by surprise. An official statement released by the club insisted that there had been no dispute behind Turnbull's decision but in fact there had been numerous disagreements between the trainer and the manager Galbraith over training methods among other things. The impetuous Turnbull had been a front-runner for the manager's job after the resignation of Hugh Shaw and was said to have been bitterly disappointed at Galbraith's appointment. It was well known that he held scant regard for the manager's ability, an opinion shared by the majority of the players. According to Turnbull, there was no single reason for his departure, he had simply had enough. His resignation severed the last remaining on-field link with the golden glory days of the late '40s and early '50s. He would not be absent from the game for long. Ten days after his surprise departure from Easter Road he was offered the job of trainer at Queen's Park.

With Tommy Preston installed as temporary trainer, on 20 March a 2-0 home defeat by Airdrie moved Hibs' relegation position into the critical category. Now six points behind third-bottom Clyde, they had four games in hand, unfortunately all away from home, against the top four sides, Celtic, Dundee, Rangers and Partick Thistle. Prospects looked bleak, to say the least.

During the second half of a particularly desperately dull and dreary game, Airdrie were leading 2-0 when the ball landed among the sparse crowd for the umpteenth time, one disgruntled fan grabbed it and made his way to the top of the extended terracing. Throwing the ball over the back, he turned to face the spectators with arms raised aloft in a gesture of defiance. The culprit was apprehended by Edinburgh's finest and taken into custody to a background of sarcastic slow hand clapping. On the Monday, Harry Swan appealed through the local press for the fan – who had been released without charge – to contact him and collect a free ticket for the rest of the season, Swan commenting dryly that 'he had been the only person inside Easter Road all afternoon who knew what he was going to do with the ball'. The fan, headlined in one newspaper as 'The Man Who Could Take No More', declined the free ticket. Things were bad!

Help in the relegation dogfight came from what may now seem an unlikely source when Hearts offered to loan Hibs several players, but such gestures were nothing new; with relegation of benefit to neither side, in the past both clubs had been more than eager to help the other in times of difficulty.

In the return fixture against Valencia a few days later, the relegation gloom that had hung over Easter Road was temporarily lifted. Instead of the jeers that had accompanied their recent performances, the players were encouraged by cheers as the fans responded enthusiastically to their favourites somewhat unexpectedly defeating the cup holders. With absolutely nothing to lose, Galbraith gambled heavily with his team formation and the gamble paid off. Goalkeeper Ronnie Simpson was recalled in place of Wilson, Eric Stevenson made his first appearance since his leg break in October, and Alex Cameron his debut at right back. Thirty-two-year-old former Scotland centre half Willie Toner, who had been signed only the previous day from Kilmarnock, was also making his first appearance for his new side.

Surprising everyone inside Easter Road, Valencia were forced to endure a first-half pounding right from the opening whistle, and after only 12 minutes Preston coolly placed the ball past the advancing Spanish international goalkeeper Zamora. The first half had belonged almost entirely to Hibs and Valencia were extremely fortunate to go in at the interval only one goal down. Looking nothing like relegation strugglers, Hibs went further ahead in the second half. Grant, in tremendous attacking form, started the move. Breaking through from the midfield he sent O'Rourke on his way down the wing. The youngster sent over a perfect centre, and before the keeper could even move, Baker had flashed a header into the net to give the home side a two-goal lead on the night.

The bewildered Zamora was forced to make several excellent saves to prevent rampant Hibs from increasing their lead, while his opposite number had little to do all evening. Mindful of Dunfermline's stirring comeback from a 4-0 deficiency in the previous round, the Hibs fans were now beginning to entertain notions of a famous comeback, but a quick move by Guillot found Nuñez completely unmarked and he wasted no time in sweeping the ball past Simpson, shattering their hopes.

There was to be no more scoring, but although Hibs had failed to progress to a third European semi-final, this had been a tremendous performance. Holders Valencia, who would retain the trophy at the end of the season, had been badly shaken, particularly during the first 45 minutes, by a team that had begun to believe in itself again. The big difference at Easter Road had been the atmosphere. With an enthusiastic crowd encouraging their every move, the Greens put up a brilliant performance that left the fans firmly believing that no matter what happened in the league, this side would roll up their sleeves and not surrender without a fight.

FINAL SCORE: HIBERNIAN 2. VALENCIA 1.

FAIRS CUP QUARTER-FINAL (2ND LEG), WEDNESDAY 3 APRIL 1963, EASTER ROAD.
HIBERNIAN: SIMPSON, CAMERON, DAVIN, GRANT, TONER, LEISHMAN, O'ROURKE, (M.) STEVENSON, BAKER, PRESTON, (E.) STEVENSON.

Two days after Hibs' gallant display against Valencia, it was announced that representatives of all four British ruling bodies would be meeting the organisers of the Fairs Cup to recommend that selection to the competition should be based solely on league position. The disagreement at the start of the season over the inclusion of Hibs and Celtic was set to continue. Then, the SFA had written to the Fairs Cup headquarters stating that in choosing Hibernian the committee had acted contrary to their express wish that selection be based solely on merit. Bob Kelly of Celtic went further, acidly stating that if invites were to go to cities that held industrial fairs, then no Scottish clubs would be entitled to participate. Regardless, the days of Hibs participating in Europe by invitation were over; in future, they, and others, would need to qualify.

In the league the relegation struggle intensified. A trip to Parkhead ended with the Edinburgh side losing the battle of the Greens 2-0 and that same afternoon Clyde gained two vitally important points to move eight ahead of Hibs. There was, however, a slight glimmer of hope in that Hibs had played four games fewer than Clyde but had a much better goal average.

At the beginning of April a 3-1 victory over Dundee at Dens Park was Hibs' first league victory since November, a total of 13 games, so it was highly unlikely to think that they could win all or even the majority of the games in hand. The next four matches, however, produced four points from the eight on offer to give renewed hope to their beleaguered supporters that relegation could still be avoided. But as Hibs were drawing 1-1 with Dunfermline at home, Clyde's 2-1 victory over St Mirren in Paisley meant that the Shawfield side were four points clear, having played only one game more, and it would now appear that the Edinburgh side were doomed. In the game against Hearts at Tynecastle postponed from New Year's Day, an unexpected point was gained when the Gorgie side, two goals ahead at the interval, allowed Hibs to score three times inside a six-minute spell to storm into a fighting 3-2 lead, only for Norrie Davidson, one of the players earlier offered to Hibs on loan, to level things late in the game.

A few days before the game against Hearts, Hibs had lost the services of the experienced centre half Willie Toner for the rest of the season as the result of a freak training ground accident. Playing in a bounce game at Easter Road with makeshift goals, the centre half scored at the main terracing end. Throwing up his hands in celebration, Toner overbalanced and fell backwards over the retaining wall, dislocating his shoulder and severely lacerating his face in the process.

With three games left to play, Hibs announced that they were to put forward a motion to increase the number of teams in the First Division to 22 at the General Meeting of the Scottish League at the end of the season. This prompted allegations that Swan was attempting to create an escape route for his own side, particularly given that in the past he had proposed that the First Division should be reduced in numbers. Swan refuted all claims of inconsistency, stating that he had also recommended a new cup tournament to supplement the number of games. He was adamant that in light of the present fall in attendances it would be financial suicide to reduce the number of games played. Still in with a slight but mathematically possible chance of saving their First Division status, a 2-1 win against St Mirren at home and another at Palmerston by a 4-0 scoreline meant that Hibs had to win against the already relegated bottom club Raith Rovers in Kirkcaldy in the final game of the season to almost guarantee inclusion in First Division football next season. The positions at the bottom with one game remaining were:

	P	W	L	D	F	A	Pts
Hibs	33	7	17	9	43	67	23
Clyde	33	9	13	5	48	80	23
Raith Rovers	33	2	27	5	35	114	9

It was now crystal clear. If Hibs lost, even a draw with champions Rangers would save Clyde. If Hibs drew, Clyde would have to win. But if Hibs won, Clyde would be required to run up a cricket score to have any hope of safety.

In front of a huge crowd, the majority of them having nervously made their way from Edinburgh determined to encourage their side to victory, three first-half goals set Hibs on the way to a 4-0 victory over Hugh Shaw's men, ensuring, barring a miraculous scoreline the following Wednesday in Clyde's game against Rangers, Hibs' First Division survival. The goals were scored by Baxter (2), Fraser and Baker in an otherwise scrappy game. Great credit must go to the Edinburgh side, who had taken seven points from their final four games, scoring 13 goals along the way, but it had been a close-run thing.

There would be no miracle for Clyde, who were defeated 3-1 on the Wednesday by Rangers and they were relegated along with Hugh Shaw's Raith Rovers.

With safety now assured, Gerry Baker, keen to try his luck again in England, submitted a written transfer request. With the exception of Baker who had scored 13 times in the league, no Hibs player had exceeded five, and the total of 47 contrasted sharply with the 106 scored three years before. It was Hibs' worst tally since season 1929–30. With the exception of Raith Rovers, only Queen of the South had scored fewer goals.

As might well be expected, there was a major clear out as Walter Galbraith issued his list of free transfers. They included Marjoribanks, Logan, Cuthbert, Blair, Morris Stevenson, Harvey McCreadie, Tom McCready, Davin, Bogie, and somewhat surprisingly, Ally MacLeod who had been club captain until losing his place around the time of Turnbull's resignation. MacLeod would retire to take up management at Ayr United, a path that would eventually lead him and Scotland to Argentina in 1978. Morris Stevenson had made 30 appearances in all competitions during the season, and could also have been considered a surprise choice to be released. Harvey McCreadie had made only nine starts, Logan one and Marjoribanks had featured not at all.

3

Swansong for Harry, a Debut for Pat Stanton and 'The Big Man'
1963–64

PERHAPS DISILLUSIONED AFTER the anxiety of near relegation, during the close season Harry Swan, now nearing 70 years of age, had sold his shares in the club to Edinburgh businessman William Harrower. One can only begin to imagine the pressure he had been under in the closing months of the previous season. After nearly 30 years as the guiding force at Easter Road, during which time he had been behind almost every innovation in the Scottish game, and possibly feeling that he could take the club no further, Swan had decided to transfer overall control of the club to someone with new ideas. Harrower was a successful Edinburgh businessman who owned over 50 betting shops in and around the city and several rented properties, including it is rumoured, the one in Danube Street used by the infamous Edinburgh madam Dora Noyce as a brothel, although it has to be said that Harrower had no involvement in the nefarious activities that took place in the house. The new chairman had been a season ticket holder at Easter Road for many years, but business commitments had limited his attendance at the stadium to mostly midweek games. Alex Pratt, managing director of the electrical engineering firm of Pratt Brothers, also joined the board. Swan's wealth of experience and expertise would not be lost to the game, however, and he was unanimously elected a lifetime director in recognition of his magnificent service to Hibernian.

To mark the occasion the *Edinburgh Evening News* ran a feature entitled 'The Harry Swan Story' in which Swan recounted various anecdotes of his time with the club. He recalled once, on handing the Rangers secretary a cheque for £400 after a match at Easter Road, the official remarking, 'You know Harry, it wasn't Hibs they came to see today, it was the Rangers.' Many years later, after a league decider played at Ibrox in front of 106,000 spectators, the same Rangers official had handed over a much larger cheque. Swan couldn't resist commenting, 'You know, it wasn't Rangers they came to see today, it was Hibs.'

In the article he also recalled that home games had often kicked off at 3.15pm because local publicans, one of them director Barney Lester who owned the Albion Bar, liked their customers to get in a final round before moving on to the match. Journalists had complained to Swan that the late start made it difficult to get the match report out in time for the evening sports editions and so he changed the start of the games back to 3pm, only to find his office invaded by a posse of protesting bar owners. He told them, 'Your customers will change their ways. We will build a bigger ground, there will be more spectators visiting the area, and in the long run your till receipts will be bigger.' And that's exactly how it turned out.

On the state of the game, Swan stated ominously, 'Whether we like it or not, there must be reorganisation. Many clubs, some with illustrious names, must go. You must face up to eventualities and progress.'

He did, however, predict a great future for Hibernian, and ended with a special word of praise for three men who had played a great part in its rise over the years.

> Willie McCartney: Full of personality and enterprise, whose sudden death in 1948 was deeply regretted by many in the game.
> Hugh Shaw: A complete contrast to McCartney's flamboyancy: Shrewd, quiet, and thoughtful, but a man with the vision to foresee great developments. To the outside world Hugh was a man who said little, but he was always ready with advice and constructive thinking in discussions behind the scenes.
> Jimmy McColl: What a wonderful assistant he has been over the years! Every one connected with the club now or in the past, has known the benefit of his advice and encouragement.

More new faces joined the club during the close season. In an off-field move that would pay major dividends in the years ahead, former Third Lanark trainer Tom McNiven replaced Eddie Turnbull. The former Stonehouse Violet player and amateur sprinter, who had become the youngest trainer in the game when joining Third Lanark five years before aged just 24, had actually joined Morton during the close season. Before he could commence his duties at Cappielow, he was approached by Hibs. He asked to be released from his contract to join the Edinburgh side, and Morton, reluctantly, agreed.

A major rebuilding programme was needed if another relegation dogfight was to be avoided in the 1963–64 season. One of the manager's first tasks was to sign inside forward Neil Martin from Queen of the South for around £6,000, a fee that would prove a bargain. The lanky former Alloa goalscorer had been in dispute with the Dumfries club since being forced to go part-time and accept a cut in wages from £22 to £14 per week; at one stage he had even threatened to quit the game altogether. The dispute centred around an incident when the player, one of only two full-time employees at the club, had missed a Scottish Cup tie against Stenhousemuir at Palmerston when bad weather had prevented him reaching Dumfries from his home in Tranent. Martin had defied the instructions of manager George Farm that he should remain in the Dumfries area overnight for the match, and the car containing himself and three other players from the Edinburgh area had only got as far as Penicuik on the morning of the game. A chance meeting between Martin's wife and a journalist in a Tranent shop led to the player joining Hibs when the reporter recommended him to Galbraith. Falkirk were also chasing his signature, making a bid for the player that same day, but their offer fell short of Hibs' valuation, and the scorer of 47 goals in just over two seasons at Palmerston moved to Easter Road, fortuitously for Martin: Queen of the South were relegated at the end of the season.

Among the new faces called up during the summer was a local youngster destined to become one of the finest ever to wear the famous green and white jersey. Eighteen-year-old Pat Stanton joined the club from juvenile side Edina Hibs and had been farmed out to Bonnyrigg Rose. While at Bonnyrigg, he had been approached by a committee member who complimented the youngster on having played more games than Tommy Connery, later of James Bond fame, who had played for the club in the 1950s. Thereafter, whenever the multi-millionaire film star was seen on TV relaxing on some sun kissed beach, Stanton would often wonder just where it had all gone wrong for Connery. Although he had been training at Easter Road in the evenings since his schooldays, he had been offered terms by clubs on both sides of the Border, including Jock Stein's Dunfermline. At one stage he might well have signed for Hearts, but there was only ever going to be one destination for Hibs fanatic Stanton. Pat would later jokingly recall Walter Galbraith and the Hibs chief scout first turning up outside his house in a huge white Jaguar, setting many of the curtains in the street twitching. At that time the only Jaguar's that were to be seen in Niddrie were police cars.

Stanton was joined at Easter Road by other new starts Billy Simpson and Jimmy Stevenson, both also from Edina Hibs, and Sandy Keay, a goalkeeper from Coupar Angus. Rumours that Hibs were about to make a move for former Hearts full back George Thomson, then with Everton, was denied by both clubs and in the end came to nothing.

Once again the annual cricket match at the Leith Oval was won by the Greens by 109 runs to 107 despite the mediocrity on show from some of the footballers. At the start of the previous season Harry Swan had been scathing regarding the viability of the annual Edinburgh Select charity match, declaring that the fixture was now losing its appeal with the fans. As already mentioned, the charities involved received little benefit from the game after expenses had been deducted, leaving Swan to suggest that it would perhaps be better if both clubs gave a donation instead. Hibs now found it difficult to supply enough players to field a team, or so they claimed, but rather than let the fundraising match drop completely, Dunfermline Athletic offered to play Hearts at Tynecastle. It was a gesture they no doubt regretted after they were comprehensively thrashed 7-0 by the home side.

With admission into the Fairs Cup now based solely on league placing, there would be no European football at Easter Road during the coming season. Instead Hearts and Partick Thistle would fly the flag for Scotland, Partick flying it a little longer. The Firhill side went out in the second round to one of Hibs' old adversaries', after Hearts' first-round exit at the hands of another of Hibs' former European opponents, Lausanne, who seemed to have overcome their earlier European difficulties.

The new season opened with a league cup-tie against St Mirren at Easter Road. Recent signing Neil Martin made an impressive start to his Easter Road career when he scored with a trademark diving header to give his side a first-half lead, only for a fighting Saints to equalise in the dying minutes to earn a deserved share of the points. Four wins and a draw in the remaining matches in a section that included Dundee United and Aberdeen meant that on the same evening, holders Hearts were making an early exit from the competition; Hibs progressed to the later stages for the first time in ten years. After the final section game against Dundee United at Tannadice, one newspaper report proclaimed that 'not since the days of the Famous Five had Hibs been seen in such devastating form, and in no way did the 4-2 scoreline reflect their tremendous performance'.

After a bright start to his Easter Road career, the fierce tackling defender Tommy Leishman, who had not featured since his injury in April, was now finding it difficult to displace left half John Baxter, and he was placed on the transfer list at his own request. In time-honoured fashion, the club revealed that they were prepared to listen sympathetically to any offers for the player. At the same time over on the other side of the city, a clearly unhappy Willie Hamilton had also tabled a transfer request. This had been immediately turned down by the Tynecastle board who were well aware of the player's outstanding abilities, but it would be no surprise to learn that Hibs had been keeping a close watch on any developments.

A 3-0 home win against Third Lanark extended Hibs' unbeaten run to seven games, but the annual visit to Tynecastle put an end to it. In a thrilling game, two goals by Gerry Baker, the second as Hibs were mounting a storming comeback from 3-1 behind, were not enough when Hearts scored late in the game to secure a 4-2 win.

Another vintage performance by the Edinburgh side in the first leg of the League Cup quarter-final at Dens Park saw them secure a 3-3 draw against Dundee and they were now clear favourites to advance through to the semi-finals. In the return fixture at Easter Road, Dundee never really recovered from missing two gilt-edged chances early in the first half, and the home side turned round at the interval leading by a Neil Martin goal, his sixth in 11 games. Any thoughts harboured by Dundee of a comeback after the break were shattered when Gerry Baker, surely at that moment the most improved player in the country, scored from what appeared to be an almost impossible angle near the touchline. The goal knocked any remaining fight from the Angus side and was enough to secure Hibs a place in the last four against the exciting up-and-coming Second Division side Greenock Morton.

Hibs being Hibs, the exhilaration of reaching the semi-finals would be brief. Three days after the victory over Dundee, they travelled through to Ibrox to face Rangers in the league. In what was labelled a likely Cup Final rehearsal, they were murdered 5-0, and in the words of the old saying, were lucky to get nothing. Second to every ball, the Greens relied too much on the fast break of Baker who, like most of his colleagues, had a poor afternoon. It was the first time that Hibs had failed to score that season.

Although much improved since the defeat at Ibrox, defeats by both Kilmarnock, their first home reverse of the season in either competition, and Motherwell, saw them drop to 16th place in the table and rekindle frightening memories of the relegation dogfight of the previous year. Yet again, something had to be done.

Earlier in the week Hearts had rejected an audacious double bid by Hibs for both full back Davie Holt and inside forward Willie Hamilton, the latter still clearly unhappy at Tynecastle. England had also been scoured in a vain attempt to freshen up the side; instead, Hibs gave a debut to Pat Stanton at inside right against Motherwell at Fir Park on 5 October 1963. Called up only two months before, the teenager who was destined to become a legendary figure at Easter Road made a dream start to his first-team career when scoring one of Hibs' goals, although it was not enough to prevent the visitors suffering a 4-3 defeat. Although understandably tiring late in the game, the youngster did more than enough to suggest that he was a likely star of the future. Left back Billy Simpson was also making his first-team debut that same afternoon. After the previous two lacklustre defeats, at least this had been a fighting display by Hibs, the only difference between the sides a brilliant hat-trick by centre forward Joe McBride, who would be lining up alongside Stanton at Easter Road before too long.

Meanwhile, Hibs could look forward to a cup-tie against lower league opponents that on paper should have provided no problems. On Monday 7 October 1963 Hibs took the field at Ibrox for their first League Cup semi-final for ten years. Their opponents, Second Division Morton, were at that time taking the lower division by storm.

HIBERNIAN: SIMPSON, FRASER, MCCLELLAND, GRANT, EASTON, BAXTER, SCOTT, STANTON, BAKER, MARTIN AND (E.) STEVENSON.

MORTON: BROWN, BOYD, MALLAN, REILLY, KEIRNAN, STRACHAN, ADAMSON, STEVENSON, BYRNE, MCGRAW, WILSON.

Facing the Edinburgh side was former player Morris Stevenson and Alan 'Mr Goals' McGraw, who would score over 60 before the season was out. The 1-1 final scoreline in no way indicated the tremendous pressure and pummelling that Hibs endured and only a sterling performance by an overworked defence avoided the embarrassment of yet another humiliating defeat by a so-called lesser side. The Second Division side took the lead after only three minutes when danger man McGraw opened the scoring. Thousands of Hibs fans who had travelled through from Edinburgh on a football special, missed the goal and much of the first half after a delay in leaving Waverley Station. Neil Martin equalised against the run of play in the first half but there was to be no more scoring. Pat Stanton, who had kept his place in the side after his debut only two days before, had been switched to a deep-lying role, but still made time for the occasional foray up front in a more than satisfactory cup debut. During some hectic action, Neil Martin fractured his wrist when falling awkwardly. Although in some discomfort, he managed to finish the game but would miss the replay and around six weeks of the season.

With Neil Martin's enforced absence from the side, it was obvious that another experienced player was needed before the replay. At a hurriedly convened board meeting the following day, several names were considered, including the former St Mirren cup winner Tommy Bryceland who was then with Norwich, George Herd of Sunderland and Bobby Hope of West Bromwich Albion. Former Motherwell Ancel babe Pat Quinn, however, was seen as the ideal candidate and he was signed from Blackpool for a fee in the region of £30,000, then a record fee by a Scottish club, beating the previous record paid by Dundee to Derby County to bring Billy Steel back to Dens Park in 1950.

Just days before the cup replay, the alarm bells were once again ringing. With new signing Pat Quinn and right back Bobby Duncan, making his debut, in the Easter Road line-up, a 3-0 defeat by Dunfermline at Easter End Park saw Hibs drop to second-bottom of the table.

On Monday 14 October 1963, both Morton and Hibs met in the League Cup semi-final replay, again at Ibrox. Quinn for Martin was the Easter Road side's only change from the first game. For long spells neither team seemed capable of scoring, and in the end the final result hinged on two penalty decisions. After a dull, no-scoring first half, McGraw scored from the spot with 26 minutes remaining to give his side a 1-0 lead. In the dying minutes of the match, Quinn was blatantly fouled inside the box. The referee waved play on, much to the dismay of the Hibs supporters who were convinced that they had been denied a stonewall penalty. For the second time in 14 years, a Second Division side had advanced to the League Cup Final at the expense of Hibs. British Rail had again laid on a football special for the replay, with the return fare from Edinburgh setting the supporters back the princely sum of 7/6. On the journey back from the game, five of the nine carriages were totally wrecked in a frenzy of unmitigated vandalism by a section of the Hibs support who just could not take defeat. As well as the smashed windows, mirrors had been broken and seats slashed to pieces in an orgy of destruction that began even before the train left Glasgow. Clearly it was a situation that the club could well do without and immediate steps were taken to distance themselves from the conduct of the morons who had been responsible for the damage.

On the Saturday, an outstanding performance by Gordon Smith against his former club helped Alan Gilzean to score all four Dundee goals, totally demoralising hapless Hibs in Edinburgh without reply. In the previous four weeks only a draw in the first semi-final had interrupted six straight defeats and only four goals had been scored against the 20 conceded. Once again Hibs' future was beginning to look bleak. After a positive start to the season, the Easter Road side were finding it nigh on impossible to pull themselves away from the lower reaches of the table. It was now imperative that more quality signings were made.

Pat Stanton had made his home debut in the Dundee game, and after an illustrious career spanning just over 23 seasons, it was Gordon Smith's last ever at Easter Road. Stanton would relate in later years that such was his awe of the legend, that when the veteran turned to smile at him early in the game his legs turned to jelly.

A few days later Irishman John Parke became Hibs' second acquisition inside eight days when he was signed from Linfield. The full back had made his international debut for Ireland in a 2-1 win against Scotland in Belfast only the previous Saturday, completely snuffing out the danger of Willie Henderson, and had also been attracting the attentions of Celtic, Dundee and St Johnstone. Hibs, however, had travelled over to Ireland to sign him immediately after the Scotland game and the defender made an outstanding impression in his first outing in Hibs colours in a 4-1 home win over St Johnstone. The Easter Road side's first win in eight games lifted them two places nearer safety in the league table.

At the beginning of November the unsettled Willie Hamilton was signed from Hearts for a fee of around £5,000, just in time to make an appearance at Firhill as part of a 'big-money' inside trio of Quinn, Baker and Hamilton, who had cost the club almost £55,000 between them. Only the brilliance of goalkeeper Simpson, however, kept the scoreline down to a respectable 2-1 defeat. Once again Hibs had second-bottom position all to themselves.

Among the items listed for discussion at that month's board meeting was a written transfer request from Gerry Baker. It had been common knowledge for some time that Baker was unsettled at Easter Road and was keen to try his luck again in England. Also on the agenda was the question of the impending winter and the memory of the fixture fiasco of the previous season. The pros and cons of using straw to protect the pitch were discussed, as was the equally archaic use of braziers to melt the frost. The installation of a costly underground electric blanket was rejected after it had been pointed out that it was pointless protecting the playing surface if the safety of the fans on the terracing could not be guaranteed.

A few days later, English Second Division side Bury tabled an offer of £15,000 for Baker and it was widely accepted that he would join the Lancashire club, when out of the blue it was announced that he had been transferred to First Division Ipswich Town for a fee in the region of £18,000, teaming up with former Hibs player Doug Moran. Ipswich had made a meteoric rise under the guidance of former Spurs and England full back Alf Ramsey, gaining almost consecutive promotions from the Fourth Division to the First. Ramsey had since left to take over as England manager, to be replaced at Portman Road by the legendary former Newcastle United centre forward Jackie Milburn. Now, only two years after winning the First Division Championship, they found themselves in a perilous position and would end the season bottom of the table and relegated back into the lower division.

In the early stages of a game at Broomfield at the beginning of December, Airdrie looked more than capable of gaining revenge for the record-breaking 11-1 humiliation a few years back, but the visitors fought back well to go in at the break only 4-2 down, both teams missing penalties. In the end the Diamonds settled for a 5-3 win. Hibs finished the game with only nine men after John Parke was carried off injured with 30 minutes remaining, before Neil Martin and Reid of Airdrie were both sent off for fighting.

There was more bad luck for Hibs the following week when the unlucky Jim Easton broke a leg against East Stirlingshire. It was only the latest in a string of injuries – according to the official programme, no other side in the country had suffered such a horrific list of injuries. Both Easton and Eric Stevenson had broken an ankle within weeks of each other during the previous campaign. Now, although the present season was only half way through, Duncan Falconer had become an almost permanent casualty, with Toner and Leishman also missing for long periods. O'Rourke had severely damaged his ligaments, Neil Martin had first broken his collar bone and then his wrist, and Baxter, McClelland, Fraser and Grant had all been absentees at some time or other. John Parke, recovering from a recent cartilage operation, had been carried of at Airdrie. The long casualty list and the impending suspension of Martin had obviously made it almost impossible for manager Galbraith to field a settled side.

The New Year began with the traditional joust against near neighbours Hearts at Easter Road, Hibs still clinging precariously to second-bottom place in the table. However, looking nothing like relegation candidates, the home side had the better of the play, but could only manage a share of the points thanks to a second-half goal from the penalty spot by Martin to level the scores at 1-1 after he had been brought down by centre half Roy Barry. Although not listed in the match programme, Johnny Grant, a recent signing from Kilwinning Rangers, made his first start for the club. The diminutive five foot nothing outside right with a huge heart was an instant hit with the fans, but even he could not spur his new side to victory over Hearts for the first time in 12 years at Easter Road. The petite Grant followed up his impressive display against Hearts with another five-star performance at Brockville, scoring a fine solo goal in Hibs' 4-1 victory. The Hibs fans, who had had precious little to enthuse about for some time, appeared to have discovered a new hero.

For the second time in three years there was an exit from the Scottish Cup at the first time of asking, this time a defeat by Aberdeen. The 5-2 Pittodrie demolition allowed Hibs, in manager's parlance, to concentrate on the league, which in light of the anxiety of the previous year's relegation worries, now remained the major priority. A win at Motherwell and a share of the spoils at Dunfermline during the next few weeks saw the club start to claw themselves to safety and although they were not yet immune from the spectre of Division Two, the signs were that they could yet climb clear of the basement dogfight.

In mid-February there was an unexpected break from the worries of relegation when Hibs were invited to the French Riviera as Scotland's European ambassadors. This time, instead of the European or Fairs Cup competitions, or even the Cup Winners' Cup, they would be competing for the far from illustrious Cannes Festival of Sport Trophy, a two-team tournament between themselves and FC Cannes. A 3-2 victory with goals from new centre forward Stan Vincent, a recent acquisition from Cowdenbeath, and a double from Neil Martin saw Hibs emerge victorious after a disappointing start. Two down at one stage, the first scored as early as the fourth minute, two goals by Martin had put Hibs level before Vincent scored the winner with a brilliant header late in the game. Unhappy at the Scottish side gradually taking control of the match after their bright start, the home side soon resorted to punching and kicking their opponents. There was even an attempt to assault the referee after he had intervened at one potential flashpoint and at one stage both managers had entered the field of play to prevent the behaviour of some of the Cannes players from getting completely out of hand. Commendably, Hibs had stayed cool and were cheered from the field by the spectators, who, clearly disgusted at the behaviour of some of the home players, jeered their favourites from the field.

A handsome trophy was to have been presented to the winners, but in the circumstances, the planned presentation on the pitch was cancelled and the trophy was handed to Hibs captain John Fraser in the dressing room after the game.

In February there was a debut for former Holy Cross schoolboy Davie Hogg in a 3-0 defeat at Dens Park, the third player from the school on the books alongside Pat Stanton and Jimmy O'Rourke. Admirable wins over St Johnstone, Partick Thistle and Queen of the South in the coming weeks, saw Hibs climb to 12th place in the table.

Safe from relegation and with the injury situation rapidly clearing up, after just 28 months in the Easter Road hot seat, on Wednesday 11 March 1964, Walter Galbraith announced that he would be resigning with immediate effect. In a prepared statement, he revealed that he had wanted to leave 'for some time' but had 'waited for the succession of injuries to clear up and the team to climb to a position of league safety'. That position I believe has now been reached and that is why I am leaving immediately. I leave the team with good players, and have no other job in football in mind.' For all its suddenness, it seemed to the supporters that after the results over the past two horrendous seasons, the manager must have been sacked, but nevertheless the chairman wished him all the best, adding, 'Now that we are safe from the drop, we may even wait until the end of the season before appointing a successor to Galbraith. In the meantime the board of directors will pick the team.'

In truth, Galbraith had never been particularly popular with the players, who had not taken long to realise that his knowledge of football was extremely limited. Indeed, during his time at Easter Road he was rarely seen on the training pitch, electing to leave that side of things first to Eddie Turnbull and now to Tom McNiven. One player's principal memory of Galbraith was seeing him preen himself admiringly in the huge dressing room mirror prior to giving the team talk before games.

A few weeks before Galbraith's sudden exit from Easter Road, Dunfermline manager Jock Stein had announced that he would be leaving East End Park at the end of the season. Quizzed by reporters, Stein had said that he had no plans for the future in mind; it seemed fairly obvious that the former Celtic player would be a candidate for the vacant manager's position at Easter Road, and in all probability had already been contacted.

Meanwhile, managerless Hibs made the trip to Glasgow to face Celtic at Parkhead. The directors had made three changes from the side that defeated Queen of the South the previous week, two of them positional, with John Grant preferred at centre half in place of Falconer. But in the end the changes were to no avail. Taking the lead after just three minutes, the home side found great difficulty in penetrating the visitors' stout resistance, and it was nearly an hour before Celtic scored a second. It was only then that the Glasgow side began to seriously threaten, scoring a further three goals in the final four minutes in front of a disappointingly small crowd of around 12,000, to record an emphatic 5-0 victory.

After a victory over St Mirren, which he missed owing to a bout of flu despite the rumour that the famous Fulham chairman Tommy Trinder was in the stand to watch him in action, Neil Martin, by this time a huge favourite with the fans, dropped a bombshell by demanding a transfer. Despite the transfer request, the former Queen of the South centre forward was included in the side that defeated Airdrie 2-1 at Easter Road on Saturday 4 April 1964, Jock Stein's first game as manager of Hibs.

Signed in midweek from Dunfermline, and reputed to be on a salary in excess of £3,500 per annum, Stein, or the 'big man' as he was known in certain quarters, made several changes for his first game in charge. Wilson replaced the injured Simpson in goal, and out went Preston and Vincent to be replaced by Leishman and McClelland. Leishman was the seventh player in the past eight months to occupy the number five jersey which had become a problem position either because of injury or poor form. Several positional changes were made in the formation, but when the drab game still remained goalless at the interval, several more were tried that had a positive effect on the end result. All five forwards were interchanged. Martin was moved into the centre forward position and had an outstanding final 45 minutes, setting up a goal for Scott before scoring what proved to be the winner himself in a 2-1 victory. The second half changes gave an early indication that the new manager had an incisive tactical brain worthy of the reputation he had already acquired in his short but mercurial managerial career. Stein had started his professional career as a centre half at Albion Rovers in 1942, and had played in the Rovers side that faced Hibs in Willie McCartney's last game before his untimely death in 1948. Unsettled at Cliftonhill, he moved on to Welsh non-league team Llanelly in 1949, before surprisingly being signed by Celtic nearly two years later. A member of the Celtic side that defeated Hibs in the famous Coronation Cup Final, as captain he had also led the Parkhead side to a League and Cup double in 1953–54. After injury forced his premature retirement from the playing side, the following few years were spent on the coaching staff at Parkhead before he moved into management. When first appointed as manager at East End Park, Dunfermline were a team all but mathematically doomed to relegation, but within a short period of time Stein had led them to safety and inside two years they had won the Scottish Cup for the first time in the club's history. A keen student of the tactical side of the game, with a great interest in modern training techniques, Stein had travelled to Italy several times to study the methods of the great Hellenio Hererra. He was also a strict disciplinarian. Although he could interact with the players when required, he also knew when to draw the line, as witnessed when one senior Easter Road player addressed him by his first name in front of the others after training one morning soon after he had joined the club. The miscreant was informed that he was to be addressed as 'Boss' or Mr Stein, leaving all present in no doubt that he was not a man to be trifled with. During his first few weeks at Easter Road, Stein displayed his man-management skills to perfection. Having lost patience with the indiscipline and irregular timekeeping of the mercurial Willie Hamilton, Stein decided to teach the player a lesson. After notifying captain John Fraser beforehand of his intentions, at the next training session Stein deliberately humiliated Hamilton in front of his teammates. Told that he was a disgrace not only to himself but to his colleagues, Hamilton was ordered to go home and not report back until he was called. The embarrassing rebuke, as might be expected, did result in Hamilton posting yet another transfer request, but on his return to Easter Road a couple of weeks later he was a markedly changed man.

Recognising the urgent need for a reliable centre half, Stein returned to his former club Celtic to sign John McNamee, who was then languishing in the reserves at Parkhead. McNamee had made his Celtic debut against Hibs, and Joe Baker, at Parkhead in February 1961 when deputising for the injured Billy McNeil, but had featured in only a handful of games for the Parkhead side since. It was an inspired signing, the player soon achieving almost legendary status among the Easter Road fans during his relatively short time with the club. Although understandably hesitant and ponderous on his Hibs debut owing to his lack of first-team football, McNamee, at one time a target for Manchester United, although badly at fault for both of the East Stirling goals, improved the longer the game went on, and in the end he looked a reasonable acquisition when helping his new side to a deserved 5-2 win.

Immediately after the game it was announced that Willie Hamilton had joined Neil Martin on the transfer list. The talented but often headstrong genius Hamilton had rarely stayed long with any of his senior clubs before becoming unsettled, and in his case it was not thought likely that Hibs would be hard to deal with.

In the final game of the season, centre half McNamee started to repay his transfer fee, scoring the equaliser in the last few minutes that earned ten-man Hibs a point at Tannadice. Although he had only been at the club a matter of weeks, the rugged giant had already become a huge favourite with the fans and his frequent excursions into the opposition penalty area at corner kicks were keenly anticipated.

Despite the fear of relegation that had haunted a major part of the season, Hibs had made a tremendous recovery. In the nine home games since the turn of the year, six had been won, and only one lost – a 1-0 defeat to Rangers. Finishing the season a credible (in the circumstances), tenth in the table, the signings made during this period, together with the crop of talented youngsters already at the club, gave promise of a bright future just ahead.

A summer competition that would generate some much-needed revenue during the close season had been proposed on numerous occasions since the war without really creating much interest. Hearts chairman Nicol Kilgour had raised the subject yet again at a meeting of the clubs held earlier in the season, but somewhat surprisingly, this time the motion was successful. It was somewhat bizarre that the suggestion for a close season tournament should come from Hearts as the Gorgie side would be unavailable for the later rounds were they to top their section, having previously agreed to tour Canada during the summer. It goes without saying that Rangers and Celtic immediately disassociated themselves from a competition which was to take place immediately at the end of the present season and would be called simply 'the Summer Cup'. With the absence of the Old Firm, the remaining top 16 First Division sides would be split into groups of four, each playing home and away in a mini-league format, the winner of each section advancing to the semi-finals, which would again be played on a home and away basis. Hibs were drawn in a regional group that included Hearts, Dunfermline and Falkirk.

After three games, the Easter Road side found themselves firmly anchored at the foot of a section led by Hearts, their solitary point coming against Jock Stein's former side Dunfermline at East End Park, a point owed largely to a quite outstanding performance by goalkeeper Willie Wilson. A 3-2 defeat at Tynecastle and a disastrous 4-2 reverse at Brockville, with Jack Reilly making a debut in goal in place of the injured Wilson, made it unlikely that Hibs could even attain the second place needed to take them through to the last four if, as expected, Hearts were to win the group. With only one game left to play they were still rooted to the foot of the table with four points, although they had beaten Hearts 1-0 at Easter Road. However, if they could manage to beat Falkirk at Easter Road in the final game, and Hearts were to overcome Dunfermline, then Hibs would qualify for the semi-finals.

Neil Martin chose the game against Falkirk to fully demonstrate his prodigious goalscoring talents by claiming a hat-trick in Hibs' 4-0 victory. Late in the game the same player missed an absolute sitter from only two yards, a miss that would prove crucial when it was discovered that Dunfermline had drawn 0-0 with Hearts, leaving both Hibs and Dunfermline level on points with exactly the same number of goals both for and against. Because Hearts had already won the section, a play-off match would now be needed to see who would advance into the later stages.

Unfortunately Neil Martin would miss the play-off at Tynecastle on the Saturday, having been selected to represent the Scotland Under-23s against France in Nantes the same day in what would be his second representative honour. The unsettled Willie Hamilton took his place.

Dunfermline had the better of the opening exchanges and took the lead midway through the first half. Scott equalised from a Leishman pass before the interval and the result was never in doubt after the same player scored again with a tremendous right-foot drive 13 minutes from the end. Vincent put the result beyond doubt when he scored a third late in the game to set up a semi-final meeting with Kilmarnock.

The first game took place at Rugby Park, rarely a happy hunting ground for Hibs, and so it would prove once again. Over 10,000 spectators, Kilmarnock's biggest crowd for some time, remained to applaud both teams from the field at the end of what was considered possibly the best game seen at Rugby Park all season. Kilmarnock just edged it to take a slender 4-3 lead through to Edinburgh after McLaughlin saved Martin's penalty kick with just two minutes remaining on the clock, the striker's first miss in seven attempts from the spot. Minutes earlier Vincent had rattled the bar with the keeper beaten. Vincent, Martin, Hamilton and McNamee all managed to get their names on the scoresheet, but unfortunately for the centre half, his was an own goal to nullify Vincent's opener in the first few minutes. Tommy McLean, a promising 16-year-old, made his first-team debut for Kilmarnock at outside right, supplying the cross for the winning goal just after the interval.

In the return leg at Easter Road, Hibs' 59th game of the season, the home side ran out comfortable 3-0 winners to reach the final. Martin opened the scoring with a magnificent strike to put the Greens level on aggregate after 18 minutes. Receiving the ball on the penalty spot with his back to goal, the inside left turned all in one movement before crashing the ball high into the corner of the net past the helpless goalkeeper to bring the Hibs fans to their feet. Vincent again raised the roof when he scored a second from a Martin pass, and shortly after the restart, Martin scored his second of the game, his 35th of the season, to deny Kilmarnock any hopes of a comeback. Twenty thousand fans had packed into Easter Road to prove the doubters who had predicted that the competition would be a flop and of little interest to the fans, well wide of the mark. Despite the absence of Rangers and Celtic, there had been reasonable gates at most of the other matches and already the competition had been considered a first-rate success.

Aberdeen had defeated Partick Thistle in the other semi-final to set up a meeting with Hibs in the final, the home and away fixtures due to be played the following week. Unfortunately, the final had to be postponed until the start of the following season due to the typhoid epidemic that was raging throughout the Aberdeen area at the time.

Within the space of a few months, Jock Stein had worked wonders with a team that had been totally lacking in confidence on his arrival. Hibs were now a far more resolute side, playing attractive, attacking football. Martin had ended his first season at Easter Road as the club's top scorer with a highly credible 35 goals in all competitions, 20 in the league, a total that more than represented a satisfactory return on his transfer fee.

With the task of rebuilding the side his first priority, Stein released the long-serving Tommy Preston, who would soon join St Mirren, John Grant who would sign for Raith Rovers, and Joe McClelland, signed by English side Wrexham. They were joined on the list of 'frees' by Hughes, Cameron, McGlynn, Keay and Docherty. Willie Hamilton and Ronnie Simpson, who had been at loggerheads with the manager for some months and had been told bluntly that he would never play for Hibs again, were placed on the open-to-transfer list. John Fraser, called up to the manager's room at the end of the season expecting to be released, was stunned to be offered the captaincy for the coming season.

4

The Summer Cup
and Victory over Real Madrid
1964–65

WITH THE TYPHOID OUTBREAK in Aberdeen under control, season 1964–65 opened at Pittodrie with the first leg of the Summer Cup Final postponed from the previous season. In bright summer sunshine, Aberdeen dominated the opening 30 minutes of the game taking a deserved lead. Missing several chances to increase their advantage, the home side were stunned in the 33rd minute when Jim Scott equalised with a speculative lob. The Dons soon restored their lead, but immediately after the break Hibs took the game to Aberdeen and a Vincent thunderbolt was twice cleared off the line with the keeper stranded. The visitors, now well on top, levelled when Scott scored his second goal of the afternoon. Aberdeen regained the initiative, taking a slender lead into the return game in Edinburgh. A draw, however, would not have flattered Hibs, who almost scored twice late in the game when a clever lob by Martin was cleared off the line, Vincent striking the bar with a tremendous drive seconds later.

The return at Easter Road had everything: extra time, brilliant goals and intense excitement. Goalless at the interval, Stan Vincent scored late in the game to force an extra 30 minutes just as Hibs' chances of overhauling Aberdeen's lead had begun to look beyond them. With just seven minutes remaining, Hamilton intelligently flicked the ball to Eric Stevenson who had only been called into the side at the last minute in place of O'Rourke, who had been injured in the first game. Quickly bringing it under control, Stevenson crashed the ball into the net for what appeared to be the winning goal. For the remainder of the game play raged from end to end with near things in both penalty areas, and with the home fans nervously whistling for the referee to call a halt to the proceedings, Charlie Cook latched onto a careless clearance, his mishit header totally deceiving Fraser and Wilson as it crossed the line. For Willie Wilson, who had been in tremendous form all evening, it was a personal tragedy that such a scrappy goal had forced a third play-off.

In the Easter Road boardroom after the match, the venue for the third game was decided by the toss of a coin that spun in Aberdeen's favour, and Pittodrie it was for the play-off. The game, however, would not take place for almost a month because of League Cup commitments. Despite its critics, who were mainly from the west side of the country, the tournament had proved a great success. Already over 48,000 had attended both legs of the final, with another huge gate guaranteed for the third game play-off.

Goalkeeper Thomson Allan had been called up from Edina Hibs during the close season as had George McNeil, a tremendously fleet-footed outside right from Tranent Juniors. Yet another newcomer to the ranks was trainer Jimmy Stevenson, who had joined the club from Dunfermline. Stevenson would share his Easter Road duties with Tom McNiven, while renewing a successful backroom partnership with manager Jock Stein. As always there was still a place for the faithful Jimmy McColl, who had now been given the important task of spotting Hibs stars of the future in his new role of talent scout.

Hibs' League Cup campaign got off to a successful start with a fine 3-0 home win against Third Lanark. Long-term injury victim John Parke made his first appearance since March in a 5-0 demolition of Airdrie and yet another victory over Third Lanark, this time at Cathkin, set Hibs up for the visit of Dunfermline who had already defeated the Edinburgh side 2-0 at East End Park. Unfortunately for Hibs, a solitary goal by McNamee was not enough and the 1-1 draw left the Fifers two points ahead at the top of the group with only one game remaining.

Inside forward Quinn had featured only once in the starting line-up since the beginning of the season, and he became yet another Hibs player to be placed on the transfer list at his own request. There still remained a slim chance of topping the group were they to win at Airdrie in the final section game. Dunfermline needed only a point and in the end Hibs' 4-1 victory was not enough to enable them to advance into the later stages of the competition. Hibs finally finished in second place as the Fifers' progressed to a money spinning quarter-final tie against Rangers, who would ultimately go on to defeat Celtic 2-1 in the final.

On 3 September 1964, almost three months after it had originally been scheduled, goals from Hamilton, Scott and Cormack gave Hibs a decisive 3-1 victory in the Summer Cup Final at Pittodrie. Man of the Match Willie Hamilton chose this game to display his formidable talents and it was perhaps only fitting that he should open the scoring early in the game. Although Winchester equalised midway through the half, there was only ever going to be one winner. Stanton missed the opportunity to give his side an interval lead from the penalty spot, but this state of affairs was rectified in the second half when, again prompted from the middle of the park by the genius of a sweat-soaked Hamilton, Hibs scored twice more and hit the bar on three occasions. The scoreline failed to give an accurate reflection of the game with the visitors totally dominating the entire second-half. At the end of the day Aberdeen must have been relieved that the winning margin had not been greater. The trophy, Hibs' first cup success since beating Rangers 6-5 on corners in the final of the Southern League Cup during the war, was presented to captain John Fraser by the then Hearts chairman and Scottish League President Nicol Kilgour, who had been the main mover behind the plans to reintroduce the

Summer Cup that year. Such is the luck of the game, the unfortunate Tommy Leishman, who had figured in every match up to the final replay, was denied the opportunity of collecting a winner's medal when he was replaced by John Parke, making his first start in the competition.

FINAL SCORE: HIBERNIAN 3. ABERDEEN 1.

SUMMER CUP FINAL, 3 SEPTEMBER 1964, PITTODRIE.

ABERDEEN: OGSTON, BENNETT, SHEWAN, COOKE, COUTTS, SMITH, KERRIGAN, BURNS, FRASER, WINCHESTER, MCINTOSH.

HIBS: WISON, FRASER, PARKE, STANTON, MCNAMEE, (J) STEVENSON, CORMACK, HAMILTON, SCOTT, MARTIN, (E) STEVENSON.

With Celtic and Rangers absence from the competition, and not least the omission of section winners Hearts, it would be futile to hail the win as a major triumph, but nonetheless the players, staff, and perhaps more importantly the fans at Easter Road were ecstatic that after an interval of 12 years, silverware was once again adorning the boardroom table. Stein, with his 'Midas' touch, had done it again and it was difficult to believe that this was the same team that had flirted so dangerously with relegation just a short time before. In the space of just a few short months the manager had accomplished a truly tremendous feat, performing miracles in transforming an ordinary side totally lacking in confidence into a hard hitting and skilful outfit.

The Summer Cup was paraded before the fans at Easter Road the following week just prior to the derby with Hearts, but there was little cause for celebration at the end of the game when the Gorgie side emerged from a thrilling contest that at times spilled over with excitement and drama, with a somewhat flattering 5-3 scoreline. The visitors took a two-goal lead into the interval, but Jim Scott pulled one back for Hibs in the second half with a brilliant header before a shot by the same player was cleared off the line by Shevlane. Hearts restored their two-goal lead, but Scott scored again within a minute to set up a storming finish. Late in the game the Maroons scored twice more to take a 5-2 lead, before Martin added a consolation goal right on the final whistle.

At that time Wilson was displaying the best form of his career, with the youngsters Jack Reilly and Thomson Allan sharing the reserve goalkeeping duties between them. With Hibs well covered in that department, Stein was prepared to release the veteran Simpson from his contract and allow him to take over as player manager at Berwick Rangers. On learning of Simpson's imminent release from Easter Road, Celtic quickly stepped in and a £2,000 transfer fee plus a lump sum of £1,000 for the player himself secured the services of the goalkeeper at Parkhead as cover for John Fallon and Frank Haffey. It was well known that Stein and Simpson did not get on; the goalkeeper being told on more than one occasion that he would not play for Hibs again, but it was not the last the pair would see of each other.

Apart from the defeat by Hearts, Hibs had taken full points from their opening five league games and they were now fourth in the table, their highest position for quite some time. Although it was early days, they were now being considered by some as potential league challengers. On the downside, the recent run of rich form had started to attract the unwanted attention of predators. Wolves had enquired about Jim Scott and it was well known that the Arsenal manager Billy Wright had left Easter Road after the recent match against Partick Thistle highly impressed by Peter Cormack. More worryingly, it was also common knowledge that several other players, including Quinn, Martin and Hamilton had all recently posted transfer requests.

Shortly after Hibs' great run in the inaugural European Cup during the 1955–56 season that had seen the club reach the semi-finals of the tournament, Real Madrid, the eventual winners of the competition, had contacted Harry Swan with the offer of a friendly in the Spanish capital. Commitments at the time had made it impossible, but as part of Swan's policy of bringing glamour sides to Easter Road, he had invited Real to take part in a prestigious friendly in Edinburgh in the near future. A few months later the Spanish giants had accepted the offer. There was, however, the slight problem of the financial guarantee required by Real, which turned out to be far more than Hibs, or indeed any other Scottish club, could afford and for the time being no more was heard about the matter.

Now, as evidence of the ambition that was then permeating throughout the club, with no competitive European football in the city that season, Harrower and Stein flew to Spain in an enterprising attempt to bring the world famous Spanish club to Edinburgh for a challenge match. Fully aware that it was a huge financial gamble for the club, Stein was keen to again test his talents against top European opposition and was also extremely well aware of the great prestige that such a game would bring.

Their efforts were successful. The five-times winners of the European Cup arrived in the capital for the match on 5 October 1964. Because of the astronomical guarantee that had been demanded by the Spanish giants, said to be in the region of £10,000 plus expenses, admission prices were increased dramatically and even then a crowd of over 30,000 was needed just to break even. Instead of the normal 4/- for the terracing, this was increased to 6/- but by far the biggest increase was for the Centre Stand, which jumped from the usual 7/6 to a staggering £1 5s, more than three times the normal price.

One of the many demands made by Real was that Hibs should show no white on their outfit to avoid any clash with the all-white strip worn by the Spanish champions. Harrower had suggested that Hibs could wear red shorts but this was disregarded by Stein who ordered green shorts instead. The manager did, however, insist that Hibs wore their own familiar green jersey with its white collar and sleeves. The visitors had also insisted that a Spanish referee should be brought over to take charge of the match, but this was refused and Hugh Phillips of Wishaw, Scotland's top referee at the time, was allocated the task of adjudicator. In yet another of their many contractual demands, Real even went as far as demanding that a Spanish ball be used; it was eventually agreed to play one half with a Spanish ball and one half with a local one. In the end the traditional British ball was used throughout the entire 90 minutes.

On the night, bad weather helped keep the attendance below the break-even figure, but such was the reputation of Real Madrid that just under 30,000 were inside Easter Road as Francisco Gento led his team, including the famous but now ageing Ferenc Puskas onto the field. Among the nine Spanish and one French full internationals facing Hibs, Grosso being the odd man out, were seven members of the Madrid side that had lost to Inter Milan in the European Cup Final the previous season. Four of the side – Puskas, Gento, centre half Santamaria and left back Pachin – had played in the famous European Cup Final victory against Eintracht at Hampden just four years before. The full Real Madrid line-up was: Araquistain, Miera, Pachin, Muller, Santamaria, (Santos) Zoco, Amancio, Ruiz, Grosso, Puskas and Gento.

Right from the start Hibs harried Real, refusing to allow their illustrious visitors the opportunity to settle. Willie Hamilton, in superb form, quickly took control in the middle of the park and in the end his performance overshadowed even that of the great Puskas as Hibs humbled the famous 'All Whites' in a match that must be considered one of Scotland's greatest ever displays, friendly fixture or not.

Full back John Fraser had been earmarked to snuff out the threat of Gento on the Madrid left, and this he did successfully, although he was surprised to be spat at on several occasions by the great man. Stein's masterstroke was to play the recalled Pat Quinn in a deep-lying role alongside Hamilton, Martin moving out to the left wing.

Cormack opened the scoring after 13 minutes when he smashed a tremendous first-time drive past Araquistain in the Real goal after an inch-perfect Martin cross and Hibs continued to dominate proceedings with a display of superb and silky football. Real Madrid were seen only in patches and even then they just could not find a way through a stuffy home defence.

In the second half, their pride clearly hurt, the visitors stepped up a gear in an attempt to get back into the game, but so did Hibs to rebuff them, and the real winners were the fans who were enjoying an enthralling and exciting contest.

Ten minutes from time it was all over when Real defender Zoco deflected a Quinn free kick from 20 yards beyond his own goalkeeper to give Hibs a famous victory.

Stanton, who even this early in his career was beginning to look an extremely exciting prospect, recalls that near the end of the game, as Hibs were preparing to defend a corner, the enigmatic Willie Hamilton strolled over to him. Thinking that the experienced Hamilton was about to impart some tactical advice to the youngster, Stanton was amazed when the bold Willie retorted: 'Hey son, they tell me you get a watch for playing this lot.' Stanton was left with yet another lasting memory from the game when the ageing Puskas went over the top as both players challenged for the ball; the scar from the tackle can be seen on his ankle to this day.

At the final whistle Easter Road erupted in a frenzy of excitement, with the elated fans refusing to leave the stadium until their heroes had returned to take a lap of honour. The players duly obliged, some in various stage of undress as they circled the pitch to a backdrop of ecstatic celebration.

Although it had been billed as a friendly, it was an accepted fact that Real Madrid did not play any game in a friendly fashion and there should be no doubt that this was a great and prestigious night for all of Scottish football.

Interviewed immediately after the match, Gento, the Real Madrid captain, said Hibs played 'like World champions'. Chairman Harrower, who deserved great praise for his enterprise in bringing the Spanish giants to Scotland, was understandably ecstatic, noting, 'We had to take a small financial loss because of the weather, but the prestige of the win more than compensated for any shortfall.'

Hibs captain John Baxter later revealed that the meticulous Stein had worked out a tactical plan on the blackboard, but it had worked out even better during the game. Hearts manager Tommy Walker watching from the directors' box, had been equally impressed, and was of the opinion that 'with any luck Hibs could well have scored more'. In the boardroom after the game the President of Real Madrid was presented with a silver quaich and the players with silver tankards. The Hibs players and staff each received Real Madrid's traditional presentation of an inscribed watch, no doubt to the satisfaction of Willie Hamilton.

Before the game, *The Scotsman's* chief sports reporter, John Rafferty, had been scathing regarding Hibs' efforts to bring the Spanish giants to Easter Road. He condemned it as ridiculous, one of the craziest thing he had ever heard, to even contemplate playing a team of Real Madrid's stature, and was convinced that Hibs would be comprehensively beaten. Bumping into the reporter in the tunnel at the end of the game, Stein insisted that Rafferty accompany him into the home dressing room where the players were enjoying a welcome hot bath. Gripping the reporter by the arm, Stein announced to the surprised players that Rafferty had something to say to them. To give the now extremely embarrassed Rafferty his due, he apologised profusely for his lack of faith in the team, adding that the victory had been well deserved.

FINAL SCORE: HIBERNIAN 2. REAL MADRID 0.

CHALLENGE MATCH, 5 OCTOBER 1964, EASTER ROAD.
HIBERNIAN: WILSON, FRASER, PARKE, STANTON, MCNAMEE, BAXTER, CORMACK, HAMILTON, SCOTT, QUINN, MARTIN. SUBS, NOT USED: O'ROURKE AND (E.) STEVENSON.

Not surprisingly, three days later, the same 11 players that had humbled the mighty Real Madrid took the field at Ibrox for a game against Rangers. It had been 12 years since Hibs' last win at the Rangers ground. The home side started at their usual frantic pace and deservedly took the lead after only nine minutes. Shortly after, Shearer brought down Martin at least three yards inside the penalty box. As often happens in Glasgow, the referee completely ignored the incident and Jim Scott was booked for complaining over-vigorously.

Slowly but surely, Hibs began to assert themselves and Cormack levelled things a minute before half time when he smashed a great shot past keeper Ritchie. Shortly after the resumption of play, Rangers retook the lead only for Cormack to equalise for a second time two minutes later. The confident Hibs were the better side now and a Martin shot was cleared off the line by Greig. Full back Provan rugby-tackled Cormack after the youngster had skinned him but escaped punishment. Ten minutes from time Hamilton scored from a Scott cross, and Quinn put the result beyond doubt when he smashed home a fourth six minutes from the end to give Hibs their first win at Ibrox in any competition since goals from Lawrie Reilly and Eddie Turnbull had allowed the Edinburgh side to take both points in season 1952–53.

Playing with a confidence born from success, only one game was to be lost between then and Christmas, with seven victories and two draws, results that saw Hibs sitting proudly in third place at the turn of the year.

In mid-November, left back Joe Davis was signed from struggling Third Lanark to replace John Parke, who was transferred to Sunderland the same day for just under £40,000, a not inconsiderable sum for a full back at the time, even one of international stature. Parke had missed a major part of the previous season. His knee injury had required three operations and the astute Stein was not convinced of his long-term fitness. For Davis, who had impressed Stein with his solid performances against Hibs in the League Cup section earlier in the season, it would prove a timely move. His former club Third Lanark would end the season at the foot of the table and suffer the ignominy of relegation. Within another two years they would resign completely from the League.

As often happens, Davis made his Hibs debut against his former teammates in an emphatic 5-0 whitewash of Thirds at Easter Road, but the unlucky player, after an outstanding first appearance for his new side, was rushed to hospital midweek suffering from appendicitis. He made a remarkable recovery, amazingly missing only three games, and returned to the side in time for a 2-1 home win over Partick Thistle in December.

At Tynecastle on New Year's Day, Hibs dealt Hearts their first home defeat of the season in front of 38,000 spectators, toppling their great rivals from the top of the table. In an exciting, fast and furious game with near things at either end, the winning goal came 17 minutes from the end. Neil Martin was fouled by centre half Anderson just outside the Hearts penalty area, on the stand side. Hamilton took a quick free kick to Quinn who returned the ball. The former Hearts man then evaded a robust challenge from an opponent which forced him well wide, but from a seemingly impossible angle near the bye line at the edge of the 18-yard box, Hamilton crashed a brilliant drive past the bewildered Cruickshank and into the far corner of the net for the winning goal. During the goal celebrations, the delighted Hibs players were joined in the melee by several over-enthusiastic spectators who were eventually escorted back into the crowd by the police.

With Willie Hamilton again in influential mood in midfield, 24 hours later Falkirk were destroyed 6-0 in the then traditional holiday fixture, but the undoubted man of the match was four-goal Neil Martin. Stan Vincent added the others in a result that saw Hibs go joint second in the table alongside Hearts, but with a game less played. Martin had now scored 15, one behind leading scorer Scott, but more importantly the goals were being shared among several players, with even centre half McNamee getting in on the act. Long gone was the uncertainly of the previous season. This was a side playing with almost complete confidence in their ability, and although no one would be shouting it too loudly just yet, there were many who were confident that perhaps the coveted double could be achieved that season.

At the end of January, a solitary strike by Neil Martin gave Hibs their first league double over Rangers for 62 years, a feat unsurpassed by the famous teams of the '20s or even during the halcyon post-war years. Not since the League Championship winning season of 1902-03 when Hibs had triumphed 1-0 at Ibrox and 5-2 at home, had the Greens beaten the Light Blues twice in the same league campaign.

Both teams took the field at Easter Road wearing black armbands as a mark of respect for former Prime Minister Winston Churchill who had died earlier in the week. People were now starting to sit up and take notice of what was happening at Easter Road and a huge crowd of almost 45,000 turned up to witness a titanic struggle by both sides who at times had difficulty mastering the tricky underfoot conditions owing to the heavy blanket of snow that covered the pitch. The winning goal came with 14 minutes of the first half remaining when Martin rose majestically to bullet home a trademark header off the underside of the crossbar from a measured Quinn cross. Not even the heralded return of Henderson from injury could inspire Rangers to an equaliser although they came close on a couple of occasions near the end, particularly when a Miller drive caused the home supporters' hearts to miss a beat when it struck the post, but Hibs survived to take both points. The result kept them in second place and in touching distance of leaders Hearts who were then two points ahead, but had played two games more. Unfortunately for the huge Hibs support making their way home from the game, the euphoria of victory was tempered by the devastating announcement that Stein would be returning to Celtic as manager at the end of the season.

In the Scottish Cup Hibs were given what at first appeared to be an easy first round tie against lower league opponents at home. ES Clydebank was then Scotland's newest side, formed only the previous year when East Stirlingshire had been bought by the entrepreneur Steedman Brothers. Amalgamated with junior club Clydebank, they were moved to a new home at Kilbowie Park, but public outrage and appeals to the football authorities soon led to East Stirling being reinstated in Falkirk and Clydebank forced to resign from the League. Clydebank appealed successfully to join the league in their own right, and by the start of the following season both they and East Stirling were playing in the Scottish Second Division.

At Easter Road a fantastically spirited performance by the lower league side in their first ever Scottish cup-tie, and up against the previous weeks conquerors of Rangers at that, earned them immediate public acclaim and a deserved midweek replay at Clydebank. The goalless first half had produced little in the way of excitement, but after the break Hibs started to exert sustained pressure, and it was no surprise when they took the lead after 63 minutes when Martin scored with a header. Within five minutes, however, the fighting Bankies, who included future Scotland manager Andy Roxburgh in their line-up, scored a deserved equaliser to give Hibs a scare and it was on to Kilbowie Park on the Wednesday.

Cup-tie fever had gripped Clydebank all week and the newcomers did not let themselves down in the replay. Make no mistake, the men from Edinburgh were given a real fright, with the lower league side so much on top at one stage that their supporters could be heard chanting the traditional rendition of 'easy, easy'. In the end it all came down to the superior stamina of the full-time team and the brilliance of Hamilton. Goalless at the interval, manager Stein made a half-time tactical change in moving Quinn to the right wing and Cormack to the left, and within minutes the visitors had taken the lead when Hamilton crashed home a magnificent drive. Cormack scored a second to avoid the embarrassment of a second replay, and it was a mightily relieved Hibs side and their supporters who made the long trip back to Edinburgh later that evening.

In the second round the Easter Road side were drawn against Partick Thistle at home. After a shaky start Hibs eventually ran out comfortable 5-1 winners at the finish, to set up a money spinning home tie against holders Rangers. Seven days before the cup meeting with the Glasgow giants, and following a 4-3 reverse at Rugby Park, another defeat, this time at Cappielow, made a huge dent in Hibs' title aspirations. It was the first time that season that back to back losses had been suffered in the championship, and although it was a major setback they still remained in second place behind Edinburgh rivals Hearts.

It was around this time that the potential of trainer Eddie Turnbull was finally recognised at a higher level, and he took a step nearer, returning to Easter Road when, on 1 March 1965, he accepted the manager's job at Aberdeen. In his short time as trainer at Queen's Park, Turnbull had played a major part in the amateur side's rise from 14th place in the Second Division to within touching distance of promotion, and it was obvious to many in the game that he was destined for far better things.

Severe weather had put the cup-tie between Hibs and Rangers in serious doubt, but although mounds of snow still remained on the Easter Road trackside after it had been cleared from the field by the players the previous day, the pitch itself was in perfect condition and the game went ahead as planned. The visitors were boosted by the return of Jim Baxter after a lengthy absence owing to injury, and another huge crowd of 47,363 paid the then magnificent total of £11,176 for admission. Hibs, bidding to defeat Rangers for an unprecedented third time in the same season, took the lead after only four minutes when Hamilton headed home after goalkeeper Ritchie could only parry a Baxter header. Thereafter, Rangers started to come more into the game and a bout of sustained pressure led to the equaliser with just under half an hour of the game played. Under severe pressure for the remainder of the half, the Hibs defence stood firm and there were no more goals before the break. In the second half play raged from end to end with near things in both penalty areas without further scoring, but with only two minutes left to play and the fans making arrangements for the replay at Ibrox in midweek, Willie Hamilton scored what proved to be the winner when he managed to get the slightest of touches to a John Fraser shot that had evaded a crowded penalty area and appeared to be net bound anyway, to divert the ball past goalkeeper Ritchie to give Hibs another famous victory over the Govan side and a place in the semi-finals.

On the Monday morning, as the joyous Hibs fans were still celebrating the momentous win over Rangers, they were brought crashing back to earth when their manager announced that he would be joining Celtic, not at the end of the season as first planned, but immediately. That morning Stein had called Fraser into his office to notify the Hibs captain. To put it mildly, the news was a stunning blow, not just for the supporters but also for the players, many of them convinced that the league and cup double was now within their grasp. Some were not only disappointed, but angry at Stein's decision, feeling that they had been let down. That morning he had admitted to Fraser that it was his life's ambition to manage Celtic. Concerned that the Celtic directors would look elsewhere, he could not risk allowing the opportunity to pass.

Since taking over at Easter Road in April the previous year, Stein's time in charge had been nothing short of phenomenal. In the 37 competitive games played during this period, Hibs had won 25, with six drawn. Only six had been lost with 88 goals scored against just 37 conceded. In just over 13 months, aside from the Summer Cup win, the famous victory over Real Madrid and the unprecedented treble of wins against Rangers, Stein had transformed the side from relegation candidates into genuine league title contenders.

Recommended earlier by the now Celtic manager, the Hibs board had agreed that the Dundee manager Bob Shankly would succeed Stein. Probably aware of his great friend's impending departure, Shankly had watched the game against Rangers from the stand on the previous Saturday and had been impressed with the performance of his new charges. Shankly was from a well known footballing family. His brother Bill, as manager of Liverpool, had recently started out on a journey that would soon see the Merseyside team firmly established as one of the finest club sides in the world. The former Falkirk centre forward and Scottish League cap, had himself established a credible reputation in the game, with previous managerial experience at both

Falkirk and Third Lanark before moving to Dens Park in 1959. Forming a successful partnership with former Hibs player and trainer Sammy Kean, Shankly had led Dundee, including the evergreen Gordon Smith, to the League Championship title in 1961–62, and to the later stages of the European Cup the following year, losing only by the slightest of margins to Inter Milan, the eventual winners, in the semi-final.

Shankly officially took over the reins at Easter Road on Monday 18 March 1965, his first game in charge a Second XI Cup replay against Celtic at Parkhead that same evening. Goalkeeper Ronnie Simpson lined up against his former teammates as Hibs' inexperienced second team were defeated 5-0.

The players soon realised that the new manager was an entirely different proposition to Jock Stein. Whereas Stein had been one of the first of a new breed of young tracksuit managers, a great motivator who made great use of the blackboard for tactics – then a novelty for most of the players – Shankly was more likely to be found in the office, preferring to leave the day-to-day involvement to Tom McNiven and Jimmy Stevenson.

The new manager's first four league games in charge saw Hibs take seven points from a possible eight, including both points in a sweet 4-2 victory over Celtic in Glasgow. The magnificent display by the Edinburgh side gave them their first win at Parkhead for nine years when a Martin hat-trick, his third of the season including the four against Falkirk earlier in the season, accounted for most of the damage. The goal of the game, however, was scored by the Celtic full back Jim Young, who in attempting to clear a Hibs attack, headed into his own net what was generally accepted to be one of the most spectacular own goals seen for some time. During the game Neil Martin, who like the rest of the players had been bitterly disappointed at Stein's abdication to Glasgow, could not help in venting his feelings. After scoring his third goal, Martin made a bee line for the Celtic bench to give a stony-faced Jock Stein the v-sign accompanied by the words of the old Scottish saying – 'F*** Y**'.

The same 11 who had defeated Celtic in midweek took the field against Dunfermline at Tynecastle on Saturday 27 March 1965 in the semi-final of the Scottish Cup. After a bright start, with Quinn and Hamilton in superb form in midfield, Melrose silenced the huge Edinburgh support when he opened the scoring after 17 minutes. That effectively put paid to Hibs' hopes of capturing the old trophy for at least another year. From then on the Hibs attack was so ineffectual, creating virtually nothing of danger, that Dunfermline's second goal midway through the second half was not really necessary. In the later stages Hamilton did manage to beat keeper Jim Herriot from close range, but the effort was rightly disallowed for offside.

FINAL SCORE: DUNFERMLINE 2. HIBERNIAN 0.

SCOTTISH CUP SEMI-FINAL, SATURDAY 27 MARCH 1965, TYNECASTLE.

HIBERNIAN: WILSON, FRASER, DAVIS, STANTON, MCNAMEE, BAXTER, MARTIN, QUINN, CORMACK, HAMILTON, (E.) STEVENSON.

DUNFERMLINE: HERRIOT, (W.) CALLAGHAN, LUNN, THOMSON, MCLEAN, (T.) CALLAGHAN, EDWARDS, SMITH, FERGUSON, MELROSE, SINCLAIR.

Any lingering hopes of success in what had been up until then a truly magnificent season now lay solely in the championship. With five games left to play Hibs were lying handy in second place, three points behind leaders Hearts, but with a game in hand. In a display that was far removed from the dismal performance at Tynecastle on the Saturday, Hibs' title aspirations were kept alive with a slender 1-0 win over their semi-final opponents at Easter Road. Unfortunately back-to-back defeats by first Dundee, then a 4-0 hammering at home by Celtic destroyed the remaining half of a dream 'double', which at one stage had seemed well within their reach. In the end the Easter Road side had to content themselves with fourth place, four points behind champions Kilmarnock who had made a late challenge in the final few weeks of the season to pip Hearts for the title on goal average, and third-placed Dunfermline.

In a dramatic climax to the season at Tynecastle, Kilmarnock had needed to defeat Hearts by at least a 2-0 scoreline to take the title. Almost any other result, as long as Hearts scored, would give the Gorgie side the championship, but in the end it was Kilmarnock who scored the vital goals that mattered to take a 2-0 lead. In the dying minutes of the game, Ferguson in the Kilmarnock goal made a stupendous, title-winning save from Alan Gordon when the inside forward seemed certain to score. The miss would haunt Gordon for the rest of his days.

By a strange twist of fate, considering the events on the final day of the season at Dens Park in 1986, during season 1964–65, Hearts had unexpectedly dropped both points, and suffered severe damage to their goal average, when beaten 7-1 at Tynecastle by Dundee. It was a result that probably cost them the championship, and even Hearts' solitary strike had been an own goal by a Dundee defender.

Ironically, Hearts would be one of the main players behind a move to force a change from the goal average that was then in operation to goal difference. Had goal difference been in operation then, Hearts would have won the championship that season. The change would take place a few years later, but incredibly the Maroons would lose out again at the end of the 1985–86 season when a 2-0 defeat at Dens Park meant them missing out on the last day to Celtic. Had goal average instead of goal difference still been in operation, Hearts would have won the title.

Incredibly, neither Rangers nor Celtic had finished the season in the top four, something that had never happened before in the 74 years since the inception of the Scottish League in the 1890–91 season.

On 4 April 1965 news was received at Easter Road that Tom Hartland, a director of the club for over 30 years until his retirement at the age of 83 just 18 months before, had died after suffering a heart attack earlier in the week. Although Harry Swan had been the main figurehead at the club during this time, Hartland's contribution to the success of the team, along with Wilson Terris, particularly in the halcyon days of the late '40s and early '50s, had been of incalculable value to the club.

Neil Martin, ended his second season at Easter Road as the second top goalscorer in Scotland with 29 goals overall, 25 of them in the league, and there was more good news for the Tranent man when he was included in Scotland's World Cup party for the matches against Poland and Finland. Willie Hamilton's brilliant form had not passed unnoticed either and he too was included in the party of 22 players whose names had been submitted to FIFA for the World Cup Finals should Scotland qualify.

Any new manager obviously needs time to adapt to a fresh situation, therefore Shankly's record in the short time he was in charge at Easter Road that season was probably reasonable in the circumstances. Five games had been won, four including the cup semi-final lost, and one drawn, but one has to wonder as to the eventual outcome of the season had Stein seen out his Easter Road tenure as he initially promised. It is highly likely that he had wanted to stay at Easter Road until after the last game, but had been persuaded by Celtic chairman Bob Kelly, alarmed at the Parkhead side's failure to win silverware since defeating Rangers 7-1 in the 1957 League Cup Final, to take over in Glasgow sooner rather than later.

In the Summer Cup, holders Hibs were again drawn in a regional group containing Hearts, Dunfermline, and Falkirk. Four wins, a draw and a solitary defeat at the hands of Dunfermline saw the Easter Road side topping their section to progress into the last four for the second successive year. In the semi-final they were paired against a Motherwell side that had dropped just a single point in a group shared with Airdrie, Kilmarnock, and Third Lanark. Goals from Cormack and Stevenson at Fir Park gave Hibs a comfortable 2-0 first leg lead to boost their confidence for the return game at Easter Road, particularly as Motherwell had failed to win either of the league games between the sides that season, Hibs winning both by a 2-0 margin. Motherwell had other ideas and ran out decisive 6-2 winners after extra time to deny the capital club a second consecutive Summer Cup.

As for Jock Stein and Celtic, the Glasgow side would face Hibs conquerors Dunfermline in the Scottish Cup Final at Hampden. Celtic's 3-2 win would herald the start of the Parkhead club's miraculous run of nine league championships in succession, and the fantastic European Cup victory against Inter Milan in Lisbon in 1967. The first British club to win the competition.

5

Shankly, a Glorious Ten Minutes at Tynecastle and a Record Win
1965–66

AFTER WHAT HAD been another tough but ultimately disappointing season, during the summer the players embarked on an extensive tour of Mexico, Canada and America. It was Hibs' first visit to the American continent since the famous journey to Brazil in 1953, and a change from the usual habit of touring Europe or Scandinavia.

It turned out to be a hugely successful trip. Only eight games had been planned but the Edinburgh side proved so popular that another fixture was hastily added to their busy schedule. In all, 72 goals were scored against only six conceded, but it has to be said that, apart from the game against English First Division side Nottingham Forest, all had been against inferior, amateur opposition. For the match against Ottawa, Hamilton, initially delighted to have been given the day off, begged for inclusion in the side after discovering that a silver tray was on offer by the sponsors for the Man of the Match. His wish granted, he proceeded to turn on a dazzling performance of virtuosity. At times refusing to pass the ball to his teammates in order to score himself, he won the award hands down, scoring seven of Hibs' 15 goals in straight succession. It is now part of legend that, the following morning, on finding that the silverware did not fit into his holdall, he promptly bent it in two to transport it home. This rumour is denied by his family, who still have the apparently undamaged trophy at home today; but one Hibs player, allegedly witness to the incident, is adamant that it did happen.

The trip was not without incident. One balmy evening John Fraser and Pat Stanton were joined in their hotel room by John McNamee and John Baxter. Ordering soft drinks from reception the players were surprised to find that the refreshments had been delivered in buckets of ice. Soon the players, larking about, were throwing lumps of ice at each other, some of it finding its way through the open window. A few minutes later, urgent banging on their door revealed a couple of far from happy policemen brandishing drawn guns demanding to know who had pelted them with ice. Needless to say, Shankly was not amused at being wakened from his slumbers to calm the situation.

Hibs arrived back from North America to discover that the draw for the Fairs Cup in Basle had again paired them against Spanish side Valencia, 6-2 overall winners in Hibs' last European venture three years before. It was the first time that the Edinburgh side had been included in a European draw solely on merit. In the inaugural European Cup campaign of 1955 and the Fairs Cup competitions since, Hibs had entered only by invitation. Now involvement in all three major European tournaments had been unified and based either on league placing, or in the case of the Cup Winners' Cup on ultimate performance in the national cup competition. By this time the Fairs Cup had been expanded to include 48 teams, but on a straight knock-out basis instead of the preliminary mini-leagues of four as before. Everton, Chelsea and Leeds United were all selected to represent England, with Dunfermline and Hearts, who both received a first round bye, representing Scotland alongside Hibs.

Among the newcomers lining up alongside the senior players on the first day of pre-season training was 18-year-old Colin Stein, a centre forward signed from Armadale Thistle, who would soon make a telling contribution in the first team. Stein was joined at Easter Road by inside forward Colin Grant, scorer of one of the goals that had helped Linlithgow Rose lift the Scottish Junior Cup the previous season, and Bobby Hogg, who had stepped up from Sauchie Juniors. John Murphy and John Blackley, both still on the ground staff, were not exempt from the rigours of the first day's endeavours, and they joined their more senior colleagues in the traditional run around Holyrood Park. John Baxter, then the second longest serving player at the club took over the captaincy from John Fraser.

Before a ball had even been kicked, there was a minor outcry over a newspaper article that highlighted a situation that had been a sore point among the refereeing fraternity on the east coast for many years. The argument centred around an unwritten rule that prevented a referee from Edinburgh or Dundee officiating at games that involved teams from their respective cities, while allowing those who lived in Glasgow and its surrounding areas to take charge of matches involving local sides. One unnamed official was said to have regularly refereed at games involving west coast sides less than a mile from his Glasgow home, and Hugh Phillips from Wishaw had often officiated at games involving Motherwell. Of the 28 grade-one whistlers then on the list, only newcomer Eddie Thompson was from Edinburgh, while 18 were from Glasgow or its environs, the article suggesting that perhaps the same bias that often affected the chances of a player from the east being selected for the full international side, also applied to referees. The issue quickly died down, but the point had been made. The ruling would change, but like many others in a blinkered Scottish game, it would not happen for some time.

For the second time in three years Hibs would progress into the qualifying stages of the League Cup, but on the opening day of the 1965-66 season former Easter Road player Doug Moran made a huge dent in their cup aspirations by scoring twice in Falkirk's 3-1 victory at Brockville. Willie Hamilton had performed particularly poorly at Brockville and was dropped for the following game against St Mirren at Easter Road on the Wednesday. The demotion, however, was academic. Hamilton, who had repeatedly asked away during the previous 12 months, was transferred to Sheffield United on the morning of the St Mirren game for a fee in the region of £22,000.

Willie Wilson was recalled to the side in place of Jack Reilly who had also performed poorly at Brockville but the unfortunate goalkeeper was forced to leave the field for treatment midway through the first half after receiving a nasty head injury when diving bravely at the feet of an opponent, leaving his teammates in those pre-substitute days to play out the first 45 minutes with ten men. For the remainder of the game Peter Cormack took over in goal and gave a first class demonstration of his prowess between the sticks by making several excellent saves to prevent the visitors from taking the lead. In the second half the courageous Wilson returned to take his place on the right wing wearing a skull cap to protect his wound and, with what can only be described as unorthodox wing play, repeatedly confused the opposition left back. The goalkeeper's dizzy runs caused havoc in the St Mirren penalty area and on a couple of occasions almost resulted in a goal, much to the delight of the 9,000 crowd. Eric Stevenson scored the only goal of the game midway through the first half, Jim Scott missing the chance to increase the lead when the keeper saved his spot kick just before the interval. It was the third time in four years that St Mirren had been drawn in the same League Cup qualifying section as the Edinburgh side and they were yet to record a victory, losing four and drawing two. Five straight wins after the opening day defeat at Falkirk saw Hibs sitting comfortably at the top of the group, and they advanced into the quarter-finals to face Second Division Alloa.

In between the League Cup victories, Hibs' championship challenge had also received a boost when they overwhelmed Morton 5-1 at Cappielow. The visitors opened the scoring after only three minutes and should have scored again shortly after, but Sorensen saved Cormack's spot kick, Hibs second penalty miss in four games. With the game well won, Quinn scored Hibs' fifth goal direct from a corner kick on the hour mark, inspiring jeers of derision from Morton fans unhappy at the home side's lacklustre performance. Playing against Hibs that day were several individuals who would sign for the club in the near future: Alan McGraw, a very young Joe Harper and centre half John Madsen, a new Danish import who had what could best be described as a nightmare debut.

With qualification to the later stages of the League Cup assured, Neil Martin renewed his demand for a transfer, but because of the forthcoming European games there was no way that he would be allowed to leave the club at that moment in time. In a recent newspaper interview the unhappy 24-year-old had revealed that part of the reason for his unrest was the lack of atmosphere at Easter Road, a statement that bewildered Shankly to say the least, the manager confessing that he failed completely to understand the player's grievances.

The Martin situation apart, six successive victories and 19 goals had given Hibs the confidence to face Valencia. Twice winners of the Fairs Cup and once losing finalists during the previous four seasons, it goes without saying that the Spanish side's impressive pedigree made them dangerous and daunting opponents. Hibs had proved in the past, however, that with victories against

Barcelona, Real Madrid and Valencia themselves in the last meeting of the clubs, they had the beating of Spanish sides, at least on home ground.

Only four members of the Valencia side remained from the last match in Edinburgh sharpshooter Waldo, Mestre, Urtiaga, and keeper Zamora. Guillot, while still on the books would not feature at Easter Road. There had been an even bigger change of personnel at Easter Road – only Eric Stevenson and Jimmy O'Rourke remained from the side that had won in Edinburgh 29 months before.

Centre half John McNamee became Hibs' unlikely last-minute hero when his header from close range gave the home side a two-goal advantage that their play had richly deserved. Trailing only 1-0 late in the game, the visitors were under the impression that they had secured a satisfactory result to take back to Spain, when the former Celtic centre half turned up in the penalty area to bullet home a Cormack cross.

Jim Scott had given Hibs the lead with a header after only five minutes, stirring the 22,000 crowd into unrealistic expectations of a goal rush, but prompted by the early setback, Valencia came more into the game after the opening goal, although their inventive and accurate short-passing game lacked penetration and they failed to trouble a disciplined home defence.

Referee Burguet earned the displeasure of the supporters by turning down what appeared to be at least three cast-iron penalties for the home side in the first half, when Martin, twice, and Scott appeared to be brought down inside the box, his interpretation of the penalty rule differing from that of almost everyone else inside Easter Road.

Satisfied with the performance of the home side in the first half, despite the shortage of goals, the large Hibs support were prepared for more of the same, but the second half was ruined as a spectacle when Valencia continually employed defensive tactics, both legal and unlawful, designed to deny Hibs both the space and the opportunity to add to their lead. As could be expected, the time-wasting tactics were met by a barrage of jeers from the large partisan crowd who had paid their 4/- and demanded to be entertained. The end justified the means for the visitors, however, and they appeared content to play out time holding on to what they thought was an acceptable deficit to take back to Valencia.

It was obvious that a one-goal lead was never going to be enough in Spain, and Hibs put in a concerted effort to increase their tally. Late in the game, with the visitors starting to show signs of nerves and fraying tempers, Cormack set off on one last-ditch effort down the flank. With just 60 seconds of the game remaining, and Valencia confident that they had achieved a respectable scoreline, many of the crowd were starting to drift towards the exits when the unmarked McNamee arrived in the six-yard box and bulleted a header past Zamora from Cormack's cross to shatter the white shirted continentals. It was the centre half's third goal of the season, and so far the most important.

FINAL SCORE: HIBERNIAN 2. VALENCIA 0.

FAIRS CUP 1ST ROUND (1ST LEG), WEDNESDAY 8 SEPTEMBER 1965, EASTER ROAD.
HIBERNIAN: WILSON, SIMPSON, DAVIS, STANTON, MCNAMEE, BAXTER, CORMACK,
QUINN, SCOTT, MARTIN, STEVENSON.

Three days later at Easter Road, champions Kilmarnock snatched a somewhat fortuitous 3-3 draw when goals from Martin, Cormack and Scott were cancelled out by a McIlroy hat-trick. The main talking point for the home side was Hibs' fourth penalty miss from five attempts that season, one newspaper headline proclaiming 'Wanted Urgently, a Penalty Kick Expert'. They were not to know it, but they already had one in their midst.

Still to suffer defeat since the opening day reverse against Falkirk, confidence was high at Easter Road, and the first Edinburgh derby of the season was eagerly awaited. Tynecastle was bathed in bright summer sunshine as the teams took the field on Saturday 18 September 1965. There was a disappointingly small crowd of only 23,000, no doubt due to the fact that the fixture fell on the traditional Edinburgh holiday weekend. A pre-match announcement that the popular Neil Martin would miss the game because of injury was met by groans of disappointment from the thousands of Hibs fans. Jimmy O'Rourke, who had not featured in the first team so far that season and had been about to spend the weekend with friends at Blackpool, was drafted into the side as a last-minute replacement. The initial groans of disappointment from the fans were not long in turning into cheers when the youngster celebrated his 19th birthday in style by scoring twice in the opening minutes. Eric Stevenson quickly added another two, and with only ten minutes of the match played the visitors were already 4-0 in front, much to the consternation of any Hearts fan arriving late.

O'Rourke had opened the scoring in the very first minute of the game. Receiving a pass from Cormack on the right, the teenager hesitated only briefly before sending a well struck shot past the surprised Cruickshank in the Hearts goal. In the opening minutes the blitzed Gorgie men just didn't know what had hit them, and although they recovered some of their poise later in the match, the damage had already been done. It was the first time that Hibs had scored four goals against Hearts in a league match since 1938–39, not counting the fog-bound unofficial wartime derby in 1940 that had ended 6-5 in Hearts favour, and the first time at Tynecastle since 1925–26. The victory saw Hibs sitting proudly at the top of the league table.

HIBERNIAN: WILSON, SIMPSON, DAVIS, STANTON, MCNAMEE, BAXTER, CORMACK,
QUINN, SCOTT, O'ROURKE, STEVENSON.
HEARTS: CRUICKSHANK, FERGUSON, SHEVLANE, BARRY, ANDERSON, POLAND, FORD,
GORDON, WALLACE, TRAYNOR, HAMILTON.

In the corresponding reserve fixture at Easter Road the previous evening, two goals by the promising Colin Stein had helped his side to a 3-1 victory and the first half of a fantastic weekend capital double over the Gorgie side.

Hibs' 11-game unbeaten run since the opening day defeat by Falkirk continued when the unfortunate Alloa were demolished 11-2 at Easter Road in the second leg of the League Cup quarter-final. In the first leg at Recreation Park a Pat Quinn goal after only 60 seconds had dashed the Second Division side's hopes of an early upset, and another first half strike by Martin against his former teammates had made the return leg in Edinburgh a mere formality.

At Easter Road the writing was on the wall when Scott scored Hibs' first goal after only three minutes, and at half time the Greens led 8-0. The home fans had enthusiastically encouraged their team to emulate the scoring of the previous Saturday at Tynecastle, but against Alloa it had taken their favourites all of 15 minutes to reach this four-goal target. Left back Joe Davis, the newly nominated penalty taker, scored number seven from the penalty spot, but for some reason McNamee had decided to take another spot kick in the second half himself. Unfortunately, like the majority of his teammates before him that season, he failed dismally when the keeper saved his poorly taken effort. Although without exaggeration Hibs could well have scored 20, plucky Alloa never gave up trying and gained some reward for their industry by scoring twice in the second half, courtesy of some poor defending by the home rearguard. It was Hibs' highest ever League Cup score, almost doubling their previous best of six, which had been achieved on five occasions over the years. Hibs' goalscorers were Martin (4), Scott (4), Stevenson, Quinn, and Davis (Pen).

Although still unsettled at Easter Road, 'want away' Neil Martin was then probably playing the best football of his career, and he continued his rich vein of form by scoring his second 'foursome' inside four days as Hibs continued their high-scoring run by gaining revenge for the opening day defeat at Brockville. Scott added another as Hibs ran out comprehensive 5-1 winners. Martin and Scott were beginning to form a flourishing and lucrative partnership, and had already scored 26 goals between them since the beginning of the season.

In the game against Clyde at Shawfield the following week, John McNamee scored his fourth goal since the beginning of the season, an impressive statistic for a centre half. The goal enabled the Edinburgh side to scrape through a scrappy game with a 2-1 victory and it appeared that their minds were on the forthcoming League Cup semi-final against Celtic just two days later.

The huge travelling support that made its way to Ibrox for the semi-final on Monday 4 October 1965 witnessed what was probably one of the best and most exciting cup-ties seen at the ground for many years. The fantastic atmosphere generated by the over 46,000 supporters packed inside the stadium was electric as Celtic took the lead in the eighth minute when Joe McBride beat McNamee to a cross to head past Wilson from eight yards. Regaining their composure immediately the confident Easter Road side started to play some exciting attractive football, and they equalised when a beautiful move between Stevenson and Scott ended with Martin powering a header past Simpson from Scott's magnificently flighted cross. Hibs continued to play dazzling football and Martin scored again after 58 minutes, flicking home a Stevenson cutback. Celtic were far from out of it and were still proving dangerous opponents, but Hibs seemed to have booked a place in the final when, with just 60 seconds of the game remaining, Gemmell was allowed to dribble along the bye line after evading a tackle from Stanton. The full back's shot was knocked away by Wilson but landed at the feet of the inrushing Lennox who squeezed the ball home to force extra time, to the almost tangible disappointment of the huge Hibs support. There was no more scoring in the extra 30 minutes, but neither side, who had both given their all, deserved to lose, and for the 22 weary players who trudged off a rain-soaked Ibrox pitch there would be a replay at the same venue a fortnight later.

Meanwhile, Hibs had Valencia to contend with in Spain, but before then, a league game against Motherwell at Easter Road would finish in controversial circumstances. The visitors took the lead early in the game but were in front for only six minutes. Cormack, chasing what appeared to be a lost cause with the ball going out for a goal kick, managed to stop the ball on the bye line and, catching the Motherwell defenders completely by surprise, the teenage outside right sent over a cross for the incoming Martin to score easily from close range. The visitors again took the lead in the first 45 minutes but a positive second-half effort from Hibs gained its reward when Davis equalised for a second time from the penalty spot. The left back's accuracy from the spot now seemed to have solved the long-standing penalty kick problem, and Davis had been given the job permanently. In an exciting climax, Jim Scott smashed home what was thought to be Hibs' winner from the edge of the penalty area, only for the referee to silence the jubilant home fans by declaring that he had blown for time a fraction of a second before the ball had crossed the line. The furious Hibs fans left the ground convinced they had been robbed of revenge for the 6-2 Summer Cup drubbing by an over-zealous official. It was an opinion shared by Scott, the player booked in the dressing room after the game for protesting too vigorously.

The Hibs' party left for Valencia immediately after the game, arriving in the Spanish city in plenty of time to take in a bull fight on the Sunday afternoon. There was an early injury concern for Shankly on the eve of the game when Peter Cormack cracked a tooth while playing with a ball in the hotel bedroom, but a visit to a local dentist for temporary treatment ensured that the 18-year-old would take his place in the starting line-up.

Valencia had still to lose a home game that season, winning 13 of the 15 played. Conceding what was their first goal at home the previous Sunday when defeating Majorca 4-1, their tight defence had been breached only five times since the season began, including the two at Easter Road.

Football fever had gripped the Spanish city. 12,000 had recently attended a reserve fixture, and the Fairs Cup match, undoubtedly the tie of the round, was expected to draw a huge crowd, possibly the first sell out at the Mestalla

Stadium since 1949. The cheapest ticket was priced at the equivalent of 5/- and the most expensive 30/-; with the Valencia players reputed to be on a bonus of £120 a man, to take the game at the very least, to a third-game play-off.

By now, the SFA had relaxed their ridiculous ban on the use of a substitute goalkeeper for European matches, and teenager Thompson Allan, who had yet to figure in the first team, made a small piece of history by becoming the first Scottish player to be stripped for action if required in a competitive European game.

A magnificent, almost unbeatable display by goalkeeper Willie Wilson earned Hibs a third game play-off, and the custodian a tumultuous round of appreciative applause from the Valencia fans. Spanish supporters always appreciated a good performance by a goalkeeper, and Wilson fully deserved any praise that came his way. Only a magnificent free kick and a goal from the penalty spot after a soft award could manage to pierce the protective shield the custodian had placed around his goal.

An early spell of sustained pressure by the home side kept Hibs hemmed into their own half, with Waldo demonstrating his awesome shooting power on several occasions, and it was not until the 12th minute that the Scots managed to stage their first real attack of the game when a good move ended in Quinn shooting over the bar.

In the 14th minute Baxter brought down the ever dangerous Guillot just outside the box, and Waldo, who shared with Puskas the reputation of having the hardest shot in Spain, opened the scoring with a tremendous curving free kick, described somewhat exaggeratedly by several of the Spanish media as one of the best ever seen. If the visitors were expected to fold then Valencia were to be disappointed as Hibs stormed back playing controlled, intelligent football, although in truth rarely seriously troubling Zamora. The remainder of the now well contested game was played out mainly in midfield, and there was no more scoring before half time.

Hardly had the game restarted when Wilson was called into action to hold a tremendous swerving shot from Sanchez-Lage. The keeper then earned the deserved applause of the crowd by defying first Waldo, then Guillot, before making half a dozen other wonder stops in a period of severe pressure by the white-shirted home side. Never overawed, the Scots proceeded to fight back to produce their best spell of the game. Baxter almost deceived Zamora with a high lob, and the keeper had to look lively to palm the ball to safety. Shortly after, the goalkeeper again did well to clear a McNamee effort from close range with his feet. At the beginning of the game, Hibs had attempted the 'Roma' ploy, of Martin and Quinn switching jerseys, but the move failed to hoodwink the Spanish defenders who kept a tight grip on danger man Martin throughout the game.

Wilson was again called into action to save from Sanchez-Lage, before the Latin temperament surfaced with 20 minutes of the game remaining. The Swiss referee who had been overly fussy throughout, although consistent, correctly chalked off a goal by Waldo after Guillot had clearly run the ball over the bye line before crossing, and this provoked an ugly period of pushing and gesturing by several of the home players before order was restored without the book being produced. Four minutes later Valencia were awarded a soft penalty when Simpson was adjudged to have brought down Guillot, and leading scorer Sanchez-Lage made no mistake from the spot. The award was rather harsh considering the penalty claims by Hibs that had been ignored in the first game at Easter Road.

Hibs finished the match brightly with Scott just missing the target with a great shot in the final minute, but there was to be no more scoring and both teams were left to settle for a third game play-off. In the boardroom after the game, the toss of a coin dictated that this would take place back in Valencia. Although bitterly disappointed that fate had conspired against them, for Hibs there would be the consolation of a share of another big gate, this time split down the middle after expenses had been deducted. With home advantage, Valencia could now be considered to be red-hot favourites to advance through to the next round, but the Edinburgh side had done enough to prove that they should not be taken lightly. On this performance they had perhaps deserved to sneak through, and only a penalty would have beaten Wilson in the last half hour. Full back Simpson's challenge on Guillot for the penalty had been innocuous, and the Easter Road side had been terribly unfortunate that such a soft decision should rob them of one of their best ever away victories in Europe. Nonetheless it had still been a tremendous result for the visiting team, and their tireless effort and clever tactical play had earned the respect of all fair minded spectators in the stadium.

FINAL SCORE: VALENCIA 2. HIBERNIAN 0.

FAIRS CUP 1ST ROUND (2ND LEG), WEDNESDAY 12 OCTOBER 1965, MESTALLA STADIUM.

HIBERNIAN: WILSON, SIMPSON, DAVIS, STANTON, MCNAMEE, BAXTER, CORMACK, QUINN, SCOTT, MARTIN, STEVENSON.

Hibs' great 16-game unbeaten domestic run came to an end at Easter Road three days after the return from Spain when Rangers took both points in a 2-1 victory. Surviving a bout of early pressure, the Ibrox side recovered and were well on top when they took a half-time lead. On the hour mark, goalkeeper Ritchie seemed to have a shot from Jim Scott covered, but Eric Stevenson ghosted in to flick the ball over the line for an equaliser. Eight minutes from the end, the Govan side scored the winner to hand weary Hibs only their third defeat of the season including the loss in Spain. Hibs' half-back line had played particularly well but the lack of punch up front in recent games was beginning to be a major concern for Shankly, particularly Martin, who would surely not play as badly in the cup semi-final replay against Celtic on the Monday.

In the replay at Ibrox, Hibs' hopes of reaching the League Cup Final were effectively over after only 20 minutes when Celtic scored a second goal to take a 2-0 lead. The Parkhead side were never in any real danger of losing as Hibs produced yet another inferior display to go down to their third consecutive defeat, and only the form of Stanton, and McNamee in the early stages, had prevented an even bigger defeat. The writing was on the wall as early as the first minute when Hughes volleyed a cross over the bar from close range when he should have done better. A goal was merely delayed, however, and when it did arrive it was shrouded in controversy. In the 15th minute Johnstone threaded a pass through to McBride who looked at least four yards offside. To the amazement of the appealing Hibs players, both the linesman and referee Davidson let play proceed, allowing the Celtic centre forward to fire the ball past Wilson for the opening goal. Five minutes later the game was all but over when the Hibs defenders were caught flat, allowing Hughes to ghost in unchallenged to fire home a square ball from McBride.

Ten minutes from time, the game boiled over. Hibs were trailing 3-0 when McNamee mistimed a tackle on Hughes out near the corner flag and was booked. The giant centre half complained vehemently to the referee that no contact had been made, but made one remark too many and was ordered off. At first he refused to leave the field and for a moment looked as though he was about to attack the official. Persuaded by Pat Stanton and other teammates, he left, violently kicking the dugout on his way from the field. John Fraser, who had watched the game from the stand, was sent to the dressing room to pacify the giant centre half, to find McNamee inconsolable and close to tears. Celtic scored a fourth goal three minutes later to end the scoring, but by then it was immaterial.

Although it had been common knowledge that representatives from Spurs, Newcastle and Sunderland had been at Ibrox to watch Martin, it still came as a numbing shock for the Hibs support to discover that their favourite had joined Sunderland in a £45,000 deal two days after the semi-final debacle. In an attempt to placate the furious fans, chairman Harrower explained that despite Hibs' determination to keep the player, Martin had been insistent on a move; he pointed out that any cash the club received would turn out to represent a major return for a player who had cost just under £8,000 less than three years before. The prolific Martin would not be easy to replace. As well as numerous others in cup-ties, the inside forward had scored 53 league goals from just 65 appearances at Easter Road, including eight from six games already that season.

Jimmy O'Rourke replaced Martin in the team that defeated St Mirren 2-0 at Paisley the following day. Joe Davis scored one of the goals with a penalty kick, and a newspaper byline that would feature prominently over the next few yearswas born: 'Davis scored from the spot after Stevenson had been tripped in the box.' Another reverse, this time a 3-2 defeat at Firhill, one of Partick's goals scored by future Scotland manager Andy Roxburgh, saw Hibs drop to sixth place in the table, hardly a result to inspire confidence for the forthcoming European foray.

The 11 who would play against Valencia, plus goalkeeper Allan, Vincent, Fraser and Jimmy Stevenson, were joined by all five directors and the backroom team of Shankly, McNiven and Stevenson for the trip to Spain via an overnight stop in London.

Training for an hour on the pitch the evening before the game, Shankly had left nothing to chance, and even goalkeeper Wilson had been put through an extra training session that involved gathering crosses under an unfamiliar floodlighting system.

The teams took the field against a backdrop of fireworks and a crescendo of noise from the huge crowd packed inside the stadium, their spirit in no way dampened by a heavy downpour of rain.

As would be expected, the home side immediately took the impetus, and with ten minutes played there was a setback for the Scots when Valencia capitalised on the early pressure. Receiving the ball in what looked an obvious offside position, Muñoz was allowed to run on to send the ball past Wilson for the opening goal as the Hibs players waited in vain for the whistle. Despite frantic appeals to the French official, the goal was allowed to stand. It would now be an uphill struggle.

With both sides finding great difficulty in keeping their feet on a treacherous rain sodden pitch, play raged from one end to the other for the next 30 minutes, Hibs giving every bit as good as they received. Wilson in particular was again in positive mood and the defence well marshalled by McNamee. There were now definite signs that the visitors were beginning to take control in midfield, and at this stage there was little threat of danger from Valencia.

On the resumption, Hibs immediately settled into their stride and playing their best football of the match they were well on top. Still in pouring rain, Zamora was forced to look lively in dealing with a couple of good efforts from Quinn and O'Rourke, before Valencia broke away to create a chance that produced another brilliant save from Wilson. The huge crowd were clearly unhappy at the way the game was progressing and were not slow in letting the home side know. Then, midway through the half and completely against the run of play, the home side scored twice in five minutes to put the tie beyond reach. With little threat of danger, a Stanton slip in the 67th minute allowed Waldo a clear run on goal, but fortunately for Hibs his effort was scrambled away for a corner. The danger was only briefly averted, however, and from the resulting corner Guillot scored from close range after a miskick by Poli.

The Scots intensified their efforts to take something from the game and Zamora was again forced to look lively in dealing with an effort from Stevenson. McNamee had now been pushed forward into attack at every opportunity and shortly after Zamora's save from Stevenson, the centre half had a brilliant header tipped onto the bar and over by the keeper.

With 18 minutes remaining Muñoz put the game beyond the visitors when he thundered an absolute screamer past Wilson from a pass by Paquito, but in no way did the scoreline reflect the balance of play.

Although it was far too late to make any impression on the final result, Scott crashed a thunderbolt off the right-hand post with Zamora well beaten to deny Hibs even the satisfaction of a consolation goal.

FINAL SCORE: VALENCIA 3. HIBERNIAN 0.

FAIRS CUP 1ST ROUND (PLAY-OFF) WEDNESDAY 3 NOVEMBER 1965, MESTALLA STADIUM.
HIBERNIAN: WILSON, SIMPSON, DAVIS, STANTON, MCNAMEE, BAXTER, CORMACK, QUINN, SCOTT, O'ROURKE, STEVENSON.

Although a newspaper headline the following morning proclaimed: 'Storm-swept Hibs washed out of the tournament', this certainly had been no washout performance despite Valencia's seemingly emphatic victory.

The game had been watched by a massive crowd with little room to move inside the packed stadium. Conservative estimates by several of the experienced local reporters as well, many observers from Scotland estimated the attendance to be well in excess of 65,000, so the Easter Road directors were surprised to say the least when the official figure was given as only 53,800. With the gate receipts split down the middle after expenses, a shortfall of 12,000 supporters represented a substantial loss of revenue. Clearly far from happy at the situation, Hibs made an immediate complaint, both to Valencia and to the organising committee, but little could be done and no more would be heard of the matter.

Showing little sign of fatigue after their midweek disappointment, on the Saturday at Easter Road poor Hamilton Academicals were made to pay for Hibs' European elimination when the foot-of-the-table side were demolished 11-1. It was Hibs' biggest ever league win in their 90-year history, and is a club record to this day. Hamilton, which included former Hearts players Wilson Brown and Andy Bowman in the line-up, as well as former Hib Johnny Frye, created the first two chances of the game before the roof fell in. The scoring was evenly spread throughout the team and even full back Davis got in on the act; unusually for him, this time it was not from the penalty spot. Eric Stevenson scored his first ever senior hat-trick, while Davie Hogg, who had only made his debut against Partick the previous Saturday, opened his account for the club in the final minute. Hibs' goalscorers were (E.) Stevenson (3) O'Rourke (2) Scott (2) (D.) Hogg, Cormack, Davis, and Small (o.g.).

HIBERNIAN: WILSON, SIMPSON, DAVIS, STANTON, MCNAMEE, BAXTER, (D) HOGG, CORMACK, SCOTT, O'ROURKE, STEVENSON.

In midweek, centre half John McNamee was suspended for three weeks for his indiscretions against Celtic in the League Cup replay at Ibrox. Hibs fielded new signing Alan Cousin from Dundee in place of the suspended

McNamee against Stirling Albion at Anfield the following Saturday, the former Dens player supplying the cross for Cormack to open the scoring. The experienced Cousin, a league championship winner with the Tayside club in 1962, made a telling contribution in Hibs 2-1 victory, and the versatile part-timer, who was a schoolteacher during the week, would prove to be a valuable and experienced addition to the first team squad.

By this time, work was well underway on the construction of a covered enclosure at the Albion Road end of the ground. Originally expected to be completed in time for the Hamilton game, work was a few weeks behind schedule and would now not be in operation until the turn of the year. Apart from the resurfacing of the terracing and enclosure at the beginning of the decade, the new structure would be the first major development to take place at the stadium since the mid-'50s.

Still on the subject of development, the Hibernian Supporters Association Clubrooms in Carlton Terrace, opened in 1955, had proved an instant success, but with the continued growth in membership the building was now too small. The highly ambitious committee, under the leadership of chairman Jimmy McGrory, had overseen the construction of brand new clubrooms at Sunnyside, just off Easter Road. Hibs chairman Bill Harrower performed the official opening ceremony at a dinner held to mark the occasion on Wednesday 24 November 1965. The modern premises, that contained the usual function area, games room, and spacious lounge bar, had been partly built on the site of the first Easter Road Park, used by the Football Club from 1880 until the temporary disbanding of the side in 1891.

Eighteen-year-old George McNeil, who had been signed from Tranent Juniors at the start of the previous season on the recommendation of Neil Martin, made his first-team debut against St Johnstone in mid-December in a 3-0 home win. The mercurial outside left performed reasonably well and with a bit of luck might well have scored on a couple of occasions, particularly when he hit the crossbar direct from a corner. McNeil however, would have an inauspicious career as a footballer, making only a few first team appearances at Easter Road, and after a short spell with Morton he would go on to make a huge reputation for himself in the world of athletics as a world professional sprint champion.

At that year's AGM it was disclosed that a profit of nearly £20,000 had been made during the financial year ending 30 April 1965, welcome news after the losses of recent seasons. Furthermore, even without taking the Martin transfer fee into account, it was anticipated that the recent rise in attendances due to the team's great start to the season, and the revenue from both the League Cup semi-final games and the Fairs Cup run, that next years accounts would be even better.

This optimistic financial projection, however, did not apply across the board. Stewart Brown writing in the *Evening News* at the end of December highlighted the fragile economic state of the game in Scotland at that time. Brown was of the opinion that the high wages on offer coupled with small gates were crippling the majority of clubs in the First Division, and not even the weekly financial aid many clubs received from the respective development funds could bring much cheer:

> Part-time sides like Clyde could manage reasonably well, but clubs such as Partick Thistle are said to be losing £600 per week. Even in their championship year the Kilmarnock crowds rarely topped the 10,000 mark, and although the Christmas period is a bad time to judge, the recent Hibs versus St Johnstone match attracted only 6,563 paying customers, which would represent a loss to Hibs in the region of £1,500.

As a further example of the seriousness of the situation, Brown reminded his readers that at the recent game against Hearts at Anfield, Stirling Albion had taken just £500 at the gate. Once the league guarantee of £500 had been handed over to the Edinburgh side, Stirling Albion would obviously have made a crippling loss. He was now of the opinion that there were 'too many poor teams, and too many poor matches, and perhaps the clubs that had vetoed reconstruction in the past would now have changed their minds'.

In an interesting comparison to the modern game, the match programme for the Hibs versus Real Madrid match played just 12 months before the above article was written, reported that Real Madrid had a yearly income of approximately £1,000,000, a colossal sum then, and could keep the calibre of player then at the club because they were prepared to pay out almost a third of that income on wages. The figures make interesting reading today, when many of the top sides in this country pay out as much as 80 or 90 per cent of their income on wages alone, and sometimes more. You don't need to be a mathematical genius to work out the main reason for the near bankruptcy of several clubs during the late '90s and into the new millennium.

On 1 January 1966, Hibs were seeking their first league double over Hearts for 14 years, and in what must rank as one of the best derby games seen in the capital for several years, Peter Cormack gave the home side a well deserved two-goal lead inside the opening 20 minutes. With the Hibs support nervously awaiting the half-time whistle, Hearts pulled one back well into injury time to make the score 2-1, and within minutes of the restart Kerrigan had levelled the scores. The remainder of the game was played at a frantic pace with near things at either end, but Wallace sealed the points for fighting Hearts when his shot was deflected off McNamee's knee and past Wilson for the winning goal midway through the second half. Try as they might Hibs just could not force an equaliser, and the ecstatic Hearts fans left the ground singing their own version of the current chart hit by Len Barry: 'One, Two, Three. Wallace, Kerrigan, and McNamee'.

The new covered enclosure behind the north or Albion Road goal, soon to be nicknamed the 'Cow Shed' by the fans, was in operation for the first time for the game against Hearts, proving instantly popular with both sets of fans in those pre-segregation days.

On 8 January Colin Stein, who had been scoring regularly for the reserves, made his first-team debut in a 4-1 win over Morton at Easter Road. The teenage centre forward, who had been Bob Shankly's first signing for Hibs, failed to figure on the scoresheet but did more than enough to suggest that he would become a big favourite with the fans. His energetic style of play had caught the imagination, and he was cheered from the field at the end. Although somewhat premature, some were already comparing Stein's all action style to that of Lawrie Reilly and Joe Baker.

Stein kept his place the following week at Brockville, scoring both Hibs goals and only narrowly failing to score a third, but it wasn't enough to stop Hibs going down to a 3-2 defeat. His enthusiastic style of play and willingness to chase a lost cause went some small way towards making the fans forget Neil Martin, and they left Brockville convinced that Hibs had unearthed yet another goalscoring sensation.

The Scottish Cup brought welcome relief from a barren league run that had seen the team collect only two points from the five games since the beginning of the year. A home draw against Third Lanark rekindled memories of the previous occasion the sides had clashed at Easter Road in the tournament. Then, John Fraser had scored a late winning goal to clinch a 2-1 victory to set up a mouth-watering meeting with double-seeking Hearts at Tynecastle in 1958. This time the second-round draw produced another all Edinburgh derby, the first in the Scottish Cup since the young Joe Baker had stunned the hot favourites, Hearts, and their entourage in 1958 by scoring all four Hibs goals in a famous 4-3 victory before progressing to face Clyde in the final. The Hibs fans were now beginning to believe in omens.

Originally to have been played on Saturday 19 February 1966, the game had been cancelled only on the morning of the match because of the four-inch carpet of snow that covered the Tynecastle pitch. A sudden thaw over the weekend allowed the game to go ahead on the Monday evening, and a huge crowd of 31,224 packed into the ground, paying a total of £5,869.

Trailing at the interval to a 24th-minute John McNamee goal after the giant defender had prodded a Baxter cross into the net during a melee in the Hearts goalmouth, the home side staged another magnificent second-half fight back to progress through to the third round and a game against Celtic. Hibs half-time lead might well have been greater but the usually reliable Joe Davis missed with a penalty kick in the opening minutes after young Colin Grant, making his first-team debut, had been brought down in the box. It was Davis's first miss from the spot in six attempts since taking over as the regular penalty taker. Because of an injury to first choice Wilson, 19-year-old goalkeeper Thomson Allan was also making a first-team debut. The former Edina Hibs player made a brilliant start to his senior career with several fine saves, although he appeared at fault at Hearts' first goal when he hesitated in coming off his line to collect a cross, allowing Traynor to equalise. Grant proved a constant threat in the opposition half, coming close on numerous occasions, particularly when he smashed a tremendous 30-yard rocket against the bar in the opening 45 minutes. The game hinged on a dramatic 60 seconds midway through the second half. A Jim Scott thunderbolt hit the post with Cruickshank well beaten, and debutant Grant, following up, proceeded to blast the rebound high over the bar with the empty goal gaping. Still not believing their good fortune at Grant's miss, the home side immediately raced upfield from the goal kick to take the lead, and for Hibs the writing was on the wall.

All credit should go to Hearts for a spirited and courageous fight back, their two second-half goals crowning a brilliant victory, but few in the ground would have denied that Hibs' fighting performance was worth at least the draw that a magnificent Cruickshank save from Cormack in the dying minutes had denied them. On the plus side for Hibs was the display of the two newcomers, particularly Colin Grant, who on that that performance, suggested that Hibs might well have discovered yet another first-class attacker.

HEARTS: CRUICKSHANK, POLLAND, SHEVLANE, HIGGINS, ANDERSON, MILLER, HAMILTON, CUMMING, WALLACE, KERRIGAN, TRAYNOR.

HIBERNIAN: ALLAN, DUNCAN, DAVIS, STANTON, MCNAMEE, BAXTER, O'ROURKE, GRANT, SCOTT, COUSIN, CORMACK.

Out of the cup and with the championship well out of reach, the only remaining course of action for Hibs was a concerted effort to qualify for the following season's Fairs Cup. In the next six games, only one point would be dropped; but in the away trip to Hamilton, there would be no 11 goals this time, and it required an own goal by left half King late in the game to secure a slender 2-1 victory for an extremely nervous Edinburgh side.

Dunfermline, without a win in their previous four games, brought Hibs unbeaten run to an end with a 3-2 victory at Easter Road, and the fact that the rich run of form was at an end was confirmed seven days later when Dundee United won a thriller at Tannadice by the odd goal in nine.

With only four games left to play, champions elect Celtic could only manage a goalless draw at Easter Road. The recently installed Scotland manager John Prentice watched from the stand, no doubt to run the eye over the Celtic players who would make up a large part of any future squad including Murdoch, Gemmell, Johnstone, Hughes and centre half McNeill, but the new supremo would have been greatly impressed by the performance of Man of the Match, Pat Stanton. Stanton had already won his first representative honour when selected in place of the injured Murdoch in the Scottish League side that faced the English League at Newcastle.

The curtain came down on yet another promising but ultimately frustrating season with a dreary home encounter against Eddie Turnbull's Aberdeen, played out in bright summer sunshine. The visitors took both points when Melrose scored the only goal in the second half of a dull game against mainly lethargic opponents to hand Hibs their first home defeat since New Year's

Day, but by that time few in the ground could have cared less.

During the final few months of the season Hibs had flitted between sixth and seventh place in the table, eventually finishing sixth, level on points with seventh-placed Hearts, who had an inferior goal average. Hibs had scored 25 more goals than the Gorgie side, who had conceded three less. Sixth place, however, would not be enough for Fairs Cup qualification, and Edinburgh would be without representation on the European stage for only the second time in nine seasons.

Although he had only completed a third of the season at Easter Road before his transfer to Sunderland in October, Neil Martin still finished top scorer in all games, his total of 18 being one more than Cormack and Scott could muster. Joe Davis had scored a commendable ten goals, an incredible tally for a full back, although most of them had come from the penalty spot, usually with more than a little help from Eric Stevenson.

Despite taking Valencia to a third game and reaching the semi-final of the League Cup, it had been another hugely disappointing season for everyone at Easter Road and attendances had fallen drastically after the turn of the year. There was now no doubt whatsoever that a major improvement was required if the crowds were to be encouraged back in any worthwhile numbers.

Only Davis and Stanton had taken part in every game, with Cormack, Scott and McNamee not far behind. In total, 24 players had been used during the season, but on the positive side, several outstanding prospects had been unearthed in Colin Stein, Colin Grant, Thomson Allan and Bobby Duncan, all of them featuring prominently during the latter part of the campaign.

The season was not quite at an end, however, and Hearts gained a modicum of revenge for finishing below Hibs in the league table for the first time in many years by defeating their rivals twice inside four days in the final of the East of Scotland Shield. A Davis penalty was all that Hibs could muster against the three scored by Hearts in the Easter Road game held back from the 1964–65 season, while goals from Stein and Scott were not enough to prevent Hearts winning 4-2 on the Saturday at Tynecastle in the 1965–66 fixture. There was a slight consolation for the fans when the reserves won the Second XI League Cup seven days later with an aggregate 4-1 victory over Aberdeen, captain John Fraser receiving the trophy after the second leg at Pittodrie.

Morton had made a half-hearted attempt to resurrect the Summer Cup competition, despite an earlier agreement not to compete for it that year, but the proposal met with only lukewarm interest. Greenock chairman Hal Stewart had suggested an eight-team tournament, without the participation of Rangers, Celtic, Kilmarnock and Dunfermline, who would all be representing Scotland in Europe in the coming season, but it was questionable if the public would now support the competition in sufficient numbers to make it worthwhile. Hibs were moderately interested in taking part, but in the end the proposal was defeated.

Earlier in the season both Jim Scott and Pat Stanton had featured in a

Scotland XI that faced Leicester City at Filbert Street in a testimonial match for former Scotland trainer Alex Dowdells, and 11 days after the season's end both players won their first full caps in a humiliating 3-0 defeat by Holland at Hampden, thought by many of the media to be Scotland's worst ever home defeat by a foreign country. This was not the great Dutch side of a few years later, although it featured Keizer and Shryvers, but a team of part-timers, only one of them a full-time professional.

As part of their preparations for the 1966 World Cup Finals due to be played during the summer in England, Brazil played a warm-up friendly against Scotland at Hampden. Peter Cormack, who had been included in the Scotland squad for the match against Portugal the previous week, was selected to play against the South Americans, winning his first full cap wearing the number 11 jersey in a highly credible 1-1 draw against a Brazilian side containing the celebrated Pele. The hard-working and talented youngster did his reputation no harm and looked every bit a future international prospect.

There was even more prestige for the club when Tom McNiven was chosen as trainer to the Scotland Under-18 side that reported to Largs in preparation for the forthcoming friendly fixture against England at Ibrox.

6

An Epic at East End Park

1966-67

THE GOAL THREAT of Neil Martin and particularly his lethal prowess in the air had been badly missed since his move to Sunderland at the start of the previous season. With this in mind, during the summer Alan McGraw had been signed from Morton in a £10,000 deal. Seen as a natural successor to the former Alloa player, McGraw had been a prolific goalscorer during his five years with the Greenock club. His best period by far had been Morton's promotion season in 1963-64 when he had scored 62 goals in all games, helping to eliminate his new club from the League Cup at the semi-final stage along the way. The versatile player, who could play either at wing half or inside forward, had started out as a centre half, but had long since abandoned all thoughts of preventing goals, relishing instead the idea of scoring them, and very successfully at that, with a remarkable strike rate of 87 goals from just 101 league games for the Second Division side.

Lining up alongside McGraw on the first day of pre-season training was 16-year-old Peter Marinello, called up from Salvesen Boys Club during the summer. With John Blackley now stepping up to full professional status, Marinello took his place alongside John Murphy on the ground staff.

In preparation for a difficult League Cup qualifying section that included Rangers, Kilmarnock and Stirling Albion, permission had been granted by the SFA for Hibs to play a pre-season friendly against English opposition. Brother Bill at Liverpool had been approached by Bob Shankly to open the new season, but Charity Shield commitments had made it impossible for the FA Cup holders to accommodate the game. Sunderland, with ex-Ranger Jim Baxter and former Hibs players John Parke and Neil Martin in their line-up, also represented an attractive proposition, but in the end it was decided to bring Nottingham Forest to Edinburgh, the big attraction being the return of Joe Baker to Easter Road. After an unhappy stay in Italy, Baker had teamed up with former Easter Road colleague Johnny McLeod for a spell at Arsenal before moving to Nottingham the previous season. While at Arsenal, Baker had regained his England place and had been included in the initial shortlist for the 1966 World Cup Finals, only dropping out when the pool was reduced to the final 22. So highly recognised was Baker's undoubted goalscoring reputation, that when it became known that the player was unsettled at Highbury, a petition was immediately forwarded by the Forest supporters demanding that the free-scoring centre forward be brought to the City ground, and he had repaid their faith by scoring five goals from 14 starts in his first season. Bolstered by the signing of Baker, in the coming 1966–67 season, Forest, who included the long serving Scot Bob McKinlay, Welsh international Terry Hennessey, Colin Addison, Alan Hinton and future Manchester United and England outside left Ian Storey-Moore in their line-up, would take the First Division by storm, finishing in second place behind champions Manchester United – a far cry from the lowly 18th of the previous year. Having already defeated the English side during the tour of North America the previous summer, Hibs claimed their second victory over Forest in a little over 12 months in a highly competitive match, with goals by Stein, Davis from the penalty spot, and McGraw, the latter scoring his first goal for the club. Former Easter Road hero, Baker, showed the expectant and appreciative crowd that he had lost none of his goalscoring prowess by scoring both Forest goals.

The League Cup kicked off with a difficult away fixture played in torrential rain at Ibrox with Rangers displaying their two recent signings Dave Smith from Aberdeen and Alec Smith from Dunfermline. Rangers won easily enough against a Hibs side (Allan, Duncan, Davis, Stanton, McNamee, Cousin, Cormack, Stein, Scott, McGraw, and Stevenson. Sub: O'Rourke) who almost succeeded in their aims of securing a draw with their negative and defensive strategy, the Light Blues scoring the only goal of the game with just five minutes remaining.

During the close season the Scottish football authorities had joined most of the other European football associations by allowing the use of substitutes. England had accepted the change the previous season, and now a 12th man could be used in league and cup games north of the border, but only in the case of injury. Although he had not been called upon at Ibrox, Jimmy O'Rourke became the first ever Hibs player to be officially listed as a substitute in a domestic match.

A McGraw double in a 2-1 win over Kilmarnock lifted the Edinburgh men into third spot in the group, and a hard fought 4-2 win at Anfield put them in second place. Although winning well in the end against Stirling, their opponents showed no signs of an inferiority complex after a comprehensive 8-0 drubbing by Rangers in midweek, and their stubborn and resolute display made it difficult for the visitors. Both sides took the field wearing black arm bands, and a minute's silence was observed in honour of former Hibs chairman Harry Swan who had passed away at his home in Alnwickhill Road in Edinburgh the previous day, having been in poor health for several weeks.

Swan's passing severed the final remaining link to the halcyon days at Easter Road, when Hibs had been synonymous with skilful, attacking football and were respected throughout the country and beyond as feared and formidable opponents. His funeral took Monday 22 August 1966 at Warriston Crematorium was attended by dignitaries from all walks of life including representatives from clubs north and south of the border. Players and officials past and present paid their respects and passed on their condolences to Swan's wife and two daughters as they mingled with the ordinary supporter who wished to convey their sympathy in their own humble way. Paying his own respects during the oration, chairman Harrower acknowledged:

> Harry Swan's death was a sad loss for the club and for Scottish football. His world-wide experience made him a valuable member of the board and his shrewd advice was always worth listening to. We shall miss him greatly.

Remembering the dark days of the '30s, Harrower went further in his praise of the former chairman by declaring that it was no exaggeration to say that Swan could be credited with 'saving the club from extinction'. There were numerous tributes from the media, who were well aware that they had the former president of the SFA to thank for filling countless thousands of column inches throughout the years. *The Scotsman* reminded the Easter Road fans that they:

> should raise their eyes to the floodlights and remember that it was Harry Swan who pioneered their use, and they should think of the excitement of the European competitions and remember that it was Swan who led Scotland into Europe in the face of fierce opposition.

The Express and the *Daily Mail* recognised Swan's undoubted skill as a legislator and the prominent part he had played, not just in Scottish football, or in Europe, but throughout the world. As the *Daily Record* put it:

> It is not too much to say that Harry Swan was Hibs, but he was much more than that. He predicted the shape of things to come long before anyone else in Scotland. He saw before anyone the sickness that was creeping over Scottish football, and it is a tragedy that he died without seeing his dream of a British Super League that he had advocated for over ten years, come into being. A self-made man, he was blunt, almost pugnacious at times, someone who called a spade a spade, but without malice. He had given outstanding service to his club and country, including a term as president of the SFA from 1952 to 1956. A past chairman of the International Board and a member of the Fairs Cup committee, he will always be associated with the most successful period ever in the history of Hibernian Football Club.

Perhaps Stewart Brown, of the *Evening News* summed it up best:

> Whatever the headlines of the day, Harry hit them all. Occasionally wrong, he was more often right. Up to his neck in argument, like a great player he was usually several moves ahead of those around him… truly, a man ahead of his time.

It would appear, however, that Harry Swan was reluctant to leave the scene of so many of his greatest triumphs and happiest memories. Throughout the years there have been several reports of loud banging noises in the stadium late at night with no one in the immediate vicinity, particularly after a bad defeat. Several sightings have also been claimed. Former stadium manager David Brown, a level-headed individual, reports of encountering Swan on more than one occasion as he was preparing to lock up for the night, usually on the stairway leading to the boardroom or entering the boardroom itself, the former chairman sporting a wry smile as he passed silently by. Allegedly, in fairly recent years a female cleaner working alone in the Centre Stand, angry at being reprimanded by an elderly gentleman wearing a trilby hat, subsequently identified Swan from old photographs. With the old grandstand now gone, there have been no reported sightings so far in the new construction that stands on the site.

It was somehow fitting that Hibs first game after Swan's death should be an encounter against old adversaries Rangers at Easter Road. During Swan's term at the helm in the tremendously successful late '40s and early '50s, the Glasgow giants had become, after Hearts, the club's most bitter opponents in many a fierce encounter. It was also fitting that, just as Swan would have wished, Hibs recorded a well deserved victory after twice coming from behind to top the group, McGraw scoring the winner in the dying seconds when rising to head past Ritchie, Rangers' keeper. It was McGraw's third goal of the season so far, all scored with his head.

A 3-0 defeat at Kilmarnock allowed Rangers to leapfrog Hibs to the top of the section and qualification for the later stages of the competition. The game, noted for its goalkeeping blunders and controversial penalty decisions, culminated in McNamee's dismissal late in the game. In one of the most sensational games seen at Rugby Park for many years, Hibs completely dominated the opening 20 minutes, but totally against the run of play, goalkeeper Allan dropped a simple cross to allow Kilmarnock to take the lead. The visiting side stormed back but were stunned when the referee awarded a penalty after an innocuous tackle inside the box by Stanton. Allan redeemed himself by saving the spot kick to atone for his earlier error, but five minutes before the break the referee awarded yet another controversial penalty. Allan again guessed correctly to save the kick, but unfortunately for Hibs, Killie netted from the rebound, and a third Kilmarnock goal two minutes after the restart, with the goalkeeper again at fault, put the game and the League Cup quarter-finals beyond Hibs. In the late stages of the game the visitors were preparing to take a free kick just outside the Kilmarnock penalty area when McNamee was sensationally ordered off after an off-the-ball incident. The centre half later claimed, with some justification, that he had been the innocent party. Boxed in at the free kick by several defenders, he had accidentally clashed with a Kilmarnock player in attempting to break free from their attentions. It now seemed apparent, as McNamee himself was suggesting, that the rugged centre half was in danger of becoming a marked man by many referees who were perhaps guilty of being influenced by his huge bulk whenever he was involved in a physical challenge.

There was a positive start to the League Championship when Hibs defeated Hearts for the first time in 14 years at Easter Road. A Davis penalty after only six minutes set the game alight, and McGraw increased Hibs lead on the half hour after Cruickshank failed to gather a shot. Thomson Allan, who was making a habit of saving penalty kicks, denied the Maroons the opportunity to haul themselves back into the game when he saved a spot kick from Wallace just before the interval, and Scott scored a decisive third for Hibs after the break to ensure victory for the better side on the day. Hearts scored what was merely a token consolation goal two minutes from time.

Hibs were now playing the best football of Shankly's short reign, and the crowds had started to return to Easter Road in significant numbers. At that time the average attendance was 17,000. While this figure fell far below the magnitude of the huge post-war attendances, it represented a reverse in the trend of falling gates at many other Scottish grounds.

In mid-September, thousands of Hibs fans made their way over the recently opened Forth Road Bridge for a quite amazing game against Dunfermline at East End Park that ended in perhaps the most exciting climax ever witnessed by the supporters of either side. With only 28 minutes of the game remaining, Hibs held a seemingly unassailable 4-0 lead. Dunfermline, who had conceded five first-half goals at Parkhead in midweek, threatened a brief resurgence by scoring twice, but when Alan McGraw scored a fifth for the visitors the result seemed beyond doubt.

Refusing to accept defeat, the home side put the Hibs defence under extreme pressure in the closing minutes with the wholehearted play of centre forward Delaney and future Aberdeen and Manchester United manager Alex Ferguson causing all kinds of panic in the visitors' penalty area. Incredibly, the Pars pulled the score back to 5-5 with the assistance of a couple of blunders by keeper Allan, and with only seconds remaining, McNamee cleared off his own goal line with the keeper beaten and Dunfermline claiming furiously that the ball had crossed the line, but their appeals were waved aside. With the Dunfermline players still appealing to the referee, the ball was swept upfield, and with the official about to blow for full time, McGraw scored his own second of the afternoon to give his side a thrilling 6-5 victory and bring to an end one of the most fantastic games ever seen at the stadium. It was Hibs' first win at East End Park since November 1958.

The pulsating victory in Fife lifted Hibs to third place in the table. Seven days later they brought their goals tally to 16 in three games when they defeated struggling Partick Thistle 7-0 in Edinburgh to go top of the table.

If things were going well at Easter Road, the same could not be said over at Tynecastle. The tremendous run of league titles and cup wins during the late '50s and early '60s were now a thing of the past. Tommy Walker, who had led the club through its most successful ever period and at that time the longest serving manager in the country, shocked the football world when he announced his resignation… or was that merely a boardroom euphemism for the sack?

A win at Fir Park kept Hibs at the top of the table on goal average above Celtic before the clash of the Greens in Edinburgh. With McNamee suspended for his part in the Rugby Park fiasco, Alan Cousin again lined up at centre half, but four-goal Joe McBride came out on top of that particular dual. Surviving an opening spell of pressure by the Parkhead side, Cormack opened the scoring after ten minutes, but the visitors scored twice before a trip on Stevenson inside the box earned Davis his now almost obligatory goal from the penalty spot. Celtic had been by far the better side in the first half and they scored twice more to take a 4-2 interval lead. The Hoops scored a fifth midway through the half before McGraw scored a consolation goal in the dying seconds. Hibs had undoubtedly missed the presence of McNamee, who had been serving a 28-day suspension, but even 'Garth' would have had great difficulty in denying the rampaging Celtic, who were on the brink of a clean sweep of domestic and European honours. As it was, McNamee's suspension would prove to be the beginning of the end for the player at Easter Road. Although he would remain in Edinburgh for a few more months, he was now more than ever determined to further his career in England.

As Hibs prepared to face Dundee United at Easter Road the significance of the outcome of the match paled into insignificance against the news of the previous day's disaster at Aberfan. On Friday 21 October 1966 just under 150 adults and schoolchildren had lost their lives when a pit waste heap, destabilised by heavy rain, had slid down a hillside to engulf part of the close-knit mining village, including the local primary school. The news of the catastrophe in Wales stunned the entire world and for football fans it brought home the relative triviality of winning or losing points on the field of play.

John McNamee returned from suspension at the beginning of November in time for the visit of Falkirk, who included two recent signings from Easter Road in their line-up. A short while before, former captain John Baxter had ended a 12-year association with the club when he signed for the Bairns along with teammate Stan Vincent. Like Baxter, Vincent had found it difficult to secure a regular first-team spot at Easter Road since the arrival of McGraw and Cousin. Spurred on by the former Hibs players, who were desperate to turn the tables on their erstwhile colleagues, Falkirk had proved the equal of the hosts throughout, but their efforts were in vain when Hibs scored three times in a five-minute spell during the second half to run out 3-1 winners.

The temporary reprieve from a mini-slump that had seen Hibs take just five points from a possible ten since the defeat by Celtic was to prove only fleeting, and a meagre crowd of fewer than 2,500 at Shawfield a week later saw part-time Clyde embarrass a poor Hibs side who were handicapped by the absence of flu victim Pat Stanton. Hibs seemed well in control in the early stages when Stanton's replacement O'Rourke scored with a tremendous 25-yard drive after only seven minutes, but little was seen of the visitors as an attacking force thereafter. With new signing Harry Hood from Sunderland managing to get on the scoresheet, the home side cantered to a comprehensive 5-1 victory. With 13 minutes of the match remaining, Pat Quinn became Hibs' first ever competitive substitute when he replaced the injured Joe Davis.

From then until the turn of the year it was the same old inconsistent story, Hibs winning four of the seven games, including a 6-0 whitewash of Stirling Albion, and losing three, culminating in a humiliating 5-2 home defeat by lowly St Johnstone. On a snow-covered pitch that bordered only on the side of playable, Saints got off to a flying start by scoring after only 20 seconds. Hibs persisted with their usual passing game on a treacherous surface while St Johnstone employed a more direct strategy in the farcical conditions. The home side had no answer to these simple tactics and in the end the final whistle could not come fast enough for both the team and the dwindling band of supporters who had remained under the winter gloom until the very end.

In Europe, Dundee United flew the flag for Scotland when defeating Barcelona in both legs of the Fairs Cup, although by this time the Catalan side were a far cry from the team beaten by Hibs at the start of the decade. The mighty Liverpool, playing in the European Cup for the first time, were drawn against an unknown Dutch side with a strange sounding name. AFC Ajax, however, proved that they were no soft soapers by defeating the English champions 5-1 on a fog-bound Amsterdam pitch, drawing the return leg at Anfield 2-2. The result stunned the whole of Europe and perhaps put Scotland's so-called embarrassing 3-0 defeat by Holland the previous year at Hampden into perspective.

Still on the international front, Pat Stanton, Peter Cormack and travelling reserve Bobby Duncan, were all selected for the Scotland Under-23 squad to face Wales at the turn of the year. Future Hibs player Alex Edwards, then with Dunfermline, scored one of Scotland's goals in a one-sided 6-0 victory.

Financially things were far from well within the game. Figures released from Easter Road revealed that an income of just over £2,000 per week was needed just to break even, considerably more than the takings from an average game. Based on the previous 12 months' accounts, Hibs' income, including transfer fees and gate money, totalled £153,000, while wages, upkeep of the stadium, outgoing transfer fees and general administration costs amounted to £112,000 – figures that made it obvious that only the sale of both Neil Martin and Willie Hamilton had prevented a horrendous loss. As it was, the sale of both players left a profit of over £40,000, but the directors' report exposed the sobering reality that in a city with a population of over 400,000, a club could not survive on gate receipts alone. The perilous financial situation was not unique to Easter Road. On the other side of the city, Hearts had sold the popular centre forward Willie Wallace to Celtic at the beginning of December, much to the fury of the Gorgie fans, but before the month was out it would again be the turn of the Hibs supporters to lament the departure of yet another huge favourite when John McNamee was transferred to Newcastle United for £25,000 on the penultimate day of the year. Although the player was reportedly happy at Easter Road, it was common knowledge that the giant centre half was concerned at what he saw as a victimisation campaign against him by referees, and he now felt his immediate future lay in England.

The transfer of McNamee was put on hold to allow Hibs time to secure a replacement, and 24 hours after the initial bid by Newcastle, the target of an earlier mystery spying trip by manager Shankly was revealed when Hibs swooped to snap up pivot John Madsen from Morton for a fee in the region of £10,000, leaving the Easter Road club with a substantial profit from the double transaction.

Meanwhile Eric Stevenson, unhappy at being dropped after the 2-1 defeat by Rangers at the end of the previous month, his first omission of the season, had posted a transfer demand even although he had been reinstated to the side the following week. The request was joined by a similar demand from goalkeeper Willie Wilson, at that time unable to secure a regular first-team place because of the outstanding form of Thomson Allan. Considerable speculation also surrounded the future of Jim Scott, who had been watched recently by representatives of several English clubs. A rumour that a swap deal had been arranged with Rangers' transfer-listed George McLean was strenuously denied by Bob Shankly, who angrily insisted that his desire was to build a team, not sell one. But despite these protestations, Scott had at one stage literally been about to board a train at Waverley Station to travel south for talks with Wolverhampton Wanderers, only to have been informed at the very last minute that the prospective £40,000 deal had been called off.

Another rumoured move, in this case to Hibs by Ibrox veterans Jimmy Millar and Davie Wilson, turned out to lack any substance.

As McNamee prepared to line up for his new side against Alan Gilzean at White Hart Lane on the final day of 1966, both John Madsen and Jim Scott faced Airdrie at snow-swept Broomfield. Scott, possibly unsettled by the ongoing transfer speculation, had an otherwise unimpressive outing. Late in the game he was tripped in the box, probably to the envy of Eric Stevenson, allowing Davis to score the only goal of a drab game from the resulting penalty. The Hibs team around that time was along the lines of: Allan, Duncan, Davis, Stanton, Madsen, Cousin, Scott, Quinn, Cormack, O'Rourke, and Stevenson. Sub: McGraw.

No-score draws were a rarity in games between the Edinburgh rivals throughout the years, but the New Year game at Tynecastle on 2 January ended with neither side managing to breach their opponent's defensive shield. Hearts keeper Jim Cruickshank was the hero of the hour when pulling off several magnificent saves, including a double stop from a penalty taken by the normally reliable Joe Davis and the follow-up from McGraw, to deny a rampant Hibs, inspired by midfield general Pat Quinn, a thoroughly deserved victory. Somewhat predictably, the penalty was awarded when Stevenson was brought crashing down in the box by right half McDonald after a brilliantly tormenting run by the outside left had bewildered the Hearts defence. Cruickshank, credited after the match by Hearts manager John Harvey as having been 'absolutely marvellous', also managed to save two thunderbolts from O'Rourke that would have beaten most custodians, but on his form that afternoon it would have taken something extraordinary to have beaten the keeper. Just before the end, the home side were convinced that they had secured both points, but referee Davidson silenced the hordes of rejoicing Hearts fans among the 31,000 crowd when he disallowed the goal for offside. Incredibly, although it was the first no-score league game between the sides for 33 years, there would be another five in the following five seasons.

Perhaps influenced by similar events at Easter Road in the years immediately following the war, Aberdeen, emerging as a side to be reckoned with under the astute guidance of former Hibs player Eddie Turnbull, were heavily criticised for adopting the then fairly unusual policy of charging more for entry to the Main Stand for certain league games. Against Rangers at Pittodrie in January the prices had been increased from the usual 10/- to 12/6, a practice normally only adopted for important non-domestic games such as European ties. The Rangers fans vociferously denounced the increased cost, and some in the media denounced the move as an abuse of the ordinary fan who supports his team through thick and thin. Both the supporters and the press insisted that any increase should have been implemented by Aberdeen at the beginning of the season and not halfway through when they were suddenly faced with success.

In a sign of the times, there was an added dilemma for any British player who was interested in trying his luck across the Atlantic in the recently formed American Soccer League. A statement released by a spokesman from the United States Embassy warned that any player under the age of 26 who was considering joining the then outlawed American Football Association, would be eligible for call up to the US armed forces, and risked being sent to fight in the Vietnam conflict, which was then at its height.

By now, centre half John Madsen was beginning to look every inch a real bargain buy, and only a 2-0 defeat by Celtic in Glasgow marred a run of seven straight victories inspired by the blond-headed Dane as Hibs climbed to fourth place in the table and within touching distance of a Fairs Cup place.

In the Scottish Cup, a tense 2-0 win over Second Division Brechin City, with visiting goalkeeper Sandy Henderson repeatedly defying the home side almost single-handedly throughout the 90 minutes, earned Hibs a home tie against Berwick Rangers in the second round. Incredibly, the 'Wee' Rangers had brought off one of the greatest cup upsets ever in Scottish football history by defeating Glasgow Rangers 1-0 at Berwick in the previous round. It was a result that reverberated through the country and would eventually lead to the sacking of manager Scott Symon and the exit from Ibrox of several of the Rangers players involved in the humiliating defeat.

Although there were several all First Division clashes in the second round of the competition, there was no mistaking the game that aroused the most interest: all eyes were firmly focused on Easter Road, wondering if the lowly 'English' side, who were currently lying mid-table in the Second Division, could continue their giant-killing act at the expense of First Division Hibs. Cup-tie fever had gripped the Border town. As well as a huge fleet of cars, dozens of buses and even a special train had been hired to transport the large contingent of Berwick fans to the capital, all desperate to see if their favourites could prolong their Scottish Cup adventure. Led by goalkeeper and player-manager Jock Wallace, Berwick offered a brave and stout resistance at Easter Road and only a Scott goal three minutes from the interval separated the sides at the end. Nervous Hibs had missed the chance to put the game beyond doubt midway through the second half when Wallace brilliantly saved a Scott penalty, and one can only wonder what the outcome would have been had a first-half effort by Berwick's Dowds not been cleared off the line by full back Duncan.

After the game, Peter Cormack, perhaps with the naivety of youth, impetuously declared that second-favourites Hibs 'would now win the Scottish Cup'. Before the first-round draw, the bookies had made Hibs 10-1 third favourites to lift the trophy, a long way behind Celtic at 6-4 and Rangers at 9-4. The sizeable number of bets placed on the Edinburgh side suggested that the punters could see no further than one of the three lifting the trophy. A mystery individual, described only as a well known gambler, laid a £400 stake with Glasgow bookie Tony McQueen at odds of 9-1 on Hibs winning the trophy, easily the biggest bet placed outside the Old Firm. The mystery punter stood to collect £3,600 if Hibs won the cup, a colossal sum in these days, but with Hibs' horrendous Scottish Cup record, the bookies were well satisfied that their money was secure.

By now, a consistency of both selection and performance had made Hibs one of the most attractive and improved sides in the country, and with eight wins from the previous ten games, this enhanced form had been reflected by increased turnover at the turnstiles. Over 43,000 fans watched the league encounter against Celtic, 20,000 the recent championship game with Aberdeen, and over 30,000 paid to see the cup-tie against Berwick. One of the main reasons behind this upsurge was the impressive form of centre half John Madsen, which had been a significant factor in transforming a previously erratic side into what was now one of the most dependable in Scotland.

At the beginning of March, Peter Cormack, another of Hibs' rising stars and rated by many as the most exciting talent produced by Scotland since Denis Law, was on target as the Scotland Under-23 side defeated England 3-1 at Newcastle. Both he and teammate Pat Stanton enhanced their already growing reputations with a fine performance in a brilliant win over the 'Auld Enemy'. With just seven minutes remaining and the game level at 1-1, Cormack unleashed a tremendous 25-yard drive that flew past Peter Shilton in the England goal. Two minutes later, debutante Jim Smith of Aberdeen put the issue beyond doubt when he scored a third to cap a satisfying evening for the Scots.

Only one defeat in the previous 15 games made Hibs hot favourites to reach the semi-finals of the Scottish Cup, but first there was a third-round game against old adversaries Aberdeen at Easter Road. After a tentative start by both sides, an Eric Stevenson drive after 16 minutes looked like being the winner until Smith levelled with a header four minutes from time to earn Aberdeen a replay that they probably deserved. In a real blood-and-thunder cup-tie that was spoiled as a spectacle by the blustery wind, Hibs' normally free-moving forwards were given little scope against a tight and disciplined Dons rearguard, a characteristic of any team organised by Eddie Turnbull. Interviewed for the *Evening News* after the game by the self-confessed Hibs fan Stewart Brown, who had known Turbull since his days as a player at Easter Road, the confident Aberdeen manager advised the reporter in his own inimitable style not to even waste his time turning up for the midweek replay at Aberdeen, as his team had no chance. As usual, Turnbull would be proved right.

On Wednesday 22 March 1967, over 44,000 packed inside Pittodrie for the replay, 2,000 more than the previous midweek record attendance for the ground, with hundreds more locked out. Eager for a better view, several fans dangled precariously halfway up the floodlight pylons, with many more on top of the TV gantry, and the police removed countless dozens from the enclosure roof. Aberdeen set their stall out early when an over robust challenge by the rugged Ernie Winchester, one that had been recommended in the dressing room before the game by manager Turnbull, knocked the heart out of the influential Madsen inside the first few seconds. The slick-moving home side scored after only three minutes, and the game was already over. It was played under a driving torrent of sleet and rain, but the conditions failed to dampen the spirits of an Aberdeen side who totally outclassed the visitors, storming to an eventual 3-0 victory to progress through to a semi-final meeting with Dundee United.

HIBERNIAN: ALLAN, DUNCAN, DAVIS, STANTON, MADSEN, COUSIN, QUINN, STEIN, SCOTT, CORMACK, STEVENSON. SUB: O'ROURKE.
ABERDEEN: CLARK, WHYTE, SHEWAN, MUNRO, MCMILLAN, PETERSON, STORRIE, SMITH, JOHNSTONE, MELROSE, WILSON.

Just four days after the mauling at Pittodrie, an Alec Smith goal from a Willie Henderson cross midway through the second half gave Rangers an overdue goal and both points against one of the poorest Hibs sides ever to make their way through to Glasgow. A defence well marshalled by centre half Madsen, who had recovered from his midweek pummelling, received little help from their forwards and were found to be totally lacking in the required cohesion, spirit and attacking flair that had been evident in abundance earlier in the season. Goalkeeper Thomson Allan again performed well; on current form he was being tipped for inclusion in the Scotland set up for the forthcoming Home International match against world champions England at Wembley. As it would turn out, former Hibs goalkeeper Ronnie Simpson was selected for the game, the evergreen goalkeeper capping a great season and an illustrious career by playing his first full international match at the age of 36 as Scotland defeated the world champions 3-2. Simpson had been an outstanding player since making a debut for Queen's Park against Clyde in the Summer Cup in 1945 as a 14-year-old, before moving to Third Lanark, Newcastle United and then Hibs. The cynics among us may wonder why it was only when he moved to Glasgow at the tail-end of his career, that Simpson would win long overdue international recognition!

With Aberdeen in the final of the Scottish Cup and assured of a place in the Cup Winners' Cup even if they lost to champions elect, Celtic, and Rangers all but certain to finish the season as runners-up in the league, Hibs, Clyde, Kilmarnock and Dundee were all in direct competition for the remaining two Fairs Cup places. In a game that was vital to the European aspirations of the former, part-time Clyde stunned their full-time opponents by taking a second-half lead in Edinburgh, and it required a McGraw header a few minutes later to give Hibs a share of the points. Worse though was to follow. Despite an easy 6-0 victory at Easter Road earlier in the season, Hibs stumbled to an embarrassing 1-0 away defeat to a Stirling Albion, a side that would finish the campaign third-bottom of the table. Although they had seen off the challenge of Ayr United at Easter Road, yet another dropped point, this time against St Mirren, meant that they now had to win their remaining two games to have any real chance of qualifying for Europe. Two goals by McGraw, the winner coming with only minutes remaining, gave Hibs victory against Willie Ormond's St Johnstone at Muirton Park, but any lingering hopes of a European place disappeared completely when lowly Airdrie, who had won only one of their last 14 outings, defeated a lethargic Hibs side 2-0 in the final game of the season at Easter Road. Despite commanding almost all the first 45 minutes, Hibs were rocked when Fyfe opened the scoring with the last kick of the half. Surprisingly lacking the expected urgency considering the importance of the situation, the listless home side were stunned again when a defensive blunder gave the Diamonds a 2-0 victory.

After the game a distraught Bob Shankly confessed to being 'absolutely heartbroken'. 'We had plenty of chances but failed to take them,' he stated, 'and in the end we paid dearly for two defensive mistakes.'

Hibs eventually finished the season in fifth place, on the same number of points as Aberdeen but with a far inferior goal average. Both had scored 72 goals but the Easter Road side had conceded 11 more. Celtic, who within a few weeks would become the first British side to win the European Cup, finished 16 points ahead of both, winning the championship for a second successive year under the leadership of former Hibs manager Jock Stein. Hearts finished in 11th place.

Although Hibs had failed to capture a European spot, in many ways it had been a season of progress. The exciting football displayed through a large part of the season suggested that Hibs were a side on the ascendancy. The signing of John Madsen had been a masterstroke, and the campaign just ended had seen Peter Cormack come of age in the footballing sense. Full back

Bobby Duncan had established himself as a first-team regular, as had Colin Stein and Thomson Allan. The acquisition of the experienced Alan Cousin had helped to stabilise the halfback line, with midfield general Pat Quinn – who had been unsettled midway through the term, requesting a transfer at one stage – rediscovering the form that had earned him Scotland caps earlier in his career.

Apart from a few appearances by both Wilson and Grant, and one by goalkeeper Reilly, Shankly had called on only 14 players in all three competitions, including McNamee, who had shared the centre half position during the season with Madsen. Although McGraw, with 14 goals, had finished top overall goalscorer in his first season, somewhat surprisingly, defender Joe Davis had the unusual distinction of sharing first place in the league charts with Peter Cormack, both players on the 13 mark. It is not often that a full back can lay claim to finishing joint-top goalscorer, whether with the assistance of penalties or not. Had it not been for failing three times from the spot, Davis could well have been out on his own.

Thirty-three players were retained for next season; Jimmy Stevenson, Reilly, Gartshore, Bobby Hogg, Binnie and Whiteford were released.

At this time the game was in a precarious state with many clubs struggling financially. Something just had to give. Earlier in the season, Rangers had taken the unprecedented step of attempting to dissolve the Scottish League. They and 26 other sides, including Hibs, Hearts, Celtic, Dundee and Dunfermline, sought the power to end the league in its present form and replace it with a top division of 12 teams, and two of ten. The Ibrox club proposed that the voting rules be changed from a fixed number to a majority vote, with a ballot taken to wind up the league. An appeal forwarded by the five clubs which would have been excluded from the new set-up under the Rangers blueprint – Berwick Rangers, Albion Rovers, Stranraer, Stenhousemuir, and Brechin City – was rejected and the case went forward to the Court of Session. But the status quo would continue, at least for the present.

7

See Naples and Die, a Debut for Colin Stein and a Four Step Fiasco
1967–68

AS A CONSOLATION for the disappointment of missing out on a Fairs Cup place, Hibs embarked on an exhausting but nonetheless enjoyable six-week tour of North America. The Football Associations of both America and Canada were by now been recognised by FIFA and in a bid to popularise the game in those countries teams from Uruguay, Brazil, Holland, Scotland, England, Ireland and Italy, had been invited to compete in a North American League Competition, each side competing under the adopted name of a host city – in the case of Hibs, Toronto. Although at times hectic and involving a tremendous amount of tedious travelling, the 12-game tour was a relative success with the Edinburgh side finishing in third place in the Eastern Division. Progress to the final had seemed well beyond them after the opening few games, but several decent results since meant that full points from their last two games against what was seen as relatively easy Irish opposition would have been enough to secure them a place at the ultimate stage. Unfortunately, after a comfortable 6-1 victory over Shamrock Rovers, a crucial point was dropped when they could only manage a 1-1 draw against Glentoran. The result allowed Wolverhampton Wanderers to face Eddie Turnbull's Aberdeen in the final, the English side eventually winning an exciting game 6-5 after extra time.

In the interim, the number of directors at Hibernian had been expanded to the full complement of five when Sir John Bruce, a respected and eminent Royal Surgeon and Hibs supporter of long standing, was elected to the board, filling the void that had been created by the death of Harry Swan.

Pre-season training began in late July 1967, but only for those who had not been involved in the transatlantic tour. The others were allowed a few extra days rest to recuperate from their travels, but Eric Stevenson and young John Murphy surprised their colleagues by joining them on the demanding traditional run round Arthur's Seat on the first day. New signings Alex Pringle, a Scottish youth cap from Glasgow United, and Mervyn Jones, a nephew of Rangers' John Greig, were joined on the arduous run by reserve defender John Blackley, now completely recovered from his cartilage operation the previous season. Fans' favourite, Willie Hamilton, was a surprise face on the opening day. Recently freed by Aston Villa, according to Hamilton himself, he had no immediate signing plans but was merely keeping in shape. As it turned out, it was perhaps felt that the player's best days were behind him, and he was not offered the signing terms that he probably desired, despite the denials. He would rejoin Hearts a short time later on a month-to-month contract.

The remainder of the first-team squad caught up with their teammates over the next few days, including Joe Davis, recently appointed club captain, and Jim Scott, who had put pen to paper on a new contract at the end of the previous season only on the understanding that the club would listen sympathetically to any enquiries. The offers were not long in coming, and before the season had even started the Falkirk born player joined former Easter Road teammate John McNamee at Newcastle United for a fee believed to be in the region of £38,000. United's Scottish manager, Joe Harvey, had long been an admirer of Scott and was reportedly delighted to have added the tricky forward to his squad. Both Scott and McNamee would win a Fairs Cup medal the following season in Newcastle United's first ever venture into European competition. After defeating Rangers in an all British semi-final – the second game in Newcastle disgracefully marred by crowd trouble by the visiting support after Rangers had conceded a second goal – Scott scored one of the Newcastle goals as the Magpies defeated Ujpest Dozsa 6-2 on aggregate in the two-legged final.

After his earlier differences with the club, Pat Quinn was now happily settled in Edinburgh and a £5,000 bid by Southend United for the midfield schemer was rejected. Quinn would have a valuable part to play in the season ahead. Alan Cousin, however, missed the first few months of the season. An injury received during the trip to America was worse than originally feared and he needed a cartilage operation.

There was great jubilation at Easter Road when the surprise news was received that Hibs had been included in the Fairs Cup draw in place of Clyde, who had finished the season in third place, two above Hibs. A major row threatened to erupt. Clyde complained to the SFA, who took their side. The football authorities in Scotland, in line with most of the other affiliated Associations, had long insisted that qualification for the European and Fairs Cup competitions should be on merit of league position and on merit alone. This argument was countered by the Fairs Cup committee, who explained that a rule had been in place for three years that prohibited two sides from the same city taking part in the tournament. In this particular case, second-placed Rangers, who had been drawn against Dynamo Dresden, were accepted as Glasgow's representatives to the exclusion of Clyde. The argument didn't make much sense considering that both Hibs and Hearts had taken part in the same competition only two years before, but that was of no concern to the Easter Road side, who were delighted to take their place in the European competition once more, even if by the back door. There was to be even more bad news for Clyde when a late extra place went to Dundee, who had finished the season in sixth place. The heated dispute raged on for some time, with the SFA demanding the reinstatement of the Shawfield side, but the

European authorities remained firm and Hibs prepared for their fifth Fairs Cup competition, the draw in Frankfurt pairing them against Portuguese side Porto.

Only one pre-season friendly had been arranged before the start of the 1967–68 season. On a rain-swept Bloomfield Road pitch five days before the official opening day, Joe Davis scored from the penalty spot in the 62nd minute, but with Second Division Blackpool already leading 6-1, this turned out to be merely a consolation goal. The scoreline prompted a local newspaper to comment: 'Thunderstorm greets Hibs on their arrival in Blackpool, but it was nothing compared to the Hurricane that blasted them during the game!' An absolutely furious Shankly immediately barred the players from going out on the town afterwards, but young men being what they are, the delights of Blackpool were sampled after most of the squad managed to slip out of the hotel unnoticed.

The following day the manager had words of warning for the forthcoming opposition: 'Nobody should believe that points will be won easily off Hibs, especially at Easter Road during the coming season. The competition will be tough, but I am confident of Hibs holding their own.' It was a view shared by Hugh Taylor of the *Daily Record*:

> Both Edinburgh teams have the chance to make good again but frankly I see Hibs as the better prospect, and they could certainly be well on the way to greatness, especially if they sign outside right Alec Scott.

Hibs were rumoured to be interested in signing ex-Rangers Scott, then with Everton, brother of the recently transferred Jim.

In a League Cup section comprising of Motherwell, Dundee and Clyde, the Easter Road side topped the group at the halfway stage after a 3-1 home win over Clyde and looked assured of proceeding to the quarter-finals. Hibs being Hibs, however, went down to successive defeats by Dundee and Motherwell (teenager John Murphy making a scoring first-team debut at Fir Park). These defeats made the last game of the section meaningless and for a second consecutive year Hibs had fallen at the first hurdle. In the cup game against Dundee in Edinburgh, John Fraser, then the longest serving player at Easter Road, replaced the injured John Madsen at centre half. It was to be Fraser's final first-team appearance after a senior career spanning 14 years.

With their League Cup ambitions prematurely curtailed, Hibs finally admitted an interest in signing Alec Scott, hopefully in time to face Hearts at Tynecastle, but the signing was complicated by the fact that Plymouth Argyle were also showing an interest, and it was feared that once it became common knowledge that Everton were demanding only a modest £14,000 transfer fee for the experienced former international, that other clubs would quickly enter the race.

Meanwhile, at Tynecastle the astute Shankly got his tactics just right. The danger of Willie Hamilton in midfield was nullified by 'shadow' Alan McGraw, who marked his former teammate out of the game, allowing Pat Quinn more room to dictate the game from the middle of the park. The midfield general celebrated this freedom by scoring a hat-trick in Hibs' emphatic 4-1 victory. It was the first treble by a Hibs player since Eric Stevenson had scored three in the 11-1 win over Hamilton Academicals nearly two years before, and Hibs' first hat-trick against Hearts since the four scored by Baker in the famous cup-tie at Tynecastle in 1958. Although the sides were level at the interval after a Traynor strike cancelled out Quinn's opening goal, there was only ever going to be one winner, and on this showing Hibs were now being considered a sound bet to challenge the dominance of the Old Firm.

Because of his business interests north of the Border, Alec Scott had decided to move back to Scotland and agreed to notify Hibs on the Monday if he would be joining them. The deadline passed and was changed first to Wednesday, then Thursday, but still the saga continued, and it was only on the Friday morning that Scott finally agreed to become a Hibs player. Initial plans to include him in the line-up for the game against Raith Rovers the following day had to be delayed because of a minor muscle injury received playing in a reserve game for Everton, and the vastly experienced European campaigner would now make his debut against Porto in the Fairs Cup at Easter Road on the Wednesday evening.

A 3-0 home win over Raith Rovers saw Hibs, now the competition's top scorers, sitting proudly at the top of the league table. Strikes by Cormack, Stein, and an own goal by former player Bobby Kinloch, put Hibs on easy street against the newly promoted Fifers. The bustling, all-action style of Colin Stein had impressed representatives from Porto watching from the stand and they would probably have pinpointed the fair-haired centre forward as the main danger in the forthcoming European tie. Opposing Stein that day was older brother Bobby; it was the first time that the brothers had faced each other in a senior match.

For the game against Porto, Hibs had concerns over the fitness of Stanton and Duncan, who had been injured against Raith Rovers on the Saturday, but both took their place in the line-up at the kick-off. Two substitutes were now allowed in European matches. The usual custom was for one of them to be a reserve goalkeeper, but because of the injury doubts Shankly decided to go with two outfield players instead.

With the side sitting clear at the top of the table, morale at Easter Road was high, but more than a few eyebrows were raised when Shankly announced that he wanted to win by at least four clear goals.

Alec Scott, making his debut at outside right, played for just over an hour before being withdrawn owing to a slight recurrence of his muscle injury, but what a telling contribution he made in his first game, adding a new dimension to the home attack. A classy Hibs turned in their best performance of the season so far. In absolutely devastating form, particularly during the first half, Hibs cantered to a commanding 3-0 lead and although they had failed to make the target set by the manager they could now face the return leg in Portugal with confidence. Although it had been a real team effort, with every man playing his part, special mention should go to two-goal Peter Cormack and to Colin Stein, on his European debut. At the back, marshalled by the ever-reliable Madsen, Hibs dealt effectively with everything they were required to do, the rugged Dane keeping a tight reign on danger man Djalma, who rarely threatened.

FINAL SCORE: HIBERNIAN 3. PORTO 0.

FAIRS CUP 1ST ROUND (1ST LEG), WEDNESDAY 20 SEPTEMBER 1967, EASTER ROAD. HIBERNIAN: ALLAN, DUNCAN, DAVIS, STANTON, MADSEN, MCGRAW, (A) SCOTT, QUINN, STEIN, CORMACK, STEVENSON.

Typically, manager Shankly refused to get carried away by the impressive display, but even he could not fail to have been pleased by the performance of his team:

It was a wonderful game, but it was impossible to keep up the remarkable pace in the second half although I thought Hibs should have scored more goals. Scott played exactly as I visualised when I bought him, and he will get even better. With luck we could go on to have a reasonably good season and finish near the top of the league.

Interviewed after the match, the Porto secretary admitted that the Portuguese side had made the mistake of underestimating Hibs:

We never expected such a terrific pace. The speed of Hibs stunned us but it will be a different story in Portugal with a 30,000 home crowd behind us. Although the second leg will be difficult, the tie is far from over!

As they prepared to make their way to Portugal for the return leg, there was a worry for Hibs on arriving at Turnhouse Airport when it was discovered that Alec Scott's passport had failed to arrive from his home in Liverpool. A temporary visa was finally arranged, allowing him to make his way to Portugal with his new teammates.

On arriving at Porto, Hibs became a victim of the disruptive tactics that were employed by many continental sides at that time, when their request for training facilities on the Dash Antas pitch was refused. This decision took the Hibs officials, who had done everything possible to assist Porto before the first game at Easter Road, completely by surprise, but it was only after strong insistence by Shankly that permission was eventually granted.

Although they would both play, there had been a slight doubt over the fitness of Stanton and Stein, but of more concern was the condition of Eric Stevenson, who required treatment from Tom McNiven right up to the kick-off. McNiven had arrived in Portugal with his new 'Secret Weapon', a recently acquired, extremely expensive and bulky portable treatment machine that was being used for the first time on the continent, although it had been taken on the club's close season trip to America.

Although Hibs were currently joint league leaders as well as Scotland's top goalscorers, the much-travelled Shankly warned his players of the danger of complacency against a side that had yet to lose a domestic game that season and would pose a strong threat in front of their own fans. The referee was from neighbouring Spain, and although there would be no doubts as to his bias, he was likely to officiate in the continental style, which was often contrary to that expected by British teams.

The announcement that Stevenson was fit to play was great news, and Hibs' confidence was boosted even further when they were awarded a penalty inside the opening three minutes after Stein was brought crashing down inside the box, leaving the referee no option but to point to the spot. After several minutes' delay caused by the Porto players jostling and arguing with the referee, Davis expertly placed the ball past goalkeeper Americo to give his side what looked like an unassailable four-goal aggregate lead.

There was a sensation in the 35th minute when Cormack and his marker Rolando were sent off for fighting. After being tackled by the fiery Cormack, the Porto midfielder threw a punch at the Hibs man and in the ensuing melee several other Porto players started to jostle the Scot, who was rescued by his teammates. After the pandemonium subsided, both players were sent off.

Four goals behind on aggregate, the home side were now left with no other option than to throw caution to the winds, and they managed to pull a goal back inside nine minutes. The goal gave Porto fresh inspiration, and there was a feeling that the game was far from over when Valdir scored a second goal just 60 seconds later.

The still dangerous Hibs attack almost increased their lead when a Quinn drive struck the bar with a fierce shot, but with 20 minutes remaining Valdir scored a third and from then until the final whistle any composure previously shown by the Edinburgh side had completely evaporated, their play becoming anxious and disjointed as they were forced into a ten-man defensive shell. Despite intensive pressure, Porto just couldn't score the vital fourth goal that would have earned them extra time, although right on the final whistle Stanton was forced to head clear from under the crossbar with goalkeeper Allan beaten.

FINAL SCORE: PORTO 3. HIBERNIAN 1.

FAIRS CUP 1ST ROUND (2ND LEG), WEDNESDAY 4 OCTOBER 1967, DAS ANTAS STADIUM.
HIBERNIAN: ALLAN, DUNCAN, DAVIS, STANTON, MADSEN, MCGRAW, SCOTT, QUINN, STEIN, CORMACK, STEVENSON.

Shortly after the final whistle Hibs were informed that the Portuguese side were claiming the tie on the grounds that they had failed to present proper player identification to the referee before the game, presumably a reference to Scott's temporary visa. However, on contacting the Fairs Cup secretary in Basle that same evening, Hibs officials were told that while a referee could ask for identification there was no hard-and-fast rule, and in the end no more was heard about the ludicrous complaint, the Edinburgh side going forward into the draw for the second round.

Hibs themselves had been unhappy at the overall performance of the referee and lodged an official complaint. According to Shankly, some of the official's decisions were the worst he had seen in all his years in the game, particularly the sending off of Cormack. The player himself considered his tackle on Rolando 'no different to any made at home, and the Portuguese player had 'simply overreacted'. Cormack would now automatically miss the next European match as the referee's decision was deemed final, the rules of the tournament disallowing an appeal.

Hibs' opponents in the second round of the Fairs Cup would be either Hanover of Germany or Napoli, who had yet to play the second leg of their tie. The Italians led 4-0 from the first game in Naples, and for the first time in his managerial career Bob Shankly decided to travel to Germany to watch both teams in action. Even during Dundee's great European run of the early '60s, the manager had preferred not to spy on future opponents, concentrating instead on the strengths of his own team.

At the end of October, Hibs officially unveiled their new floodlighting at an East of Scotland Shield game against Hearts. The £8,000 system was considered to be the best in the country at that time, and players and supporters were impressed at the enhanced brightness. Goals from both O'Rourke, and Davis from the penalty spot, cancelled out a strike by Ford as Hibs won one of the most hotly contested and controversial fixtures for many years. For entertainment and excitement, the fans, who were now being asked to pay 5/- for admission to the terracing, certainly got full value for their money in a hard-fought encounter, but the intensity of the tackling of both sides saw several players requiring treatment the following morning. Hearts manager John Harvey summed up the mood: 'It was a good, hard game, and although the trophy itself isn't all that important, a lot of prestige was at stake and it showed in the wholehearted and sometimes over vigorous performances of the players.'

Statistics released around that time revealed that for a second consecutive season, attendance figures in Scotland were on the increase. In the League Cup alone, the crowds had swelled by over 100,000, although most of this was due to the fact that both halves of the Old Firm had been drawn in the same section. Gates at most major grounds had shown a marked increase, but there were still exceptions such as the Motherwell versus Dunfermline League Cup tie at Fir Park, which had been watched by a hugely disappointing 3,200.

It was also around this time that Professional Footballers' Association chairman John Hughes met with the referees' committee to discuss proposals to amend the application of the disciplinary suspensions meted out to players found guilty of an indiscretion. The fact that they were banned for a number of days rather than games meant that a player banned for four weeks would miss no games at all if bad weather prevented any matches being played during the period, while a player suspended for two weeks could miss four games if his club was involved in midweek competitions. The PFA's preferred option to eliminate this anomaly was for a player to sit out a set number of games. Although this would take some time to implement, the system would eventually become accepted practice and is still in use today.

A 4-0 defeat at Parkhead by European Cup holders Celtic, who had surrendered their European crown at the first hurdle against Dynamo Kiev earlier in the week, saw Hibs slip to third place in the table, but three consecutive victories saw them rise to second place and consequently grow more than confident of upsetting the challenge of Stirling Albion at Anfield. As it turned out however, a woefully incompetent 90 minutes by the Easter Road side enabled bottom-of-the-table Stirling to beat the hapless Fairs Cup hopefuls by an emphatic and embarrassing 4-1 margin and collect their first win bonus of the season, one of only four that term before they suffered the ignominy of relegation in April. Even worse, it was Albion's second consecutive home victory against Hibs in two seasons.

Victories over Aberdeen and Dundee after the Anfield debacle saw the Greens in confident mood to face the forthcoming European challenge. At Dens Park there was a sensation just seconds after Cormack gave his side a 3-1 lead with little over an hour played. Near the far side touchline Alan McGraw fouled a Dundee player who angrily remonstrated with the wing half, the incident ending with the Hibs man swinging a wild kick which, fortunately for his opponent, was wide of its target. McGraw was sent off for his part in the fracas and the Dundee player booked. The use of red and yellow cards was still not universal practice, and at first it seemed as if McGraw had only been booked. The Hibs player ran as if to take up position in his side's defensive set-up for the free kick, but stunned his teammates and the supporters by continuing his run right off the field and up the tunnel at the corner of the ground.

The two goals scored by Colin Stein in the 4-1 victory, took the centre forward's tally to eight in the last four outings, including a hat-trick in the 5-0 demolition of Airdrie at the end of October. The former Armadale Thistle defender, by now Scotland's top goalscorer, with ten league goals, was beginning to earn deserved acclaim as a prolific marksman.

In Hanover, with Shankly watching from the stand, a 1-1 draw was enough to see Napoli safely through to the second round and a game against Hibs, the first leg to be played in the beautiful city of Naples. Cormack would obviously sit it out after being sent off in the previous round, and it was first thought that McGraw's dismissal at Dens Park would also mean Hibs missing his services. However, because the disciplinary committee would not meet until after the game in Naples, the wing half was cleared to play.

Shortly after arriving at their hotel in Naples, where they were billeted on the top floor with spectacular views over the city, Pat Stanton was packed off to bed suffering from flu. This was a real blow for Shankly in view of his already badly depleted side, but another potentially more serious problem soon presented itself. Shortly before the team had left Edinburgh the pound had been devalued, and on arriving in Italy, the players found that the banks were refusing to change their traveller's cheques until the rate of exchange had been determined. Luckily, help was near at hand – an Edinburgh restaurant owner of Italian extraction who also owned snack bar facilities inside Easter Road and had travelled over for the game on the team plane, managed to borrow enough lira from friends and relatives, averting calamity.

Napoli had experienced a difficult start to the '60s, twice suffering the ignominy of relegation, but since the signing of the brilliant Brazilian international Altafini in 1965 they had flourished, finishing fourth in the Italian League the previous season. The 2.30 kick-off was good news for Hibs, as the afternoon start would prevent many home fans from attending the game because of work commitments. Given the hostile reputation of the natives, who were reputedly a fearful sight in full flow, the sparsely occupied terraces would clearly act in the visitors' favour. In view of his weakened team selection, Shankly had no option but to consider a defensive strategy, and would happily have settled for a two-goal deficit as long as Hibs scored at least once.

The teams took the field with Hibs wearing their normal colours, the home side wearing their change strip of red shirt and white shorts instead of the usual dark blue. As expected, the crowd – who had paid between 15/- and £2 for admission to the arena, much more than the minimum 5/- paid at that time by their Scottish counterparts – numbered well under 20,000, far short of the average crowd of over 65,000 that normally all but filled the 82,000 capacity stadium.

Surprisingly, Stanton had recovered enough to take his place in the starting line-up, but with Cormack already an absentee, Shankly was dealt another blow when Eric Stevenson failed his fitness test shortly before the kick-off. Colin Grant, making only his fourth start of the season, replaced Stevenson. Jimmy O'Rourke, who had been the youngest ever player to take part in a competitive European competition when he turned out against Utrecht in 1962, replaced Cormack.

Spurred on by the relatively small but partisan home crowd, Napoli swept into the attack from the off, and within minutes Allan had to produce a wonderful save to deny Altafini the opening goal. Apart from the Brazilian Altafini, who looked a polished world-class performer, the Napoli side looked anything but superstars and the visitors were far from outclassed. After a sluggish opening, Hibs began to settle and for long periods of the first half they were the better side and only poor finishing prevented them from taking the lead. Inspired by the prodding of Pat Quinn, the visitors were beginning to look the more dangerous side when disaster struck midway through the opening period. A soft free kick awarded after an innocuous tackle by Stanton proved costly when Cane lashed in a drive that Allan should have saved, the

Joe Baker and Johnny McLeod bid farewell to Easter Road 1961.
From left: (E.) Stevenson, McLeod, Davin, Baker.

Easter Road at the beginning of the 1960s.

Willie Ormond, whose signing for Falkirk severed the last remaining on-field link with the Famous Five.

Eddie Turnbull oversees training at Easter Road. From left: Turnbull, Baxter, Grant, Preston.

Scottish Juvenile Select. Hibs' Eric Stevenson second left in front row. Willie Henderson is at the extreme left of the front row, next to Alex Ferguson.

The Baker brothers at home. Gerry (left) would take over from Joe in the Hibs line-up during the 1961–62 season.

Jimmy O'Rourke, who became the youngest player to take part in a competitive
European game for Hibs when facing Utrecht in 1962.

Action from a Hibs versus Hearts match at Easter Road in the early '60s. Hibs players from left: Simpson, Grant, Leishman, Fraser.

Action from a Hibs versus Queen of the South match at Easter Road, 1960s.

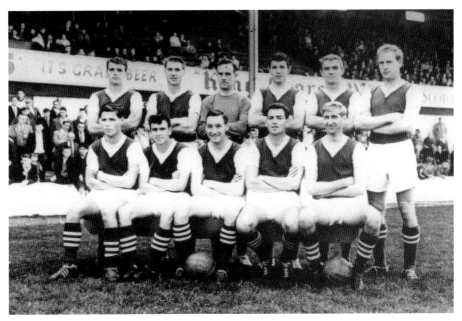

Hibernian, season 1961–62. Back row left to right: Fraser, Grant, Simpson, Baxter, Easton, Baird. Front row: Bogie, (E.) Stevenson, Kinloch, Preston, (A.) MacLeod.

Hibernian, season 1963–64. Back row left to right: Easton, Baxter, Docherty, Preston, Duncan. Second-back row: Fraser, Scott, Cormack, Wilson, O'Rourke, Keay, Leishman, Grant, (R.) Simpson, Gartshore, Hughes. Second-front row: Byrne, McClelland, McGlyn, Cameron, (J.) Stevenson, Toner, Falconer, Baker. Front row: Seaton, Martin, Stanton, (B.) Simpson, (E.) Stevenson.

Harry Swan ended a 29-year period as Hibs chairman when he sold the club to William Harrower. From left: Smith, (H.) Shaw, (A.) Buchanan, Swan.

Pat Quinn not long after he joined Hibs from Blackpool.

HIBERNIAN

FOOTBALL CLUB

OFFICIAL PROGRAMME

6D

Summer Cup Final

Wednesday, 5th Aug., 1964

No. 1 HANDBOOK EDITION   Kick-Off 7.30 p.m.

Aberdeen

Programme for Easter Road leg of the Summer Cup Final against Aberdeen.

Action from the Summer Cup Final play-off at Pittodrie; Hibs won 3-1.

Hibernian, season 1964–5. Back row left to right: (E.) Stevenson, Meechan, (D.) Hogg, (B.) Simpson, Allan, Duncan, Whiteford, Fraser, Hamilton. Middle row: McNeill, Martin, Parke, Reilly, Wilson, Baxter, Wilkinson, McNamee, Easton, Stein (manager). Front row: (J.) Stevenson, (trainer), Quinn, O'Rourke, (J.) Grant, Cormack, (J.) Stevenson, Vincent, Scott, Cullerton, Stanton, McNiven (physio).

The maestro, Willie Hamilton.

HIBERNIAN

FOOTBALL CLUB

6ᴅ

OFFICIAL PROGRAMME

Challenge Match

Wednesday, 7th Oct. 1964

No. 8

Kick-Off 7.45 p.m.

REAL MADRID

Programme for the Hibs versus Real Madrid game.

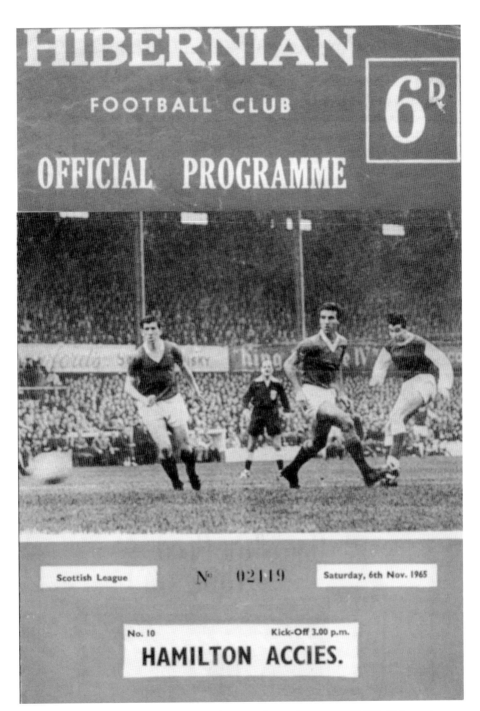

Programme for the game against Hamilton Academicals, 1965, still Hibs' biggest home league win.

Hibernian, season 1964–65. Back row left to right: Simpson, Fraser, Davis, Wilson, Stanton, McNamee, Baxter. Front row: Scott, Hamilton, Quinn, Martin, Cormack, Vincent, (E.) Stevenson.

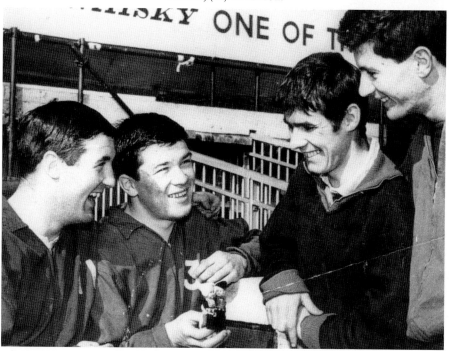

(J.) Stevenson, O'Rourke, (D.) Hogg, and Reilly at Easter Road after training.

Neil Martin.

Opened in time for the 1966 New Year's Day derby against Hearts, the 'Shed' was soon to be a source of concern for the police. (Pictured in the 1990s.)

John McNamee.

ball squirming from his hands and over the line. The setback failed to dispirit Hibs, however, who were every bit as good as the home side for long periods of the game, although squandering several good opportunities to equalise.

Soon after the restart, Napoli doubled their lead and scored again in the 68th minute when Man of the Match Altafini headed past Allan, and another goal by Cane left the visitors with it all to do. Hibs were thrown a lifeline ten minutes from the end when Stein scored a vital away goal, his first in Europe, but five minutes from time outside right Cane scored his third goal of the night to give his side a commanding 4-1 lead.

FINAL SCORE: NAPOLI 4. HIBERNIAN 1.

FAIRS CUP 2ND ROUND (1ST LEG), WEDNESDAY 22 NOVEMBER 1967, STADIO SAN PAOLA.

HIBERNIAN: ALLAN, DUNCAN, DAVIS, STANTON, MADSEN, MCGRAW, SCOTT QUINN STEIN, GRANT, O'ROURKE.

The final scoreline flattered the Italians. For Hibs it was the old story of missed chances proving costly in European competition, particularly with away goals now counting double in the event of a draw.

The main difference between the sides had been Altafini, a player of genuine quality, and Shankly would desperately need to devise a plan to subdue him in the second leg at Easter Road. Shankley's view was that his team 'had not done themselves justice by their overall performance'. Hibs obviously now faced a mammoth task in Edinburgh, and even with a full squad at their disposal, very few, apart from the manager, were of the conviction that Hibs were capable of reversing the result.

After a poor showing in Naples, goalkeeper Thomson Allan was dropped for the trip to Ibrox on the Saturday and his place taken by Willie Wilson who was making his first start for more than a year. Despite a quite magnificent display by the Wallyford player, Rangers won comfortably in the end, but early on it had all been so different. Far from overawed, Hibs did well until they allowed the award of a soft penalty midway through the first half to upset their rhythm. Tempers frayed and things came to a head after 50 minutes when Colin Stein and Alex Ferguson were both sent off after the Rangers player had fouled the fiery Hibs centre forward, who lashed out in retaliation. Thereafter, it was mainly all Rangers, who scored a second goal in the final few minutes to put the result beyond doubt.

Hibs' chances of overturning the Fairs Cup result in Italy were boosted with the news that Napoli would be travelling to Edinburgh without two of their established players. Wing half Stenti, who had played in the first game, was injured. But it was the news that Altafini, who had caused so much damage in that game, was also unfit that was the most encouraging. It turned out later that the Brazilian superstar could have played, but it was felt that with such a commanding lead, his presence in Edinburgh would not be required. It was to prove a disastrous decision for the Italians. While the media were of the opinion that the Edinburgh public were the losers, being denied the chance to see a truly great player in action, the absence of Altafini would have delighted everyone behind the scenes at Easter Road. The Hibs supporters, however, would have the opportunity to see the great Altafini for themselves a few years down the line, with devastating consequences for their team.

The Italian side made a puzzling change to their travel arrangements. They were expected to arrive at Turnhouse Airport on the Monday afternoon and a representative from Easter Road was there to greet them. On their non-appearance, he made frantic enquires and discovered that Napoli had decided to stay overnight in London to relax the players. The visitors, whose victory over Bologna on the Sunday meant they now headed the Italian table, eventually arrived in the capital 24 hours later than first planned. The decision to delay their arrival in Edinburgh perhaps indicated that Napoli was already taking the result for granted.

With the possible exception of Eric Stevenson, Hibs had a full complement to choose from, but Shankly had the dilemma of whether he should risk the temperamental but influential player who relished the big occasion. Although far from 100 per cent ready, Stevenson was improving in fitness every day and it was eventually decided to take a gamble and include him in the starting XI.

Hibs faced what some thought an impossible task to overcome their three-goal deficit against one of the best sides in Europe, but in one of the most incredible nights ever seen at Easter Road in the 92-year history of the club, they achieved a miracle by beating Napoli 5-0 to go through to the quarter-finals. The absolutely magnificent and rampaging Hibs wrote perhaps the greatest chapter in their long and illustrious history, prompting one newspaper to proclaim that the saying 'see Naples and die' should be changed to 'see Edinburgh and die'.

Such was Hibs' overwhelming dominance that Dino Zoff in the Napoli goal was involved in flurries of activity throughout the 90 minutes, while his immediate opposite, Willie Wilson, did not have one single save of note to make in the entire game. Zoff, the understudy to Fiorentina's Albertosi in the Italian side, was certain to take over from his countryman in the near future, and only the previous week he had been voted the best goalkeeper in Italy.

For Hibs it was imperative to score an early goal. Kicking up the slope, the Greens went on all-out assault straight from the start and earned a free kick just inches outside the penalty area in the very first minute when the heavily bandaged Stevenson was brought down as he tried to wriggle into the box. The free kick from Quinn came to nothing. Two minutes later the Italians ought to have conceded a penalty when Cormack was brought down well inside the box. The referee awarded an indirect free kick, an outrageous decision, but this also came to nothing.

The fairy-tale began as early as the fifth minute. Right back Bobby Duncan received the ball just inside his opponent's half. Charging forward near the right stand-side touchline he evaded two tackles before finding himself not far from the penalty area. Without glancing up, the defender stunned the unsuspecting Zoff and every single spectator in the ground when he let fly with a spectacular left-foot rocket from all of 25 yards that screamed past the helpless keeper and into the roof of the net to bring the house down. Such was the power of Duncan's shot that Pat Stanton would later recall that if it had not been stopped by the net, the ball would have ended up in Lochend Loch. It was Duncan's first goal for the first team and one that was to achieve legendary status. It is still spoken about fondly to this day, and with the exaggeration of time, the distance of the strike is now described as being anything from the half-way line, to a spot halfway down Albion Road itself.

Now on the back foot, the bewildered visitors were forced to resort to persistent fouling and body checking in an attempt to stem the tide of green and white attackers, but the referee was alive to this and clamped down consistently.

Stanton almost scored with a brilliant header from a perfectly flighted Quinn free kick only for Zoff to save spectacularly, before a dangerous McGraw shot was deflected for a corner with the keeper beaten.

Amid unbelievable excitement, Stein almost scored when his perfectly judged lob beat Zoff, only to see Bianchi appear on the line to head clear.

It was all Hibs. A second goal just had to come, and it did. Just before half time Stein somehow managed to evade a couple of robust tackles and found himself on the edge of the penalty area near the bye line. His cut back was intercepted by Zoff who fumbled the ball, allowing the inrushing Quinn to crash the ball low and hard into the net off the post.

The ecstatic Hibs fans sensed that a remarkable comeback was on. In a desperate effort to save the game, Napoli now substituted an attacker with a defender at half time, but it made absolutely no difference to the pattern of the match. The pace was hectic and relentless as Hibs charged down the slope time after time. It was nonstop attack, and Easter Road went wild in the 67th minute when their favourites scored a third. The industrious Stein won a corner on the right. Scott flighted over a perfect cross and Cormack rose above the Italian defenders to power a header into the net.

Two minutes later the fans were chanting 'easy, easy' after Stanton scored with a typical header from close range. Napoli were all over the place now and almost conceded another straight-away but Zoff was on hand to collect a Stein header.

With just under a quarter of an hour to go, Stevenson and Girardo clashed near the touchline in front of the Main Stand. The Italian player had a kick at the Hibs player as he lay on the ground and was sent off.

With 11 minutes remaining, Stein intercepted a clearance and went through to score a fifth, a scoreline that would reverberate around Europe and cement possibly Hibs' most impressive ever performance in Europe. No team could have lived with them in this irrepressible mood and the end of the match just couldn't come quick enough for Napoli.

As the Italian team slumped dejectedly from the pitch, the excited Hibs players remained to take a deserved bow in front of their delirious supporters. In the next round, they would now face either Partisan of Belgrade or Leeds United, who were still to play the second leg of their tie.

FINL SCORE: HIBERNIAN 5. NAPOLI 0.

FAIRS CUP 2ND ROUND (2ND LEG), WEDNESDAY 29 NOVEMBER 1967, EASTER ROAD. HIBERNIAN: WILSON, DUNCAN, DAVIS, STANTON, MADSEN, MCGRAW, SCOTT, QUINN, STEIN, CORMACK, STEVENSON.

Interviewed after the game an ecstatic Bob Shankly revealed:

From what I saw in Italy I knew we could do it, but never as completely as this. I can't remember being so delighted about a result since Dundee beat Cologne 8-1 in the European Cup at Dens Park. It must be a long time since the Italians have seen one of their top sides humbled so convincingly.

The Scotland manager, Bobby Brown, who was present at the match, congratulated Hibs on a tremendous performance. He was not alone in his praise. The Napoli president confessed: 'Hibs were another team altogether from the one seen in Naples. Their power, speed, and force were far too much for us.' The last word should go to right back Bobby Duncan whose incredible goal had been the catalyst for the famous victory: 'It was my first ever goal for Hibs, with my left foot too, and I could hardly believe it when I saw the ball sailing into the net.'

After the exhilaration of the fantastic European triumph on the Wednesday Hibs were brought crashing back to earth a few days later at Cappielow. Although exerting severe pressure on the Morton goalmouth after losing an early goal, a home side containing former Hibs player Morris Stevenson held out to deny the visitors two important points in their quest for a European place the following season. Hibs were now lying in third place, a position they had held for the past few weeks, six points behind leaders Rangers, and five behind Celtic.

By now Hibs knew that their next Fairs Cup opponents would be Leeds United. Leeds had drawn 1-1 against Partisan Belgrade at Elland Road, winning 2-1 in Yugoslavia, but the meticulously thorough Don Revie and his backroom staff had already had Hibs watched on several occasions, and were reportedly extremely impressed by what they had seen.

Since taking over as manager of United in the late '50s, the former Leicester, Hull and Sunderland centre forward Don Revie, a colleague of Bobby Johnstone in the Manchester City cup-winning team of 1956, had assembled a formidable side. Promoted from the Second Division as champions at the end of the 1963–64 season, they had reached the FA Cup Final the following year, losing 2-1 to Liverpool only after extra time. Although a major prize had eluded them so far, they had come near on several occasions, never more so than in their first season back in the top flight when they lost the championship to Manchester United only on goal average. Several of the squad were already full internationals, including the one-time Hibs target Billy Bremner. Others such as Welsh cap Gary Sprake, Eire's Johnny Giles, England's Norman Hunter and 1966 World Cup winner Jack Charlton, were vastly experienced on the international front. Most of the rest were already Under-23 caps, including centre forward Mick Jones, a £100,000 buy from Sheffield United earlier in the season.

As well as attracting many admirers for their skilful play, Leeds under Revie had also gained a reputation as solid competitors. Exponents of the cynical foul, they were not above taking the art of gamesmanship to the very edge.

Currently lying fourth in Division One and already in the semi-finals of the League Cup, Leeds had more than proved their European pedigree by going all the way to the final of the Fairs Cup the previous year, losing 2-0 to Dynamo Zagreb in Yugoslavia after a 0-0 draw in England.

Bob Shankly had been confined to bed on the Monday with a stomach chill, but although still far from fully recovered there was no way he was going to miss the match and he was among the official party of 16 players plus backroom staff and directors who made their way to England on the Tuesday morning. Brother Bill at Liverpool had earlier supplied Shankly with a dossier highlighting the strengths and weaknesses of the opposition, and the shrewd tactician would use the information wisely.

Once again Scotland could be proud of this fighting Hibs side. On a treacherous, icebound pitch, they were kicked pushed and shoved throughout the entire 90 minutes, but refused to allow Leeds to intimidate them, and in the end the English side were made to look second best. Even the loss of a goal after just four minutes, and the loss of Colin Stein 18 minutes later, failed to unsettle the visitors.

In the opening minute Hibs got the first chance of the game when Stein pounced on a Stanton clearance that had been missed by Charlton, but the centre forward was cynically fouled on the edge of the box. Madsen then made a fine interception as Leeds roared into attack, but in the very next move the home side took the lead when Gray drove a Greenhoff cross past Wilson from close range after a fortunate deflection. An enterprising Davis shot just inches past the post left Sprake sprawling, before a good move between Stevenson and Cormack brought a great save from the goalkeeper who was forced to dive bravely at Cormack's feet to prevent a certain goal. Looking anything but overawed, Hibs created several more dangerous chances and thought they had equalised midway through the half when Stein had the ball in the net, only for it to be ruled offside.

The most controversial incident of the game came just minutes later. Stein, fouled twice in quick succession by Bremner, required treatment after being crudely bundled onto the trackside by the Leeds captain. It was quickly evident that the centre forward was in some distress, and he made his way down the tunnel on a stretcher to be replaced by O'Rourke. Much to the disbelief and fury of the large number of Hibs fans who had made their way south, Bremner was not even booked for this blatantly obvious and shockingly dangerous tackle. The half ended in typical fashion with Hunter being warned for a particularly wild tackle on Cormack.

Immediately on the restart Hibs were put under severe pressure as Leeds attempted to consolidate their lead, and were desperately forced to concede several corners. Hibs, however, were far from out of it and a great shot from O'Rourke was diverted for a corner, as was another effort shortly after by the same player after good play by Stevenson.

Midway through the half a great through ball by Charlton was crashed into the net by Lorimer, but the excited roars of the home fans were stifled when the goal was correctly judged to be offside.

Playing with great confidence, Hibs continued to look dangerous in front of goal. Cormack beat two defenders in the penalty box before squaring a lovely ball to O'Rourke, only for the substitute to slice his shot past the post.

It seemed certain that Leeds would need more than one goal to take to Easter Road and Bremner was moved into the forward line in an effort to secure the elusive second, but there was to be no more scoring.

Near the end only a crunching solid tackle by Hunter prevented Cormack from bursting through to equalise, and almost on the final whistle Wilson made a miraculous save from Jones when he held a powerful effort from no more than two yards.

FINAL SCORE: LEEDS I. HIBERNIAN O.

FAIRS CUP 3RD ROUND (IST LEG), WEDNESDAY 20 DECEMBER 1967, ELLAND ROAD.
LEEDS UNITED: SPRAKE, REANEY, COOPER, BREMNER, CHARLTON, HUNTER, GREENHOFF, LORIMER, JONES, GRAY, GILES.
HIBERNIAN: WILSON, DUNCAN, DAVIS, STANTON, MADSEN, MCGRAW, SCOTT, QUINN, STEIN, CORMACK, STEVENSON.

The English newspapers were generous in their praise of the Edinburgh side, and were unanimous, as were both managers and players, that Peter Cormack had been the best player on the field by far. Coventry manager Noel Cantwell, who had watched from the stand, thought that it had been 'a tremendous all-round performance by Hibs, but Cormack was supreme and would be an asset to any English club'. Shankly was again delighted with his team's performance, particularly after the setback of losing an early goal, and in his view Hibs had deserved at least a draw.

It was not only Cormack who had taken the eye. One newspaper claimed that on this performance, centre half John Madsen was better than the England centre back Jack Charlton, and that if Mick Jones was value for the £100,000 recently paid for him, then what was Colin Stein worth? England international Norman Hunter was also unstinting in his praise for Cormack and Stanton, stating bluntly that the obvious talents of both players were wasted in Scotland. Stein's injury at Elland Road had appeared a bad one, but the striker had two weeks' enforced rest to recover after receiving 14 days suspension earlier in the week for his part in the November altercation with Alec Ferguson at Easter Road which had led to both players being ordered off.

Back at Easter Road, a penalty kick awarded after Stevenson was brought down in the box, allowed Joe Davis to score the only goal of the game from the spot to give Hibs their first home win over their arch rivals Hearts on New Year's Day for 20 years. In an often tough and torrid game, Hearts had the best of the first half, but the roles were reversed in the second, although the Maroons staged a grandstand finish after Hibs' goal, only to find Wilson in steadfast form. The result meant that the teams were now neck-and-neck in vying for third place in the title race, although the Easter Road side still had a game in hand over their oldest rivals.

The following day at Starks Park, the visiting fans were surprised to see an exciting 17-year-old prospect named Peter Marinello making his league debut wearing the number seven shirt in place of the injured Alec Scott. Lowly Raith managed to secure a commendable and thoroughly deserved 2-2 draw in an otherwise drab and dreary game. For the visitors, only Marinello received pass marks. The electrifying runs and tricky ball control of the former Easter Road ground staff boy excited the crowd throughout the 90 minutes. On this performance he was already being compared by some to the great Gordon Smith, a comparison that was highly premature.

Marinello kept his place in the 3-0 home victory against Dundee United four days later and proved he had the temperament and the ability for the big time with another dazzling performance. It now remained to be seen if Shankly would keep faith with the youngster in the event of the injured Alec Scott failing to respond to treatment before the big Scotland versus England return Fairs Cup clash at Easter Road.

Leeds had defeated Fulham 5-0 at Craven Cottage on the Saturday, thanks to a Greenhoff hat-trick and a further two goals from Jones, and they arrived in the Scottish capital the day before the match in buoyant mood. As formidable a team away from home as they were in Leeds, they had never yet lost a European tie after leading from the first leg. Interviewed before the game, Bremner was quoted as saying that one goal would be enough, as had been proved before 'in far better places than Easter Road'.

By now, Stein had completed his suspension and Hibs' injury doubts Alex Scott and Bobby Duncan had recovered sufficiently to take their place in the starting line-up, leaving a disappointed Marinello to watch from the substitutes bench.

The enormous interest in the game caused the kick-off to be delayed several minutes to allow the huge crowd still outside the ground time to enter and as the teams took the field it was estimated that fully 45,000 were packed inside the stadium. They didn't have to wait long for the opening goal. Hibs, who had won the toss and elected to kick up the slope in the first half, moved quickly into attack. After only five minutes a good move was started by Cormack, who passed to Quinn. The diminutive midfield maestro squared the ball high to Stein who appeared well covered by Cooper. The centre forward, however, spotting the goalkeeper slightly off his line, somehow managed to lob the ball over Sprake's head and into the net from the narrowest of angles. The inrushing Charlton, making a valiant attempt to clear, could only help the ball on its way into the net to level the aggregate score.

Soon after, a tremendous strike by Scottish international Eddie Gray from the edge of the box looked a certain goal all the way, but Wilson, diving to his left, spectacularly turned the ball to safety.

A last-gasp tackle by Charlton on Stein at the other end was required to prevent Hibs from going further ahead, and the same player fouled Cormack on the edge of the box after a dangerous run by the inside forward caused panic in the Leeds defence. The free kick against a well organised defence came to nothing.

From then until the interval, the game raged from end to end with several near things in both penalty areas, and the half finished with keeper Wilson narrowly winning a desperate race against Lorimer after a through ball by Charlton created the chance.

Kicking down the famous slope and encouraged by the excited home supporters, Hibs were quickly into their stride after the restart, and a great run by captain Joe Davis had the fans on the edge of their seats. Efforts by Stein and Cormack kept up the pressure on the English side, but a clever back-heeler by Bremner set up a scoring chance for Gray, whose powerful drive was deflected by Stanton for a corner.

Although it had not been an overly dirty match, things came to a head early in the second half as the tension reached both sets of players. Cormack was booked for taking a wild swing at Bremner and a minute later Charlton's name also went into the book after a crude foul on Stein midway inside the Leeds half.

A Scott corner on the left allowed Davis to rifle in a left-foot shot that went narrowly past the post, and with 20 minutes remaining, a great chance for Hibs was scorned when Scott and Stein raced clear on the right. With only centre half Charlton between them and Sprake, Scott's cross-field pass to Stein was hurriedly struck by the unmarked centre and his wild effort went well wide of the target.

Hibs were now in total control and Stein should have scored the winner after a great solo run, but his shot was blasted wildly high over the bar. Then came the controversial late goal that effectively decided the game.

The four step rule, introduced only at the beginning of the season, and it was to cost Hibs dear. Before then goalkeepers could travel limitlessly around the box as long as they bounced the ball every four paces. The new ruling, designed to stop time-wasting, decreed that a goalkeeper could only travel four steps with the ball before releasing it either by kicking or throwing.

With only 15 minutes of the game remaining, Hibs were leading 1-

o on the night and the teams level on aggregate. With extra time looming, keeper Wilson in the top goal received the ball. As he attempted to clear, he appeared to be impeded by Lorimer and forced to take an extra stride. To the amazement of the huge home support, the referee, who had ignored the constant infringement of the new rule by both goalkeepers all evening, immediately awarded Leeds an indirect free kick inside the box despite frantic appeals from the home side. Although in a dangerous position, Hibs' defence had been in total command throughout the game, and it was not expecting too much to assume that they could deal comfortably with one more attack. From the resulting free kick, however, Giles flighted the ball deep into the Hibs goalmouth to find the head of Charlton, who towered above Stanton, to power a header into the net for a cruel winning goal.

Near the end McGraw was booked for a foul on Greenhoff as desperation entered Hibs play and in the final seconds a Quinn corner was missed by Sprake, but the ball flew harmlessly past the goal with no takers. Hibs were out of the Fairs Cup for yet another year.

FINAL SCORE: HIBERNIAN I. LEEDS UNITED I.

FAIRS CUP 3RD ROUND (2ND LEG), EASTER ROAD, WEDNESDAY 10 JANUARY 1968, EASTER ROAD.

HIBERNIAN: WILSON, DUNCAN, DAVIS, STANTON, MADSEN, MCGRAW, SCOTT, QUINN, STEIN, CORMACK, STEVENSON.

LEEDS UNITED: SPRAKE, REANEY, COOPER, BREMNER, CHARLTON, HUNTER, GREENHOFF, LORIMER, JONES, GRAY, GILES.

It had been a brave effort by the Easter Road side, and but for the debatable decision by Welsh official Clive Thomas, refereeing his first Fairs Cup tie, who is to say that Hibs would not have won in extra time – they had finished the game much the stronger side. Awarding a free kick against Wilson in the circumstances had been an over-fussy decision by a referee who was no stranger to controversy – and he would go on to cause outrage in the 1978 World Cup Finals in Argentina by disallowing an injury-time winner for Brazil in the game against Sweden by blowing for full time as the ball from a corner kick was in mid-flight.

The victory meant Leeds would now be paired against Rangers in the next round, winning 2-0 at Elland Road after a dour 0-0 draw at Ibrox, before eventually going on to win the competition by beating Ferencvaros of Hungary in the final, the first of four consecutive victories for English clubs in the tournament. It would be a good season for Leeds, who would also win the League Cup for the first time when defeating Arsenal 1-0 in a dour final at Wembley.

The long-awaited clash of the Greens took place at Easter Road when champions Celtic visited third-placed Hibs on 20 January 1968. What began as a disappointing day for right back Bobby Duncan when he scored an own goal after just two minutes to give the Glasgow side the lead, deteriorated even further when he was carried off three minutes before the interval with a broken leg after a clash with the rugged John Hughes. Having dispossessed the powerful Celtic outside left near the half-way line in front of the main terracing, the defender set off on an attacking run down the slope. Hughes, still on the ground, stretched out a leg for the ball as Duncan passed, but tripped the full back, who suffered a severe fracture when he fell awkwardly. Police were forced to enter the covered enclosure to separate the rival fans immediately after the incident. The game ended in a 2-0 win for Celtic.

Colin Stein collected the second of the three hat-tricks he would score that season in the first round of the Scottish Cup against East Stirling at Firs Park. Stirling, at the time lying fourth-bottom of the Second Division, stunned their more illustrious opponents by taking the lead in the opening minutes, but the three goals by Stein, another from Cormack, and the by now almost obligatory penalty goal from Davis, gave the Greens a 5-3 victory.

The powerful, cavalier style of centre forward Colin Stein, who was already a huge favourite with the fans, had caught the eye of the selectors, and along with teammates Stanton and Cormack, he was selected for the Scotland Under-23 side against England at Hampden, his first international honour. The trio of Hibs players performed reasonably well in a 2-1 defeat that was a personal nightmare for the former Kilmarnock goalkeeper Bobby Ferguson, then with West Ham, who was found sadly lacking at both England goals.

Back in Edinburgh, a McGraw strike, only his fifth of the season, was enough to give the Easter Road side both points in a league game against Dunfermline in Fife. The previous Saturday the Pars had defeated Scottish Cup favourites Celtic in the first round of the competition and this latest result prompted McGraw to claim, somewhat rashly as Cormack had discovered the previous season, that Hibs would win the Scottish Cup.

It didn't take former Easter Road player Derek Whiteford long to prove how ill-advised McGraw's comments had been when he scored the only goal of the game to send Airdrie through to the third round of the competition, and a tie against St Johnstone. In the first half Hibs had been well on top when Whiteford scored against the run of play a few minutes before the interval. Try as they might, Hibs just couldn't breach the Airdrie defence; if anything, it was the Diamonds who looked likelier to add to their lead in the second half and only a couple of fine saves by Wilson prevented a heavier defeat.

Hibs' early exit from the Cup brought a flood of enquiries from English clubs who were keen to sign a number of the Easter Road players, particularly the trio who had represented Scotland in the recent Under-23 international. Posting a hands-off notice via the press, chairman Harrower made a resolute denial that any player was for sale, a statement, however, that would invoke little confidence among the supporters, who had heard it all before.

At the beginning of March the Scottish Cup defeat by Airdrie was avenged when an own goal by future Hibs centre half Jim Black gave the Greens both points in a 2-1 victory. An injury received by Pat Stanton during the game forced the defender's withdrawal from the forthcoming return Under-23 fixture between Scotland and England at Newcastle. Stanton's misfortune, however, was welcome news for his replacement John Blackley, who made his league debut in a 2-0 home win over Dundee, a victory that saw the Edinburgh men well on the way to European qualification. Thomson Allan, deputising for the injured Wilson, once again demonstrated his prowess from the 12-yard spot when he saved a penalty from future Dundee United manager, Jim McLean.

Third in the table, eight points ahead of their nearest challengers with only eight games left to play, suggested that a place in the following season's Fairs Cup competition was a mere formality for the Easter Road side, but Hibs being Hibs, they elected to go down the more difficult route. Only one point was secured from the next four games, which included a humiliating 5-0 defeat by Eddie Turnbull's Aberdeen, a 3-1 loss at home to Rangers, and even worse, a 2-0 reverse by relegation strugglers Morton at Cappielow. With the supporters' nerves starting to fray, consecutive victories over Motherwell, Falkirk, and Clyde, saw the Easter Road European ambitions back on track.

Yet another hat-trick by Colin Stein, his third of the season, gave Hibs a share of the points against Kilmarnock at Easter Road in the final game of the season, but perhaps the most satisfying result of the afternoon as far as the Hibs supporters were concerned was the news from Hampden that Dunfermline had won the Scottish Cup for the second time in eight years at the expense of near neighbours Hearts.

The title race itself had been a close-run thing. At one point Rangers looked capable of halting Celtic's bid for three consecutive championships, but in an exciting climax to the season, the Parkhead side edged ahead to win by two points. Hibs, as expected, finished in third place to clinch a Fairs Cup place yet again, six points ahead of fourth-placed Dunfermline, but a massive 18 behind the champions.

Only Joe Davis and Alan McGraw had featured in all Hibs' 46 games, including the Fairs Cup. The energetic Colin Stein had finished the season as Hibs' top goalscorer with 29 goals, 21 of them in the league, 12 ahead of the next best Peter Cormack and the ever-reliable Joe Davis who had scored 11 in all competitions, all of them from the penalty spot. His exciting, all-action displays had made Colin Stein one of the hottest prospects in Scotland and already it seemed certain that his stay at Easter Road would be brief. While his 38 goals in 63 league games fell far short of the impressive scoring rate of Joe Baker just a few years before, it could still be considered a worthwhile total and stood comparison with any other Scottish player at that time.

Once again there were rumours that UEFA would be taking over the running of the Fairs Cup at the start of the following season and that the new organisers would possibly limit the number of entries to one from each country. In England, Football League secretary Alan Hardaker stated that if this were indeed to be the case, then possibly a British League could be formed. This would allow the sides that failed to qualify for a European tournament to take part in a prestigious alternative competition featuring perhaps the top half-dozen clubs from both Scotland and England. As it would turn out, Hardaker's ambitious proposal was put on ice after it was learned that the status quo would continue the following season.

During the season just ended, John Madsen had revealed that he was homesick and wished to return to his native Denmark to resume his career as an architect. Despite warnings from the club, immediately after the last game of the season the centre half packed his bags and left for home. As he was still a contracted player at Easter Road, Madsen's actions resulted in his subsequent suspension from the game, effectively a *sine die* ban.

8

The First £100,000 Transfer
and League Cup Final Disappointment
1968–69

INSPIRED BY THE SUCCESS of the Hibs Supporters Club at Sunnyside, the football club now decided to build their own clubrooms in the car park at the rear of the main terracing. Work started in mid-July 1968 and it was expected that the premises would be up and running before the turn of the year. To be called simply 'The Hibernian', the clubrooms would be run under the auspices of the Development Club with all profits going directly to the football club to help fund ground improvements. The trustees included former Hibs goalkeeper Tommy Younger, who took on the role of secretary. The target of the ambitious project was to attract an initial membership of 1,200, each paying an annual subscription of 5/-. Designed to accommodate around 800, it would comprise the usual lounge and games room plus a function hall. As well as the normal travel club whose main aim would be to make it easier for supporters to travel to away games, the go-ahead committee intended to book star personalities for regular cabaret evenings, which it was hoped would make it one of the best venues of its kind in the city.

On the playing front, the former Hearts and Celtic defender Chris Shevlane, who only months before had announced his retirement from the game because of injury, took his place among the 28 players who assembled for the first day of pre-season training at Seafield. Freed by Hearts after a long fitness battle, Shevlane had been quickly snapped up by Celtic. Unfortunately, his injury failed to clear up properly at Parkhead, the full back making only a couple of appearances for the first team, and he had decided to retire from the game. Somewhat surprisingly, after a short spell on the sidelines, he felt well enough to resume his playing career, and after medical advice, had signed on at Easter Road. Also meeting his new colleagues for the first time was a 17-year-old Alex Cropley, an outside left from Edina Hibs. Cropley would make his first team breakthrough in the coming season, and would have a huge part to play in the story of Hibernian in the coming years. Edina Hibs were a recently formed juvenile side attached to and funded by the Hibs Supporters Association with the aim of attracting young talent for Easter Road. Cropley became one of the first players to make the breakthrough from its ranks.

One familiar face missing from the first day of training was that of John Fraser. Signed from Edinburgh Thistle 14 years before, Fraser, just one of the many players who had been seen as a possible replacement for the legendary

Gordon Smith, had spent most of the previous season in the reserves, and he had now decided to accept the post of player-coach at Stenhousemuir.

During the summer Peter Cormack had rejected all attempts by the Easter Road management to persuade him to sign a new contract, although he was still a registered player by virtue of the 12 months' extension clause in his contract. By now an established Scottish International, Cormack had become unsettled after watching a succession of teammates moving on to better things in England, and now he too was keen to try his luck down south.

As a warm-up to a new season, friendly fixtures were arranged against Newcastle United and Birmingham City. Shevlane, making his first appearance in a Hibs jersey, scored the winner for Newcastle when his attempted headed clearance beat his own goalkeeper late in the game. Ex-Hibs players Jim Scott and John McNamee had lined up for Newcastle against their former colleagues.

Hibs fared much better three days later when they defeated 2-0 a Birmingham City side that included future Hibs signing Jim Herriot, their first victory in England for several years. Somewhat unlucky to lose against the Magpies, Hibs turned on the style in Birmingham, and both the decisive result and performance enhanced the confidence of the Easter Road players for an extended run in the League Cup.

With Celtic and Rangers both in the same group, a leading Glasgow bookmaker had made Hibs red-hot 3-1 favourites to qualify for the quarter-finals of the competition and possibly go all the way to the final. As usual, things failed to go according to plan when St Johnstone inflicted a first-day defeat on hapless Hibs at Easter Road, their first opening day reverse for six years, to leave them stranded at the foot of the table. To compound a day of misery for the supporters, Peter Cormack limped off at the interval and the usually reliable Joe Davis missed a second-half penalty. Cormack would miss four games but by the time he had recovered enough to return to action for the last section game at Brockville, Hibs would already have progressed into the quarter-finals. At Brockville Cormack might well have been facing former Hibs player Johnny McLeod. An earlier audacious bid by Falkirk to sign the former Easter Road star had failed when they were unable to meet the players wage demands. McLeod would sign for Belgian side FC Mechelen instead.

In a 2-2 draw with St Johnstone in Perth, Pat Stanton was ordered off for the first time in his senior career when he retaliated after being fouled. Asked for his name by referee 'Tiny' Wharton, the still angry Stanton cheekily replied, 'It's Pat. That's P-A-T to you.' Wharton replying immediately: 'OK smart alec, can you spell ta -ta?'

Four days after Stanton's dismissal both Pat Quinn and Davie Sneddon of Raith Rovers were sent off at Easter Road for violent conduct. Quinn had fouled the former Kilmarnock player directly in front of the tunnel, an action that brought immediate retaliation from Sneddon. For several seconds a punch-up that would not have disgraced a lightweight boxing contest ensued, before referee Henderson called a halt to proceedings, counting out both contestants by ordering them to the dressing rooms.

The continuing impressive form of Colin Stein had earned the Hibs striker a place on the bench in the Scottish League side to face the League of Ireland at Dalymount Park. In a double honour for the club, physiotherapist Tom McNiven was once again selected as part of the backroom set-up. Both Willie and Tom Callaghan of Dunfermline had also been selected, making them the first brothers to be selected for Scotland since Davie Shaw of Hibs and Jock of Rangers had faced Switzerland 20 years before. Unfortunately for the Dunfermline player, Willie Callaghan was forced to withdraw because of injury and Pat Stanton was called into the side as his replacement.

In the opening league fixture against Hearts, former Hibs favourite Willie Hamilton was allowed to control the middle of the park as his side went on the rampage at Easter Road. Leading by a Stanton goal at the interval, Hibs never quite recaptured their first-half form and Hearts ran out deserving 3-1 winners.

In what was seen as an easy passage into the League Cup semi-finals, goals from Stein, Stevenson, Marinello and another from Davis from the penalty spot were thought to be more than enough to see off the threat of Second Division East Fife at Bayview. Although Nelson managed to pull one back for the stuffy underdogs, with the return leg at Easter Road still to come, progress into the semi-final and a probable meeting with Dundee, now seemed a mere formality.

In the Fairs Cup Hibs had been drawn against Olympia from Ljubljana, rekindling bitter memories of the trip to Yugoslavia seven years before, when they had been soundly beaten by Red Star in Belgrade. Before the tie could take place, on 21 August 1968, the political climate in Eastern Europe was destabilised when Russia invaded Czechoslovakia. The decision was made that there would be a new draw for all the European competitions, but in the end the revised ballot did not affect either the Hibs versus Olympia tie or the Rangers versus Vojvodina game, as Yugoslavia was not likely to be embroiled in the conflict. The original referee for the first game in Yugoslavia, however, became an early casualty when the Czech earmarked to take control was hurriedly withdrawn to be replaced by an official from Austria.

On the eve of departure to Yugoslavia, the chance of a confidence-boosting win against struggling Raith Rovers at Kirkcaldy hit the buffers when a quite abysmal performance ended in the Fifers winning comfortably, a result that saw Hibs plummet to second-bottom of the table as one of only three sides in the country without a solitary league point. During the game Colin Stein had become the third Hibs player to be dismissed in as many weeks when he was sent off in the first half for an offence that nowadays would be regarded as trivial. After being fouled by a Raith player, the referee overheard the Hibs centre forward swearing, either at his opponent or at the official who had refused to award a foul in Stein's favour. The referee refused to listen to Stein's pleas of innocence and he made the long walk to the tunnel.

Formed at the end of the Second World War, Olympia was one of the newest sides in Europe. Having had the misfortune to be drawn against the eventual winners Ferencvaros of Hungary in the first round in 1964-65, losing 6-3 on aggregate, this was their second venture into the Fairs Cup.

Like their Scottish counterparts, they had not made the best of starts to the season winning only two and drawing one of their five games so far, and were reputedly on a bonus of £50 per man to win the home leg. With the monthly wage in Yugoslavia around £15 per month at that time, the bonus represented a healthy incentive.

The Bezigrad Stadium itself was peculiar in that it was completely bereft of cover except for a tiny press box and a house-like structure built on stilts behind one of the goals that accommodated the directors and guests. A running track encircled the pitch, separating the players from the 4,000 or so home supporters who had paid anything from 3/- to 10/- for the privilege of being soaked to the skin by the heavy rain that had fallen since morning.

Manager Shankly included 17-year-old Peter Marinello, who would be making his European debut, in the party of 16 players, backroom staff and directors that would make the trip to Yugoslavia.

There had been yet another change to the rules. Now, three substitutes would be allowed to be stripped, although only two could be used.

A 3-0 victory in what was the 100th Fairs Cup tie involving a Scottish side, was Hibs' first away win in Europe since defeating Utrecht in 1962, and their biggest away success in the 15 European ties played since overcoming Rot Weiss 4-0 in 1955. It guaranteed, barring a disaster, entry into the second-round draw.

The heavy rain that had fallen steadily all day developed into a thunderstorm as the teams took the field, but the atrocious conditions failed to prevent Hibs from turning in as good a performance as they had ever produced in an away tie in Europe.

Starting the match cautiously, the Greens conceded a number of early corners that produced little in the way of danger and soon found the measure of their opponents. With the trickery and pace of Marinello causing problems on the wing from the opening whistle, the majority of the damage was done in a three-minute spell on the half-hour mark. After the outside right had been blatantly fouled on the edge of the box, Quinn's measured free kick found Stevenson who blasted the ball into the net. Three minutes later, Stein took advantage of a miskick by Nicolik in midfield to wrong-foot the keeper before calmly stroking the ball into the net for his fourth goal in five European matches, making the home supporters' hearts as heavy as the falling rain.

After the interval, inspired by the three-man midfield of Quinn, Stanton and Cormack, Hibs took up where they had left off with most of the play concentrated around the Olympia penalty area. Eight minutes into the half, goalkeeper Skulj was carried off after a collision with an opponent and was replaced by reserve keeper Zabjek.

With 19 minutes remaining, Marinello, who had been involved in both first-half goals, sent over a right-wing cross from a tight angle. Centre half

Soskic, in trying to clear the danger, headed past his own keeper, and the part-timers saw their hopes of the £50 bonus completely disappear. The youngster, who was denied a stonewall penalty when he was pulled off the ball in the second half, could feel well satisfied with his performance in his first ever European outing, as could Colin Stein, whose energetic, bustling style upset the home defence throughout the entire 90 minutes.

FINAL SCORE: OLYMPIA 0. HIBERNIAN 3.

FAIRS CUP 1ST ROUND (1ST LEG), WEDNESDAY 18 SEPTEMBER 1968, BEZIGRAD STADIUM.
HIBERNIAN: WILSON, SHEVLANE, DAVIS, BLACKLEY, COUSIN, STANTON, MARINELLO, QUINN, STEIN, CORMACK, STEVENSON.

After the recent run of poor results, the win was just the tonic the players had needed. The home officials were lavish in their praise of the Scottish side. Manager Konjevod, a former Yugoslavian international, highlighted Peter Cormack as the man of the match, but admitted that, 'The entire Hibs were the absolute masters of a game played in terrible conditions.'

Of the eight British and Irish sides that had been in European action that same evening, only Hibs had emerged with a victory. The 1967 European Cup winners Celtic and the 1966 Fairs Cup finalists Liverpool, both lost, while the mighty Leeds could only manage to scrape a draw against Standard Liège in Belgium. At the airport for the flight home, there was a chance encounter with Fiorentina's manager Bruno Pesalo, who had been in charge of Napoli during the 5-0 rout at Easter Road the previous season. With his side now looking likely to qualify for the next round after their away draw with Dynamo Zagreb the previous evening, an enquiry from the Scottish media asking if he would fancy meeting Hibs in the next round, elicited the curt reply, 'No thank you, once was enough.'

A narrow 2-1 win against plucky Second Division East Fife in the return leg of the League Cup at Easter Road gave Hibs a 6-2 overall aggregate and, as expected, a passage through to the last four of the competition and a meeting with Dundee at Tynecastle. But in the championship things were not going so smoothly. A 2-1 defeat by Partick Thistle in Glasgow saw the visitors slip to 17th place in the table, or second-bottom, and again the alarm bells were ringing.

Englishman Roy Baines made his first appearance in goal for Hibs' reserves in the corresponding fixture in Edinburgh the same afternoon. The former Derby County player had spent a short spell with Celtic and had initially been offered a month's trial at Easter Road. Several impressive performances for the second string would soon see the agreement extended at least until the end of the season.

Meanwhile, the Hibs Supporters Association had decided to formally recognise the most outstanding performer of the season. It turned out to be a one-horse race, with Pat Stanton the unanimous choice of all the branches.

He became the first recipient of the Player of the Year award, presented by Association chairman Jimmy McClory at a function to celebrate the occasion in the social club. A large crowd watched the presentation to an extremely popular player, including many of his current teammates, and the evening proved so successful that it had been decided to make the award an annual feature.

Because of Hibs' commanding lead from the first game, most observers were of the opinion that the return leg of the Fairs Cup tie against Olympia would be a mere formality, but Shankly thought otherwise. Since their impressive performance in Yugoslavia, Hibs had struggled to regain their early season form, while their opponents had put together a rich run of results. The home side's chances of qualifying for the next round were reinforced, however, when it was discovered that several regular Olympia players would be missing, including Skoric, whose fear of flying prevented him from travelling with his teammates. Outside left Spasojevic would also be missing. Although he had not been booked in the first game, he had been warned by the referee after a particularly nasty kick at Peter Marinello and, commendably, had been suspended by the club for his unsporting behaviour.

Goalkeeper Borut Skulj, who had been carried off injured in the first leg and was still struggling to regain full fitness, had been surprised to learn that both he and his bride of only seven days were being flown to Edinburgh on an all-expenses-paid honeymoon trip as a wedding present from the club. Although travelling with the official party, and obviously attending the game, the pair were no doubt glad to learn that they had been booked into separate accommodation.

With a conviction that the tie could still be salvaged, Olympia stormed into attack from the start and demonstrated their intent by opening the scoring inside four minutes after the tricky Popivoda ended a mazy run from his own half, leaving several Hibs defenders floundering in his wake before steering the ball past Wilson. For a while the technically gifted Slavs were well on top, but Hibs gradually clawed their way back into the game and it was only then that a different side to the Yugoslavian team came out. Olympia resorted to stop-at-nothing tactics and were lucky to survive a penalty claim after Stevenson was sent crashing inside the box. They proceeded to kick and hack, with Marinello, Cormack and Stevenson the main targets. Stevenson in particular was proving a handful, but try as they might the home side could not secure the vital goal that would surely finish the tie.

The turning point came in the 63rd minute when a Marinello cross from the right was handled by Rogic in the penalty area leaving the referee with no option but to award a penalty. The Slavs hotly disagreed with the decision, and the proceedings were held up for several minutes as the official struggled to regain control of the situation while being jostled by a horde of angry Olympia players. Order was eventually restored, and the composed Davis slotted the ball past Zabjek to give Hibs an equalising goal on the night and a place in the next round.

The goal was the catalyst for all hell to break loose and three minutes later, Jovanovic was ordered off after a vicious foul on Marinello. No sooner had the Olympia player left the field, than Stevenson was tripped on the edge of the box, and much to the delight of the 11,000 crowd, referee Russell again had no hesitation in pointing to the spot, the home side's second penalty inside three minutes. Once again, after a few minutes' delay while the Slavs argued with the referee, Davis calmly drove home the spot kick, giving Hibs an overall 5-1 lead.

FINAL SCORE: HIBERNIAN 2. OLYMPIA 1.

FAIRS CUP 1ST ROUND (2ND LEG), WEDNESDAY 2 OCTOBER 1968, EASTER ROAD.
HIBERNIAN: WILSON, SHEVLANE, DAVIS, BLACKLEY, COUSIN, STANTON, MARINELLO, QUINN, STEIN, CORMACK, STEVENSON.

Although obviously delighted to be through to the next round, Hibs' form had again been erratic and of major concern to the manager, although undoubtedly this had been due in some part to the desperate measures of their opponents.

At Easter Road on the Saturday, inspired by Pat Stanton, playing in the unfamiliar centre half position, an emphatic 5-1 victory over Airdrie in front of a disappointingly small crowd of just over 5,000 set Hibs up nicely for the forthcoming League Cup semi-final against Dundee at Tynecastle. The recalled Alec Scott, who had not featured in the first team since losing his place to Peter Marinello at the start of the season, took advantage of his reinstatement to score his first goal for the club when he first timed a tremendous drive past future Hibs goalkeeper Roddy McKenzie from 20 yards. Davis had opened the scoring early on with his third goal from the spot in two games before the roof fell in on poor Airdrie who rarely threatened throughout the 90 minutes, their consolation goal coming in the final seconds of the match. John Blackley, now well on the way to establishing himself in the first team, was injured in the second half to be replaced by Cousin, and was now considered a doubtful starter for the semi-final just four days later.

Tynecastle had not proved a particularly happy hunting ground for Hibs in cup semi-finals. Of the six League and Scottish Cup ties played on the ground since the war, five had ended in defeat, with a solitary victory against Queen of the South in 1950. Regardless of Hibs' poor record at the ground, Dundee themselves were decidedly unhappy at the choice of venue. Their possibly justified complaint that Tynecastle was almost a home game for Hibs and that there was sure to be larger support from Edinburgh, was ignored and Tynecastle it was. As expected, Blackley missed the game, his place being taken by part-time school teacher Alan Cousin. Bidding to make only their second appearance in a League Cup Final, there was an early set-back for Hibs when George McLean opened the scoring for Dundee after only six minutes to silence the huge vocal Hibs support among the 20,000 crowd inside Tynecastle at the start. The joy of the Tayside fans, however, was short-lived, and within 30 seconds the sides were level when Stein beat goalkeeper Donaldson with a volley.

Midway through the second half of a real blood and thunder cup-tie that produced numerous near things at both ends, Jimmy O'Rourke replaced Pat Quinn who had taken a knock. With their substitute used, Alan McGraw was stretchered off with little more than 20 minutes remaining. Hibs battled on with only ten men. Megraw's injury had looked so severe that there seemed little chance of the player returning to the action, which left his side to face the daunting prospect of playing 30 minutes of extra time a man short. Deciding he could be of nuisance value if nothing else, McGraw returned to the fray near the end of the game sporting a huge bandage on his injured knee. His re-appearance was met by a huge roar of approval from the Hibs fans. With just seconds of normal time left to play and with extra time looming, Hibs won a corner on the left. Eric Stevenson sent over a dangerous in-swinging cross that was twice blocked on the goal line. Somehow the heroic McGraw, who looked incapable of movement, lunged forward to force the ball over the goal line to send Hibs through to face Celtic in the final.

The Dundee side that night contained several players with past or future Easter Road connections. Centre half Jim Easton had been a regular at Easter Road until his transfer to Dens in 1964. Lining up alongside Easton was fervent Hibs fan George Stewart who would become a popular defender at the club during the Turnbull years. Goalkeeper Donaldson would spend a short spell on the payroll during the '70s, with inside forward Jocky Scott acting as assistant manager to Alex Miller in the 1990s.

HIBERNIAN: WILSON, SHEVLANE, DAVIS, COUSIN, STANTON, MCGRAW, SCOTT, QUINN, STEIN, CORMACK, AND STEVENSON. SUB: O'ROURKE.

DUNDEE: DONALDSON, WILSON, HOUSTON, MURRAY, EASTON, STEWART, CAMPBELL, MCLEAN, (S.) WILSON, SCOTT, BRYCE. SUB: SELWAY.

Four points from the following three matches still left Hibs hovering in a mid-table position. The inconsistency that had blighted a major part of their season had not been helped by the absence of John Madsen in defence, and it was welcome news that the centre half had had a change of heart and would be returning to the club. Since breaking his contract and walking out of Easter Road to return to Denmark at the end of the previous season, Madsen had been unable to sign for any other side because of the suspension imposed by UEFA. Obviously well short of match fitness, it would be some time before the Dane could even be considered for a place in the first team. In his absence, Alan Cousin had proved a more than able deputy, as had Pat Stanton who had performed exceptionally well at centre half in the Tynecastle semi-final, but the expertise of both players in other areas, particularly the inspiration of Stanton in the centre of midfield, had been badly missed.

The splendid form of the wholehearted Colin Stein meant that he could not be held back much longer and he joined the long list of full internationals supplied by the club throughout the years when he was selected at centre forward in Scotland's 1-0 win over Denmark in Copenhagen in October. Future Hibs goalkeeper Jim Herriot also made his debut that evening. Stein's teammate Peter Cormack came on as a second-half replacement for McCalliog, while Stanton had to settle for a place on the sidelines.

The following Monday, just five days before Hibs were due to face Celtic in the rearranged League Cup Final, Colin Stein's joy at making his full international debut was tempered by the news that he had been suspended for ten days as a result of his dismissal against Raith Rovers in September. He was devastated to learn that he would miss the Cup Final. Although he was not to know it at the time, Stein had already played his last game for Hibs in the 1-0 win against Kilmarnock the previous Saturday.

Semi-final hero Alan McGraw had fought a desperate battle to be fit for the final after his injury at Tynecastle, but it was all for nothing when a fire swept through Hampden in the early hours of the Tuesday morning, just four days before the big game. Around 2,000 seats were destroyed in the same section of the stand that had been badly damaged by fire in 1946. As well as extensive damage to the seating area, the building had also suffered widespread internal damage that rendered the dressing rooms, administration offices and a restaurant unusable and in the circumstances, there was no other option but to postpone the Cup Final.

By a remarkable coincidence, part of the Main Stand at Ibrox was also badly damaged by fire the following morning, although any connection between these incidents was immediately dismissed by the Glasgow Police.

John Madsen made his long-awaited return to Scotland on Tuesday 29 October 1968. That same day the news broke that Everton had offered Hibs £90,000 for Colin Stein, an enormous sum at the time. Initial talks between both parties that evening had been productive, but both the Everton manager Harry Catterick and the Hibs directors were incensed to discover later that the move was off. According to Catterick, the player had seemed satisfied with the terms that had been offered, believed to be £5,000 per annum including bonuses with a £4,500 signing-on fee and a house, but had asked for time to think it over. Stein had come back demanding a wage far in excess of any other player at Goodison, which was obviously unacceptable to the English club, who were now convinced that the player had been approached by another club in the interim. Early the following morning, Rangers – who were determined to put an end to Celtic's recent domination of the championship, and had recently failed in an attempt to sign Bobby Hope from West Bromwich Albion for £90,000, and were rumoured to be interested in Chelsea's Charlie Cooke – offered Hibs £100,000 for Stein. The deal was completed on the Thursday afternoon against the wishes of a furious Bob Shankly, and Stein, who confessed to having achieved a boyhood dream by signing for the Ibrox side, became the first £100,000 transfer between two Scottish clubs, and Rangers' first big-money signing since paying Dunfermline £65,000 for Alex Ferguson in 1967. Ferguson or Alec Smith had been suggested as part of the deal, but this was dismissed out of hand by Harrower and the deal concluded on a strictly cash only basis. Somewhat surprisingly, Stein had only become a centre forward by accident. Joining junior side Whitburn as a left back from Broxburn Strollers, he had played up front in a few practice games, so discovering his talent for scoring goals and he had been signed by Hibs after only a few games at centre forward for the West Lothian side.

A disillusioned Bob Shankly refused even to discuss the Stein move, and he would shortly resign over the sale, unhappy at the direction the club was taking. Persuaded by the chairman to withdraw his resignation, things would never be quite the same again for Shankly at Easter Road.

Several record books list Colin Stein as a Rangers player when he won his first full Scottish cap. However, his debut against Denmark took place on 16 October 1968 while he was still a Hibs player, his signing for the Ibrox side talking place 15 days later.

The following Saturday, Alan McGraw replaced Stein in a Hibs side that made its way to Paisley, with young Ian Wilkinson making his first-team debut at centre half. At that time St Mirren were the only undefeated side in Britain and held the meanest defensive record in the country. Undoubtedly missing the attacking thrust of Stein, the Edinburgh side were generally second-best and were well beaten in the end. The 3-0 win was St Mirren's first victory against Hibs in the previous 18 matches between the sides. That same afternoon Colin Stein began his Ibrox career in spectacular fashion, scoring three times inside four minutes in Rangers' 6-0 victory over Arbroath.

Things would get even better for the Phillipstoun-born player just seven days later when he scored another hat-trick, this time against his former Easter Road colleagues at Ibrox as Rangers ran out convincing 6-1 winners. Hibs' solitary goal was scored by Joe McBride, who had been signed from Celtic only in midweek for a bargain £15,000. Man-of-many-clubs McBride, who had collected two full and four league caps during his time at Parkhead, had been Jock Stein's first signing for Celtic in June 1965, for the grand sum of £27,000 from Motherwell, and was a prolific goalscorer of proven ability. In 1966 he had scored 33 goals for Celtic by Christmas, before picking up the cartilage injury that would keep him out of football for the rest of that season, including Celtic's historic European Cup win in May 1967. Unable to command a regular place in the Celtic first team since his return to full fitness, McBride saw the move to Easter Road as the perfect kick-start to his career. Although he had faced the Ibrox side on numerous occasions during his stints with Kilmarnock, Motherwell, Partick Thistle and Celtic, McBride's goal in the 6-1 defeat was his first ever against Rangers. Cormack, who had been withdrawn during the 1-1 draw with Dundee United two weeks before with a suspected dislocated shoulder and torn ligaments, made a surprise return to the side at Ibrox, but even he could do little to stem the blue-shirted tide.

The dejected Hibs fans who tuned in to the radio as they made the long journey back from Glasgow that bleak Saturday evening would have been even more depressed to hear former Arsenal player Don Roper recall one of his most memorable games, the 7-1 floodlit friendly victory over Hibs in 1952 when he had scored five of the goals, one direct from a corner.

McBride made his home debut for Hibs against Lokomotive Leipzig in the Fairs Cup four days after the Ibrox fiasco. The East German side were in the middle of a bad run. Of the 13 games played so far, they had managed to win just two, losing eight, but perhaps of even more heartening news for Hibs was the fact that they had failed to score in seven.

New signing Joe McBride celebrated his home debut by scoring a first-half hat-trick against an unimpressive Leipzig side, the first ever treble by a Hibs player in a competitive European match. The rugged centre forward, who had scored four times for Celtic against Hibs on his last appearance at Easter Road, could easily have equalled that tally but for a second-half strike that was ruled out by the Swiss referee. The home side survived an early scare when Stanton was on the spot to clear off the line with Wilson beaten, but just a few minutes later McBride scored his first after a gift from keeper Nauert, who dropped the ball at the centre forward's feet, leaving him the simplest of tasks to open the scoring. The goal meant that the former Celtic striker had now scored on his debut in all three European competitions.

Hibs' second goal, after 15 minutes, was an absolute beauty. Racing up the right flank, Scott sent over a brilliantly measured cross that was caught perfectly by the inrushing McBride, whose header flashed into the net past the helpless keeper. It was Hibs 50th goal in the Fairs Cup and their 59th overall in Europe.

Just seconds before the interval, McBride ended a Stevenson move when he smashed a left-footed shot into the net for his hat-trick.

Midway through the second half, Naumann pulled one back for Lokomotive from a suspiciously offside-looking position to give the Germans some hope in the return leg. Near the end of the game, Alec Scott was sent off for lashing out in retaliation after being fouled by two Locomotive players. He would now miss the return leg in Germany.

McBride thought he had scored a fourth, but his delight quickly turned to despair when the Swiss official ruled it offside. Worse was to come. A few minutes later O'Rourke was blatantly fouled inside the area, but the frantic appeals by the Hibs players was waved aside by the referee, who seemed to be the only person in the stadium who didn't think it was a penalty. His quite incredible decision was met by howls of derision from the Hibs support.

Before the game, the Swiss official had announced that he would be retiring at the end of the season, and on this performance, this would not be a minute too soon as far as the majority of the Hibs fans inside Easter Road were concerned.

FINAL SCORE: HIBERNIAN 3. LOKOMOTIVE LEIPZIG 1.

FAIRS CUP 2ND ROUND (1ST LEG), WEDNESDAY 13 NOVEMBER 1968, EASTER ROAD.
HIBERNIAN: WILSON, SHEVLANE, DAVIS, COUSIN, STANTON, O'ROURKE, SCOTT, QUINN, MCBRIDE, GRANT, STEVENSON.

It did not take McBride long to become a firm favourite with the fans and he followed up his three goals on the Wednesday by going one better on his home league debut as Hibs demolished Morton 5-0 a few days later. A Greenock side that featured future Hibs player Joe Harper, who had recently been re-signed from Huddersfield, and former Hib George McNeil, just had no answer to McBride's spectacular shooting power. The prolific goalscorer had now scored eight in his first three games for the club.

A delay in London as Hibs made their way to Leipzig for the return leg of the Fairs Cup meant an overnight stay in Amsterdam, with more bad weather the following day delaying the journey even further. The situation prompted Stewart Brown of the *Edinburgh Evening News*, who was travelling with the team, to wonder why Hibs had not chartered an aircraft for the trip to East Germany. By that time the private chartering of an aircraft had become a fairly normal method of travel for football clubs. Rangers and Celtic had regularly hired their own plane for their European trips, as had Dunfermline and Dundee in the past. A further advantage, one that was yet to be discovered by Hibs, was that part of the cost could be offset to a degree by allowing supporters to travel with the official party.

The eventful trip to Leipzig involved four different flights. Edinburgh to London and then on to Amsterdam, before flying to East Berlin then a further internal flight, a long and exhausting journey that had originally been expected to take just eight hours. The travel-weary party finally arrived at their destination 24 hours behind schedule, the marathon excursion ending with a 120-mile coach journey.

Lokomotive desperately needed an early goal if they were to have any hope of overturning the first-leg result, but when an early goal did come, it fell to Hibs.

Re-called keeper Friese, struggling to collect a Stevenson cross in the third minute, dropped the ball at the feet of Grant who obligingly gave his side a four-goal overall advantage. It was Grant's first European goal, his first strike since January, and with it the heads of the Lokomotive players visibly dropped.

Forced to concede numerous corners in the early stages of the game, which never at any time looked likely to lead to a goal, it was the visitors who came nearest to scoring again when McBride set Grant up with another great chance only for the youngster to be dispossessed as he was about to shoot.

Using the Roma ploy of McBride and Grant switching jerseys to confuse the East German defenders, the subterfuge paid off and with a bit of luck the duo might well have scored several goals between them.

Five minutes before half time, Frenzel had the ball in the net for Leipzig, but the goal was disallowed for a foul on keeper Wilson who required treatment after the incident.

In the second half, the bugles and horns of the 10,000 mostly German fans inside the vast ghostlike 120,000 capacity stadium, failed to inspire an insipid home side whose play by now had become vastly inferior to that of

Hibs, and the visitors really should have added to their tally, particularly when Cormack hit the post late in the game.

There was to be no more scoring, and for the first time since his move to Edinburgh, McBride, who had come in for more than his fair share of attention from the rugged Leipzig defenders, both on and off the ball throughout the 90 minutes, failed to register on the scoresheet.

FINAL SCORE: LOKOMOTIVE LEIPZIG 0. HIBERNIAN 1.

FAIRS CUP 2ND ROUND (2ND LEG), WEDNESDAY 20 NOVEMBER 1968, CENTRAL STADIUM.

HIBERNIAN: WILSON, SHEVLANE, DAVIS, COUSIN, STANTON, O'ROURKE, QUINN, CORMACK, GRANT, MCBRIDE, STEVENSON.

The 4-1 aggregate win was Hibs' fourth successive victory on the continent, equalling their best ever sequence in European competition. Not since overcoming Copenhagen and Utrecht in both legs of the Fairs Cup in 1962 had they managed to achieve the feat.

It was around this time that Willie Hunter was signed from American side Detriot Cougars, teaming up once again with former Motherwell colleagues Pat Quinn and Joe McBride. A prodigious talent, Hunter had been an integral member of the legendary Fir Park Ancel Babes during the late '50s. The Abbeyhill-born Hibs supporter had won seven full and league caps before deciding to try his luck in the States. Although only 29, Hunter was possibly past his best, and would feature in the first team only rarely before joining South African side Helenic in 1970 followed by a move to Cape Town City.

At that year's AGM, it was revealed that a loss of almost £5,000 had been made in the previous financial year, although this figure did not include the sale of Colin Stein, which fell outside that accounting period. With all available funds required to finance the building of the new social club, there had been no input from the Development Club. Hibs themselves had benefited to the tune of £12,000 from the scheme the previous year, and it was projected that within a few years, profits from the social club would outdo even this figure. During the past 12 months, £135,000 had been expended on wages, transfer fees and administration costs, and although income from gate receipts and all other avenues had risen from £102,000 the season before to £132,000, the figures still represented a shortfall being recorded for a second successive year.

At the end of the month a quite amazing battle took place at Easter Road between the European Cup holders Celtic and tenth-placed Hibs. The first half was evenly contested and both sides left the field level at the interval with goalscorer supreme Joe McBride having cancelled out an earlier penalty goal by Gemmell. Most of the drama came late in the match. In an end-to-end game Joe Davis gave Hibs the lead from the penalty spot with just 15 minutes remaining. The astute Jock Stein now switched the rugged John Hughes into the middle of the park, and Alan Cousin, who had earlier seemed so assured, had no answer to the power and aggression of the giant forward as the visitors scored four in the remaining few minutes to power themselves to a 5-2 victory against a Hibs side, who until the late scoring burst had looked every bit the equal of the champions.

There was yet another high-scoring game seven days later against Aberdeen at Pittodrie, but this time with the result in Hibs' favour. In an attempt to stabilise the centre of the defence after the heavy defeat the previous Saturday, centre half John Madsen, who had been training twice a day since arriving back in Edinburgh several weeks before, was included in the side for the first time since his return and he helped his colleagues to an emphatic 6-2 victory; 5-1 ahead at the interval, the game was a personal triumph for Peter Cormack who scored his first hat-trick in over four years, staking a strong claim for inclusion in the Scotland side to face Cyprus in midweek.

The game, however, was a personal disaster for Aberdeen goalkeeper Bobby Clark whose involvement in several of the goals would not have endeared him to manager Eddie Turnbull. That same afternoon at Easter Road, full back Bobby Duncan was making his first appearance since breaking his leg against Celtic 11 months before, in the reserves' 3-1 victory over the Dons' second team.

In the third round of the Fairs Cup, Hibs had been handed an unenviable task when they were drawn against the previous year's Cup Winners' Cup finalists, SC Hamburg. Formed in 1887 and the oldest club in Germany, Hamburg could boast no fewer than six internationals in their line-up, including the legendary Uwe Seeler, who had captained West Germany in the 1966 World Cup Final against England at Wembley, and Willie Schultz, who only a few weeks before had played for the Rest of the World against Brazil in Rio de Janeiro. Shultz, however, was still in South America with the international side and would miss the first leg in Germany.

Hamburg had also made a poor start to their domestic season, but like Hibs had gradually improved in form and by the halfway stage of the West German championship they lay in second-place in the table. The game against Hibs would be their 30th in Europe, but only their third in the Fairs Cup, their previous inter-continental excursions having been in the European Cup, and Cup Winners' competitions. At that time they were still to lose at home in European matches with 11 victories and three draws in the 14 games played. There was little doubt that they would be extremely difficult opponents for Hibs, making their 29th appearance in the Fairs Cup.

A heavy flurry of snow the day before the match had threatened to cancel the game, but on the day itself the problem had receded. Another worry was that the thick blanket of fog that lingered over the city all day would make it impossible for the spectators to see much of the action. As evening fell the fog had still not lifted and play would have proved impossible, but luckily, just before kick-off, the billowing fog lifted sufficiently to enable the match to begin. At the start of the game the spectators on either side found it impossible to identify players on the opposite side of the ground, with the goalkeepers experiencing great difficulty in seeing anything over the halfway line. To make matters worse, the white-shirted Hamburg players were doubly difficult to distinguish in the mist. Had this been a domestic game, in all probability it would have been postponed.

Pat Stanton recalls the story of how, as the Hibs team bus drew up outside the Volkspark Stadium a few hours before the game, a solitary and rather forlorn looking figure sporting a green and white scarf was spotted on the other side of the street watching the players through the gathering mist as they disembarked from the bus (this was in the days before it became the norm for fans to travel abroad). Stewart Brown of the *Edinburgh Evening News* went over to question the solitary traveller, who suddenly snapped, 'Wait a minute, you're not going to write about this in the *Evening News*, are you?' When Brown replied that indeed he was, the fan snapped back: 'F*** off, the wife thinks I'm up in the north of Scotland, working.'

Watched by fewer than 7,000 spectators, the teams took the field at the Volkspark Stadium led by a piper from the Royal Scots, who were stationed in Germany at the time. The fog made the players appear as ghostly silhouettes as they lined up on a pitch hardened by a severe ground frost.

Hamburg took the lead as early as the fifth minute when good play between Kramer and Shultz set up a glorious chance for Honig, who blasted past Allan from 12 yards. Things looked ominous for Hibs but they survived the loss of an early goal, with Shankly again getting his 4-3-3 tactics just right. Stanton and Madsen were immense at the back, extinguishing most of the danger after the early setback, and thereafter the early threat of Honig was blotted out completely. Although the power and experience of Seeler worried the visiting defenders on several occasions, there was no more scoring before the interval.

After the break Hibs were forced mainly onto the back foot, their forays upfield growing rarer as the game went on, and 15 minutes from the end the German fans peering through the murky gloom thought that their favourites had doubled their lead when Seeler scored from close range. Fortunately for Hibs, referee Hannet of Belgium, who had had a splendid game in the difficult conditions, spotted the centre forward pushing Madsen before putting the ball past keeper Allan, and the goal was disallowed.

In one of Hibs' rare attacks, Cormack forced a great save from Girschowski, who twice more had to look lively to deny the visitors. In the dying minutes of the game, McBride had a great opportunity to equalise, only to slip as he was about to connect.

Not even the numerous bonfires lit on the terracing by the freezing home supporters in the second half could brighten the realisation that one goal might not be enough in Edinburgh. In direct contrast, the obviously delighted Hibs players were now quietly confident of going through to the next round, with even manager Shankly claiming, 'Hibs will beat Hamburg at home', his opinion shared by skipper Pat Stanton.

FINAL SCORE: HAMBURG 1. HIBERNIAN 0.

FAIRS CUP 3RD ROUND (1ST LEG), WEDNESDAY 18 DECEMBER 1968, VOLKSPARK
STADIUM.
HIBERNIAN: ALLAN, SHEVLANE, DAVIS, COUSIN MADSEN, STANTON, O'ROURKE, QUINN,
MCBRIDE, CORMACK, STEVENSON.

At the turn of the year, former Hearts full back Chris Shevlane made
his first return to Tynecastle since his premature retirement and subsequent
recovery from injury several months before. The game finished goalless,
Hearts passing up the opportunity to record their first home win over their
great rivals in a New Year's Day derby match since 1955. Alan Gordon had
the miss of the match in the final few minutes when somehow he managed
to blast past the post from three yards when it seemed much easier to score.
Gordon's miss was even worse than the two easy chances that had fallen to
Joe McBride in the first half.

McBride made amends for the missed chances at Tynecastle by scoring
twice against struggling Raith Rovers the following day. Cormack scored the
other in Hibs' 3-0 win against the struggling Fifers. Bobby Duncan, making
his first-team come back after his leg break against Celtic, formed a solid
full back partnership with Joe Davis who now looked back to his best after
a lukewarm spell. Although they were now in the top half of the table, after
what could be termed an indifferent start, to say the least, it still seemed as
though a place in the following season's Fairs Cup would be beyond the
Easter Road side.

Monday 6 January 1969 heralded the official opening of the new
Hibernian Social Club, beating by just a few days a similar venture by Hearts
that had been delayed because of an electricians' strike. Within weeks the
club had proved so popular that it already had almost 3,000 members on its
books, prompting secretary Younger to boast, 'This is one of the first such
ventures in its field, and within a few years Hibs will be benefiting to the
tune of £20,000 annually from its profits.' Instead, circumstances, including
poor management and regular violence both inside and out the club, on one
occasion resulting in a death, would ensure that within a few short years
the club would cease to function, the clubrooms lying empty in a state of
disrepair and neglect for several years.

Although they had put up a brave fight to eventually win the match 2-1,
the new FIFA ruling of away goals counting double in the event of a draw saw
Hibs making a premature exit from the Fairs Cup competition.

In direct contrast to the game in Hamburg where the Belgian referee
had been exceptional, perhaps the best Hibs had ever encountered on their
European travels, Mr Johnson of Sweden had a nightmare evening. There
was confusion right from the start when the official allowed the Hamburg
goalkeeper to wear a green jersey despite repeated complaints from the Hibs
players, an error that would perhaps cost the home side dear; but his biggest
mistake came at the final whistle when he prepared to play an extra 30
minutes when even the fans knew that their team had lost on the new away

goals ruling. Entirely oblivious to the situation, the embarrassed official had to be informed by his linesmen that the game was over.

The Germans had made their tactics clear right from the start by adopting a stop-at-all-costs policy, particularly against Cormack who was forced to endure a physical hammering throughout the game. Three Hamburg players were booked for over-robust play, and a neutral observer might well have been of the opinion that a more severe punishment should have been meted out to Horst for persistent fouling, and to Kramer for kicking Stanton in full view of the stand-side linesman and the spectators on the terracing.

The first half ended goalless, but by that time two seemingly good strikes by Hibs had been mysteriously chalked off by the erratic official. In the 13th minute McBride claimed his shot had hit the roof of the net before being cleared, but despite furious appeals from the Hibs players it was disallowed. Nine minutes later, goalkeeper Ozcan did tremendously well to get a hand to a Cormack shot, which he failed to hold, with the inrushing Stanton sweeping the ball into the net. This 'goal' was also ruled off, the referee deciding that Stanton had been offside. The home players and the majority of the spectators were adamant that the official had got it wrong once again, probably confusing the green goalkeeper's jersey with that of a Hibs player.

On the stroke of half time, Cormack was brutally hacked down inside the box, but surprisingly the normally dependable Joe Davis drove the resultant penalty kick past the keeper's left-hand post. Before the kick had been taken, several Hamburg players had attempted to unsettle the normally unflappable full back, and it appeared as though Davis had allowed the gamesmanship to affect him.

Although it was far from one-way traffic, midway through the second half Hibs finally managed to score the goal their play had deserved against a German defence that had subjected the home forwards to a night of vicious brutality, when McBride scored from close range after a melee in the goalmouth. Then, with the visiting forwards threatening little danger in the home penalty area and extra time looming, disaster struck. Under no pressure, full back Duncan sent a misplaced pass from Dorfel straight to the feet of Seeler, who wasted no time in blasting the ball past Allan from 15 yards, leaving Hibs now needing two goals for victory. The goal was the signal for Hibs to reassert themselves in attack, but much to the dismay of the home fans, they persisted with high balls into the area which proved too easy for the goalkeeper and his tall defenders to deal with. In the final minute of the match McBride scored his second goal, levelling the overall scores, but it was never going to be enough, and after the ensuing confusion over extra time, it was the Germans who progressed into the next round.

FINAL SCORE: HIBERNIAN 2. HAMBURG 1.

FAIRS CUP 3RD ROUND (2ND LEG), WEDNESDAY 15 JANUARY 1969, EASTER ROAD.

HIBERNIAN: ALLAN, DUNCAN, DAVIS, STANTON, MADSEN, COUSIN, SCOTT, QUINN, MCBRIDE, CORMACK, STEVENSON.

The visiting players left the field to a background of jeers from a home support that was not enamoured of the constant time-wasting and fouling from Hamburg that had prevented Hibs from dictating the pace of the game for almost the entire 90 minutes.

Leeds United manager Don Revie had watched the game from the stand, ostensibly to run the eye over possible future opponents, but he could not fail to have been impressed by the performance of Peter Cormack, Hibs' top performer on the night. Cormack had shown great resilience in the face of some extreme provocation. The scrawny inside right with the huge heart had taken so much punishment during the game that afterwards he was almost unable to walk unaided and had to be driven home by one of the backroom staff.

Although it is unfair to blame individuals, mistakes by both full backs had proved very costly, particularly the miss from the penalty spot by the usually reliable Davis. Although it was disappointing to exit the competition, the game had nevertheless been great entertainment for the 27,399 crowd, with Hibs benefiting to the tune of almost £7,000 from the gate.

At the end of January Hibs began their latest quest for their holy grail: the Scottish Cup. In the first round against Rangers in Glasgow, centre half John Madsen had perhaps his best game for the club since his return from voluntary exile. With a defensive formation that had been geared more to bringing Rangers back to Easter Road than winning the game, the home side had their chances just before the interval, but once again it was Colin Stein who inflicted the damage on his former teammates. Despite an inspired performance by Madsen at the heart of the Easter Road defence it was only a matter of time before Hibs conceded a goal, but when it did arrive it was clouded in controversy, a far from unusual occurrence at Ibrox. With just over 20 minutes remaining, Stein, who had been comfortably held by Madsen all afternoon, was on hand to tap home from close range after a Johnston shot had come back off the post, the Hibs players appealing in vain that the goalscorer had been in an offside position. Only rarely are appeals of this nature by an away side successful at Ibrox and the goal, the winner as it transpired, was allowed to stand. Late in the game the ball ran down the entire length of Madsen's arm as he tried to clear in the box, and to the amazement of everyone in the ground the referee refused to award a penalty, much to the fury of the vigorously protesting Rangers players – yet another rare occurrence in Glasgow.

With dreams of Scottish Cup glory behind them for yet another year, there was now only a European place left to play for. Changes were made to the side that had lost at Ibrox, and against Clyde at the beginning of February Willie Wilson made a return in goal in place of the injured Allan, with a debut at last for former Motherwell player Willie Hunter. Hunter had been signed at the end of November but had been in the reserves for over two months, patiently waiting for his first-team chance. Two goals in the opening 15 minutes set Hibs on the way to victory, but the Shawfield side pulled one back midway through the half. Within minutes of the restart, Peter Cormack was sent off for retaliation after being fouled and the game died as a spectacle. The win, however, kept Hibs in seventh place and in touching distance of their target of a European place.

An interesting article by league secretary Alan Hardaker appeared in the February issue of the *Football League Review*. Hardaker felt that it was now time to go back to the original interpretation of the offside law where a player could not be penalised merely for being in an offside position, but would have to be guilty of seeking to gain an advantage, or be interfering with play. At that time it was common for most managers to adopt negative and defensive tactics, especially away from home, and a return to this format, said Hardaker, would help to bring back the goals and reduce the number of draws that were blighting the game. Although it would not take place for several years, the idea has since become the accepted practice.

At the end of February the unsettled Peter Cormack handed the club a written transfer demand, one that was instantly refused. At that time the player was operating only on the option clause of his contract, but after talks with the manager at the end of the previous year, he had signed a new deal to cover the remainder of this period. The refusal to consider his recent request led to Cormack insisting that he would definitely refuse to sign another contract at Easter Road, with the postscript that he would welcome a move to Leeds United. It was no secret that Revie was a big admirer of the player, or that he would be prepared to write a six-figure cheque to secure his services at Elland Road.

A goal by Davis from the penalty spot, and strikes from O'Rourke and McBride, gave the Greens an easy 3-0 victory and revenge for the defeat by St Mirren at Love Street earlier in the season. John Blackley, making his return to the first team since breaking a toe almost six months before, shared the limelight in an impressive all-round team performance with 18-year-old Alex Cropley in the number 11 shirt. Cropley, of whom Shankly was predicting a big future, failed to make a goalscoring start to his first-team career when he rounded the keeper only to hit the post with his shot.

A disastrous ten-game sequence without a win began with a 2-1 home defeat by Rangers the following midweek. Among the results that saw Hibs plummet from seventh to 13th place in the table, surely now banishing any lingering hopes of Fairs Cup qualification, was a 4-3 defeat at Cappielow with Joe Harper scoring a hat-trick. This was closely followed by a humiliating 2-1 home reverse by Arbroath, the Angus side's first away win of a season that would end with them firmly anchored at the foot of the table, and relegation. The young Cropley scored his first league goal for the club after seven minutes, but the suspended Peter Cormack watching from the stand, could only suffer in agony as his teammates stumbled to their worst display, and worst defeat for many years.

The League Cup Final postponed from October had now been rearranged for the beginning of April, and a Cup Final rehearsal against Celtic at

Parkhead 12 days before offered a glimmer of hope for an end to the dismal run of poor form. Behind at the interval, Hibs equalised when McBride scored in 72 minutes, with leaders Celtic fortunate to survive with a share of the points as the Edinburgh side took total control. Only a week before the Cup Final, any hope of a confidence-boosting victory were dashed when former Hibs player Davie Hogg, now with Dundee United, scored twice in a 3-0 win at Tannadice. Hogg's first goal was a tremendous 30-yard drive that screamed past the helpless Allan, after a pass from Alan Gordon, who had been signed only that morning from Hearts in an £8,000 deal.

At Hampden the following week, champions elect Celtic, then well on the way to a fourth consecutive league title, had been installed as red-hot favourites to lift the League Cup. Somewhat optimistically the SFA had notified both teams that the replay, should one be needed, would be at the same venue the following Wednesday evening.

The national stadium was bathed in bright summer sunshine on Saturday 5 April 1969 and a crowd of over 80,000 greeted the teams as they made their way onto the pitch. It was a day that was destined to end in abject disaster for the Edinburgh side as Celtic coasted to a 3-0 half time lead, and were leading 6-0 before the Easter Road side gained some semblance of respectability when O'Rourke and Stevenson both scored near the end. As strange as the scoreline would suggest, Hibs could take some credit from their performance. Fighting hard for 90 minutes, teamwork was the key, but quite simply, Celtic were far too good for them. Hibs missed a great chance to open the scoring inside the first few minutes when a Stevenson drive just shaved the post, before Celtic turned on the style, and the game was over before half time.

Pat Quinn, making his first appearance since the Scottish Cup defeat by Rangers in January replaced the cup-tied Joe McBride, with Cormack moving to centre forward, but in truth the power and aggression of McBride was badly missed against his former teammates. If the Hibs players could take any consolation at all from the game, it was the fact that on their performance that afternoon at Hampden, Celtic would probably have beaten anyone.

HIBERNIAN: ALLAN, SHEVLANE, DAVIS, STANTON, MADSEN, BLACKLEY, MARINELLO, QUINN, CORMACK, O'ROURKE, STEVENSON. SUB: HUNTER.
CELTIC: FALLON, CRAIG, GEMMELL, MURDOCH, MCNEIL, BROGAN, JOHNSTONE, WALLACE, CHALMERS, AULD, LENNOX. SUB: CLARK.

With Hibs making perhaps their final bid towards European qualification, three days after the humiliation at Hampden a crowd of just over 4,000, by far the lowest attendance at Easter Road all season, jeered when Davis missed a penalty against Dundee. Cries of 'Shankly must go' reverberated around the eerily empty reaches of the vast stadium as the Taysiders recorded an easy 3-1 win, their first victory at Easter Road since 1965. A consolation goal by Cormack in the final seconds was met by slow handclapping that quickly spread around the ground, turning to jeers as the home side left the field.

In an effort to rectify the obvious defensive problems, the former Hearts and Newcastle United goalkeeper Gordon Marshall was signed from Nottingham Forest for a fee of around £8,000 just in time to make his debut in a rearranged game against St Johnstone at Morton. Unfortunately, even the vastly experienced goalkeeper could do little to prevent the visitors from conceding the two goals inside the first six minutes that eventually gave the Saints both points. Stevenson gave Hibs a modicum of hope when he pulled one back just before half time, but all hope was dashed when Marinello was ordered off midway through the second period, the seventh Hibs player to be sent off since the beginning of the season.

Alex Pringle made his first-team debut in the 4-0 home victory against St Johnstone in the final game of the season, Hibs' first win in an 11-game spell that had lasted over two months. Hibs eventually finished 12th in the table, their lowest position for six years, and quite obviously there would now be no European football at Easter Road the following term.

Joe McBride had surely been the bargain of the season. Signed only in December, the former Celtic player ended his first term at Easter Road as Hibs' top goalscorer, finding the net 24 times, 19 in the league and the rest in the Fairs Cup, six more than the £100,000-rated Colin Stein at Ibrox. Once again Joe Davis had kept up his remarkable record of not missing a single game during the entire season, the only ever-present in the side, one ahead of his nearest challenger, Pat Stanton.

By now the chairman had promised the fans that goalkeeper Marshall would not be his last big-money signing. During the previous few weeks Shankly had taken in games at Airdrie, believed to have been watching either Sam Goodwin or Jim Black, and had also visited London on a top-secret spying mission, the target believed to have been former Celtic player John Cushley, then with West Ham. In the end Jim Black became Hibs' most expensive signing, at £32,000, when he moved the short distance from his home in Plean to Edinburgh.

With Black at the heart of the defence, Airdrie had ended the season in seventh place, six ahead of Hibs, conceding just 44 goals, a total bettered only by the top four: Celtic, Rangers, Dunfermline and Kilmarnock.

Twenty-eight players had been retained for the coming season, including the recently signed ground staff boys from Edina Hibs, John Puller, Willie McEwan and John Brownlie. In the expected clear-out, the experienced Willie Wilson, Pat Quinn, Alan Cousin and Alan McGraw were freed along with young Maurice McCabe. Alec Scott, who had failed to hold down a regular first-team place since the Scottish Cup defeat by Rangers in January, was placed on the open-to-transfer list.

9

Macfarlane In, Marinello and Cormack Out, and a Mystery Bid

1969–70

AT THE START of the 1969–70 season, Hibs abandoned the traditional use of both Seafield and Hawkhill for their pre-season training to take up the offer to utilise the excellent facilities at the Civil Service playing fields at Silverknowes. On the first day, record signing Jim Black lined up alongside youngsters Puller, McEwan and Brownlie, all called up at the end of the previous season, as the players were put through their paces by trainer Jimmy Stevenson. For 26-year-old Black it would be his first experience of full-time football. Just days before the start of the new season the unlucky Bobby Duncan, now fully recovered from the terrible leg break that at one time might well have ended his career, underwent a cartilage operation in the PMR Hospital in Edinburgh.

Former player John Fraser, who had recently retired after a short spell with Stenhousemuir, made a return to Easter Road when he was asked to look after the schoolboy signings in the evenings. He would have an unexpectedly quick promotion. Just weeks into the new season, trainer Jimmy Stevenson would return to his former club Dunfermline, paving the way for Fraser to rejoin the club on a permanent basis as reserve team trainer. The evergreen 74-year-old Jimmy McColl, who was still available to pass on a helpful word of advice to the youngsters if required, was still involved behind the scenes but these days in a far less strenuous capacity. Most of the medals and souvenirs collected during a lifetime in the game had been stolen during a burglary at McColl's home some time before, but he had recently been unexpectedly reunited with one of the medals after the Celtic manager Jock Stein had come across it in Glasgow.

At the start of the season, Pat Stanton replaced Joe Davis as club captain. Although he was still only 24, the experienced Stanton had already made over 300 appearances for the club since making his debut in 1963, and was a well respected figure in the game. Delighted to accept the position, Stanton was quick to remind the supporters jokingly that he would not be taking any penalties. It was a statement that would later come back to haunt him.

Without the distraction of a summer tour, Hibs again relied on a series of pre-season friendlies against English opposition to gain match fitness before the start of the new campaign. The Newcastle United manager Frank Brennan, a great admirer of Peter Cormack, was given an early opportunity to watch the player in action again when the clubs met for a second consecutive year in a challenge match at Easter Road. The Fairs Cup holders were known to have £100,000 to invest before the tax deadline expired in July and it was common knowledge that they had been interested in signing the Hibs player, but in a surprise move only days before, they had opted for Aberdeen's Jim Smith instead.

Recent signing Jim Black, who was making his first start for his new side, impressed on his debut against Newcastle, and more than held his own against the dangerous giant Welsh International centre forward Wyn Davies, but despite constant second-half pressure by the home side the game ended goalless, the first no score draw at Easter Road for nearly three and a half years. Early in the second half Peter Cormack was substituted suffering from a neck injury. Cormack would have ample time to recover after having received a three-game ban in midweek for bookings received during the previous campaign.

A midweek friendly at Highfield Road also ended level but only after a last-minute goal by Neil Martin, who had moved from Sunderland to Coventry, gave his new side a 1-1 draw against his former teammates. In the opening League Cup game, a much weakened Hibs side secured an easy 4-1 home win over Clyde. With McBride injured and Cormack, Marinello and Blackley all suspended, Hibs gave 19-year-old former Cumbernauld United player Johnny Hamilton the opportunity to make his competitive debut. Hamilton's aggressive style and clever play suggested that the player was well capable of making a big name for himself in the game. The fans had been intrigued as to how both new signing Jim Black and centre half John Madsen could be accommodated in the same line-up, but for the opening game of the season Madsen was relegated to the substitute's bench. For the next, against Dunfermline at East End Park he would play alongside Black in an unfamiliar wing half position. It would be his last game for the first team, and he would shortly return to Denmark to play for hometown side Esbjerg.

At the half-way stage of a group that included Clyde, Dunfermline and Aberdeen, the Easter Road side looked odds-on favourites to win the section, but with goal difference now replacing goal average, a disastrous 3-1 reverse at Shawfield meant they needed to defeat Eddie Turnbull's Aberdeen by two clear goals in the final match at Easter Road if they were to progress into the quarter-finals. As it turned out, a defence well organised by the former Famous Five icon Turnbull, coped comfortably with everything a disappointing and punchless Hibs attack could muster, and the Dons were well worth the point secured in a no-score draw that guaranteed them entry into the next round and a bumper payday against Celtic.

For the opening league match of the new season, Hibs made their way to Somerset Park to face newly promoted Ayr United, now managed by former Hibs player Ally MacLeod. A woeful performance by an Easter Road side totally lacking the spirit and determination of the newcomers saw them surrender meekly to a team forced to play with ten men for most of the game. In the dressing room after the game even the players were unanimous that the 3-0 defeat had been the worst display by a Hibs side for many years. The debacle prompted one newspaper reporter to suggest that, had a military court of law applied, Hibs would have been found guilty of desertion while under fire.

Not unexpectedly, Shankly made changes for the game against St Mirren at Easter Road. Out went Wilkinson and Grant. But the biggest surprise was the demotion of former captain Joe Davis, bringing the defender's amazing run of 273 consecutive games to an end. During this run, the former Third Lanark player had scored 47 goals, 34 in league games, a quite phenomenal total for a full back even although most came via the penalty spot. He would not play for the first team again. In came O'Rourke and Blackley, the defender making his first full appearance of the season after suspension, and young Mervyn Jones, a nephew of John Greig of Rangers, who was making his debut as a replacement for Davis at left back. Two headed goals, one in each half by Cormack, gave Hibs both points, but the major talking point was the resignation of manager Bob Shankly immediately after the game.

Interviewed by the astonished reporters soon after the final whistle, a disillusioned Shankly lamented that there was 'no fun in the game anymore, at least not at the top level. Good results are now an absolute must, and there is always a strain.' With 17 years' managerial experience at Falkirk, Third Lanark, Dundee and Hibs, Shankly had been frustrated at constantly having to sell his best players. Forced to part with Alan Gilzean and Ian Ure at Dundee, the pattern had continued at Easter Road with the sale of Hamilton, Martin, Scott, McNamee and Stein. Quitting in protest barely ten months before, after the sale of Stein to Rangers, Shankly had been persuaded by chairman Harrower to change his mind, which he later identified as a big mistake on his part. He had contemplated retiring at the end of the previous season, but had decided to honour the remainder of his contract, and was adamant that he would not have stayed after that. When asked if he had any plans to remain in the game, the discontented Shankly replied honestly, 'Not at the moment, but one never knows.' He would shortly take over as manager of Stirling Albion.

Somewhat predictably, former players Eddie Turnbull and Willie Ormond were among the names tipped to succeed Shankly for the £5,000-per-annum post, but meanwhile Tom McNiven took temporary charge of the side. McNiven decided to keep faith with the same 11 that had faced St Mirren, with the exception of Hamilton, who replaced O'Rourke. The caretaker manager became one of Hibs' most successful ever, with a 100 per cent record, Hibs winning all three games under his tenure, including a 5-1 home victory against Partick Thistle and a 2-1 win at Parkhead.

Against Celtic, Hibs had been a goal behind at the break, but Hamilton ended the best move of the game when he equalised three minutes into the second half with his first goal for the club. Captain Pat Stanton made sure of the points by scoring the winner seven minutes from time with a magnificent 25-yard drive that screamed past the helpless Fallon.

Stating a preference for an energetic and bright young manager with modern ideas, on Monday 22 September 1969, Hibs announced the appointment of Willie Macfarlane as Shankly's replacement. The former Hutchison Vale juvenile and Tranent Juniors player had spent ten years at Easter Road between 1949 and 1959, taking part in the first European Cup tie against Rot Weiss Essen at Easter Road in 1955. Since retiring from the playing side after spells with Raith Rovers and Morton he had successfully managed at a lower level. After spells with Gala Fairydean and Eyemouth, Macfarlane had seen service with Hawick Royal Albert in the East of Scotland League before joining Second Division Stirling Albion in 1967. Giving up a secure job as a manager of a construction company in Edinburgh, Macfarlane in his own words accepted 'the only job in football that I would have taken full-time. I have always been a Hibs supporter, and I will give the job 200 per cent effort.'

Macfarlane's managerial career at Easter Road got off to the best possible start when his new charges defeated city rivals Hearts in his first game. Perhaps boosted by the appointment of the new manager, over 26,000 had crammed into Tynecastle, the highest attendance for the September fixture between the sides for several years. Peter Cormack, opened the scoring just before half time, with Joe McBride making sure of the points when he scored from a dubious-looking offside position on the hour mark. The win put Hibs on top of the table after six games and level on points with Dunfermline. The new manager, well aware of the unacceptable number of suspensions incurred in recent years by Hibs players, quickly demonstrated his stance on discipline. As the players celebrated the victory over Hearts at a party later that evening, Peter Marinello was called over by Macfarlane to be informed that he was being fined for having his name taken during the game. It had been the first booking by a Hibs player that season.

In what was to prove a highly successful opening period for Macfarlane, Hibs travelled to Ibrox where two goals by Man of the Match Marinello, and another from McBride gave the Greens an easy 3-1 win. Using the lessons learned from playing behind the Famous Five, during the game Macfarlane had switched all the forwards around, a move that bamboozled the Rangers players who were a complete shambles by the second half. The Ibrox true blue and loyal faithful deserted in their droves long before the end.

One of the first tasks facing the new manager was to confront the unsettled Peter Cormack regarding his future at Easter Road. Prolonged discussions between the pair ended with great news for the anxious Hibs fans when the player announced that he was prepared to sign a new contract and remain at Easter Road, at least for the foreseeable future.

Cormack had been outstanding in the Scotland side that had been beaten 3-2 by West Germany in Hamburg the previous week, the inside forward impressing no less a judge than the legendary West German manager Helmet Schoen. Brazil manager José Soldanha, a spectator at the game, had also wanted to know more about the Scotland No 8 'who had played like a lion'.

Still on the international front, the Scotland manager Bobby Brown had included Peter Marinello in the World Cup squad to meet Austria, along with teammates Stanton and Cormack. Unfortunately, injury forced both Marinello, who had played just 58 first-team games for Hibs, and Cormack to withdraw from the squad. Marinello would not be selected for the full side again.

At the beginning of November, Willie Macfarlane returned to his former club Stirling Albion to sign full back Erich Schaedler for a fee reputed to be around £5,000. A previous attempt to sign the defender had been rejected out of hand but an increased offer had paid dividends, and Schaedler celebrated his last game for Stirling by scoring a rare goal in a 6-0 victory.

Three days later Johnny Graham was signed from Falkirk, making a scoring debut against Airdrie at Easter Road later that same evening. Few players could have made a more explosive start. After a dismal first half, Airdrie took the lead soon after half time, but two goals in a quite inspirational performance by outside right Graham, who hit the post late in the game as well as setting Cormack up for Hibs' third goal in a 3-1 victory, saw his Easter Road career off to a delightful start. As with Schaedler, several previous attempts had been made to sign Graham, but Second Division Falkirk, who were confident of securing promotion that year, were understandably reluctant to release a prized asset. In the end Macfarlane's persistence paid off, and like Jim Black before him, Graham was sampling full-time football for the first time in his career.

The Hibs line-up about this time was on the following lines: Marshall, Shevlane, McEwan, Blackley, Black, Stanton, Marinello, Graham, McBride, Cormack and Stevenson.

Seven consecutive wins during September and October, including Shankly's final game in charge, were hailed as a modern record at Easter Road and it was enough to earn Macfarlane the Bell's Manager of the Month award for October, including the accompanying gallon of whisky and a cheque for £50. However, reluctant to move with the times, the SFA informed Hibs that under no circumstances could Macfarlane accept either the award or the accompanying prizes: Article 121 of the Rules of Association prevented a manager, coach, trainer or player from accepting, or allowing his name to be associated with the acceptance of any presentation, testimonial or gift without the sanction of the Council. Initiated to prevent the threat of bribery or corruption, the rule was perfectly understandable, but in the circumstances the ban was a ludicrous absurdity. A few weeks later Jock Stein of Celtic was nominated for the November award, but by that time some sense won through and he was allowed to accept the trophy, but not the whisky or cash. In England it was quite rightly seen as a prestigious prize that reflected favourably on the entire club, with managers allowed to collect both the trophy and the ancillary rewards.

Erich Schaedler made his first-team debut in a friendly against Polish cup holders Gornik at Easter Road in December when he replaced left back

Billy McEwan in the second half. The defender quickly demonstrated what would soon become his legendary ferocious tackling skills when Cormack was carried off injured after both men had gone for the same ball near the half way line. The injury prompted some members of the press to wonder if playing friendly matches in mid-season was worth the risk, reminding their readers that Alex Cropley had also been injured during a friendly against Aston Villa just weeks before. Gornik's 2-1 win was Hibs' first defeat on home soil by foreign opposition since losing 1-0 to Red Star in the Fairs Cup eight years before.

Schaedler's career at Easter Road had got off to anything but an auspicious start. In his first game for Hibs against Dundee United reserves, he had had the misfortune to score an own goal, although considering that he had scored for Stirling Albion in his final appearance, goals by a full back in consecutive games was a pretty rare occurrence.

He made his competitive debut in the 1970 New Year derby against Hearts at Easter Road when he became the fourth incumbent of the left back berth that season, following in the footsteps of Jones, McEwan and Joe Davis, who a short time before had joined Second Division Carlisle United for a nominal fee. The full back, who gave little indication that he was soon to become a Hibs legend and a huge favourite with the Easter Road support, had a quiet game, and at one point was almost responsible for another own goal when a shot by a Hearts player was deflected from him and onto the crossbar before being cleared. The game itself soon degenerated into a bruising battle with little in the way of skill. The underlying nastiness surfaced when Cormack was sent off in the 65th minute for kicking Oliver while the Hearts player lay on the ground. For a while Cormack refused to leave the field before being ushered to the dressing room by trainer Fraser. Trouble erupted between rival fans in the covered enclosure behind the Albion Road End goal shortly after the incident and the police had their work cut out to restore order. The ill-tempered match ended goalless, although the visitors had been the better side, twice hitting the woodwork and forcing former Hearts goalkeeper Gordon Marshall into making several magnificent saves. The big talking point of the day, however, was the imminent transfer of Peter Marinello, who watched the game from the stand. It had been an open secret for some time that Arsenal were interested in the player, and they had now tabled an offer believed to be in the region of £90,000. As expected there were no snags and the transfer went ahead the following day, the chairman quite obviously failing to take any heed of the reasons behind Bob Shankly's premature departure from the club a few months before.

On the Saturday, bad boy Cormack was made captain, replacing flu victim Pat Stanton and he celebrated his promotion by turning in a five-star display in the 3-0 victory over Raith Rovers in Kirkcaldy. Johnny Graham scored twice to take his personal tally to seven goals in eight games, Macfarlane's reverse psychology paying immediate dividends when the new skipper scored the third himself.

At the beginning of January Manchester City target Arthur Duncan was signed from Partick Thistle as a direct replacement for Marinello for a new club record fee of £35,000. It would turn out be one of the best bits of business ever achieved at Easter Road. The speedy outside left would soon become an integral part of one of the best sides in the history of the club, score goals by the sackful, win five full Scotland caps, before going on to make a record number of appearances wearing the famous green and white jersey. But more of that later.

As his predecessor was making a scoring debut in Arsenal's 2-1 defeat at Old Trafford, Duncan's debut was put on temporary hold when the game against Dundee in Edinburgh was cancelled due to the weather. He made his first appearance in a Hibs shirt against Celtic at Easter Road on 17 January 1970. Willie McEwan replaced Peter Cormack, who earlier in the week had been suspended for 14 days and fined £75 after his dismissal against Hearts on New Year's Day. Such was the interest in the game between the first- and third-placed sides that the kick-off was held back for ten minutes to give the 45,000 fans time to leave the pub... er, enter the ground. Celtic made a flying start to take a deserved first-half lead, but new boy Duncan opened his account for Hibs when he fired a well struck shot past Williams through a ruck of players for Hibs' equaliser midway through the second half. Four minutes from time, however, Hughes gave Celtic both points, and Hibs their first competitive home defeat of the season.

A great run of only three defeats since the opening day reverse against Ayr United had seen Hibs sit briefly at the top of the table at the turn of the year but the defeat by Celtic had seen a drop to third place, although they were still well in touch with the leaders.

A somewhat interesting and ultimately prophetic article by John Ayres appeared in the *Pink News* around this time, instigated by a statement made shortly before by former Hearts director 'Archie' Bell QC, a well respected figure in football circles. Bell had raised the subject of an ultimate merger between the big two capital clubs, which, according to him, made sound financial sense. Ayres immediately lambasted the idea in the press as a figment of the silly season. 'Economists studying the balance sheet would be attracted by its viability,' he opined, 'but every fan of the respective clubs would soon let you know that the very idea is heresy, with very few likely to step into the chosen stadium if it was not the one used by their previous favourites. What colours to wear would create irresolvable issues, and an added problem would be the name. Yet another dilemma,' Ayres added without the slightest hint of facetiousness, 'would be what particular brand of Irish songs would the teenage choirs sing? No Mr Bell, you are just not on.' The article ended with a guarded footnote: 'Regardless of my opposition to the idea, history in all possibility could well prove Mr Bell right.' We would have to wait until 1990 for the answer to that.

The end of Cormack's suspension coincided with the first round of the Scottish Cup. For a second successive year Hibs had been drawn away to

Rangers, and once again they were destined to leave Ibrox empty-handed. With the kick-off delayed several minutes to allow the fans outside the ground time to enter, when play eventually started there were an estimated 60,000 packed inside the ground. The home side took the lead after 12 minutes but the arrogant 'easy, easy' chants that reverberated around Ibrox from the home fans were stifled when Graham levelled four minutes later after Neef had failed to hold a McEwan free kick. The respite was only fleeting, however, and a magnificent 35-yard drive by Alex McDonald restored the Light Blues' lead before half time. Rangers eventually ran out comfortable 3-1 winners, and Hibs long wait for Scottish Cup success continued.

By now the Greens' great start under Macfarlane had begun to falter, and their third-place position in the table was briefly threatened seven days after the cup exit when a similar 3-1 reverse was suffered at the hands of bottom-of-the-table Partick Thistle at Firhill. The scoreline in no way flattered the Jags, who could well have doubled their tally. One interested spectator was Spurs manager Bill Nicholson, believed to be there to run an eye over Peter Cormack. Despite regular denials by the club, that Cormack was for sale, the story broke that Hibs had contacted certain English clubs, hoping to provoke an auction. The continuing transfer activity at Easter Road was also having an unsettling effect on Pat Stanton who was concerned not only for his own future but for that of the team. There was no denying that during the past decade Hibs had quite clearly been a selling club, raking in the then considerable fortune of over £660,000 by selling Joe Baker, McLeod, Gibson, Gerry Baker, Parke, Hamilton, Martin, McNamee, Scott, Stein, Marinello and now, quite probably, Cormack. Stanton requested a clear-the-air meeting with the chairman to resolve his future, prompting Macfarlane to insist that he would resign immediately if the club captain was sold. Meanwhile, amid all the transfer speculation surrounding Stanton and Cormack, Alec Scott was allowed to join hometown side Falkirk for a nominal fee.

After the debacle at Firhill, a four-game unbeaten run that included a 2-2 draw with Rangers in Edinburgh, suggested that the title race was still far from over. At the beginning of March, Alex Cropley celebrated signing as a full-time professional by scoring in Hibs 3-3 draw with St Mirren at Love Street, while Peter Cormack celebrated the occasion by being sent off for the second time in five games, and the fourth time in his career, after clashing with future Hibs player Ian Munro. The unsettling transfer speculation was affecting the player, who had not produced his top form for some time.

Eric Stevenson, who had once again asked to be placed on the transfer list, had not featured in the first team since, but was recalled for the trip to Aberdeen in mid-March. Aberdeen manager Eddie Turnbull, a great admirer of the player, had tried to sign Stevenson during Bob Shankly's time in charge at Easter Road but had been given little encouragement. Cormack was again made captain, and once again it was an inspired selection by Macfarlane as the inside forward harried and harassed the soon-to-be Scottish Cup winners to a rare home defeat.

With the season reaching a climax, both Hibs and Hearts had the race for third place all to themselves. The battle took on a more important perspective now that only one team from each city was allowed to enter the Fairs Cup. Hearts, at one stage a massive ten points behind Hibs, were now catching up fast and only two points separated the sides with Hearts having played one game more. The challenge for the European place would go some way to ensuring that for both Edinburgh sides at least, there would be no so-called meaningless end of the season games.

League placings as usual would determine who would compete in the European and Fairs Cups, but for the rest there was the welcome news that discussions between the four home associations regarding a British Cup had now borne fruit. Six sides from England and Scotland, and two each from Eire and Ulster would meet in the as yet unnamed competition the following season. Harry Swan's pioneering advocacy of the introduction of a British Cup nearly 20 years before was vindicated. The present chairman at Easter Road was of the opinion that the new competition had great possibilities, not least because of the shorter travelling distances and consequently lesser financial outlay.

With just three games remaining, a hat-trick by Joe McBride in a 4-1 victory over St Johnstone at Easter Road all but confirmed Hibs finishing in third place and qualification for the Fairs Cup. Peter Cormack was the other marksman with what would turn out to be his last goal and his final game in a Hibs shirt for several years. On Tuesday 24 March 1970, the Peter Cormack transfer saga finally came to an end when he agreed to join Nottingham Forest in an £80,000 deal.

Cormack, fearing that the chance of achieving his ambition to play in England had passed him by, accepted terms as soon as Forest entered the frame. A few weeks before it had seemed as though he would be joining Spurs but negotiations had stalled during the final stages, and the deal taking him to Nottingham was completed much to his relief. The Hibs manager, who had done everything in his power to keep Cormack at Easter Road, had little to say regarding his transfer except to remind the supporters that the deal had been done 'by chairman Harrower, and by Harrower alone'.

In an attempt to placate the disconsolate Hibs fans, Harrower responded: 'The player's contract was up at the end of the season and because of his impending appearance in front of the disciplinary panel, it was thought prudent to sell him now.'

The transfer of Cormack left Pat Stanton even more uncertain of his own future at Easter Road and in two minds as to whether to demand a transfer himself, or wait and see what terms were offered for the coming season. He did confess, however, that constantly selling your best players certainly made the job a lot harder, and no amount of money could make up for the loss of the calibre of player that had been sold by the club during the previous few years.

An article in the *Edinburgh Evening News* around this time revealed that an American Football Club imminently intended to make a bid for Hibs. This provoked no little concern among the Easter Road support. According to the report, the wealthy owner of North American League side Atlanta Chiefs, an offshoot of the baseball team of the same name, was about to make an offer for the club. Millions of dollars had recently been invested in the newly formed North American League but this had failed to generate any great interest among the American public, and it was now felt that expanding links into Europe was the way ahead. The consortium were understood to have been locked for several months in unsuccessful discussions with Aston Villa, and it was now believed that they had focused their attentions on Hibs, the Easter Road set-up already having been thoroughly investigated. Harrower, who acknowledged that he had heard the stories, insisted that no approach had been made. The rumours proved to be unfounded, and no more would be heard on the subject of takeover bids until the summer of 1990.

With only two games left to play, Hearts' bid for a Fairs Cup place had finally faltered, and Hibs, now assured of a European spot the following season, applauded Scottish Cup winners Aberdeen onto the field at Easter Road after their victory against Celtic the previous Saturday. After surviving a pounding in the opening period of the match, Aberdeen scored against the run of play to run out 2-1 winners.

In Hibs' final game of the season, against Dunfermline at East End Park, 18-year-old John Brownlie made a competitive debut at right half in place of John Blackley. Brownlie, who had been an almost ever-present in the second team all season, had already been called up for the Scottish Professional Youth Squad and good judges considered him an extremely exciting prospect. Manager Macfarlane missed the game. He was at Love Street on a mystery spying trip seeking a possible replacement for Cormack.

At the end of the day, third place had been secured with relative ease, Hearts finishing in fourth place, eight points behind their Edinburgh rivals.

The draw for the following season's Fairs Cup had already been made. Hibs were paired with Swedish side Malmö. The one-club-per-city ruling denied Hearts a place in the competition, and also that of sixth-placed Dundee, who had finished one place below Dundee United. The final Fairs Cup place would go to seventh-placed Kilmarnock.

During the previous season it had been planned to build a gymnasium in the car park adjacent to the Hibs Social Club. Since the early days of the game, snow-covered or frost-hardened grounds during the winter months had often made it extremely difficult to find a suitable place for the players to train. An indoor gym would have made it possible for training to take place in all weathers, its locality making the need for extra dressing rooms unnecessary. Alas, like many other projects before and since, the resourceful idea came to nothing, and the problem of finding training grounds that were adequate in severe weather conditions would continue until the construction of a training complex at West Mains near Ormiston in 2007.

Tom Hart Takeover, Baker's Return and a Liverpool Fiasco

1970–71

THE TARGET OF the manager's mysterious spying trip to Love Street at the end of the previous season was revealed when centre forward Jim Blair was signed from St Mirren in June for a fee reputed to be in the region of £40,000. Blair took part in three games against Shalke, Nijmegan and Maastricht during Hibs' short pre-season tour of Germany and Holland. A ban earned during his time with the Paisley club, however, would mean the slim six-footer missing Hibs' opening three League Cup games. Blair finally made his competitive debut as a substitute when replacing Joe McBride in Hibs' 4-2 defeat of Airdrie at Broomfield. Seen as the ideal replacement for Cormack, the centre forward had been a prolific marksman during his time at St Mirren, scoring over 50 goals in three seasons. Now, with the benefit of full-time training under his belt, he was expected to improve even further.

In Germany there had been an unexpected injury crisis when Gordon Marshall, the only goalkeeper in the party, was injured during training. Cormack had been a ready-made stand-in, but of course he was no longer with the club. Luckily Marshall recovered sufficiently to play in all three matches including the game against Schalke that saw Jim Black score his first goal for the club after 47 appearances, when he was on hand to force home a last-minute equaliser in a 1-1 draw.

In recent seasons the versatile Jimmy O'Rourke had become something of a utility man, failing to live up to his early promise, although it has to be said, his progress had been hampered by injury. Realising that the prospect of a regular first-team place at Easter Road was remote, especially now with the introduction of Blair, at the start of the season the stocky inside forward had posted a transfer request and was left behind in Edinburgh as his teammates made their way to the continent. Although voted the Player of the Year by the Hibs Supporters Association at the beginning of the previous campaign, O'Rourke had since managed only six league appearances since then, scoring his only goal in Hibs' 2-1 victory over Dunfermline in the final game of the season. Hibs and O'Rourke had not seen the last of each other yet, and his part in the club's success during the following few years would be immeasurable.

After only 12 months at Silverknowes, the training camp was moved much nearer home. With the 1970 Commonwealth Games now over, Hibs were offered the use of the brand new facilities at Meadowbank, an offer they were delighted to take up. One surprise face on the first day was Arsenal star Peter Marinello, back in Edinburgh for his wedding the following day. Among the provisional signings was a young Willie Pettigrew from Bonkle Amateurs. Pettigrew would not remain long at Easter Road before being released, but after a short spell with Junior side East Kilbride he would go on to make a name for himself with Motherwell, Dundee United, Hearts, Morton, Hamilton and Scotland.

By this time the price of a season ticket for the coming 12 months had been released. and tickets for the Centre Stand would now cost £9, and £6 for the Wings. Debenture holders were entitled to obtain a ticket at the reduced price of £4. Shares were first issued by Hibs in 1924 to raise the capital to fund the building of a new Main Stand, and it was the distribution of these shares that had first encouraged Harry Swan to become directly involved with the club. Thirty years later, with the the debenture finally paid back, a new issue of £100 shares was released on 1 May 1960 in the hope of raising £30,000. As well as the cut-price season ticket, bond-holders would receive tax-deductible six per cent interest returns twice annually. The shares would finally be redeemed early and in full during Tom Hart's tenure at the club.

Pat Stanton, the inaugural winner of the Hibs Supporters Association Player of the Year statuette two years before, received an even greater accolade just before the start of the new season when he was voted the Scottish Football Writers Player of the Year for 1969–70 at a ceremony in Glasgow. It was a fairly rare occurrence for a player outside the Old Firm to receive the award but the nomination was a well deserved honour for the much respected Hibs player.

A League Cup section that included St Johnstone, Airdrie and Aberdeen, began with a 3-1 victory at Muirton on the opening day of the season. Graham, Duncan and McBride got the goals that mattered, but it was the 18-year-old youth cap John Brownlie, replacing the injured Shevlane in the second half, who was the undoubted star of the afternoon. Foraging tirelessly down the right wing, the youngster helped set up two of the Hibs goals, and the Saints defence had simply no answer to the full back's pace and trickery. Hibs had cut their travelling time fine, arriving at the ground with only 20 minutes to spare owing to heavy traffic congestion, but they refused to allow this to upset their rhythm, and after one game they topped the section.

Only two points were dropped from the following four games, but for the second year in succession Hibs needed to beat Aberdeen at Easter Road in the final section game if they were to progress through to the later stages. This time there would be no mistake. In their best display of the season so far, with Black, Stanton, McEwan, and McBride outstanding, Hibs cantered to a 4-0 half-time lead against Eddie Turnbull's Scottish Cup holders. There was no more scoring in the second half, but by then the game was already over and Hibs were through to face Rangers in the quarter-finals.

In recent years, games against Hearts had been mainly disappointing and the first derby of the season at Easter Road was no exception. A share of the points was just reward for both sides after yet another typically scrappy no-scoring affair, played out in difficult, blustery conditions that produced more effort than skill. Only two goals had now been scored in the previous four encounters between the sides.

At a windswept Easter Road in midweek, Rangers were far too good for a lacklustre home side in the first leg of the League Cup quarter-final. The Glasgow side started at a furious pace and opened the scoring in their very first attack of the game, doubling their lead shortly after the interval. Any lingering hopes of Hibs saving the game after Duncan pulled a goal back, disappeared completely when Rangers scored a deserved third shortly after. To the delight of their vast travelling support numbering almost 40,000 – a tremendous crowd for a midweek game – Rangers mounted an impressive display of skill and power, and Hibs' prospects of reversing the scoreline at Ibrox seemed doomed.

Recently appointed as PR man at Easter Road, former goalkeeper Tommy Younger made it one of his first priorities to make a renewed appeal to the authorities for the formation of a Super League based on crowd potential. Recalling that the subject had been a pet project of Harry Swan, Younger put forward the argument that if it had been a sound proposition when there had been a boom in attendances, it still remained a sound proposition now. The format had recently proved a great success in West Germany where the authorities, alarmed at falling gates, had simply selected the sides with the greatest crowd-pulling potential and transferred them to a newly created top division. The implementation of a Premier or Super League was not too far in the future, and as with many other developments in the game, Hibs would play a major part in its inception.

As already mentioned, one innovation that did come to fruition was the formation of a British Cup. The consolation tournament for sides that failed to qualify for Europe was to be contested by Hearts, Dunfermline, Morton, Dundee, Motherwell and Airdrie from Scotland, with Burnley, Nottingham Forest, Wolves, WBA, Stoke, and Spurs, from England. Irish sides Ards and Derry, and Limerick and Colerain from the Republic, made up the numbers. The competition would soon give rise to good-natured banter in Edinburgh that Hibs were in Europe while Hearts were in Britain.

Hibs made their first visit to Cowdenbeath on league business since the 1933–34 season, and two goals inside the first six minutes set the capital side up for the forthcoming European tie against Malmö in Edinburgh. Alex Cropley, who had been a substitute in the previous two games, staked a claim for a regular place with a top-class performance in a reshuffled Hibs side that ran out convincing 4-1 winners.

On several occasion over the years Hibs had encountered severe travel difficulties when using scheduled flights for European games, and the club representatives who were at Turnhouse Airport the day before the game to welcome Malmö may have been surprised that even the Swedish amateurs had chartered their own aircraft for the trip. Experienced European campaigners, Malmö had been one of Sweden's most successful and influential during the past 30 years, and had qualified for the European Cup on three occasions since 1964. They arrived in Scotland with just 14 players, rather surprising considering that five substitutes could now be stripped for European games, although only two could play. Their star man, striker Bo Larsson, was Sweden's top goalscorer. Capped 26 times, Larsson was only one of several internationals on the books.

Of the 11 Hibs players who took the field against the Swedish part-timers, Duncan, Black, Hamilton, McEwan, Schaedler, Cropley and Blair were all making their European debut. Blair would also have the dual satisfaction of scoring his first goal for the club. Against weak opposition who were found to be totally out of their depth at this level, Joe McBride notched yet another treble and it was mainly thanks to the former Celt that Hibs were able to run up their biggest ever win in a European competition. As well as scoring his second Fairs Cup hat-trick for Hibs, the centre forward set up a couple and was now Hibs' top scorer in European competitions with eight goals, overtaking Joe Baker's total of six.

After struggling for the opening half hour, and giving the fans little indication of what was to come, the home side somewhat fortuitously scored twice in two minutes with goals from Blair and who else but McBride, to take a somewhat flattering lead into the second half. The goals had brought some cheer to the supporters who had started to show their impatience, but although the home side had been unimpressive in the opening 45 minutes, Malmö had failed to even trouble Marshall or a compact Hibs defence during that time. The second half saw a distinct improvement in Hibs' performance, and a purple patch midway through the half saw them score three goals inside a four minute spell to ensure even this early a passage into the next round.

On the hour mark McBride scored with a header from a dangerous Duncan cross, the same player scoring number four 60 seconds later with a great left-foot shot off the underside of the crossbar. Two minutes later McBride became the provider when his perfectly weighted cross from the right was brilliantly headed into the net by Duncan, the inside right scoring his own second of the night and Hibs' sixth near the end.

Teetering Malmö had been totally overwhelmed by the goal-hungry second-half attitude of a cavalier home side that refused to lessen the pace, and for the remainder of the game it was all out assault on the Swedish penalty area. Despite several near things, the beleaguered Malmö defence somehow managed to hold out and there was no more scoring.

The players left the field to chants of 'easy, easy' and 'bring on the Celtic' reverberating around the ground, but one thing was certain: the match against the league leaders at Easter Road in three days time would be far more difficult than the games against Cowdenbeath and Malmö.

FINAL SCORE: HIBERNIAN 6. MALMÖ 0.

FAIRS CUP 1ST ROUND (1ST LEG), WEDNESDAY 16 SEPTEMBER 1970, EASTER ROAD.
HIBERNIAN: MARSHALL, SHEVLANE, SCHAEDLER, STANTON, BLACK, HAMILTON,
DUNCAN, BLAIR, MCBRIDE, MCEWAN, CROPLEY.

On the Friday after the Malmö game, Hibs chairman William Harrower, who had recently not even been attending the home games, reported that he had sold his shares in the club to 48-year-old millionaire businessman Tom Hart. It turned out that clandestine negotiations had been concluded in the boardroom after the Fairs Cup game. A former Royal Scot, Hart, who had been wounded at Normandy in 1944 and consequently walked with a pronounced limp, was a lifelong supporter of the club and missed very few games home or away. A regular visitor to the boardroom on match days, Hart had often travelled abroad with the official party. A new Hibs-orientated board was immediately installed including the former Hibs goalkeepers Jimmy Kerr and Tommy Younger. Hart took over the reins as managing director with Sir John Bruce as chairman and Ken McIntyre, club treasurer of many years' standing. In an amicable changeover, outgoing directors Pratt and Powrie, who had served the previous board well, were made honorary presidents of the club with an open invitation to the boardroom.

Hart had started his immensely successful building company in 1954, the business going public in 1968. As far as the Hibs supporters were concerned, they could ask for no better person to take over the running of the club. A man of drive, enthusiasm and energy, Hart would bring all the ingredients that had made him successful in business to Easter Road and it was his personal goal to take Hibs back to the top of Scottish football. At the press conference announcing the takeover, the managing director was faced with the time-honoured question: 'Will there be any money available for new players?' He replied, 'Hibs will buy at any time if the need arises.' On the subject of ground improvements, Hart felt that it was too early to comment, but an enquiry as to whether he could be a success at Hibs brought the honest response, 'Yes, but maybe its easier being a success in business than in football.'

The following day, the new owner took his place in the directors' box to watch Hibs record their first win over Celtic at Easter Road for 12 years, a victory that would see the Edinburgh side sitting joint top of the table. Goalless at the interval, Joe McBride scored twice against his former teammates in the second half, but a real team effort saw Hibs running out convincing winners in the end. McBride's opening goal, later described by the player himself as possibly the best of his career, was a 25-yard, left-foot volley on the turn from a Hamilton lob that screamed into the net past the helpless Evan Williams. It would be considered for some time as a candidate for goal of the season.

In the return leg of the League Cup quarter-final at Ibrox on the Wednesday, Hibs' hopes of overturning the two-goal deficit from Easter Road soon evaporated when Rangers scored from a free kick as early as the fifth minute to give the Ibrox side an overall 4-1 lead. McBride missed a great chance to level the game from the penalty spot before Greig gave his side a two-goal half-time advantage. The end result was never in any doubt. Rangers chalked up another 3-1 victory and a 6-2 aggregate win on their way to success over Celtic in that year's final.

Eighteen-year-old Kenny Davidson, who had scored three goals in his first outing for the second team against Cowdenbeath the previous week and another against Aberdeen reserves in only his second appearance in a Hibs shirt, was a surprise inclusion in the party that would make the trip to Malmö for the return leg of the Fairs Cup. Davidson would be the first youngster to benefit from the new managing director's desire to give the younger players at Easter Road European experience. Signed only a few weeks before from Loanhead United, Davidson had made an immediate impact, and it seemed that a brilliant future lay ahead of him. Sadly, as so often happens, after an explosive start the youngster soon lost his way at the club, his demise exacerbated by a severe injury. He would shortly join Dunfermline, before ending his career with Meadowbank Thistle.

The inclusion of Davidson was not the only surprise to be announced by Macfarlane. Bobby Duncan, who had not even been included in the squad for the first leg, and had yet to feature in the first team that season, was informed that not only would he be travelling to Sweden, he would be playing. There was a snag, however: Duncan had misplaced his passport, and after a desperate search of his house and the offices at Easter Road, a frantic trip to the Passport Office in Glasgow saw the player provided with a temporary visa.

A makeshift Hibs side with Duncan at right back, Stanton at centre half, Jones at inside right and Davidson making his first-team debut on the right wing, was still far too good for the Swedes. Trailing by six goals, and well aware that the tie was already well beyond them, Malmö themselves fielded only seven of the players who had played in Edinburgh.

With such a commanding lead and perhaps finding it difficult to raise their game, sluggish Hibs produced neither method nor industry in the first 45 minutes, and were forced to respond to a dreadful start after Bo Larsson gave Malmö the lead.

In the second half it took the visitors only 60 seconds to heed Macfarlane's half-time team talk when Duncan, who was making a satisfactory return to first-team action, scored his first goal since his strike against Napoli three years before, although not nearly as spectacular. With 13 minutes remaining, a great solo run by Willie McEwan ended in the midfield player giving his side the lead, but this lasted only a few minutes before Jonsson restored the status quo.

It was perhaps only fitting that the game's best player should score the winner five minutes from time, and only then through sheer determination. The majestic Pat Stanton, who had been head and shoulders above anyone on the park, moving forward when the opportunity allowed to assist his attackers, gave Hibs a 9-3 aggregate lead when his powerful header beat Hult after two previous drives had rebounded back to him.

FINAL SCORE: MALMÖ 2 HIBERNIAN 3

FAIRS CUP 1ST ROUND (2ND LEG), WEDNESDAY 30 SEPTEMBER 1970, MALMÖ.
HIBERNIAN: MARSHALL, B. DUNCAN, SCHAEDLER, BROWNLIE, STANTON, MCEWAN, DAVIDSON, JONES, MCBRIDE, BLAIR, (A.) DUNCAN.

The experimental Hibs side, though competent at the back, had been put under pressure several times, often through the poor distribution of Schaedler, but it was in midfield that they particularly struggled and it was obvious on this performance that the signing of an intelligent midfield player was a priority. On the positive side, Davidson had been an outstanding success. At no time overawed, the ball control and acceleration of the teenager had constantly proved a thorn in the side of the Swedish defenders, and as far as the press were concerned the Hibs fans could look forward to a star of the future.

The youngster retained his place in the side on the Saturday, making both his league and home debut, scoring his first goal for the club after only two minutes in a 3-3 scrappy draw with St Mirren, a match punctuated by defensive errors. The charitable mood of the Hibs defence continued seven days later when Motherwell were allowed to take a 4-0 lead and both points at Fir Park. Gordon Marshall was replaced in goal by Roy Baines, making his first-team debut, but this time the erratic display of the rearguard was finely balanced by the inept display of the forwards, and the watching Guimaraes players, Hibs' next Fairs Cup opponents, would have seen their hopes of a good result at Easter Road on the Wednesday bolstered considerably. The entire Portuguese League programme had been cancelled that weekend because of the international match against Denmark in the Nations Cup, and Guimaraes had taken full advantage of this unusual opportunity to spend six days in Scotland.

Entirely in keeping with their poor form at that time, the performance against Guimaraes was perhaps 11th-placed Hibs worst ever in the Fairs Cup, and the fans, spoiled by the many exciting European nights down the years, were not slow in reminding them. After almost 90 minutes of extreme monotony, it was only in injury time that the home side managed to make the vital breakthrough, and amazingly they scored again in time added on, giving them a two-goal advantage to take to Portugal.

There had been no goals and precious little excitement in a lacklustre opening 45 minutes, although Blackley, playing in an unfamiliar midfield position, had tried manfully to break the deadlock, but even his efforts proved woefully inadequate. The midfield problems that had troubled Hibs all season were again well in evidence, but fortunately for them Guimaraes were also found wanting as an attacking force. In the second half the visitors seemed content to knock the ball about in midfield to no end purpose for long periods, producing little danger and even less excitement, and slow handclapping echoed around the sparsely filled terracing.

Newcomer Davidson was again the solitary ray of light in 90 minutes of mediocrity. Running himself to a standstill in a heroic effort to inspire his teammates to raise the pace of the game, the inexperienced youngster should have been withdrawn far earlier than the 82nd minute, when he was replaced by Cropley.

A Graham effort only just shaved the post near the end in what seemed the final chance of the match, but all the action came in the closing seconds when the game suddenly burst into life. With the fans starting to drift away, there had seemed little danger as Hibs mounted one last attack, forcing a corner on the left. Schaedler swung over an inswinging cross which was met fully by McBride, only for his header to come crashing back off the bar. Somewhat fortuitously for Hibs, the rebound fell at the feet of the handily placed Duncan, who forced the ball home from close range.

With the referee checking his watch deep into injury time and the visitors congratulating themselves at having done enough to secure what they thought a satisfactory result, Stanton scored again with what proved to be the last kick of the game, crashing a tremendous strike past goalkeeper Rodrigues to give Hibs a crucial two-goal lead for the return leg. The Easter Road fans would remember the last time the club had travelled to Portugal with a seemingly unassailable lead, only to be forced to survive a late scare against Porto in 1967, but based on Guimaraes' performance at Easter Road it was difficult to visualise them scoring the three goals necessary to overcome Hibs' lead, even allowing for home advantage.

FINAL SCORE: HIBERNIAN 2. GUIMARAES 0.

FAIRS CUP 2ND ROUND (1ST LEG), WEDNESDAY 14 OCTOBER 1970, EASTER ROAD.
HIBERNIAN: BAINES, SHEVLANE, SCHAEDLER, BROWNLIE, BLACK, STANTON, DAVIDSON, BLACKLEY, MCBRIDE, GRAHAM, DUNCAN.

With the Saturday fixture against Rangers postponed because of the Ibrox club's League Cup commitments, reserve centre forward Phil Gordon, another signing from Edina Hibs, made his first-team debut against Hearts in the final of the East of Scotland Shield at Easter Road. Originally signed as a full back but quickly converted to a striker, Gordon was currently the top scorer in the reserves, and as a reward for his goalscoring prowess he was included in the party that would make its way to Portugal for the return leg. A Blackley penalty in the later stages of an uninspiring game was enough to bring the Shield back to Easter Road and increase Hibs' winning margin in the series to 43 against Hearts' total of 41.

Failing to take heed of the experience of Bobby Duncan the season before, Hibs were again dogged by a passport problem before the trip to Portugal. Discovering only at the airport that his permit had expired, Willie Hunter was forced to make a mad dash through to Glasgow to obtain a temporary visa before catching the next flight to Portugal, finally arriving five hours after his teammates and missing the opening training session.

A tremendous second-half fighting display under the sweltering Portuguese sun stunned their opponents and eventually gave the Scots a deserved passage into the next round. Two first-half goals from the home side in conditions more suited to sunbathing than football, cancelled out Hibs' lead from Easter Road and at that stage the Scots were facing an early European exit. On a partly tree-lined pitch with a liberal but adequate covering of greenery which was unusual for that part of the country, the visitors looked down and out after an insipid first 45 minutes but in the second half it was a different story: a Graham goal, his first in Europe, was enough to give his side an overall victory.

Beginning the second half much the better side and playing some fine football, Hibs took control of the midfield with Stanton and Hunter in particular in inspirational form. The visitors had several early chances to take an overall lead, none easier than when Hamilton missed an open goal just before Graham fired narrowly past with only the keeper to beat. With Guimaraes still capable of posing a serious threat, goalkeeper Baines, making his first European appearance, was required to demonstrate his bravery and agility on more than one occasion.

Davidson replaced Hamilton on the hour mark, and his introduction provided the Hibs forward line with a guile and intelligence that had been sadly lacking earlier.

A great run by Graham came to an undignified end when he was brought down just outside the box, and it was from the resulting free kick that Hibs scored the goal that would earn them a passage into the third round draw. Spotting the keeper out of position as he lined up his defensive wall, McBride cleverly sent a low cross to the unmarked Graham, who had little difficulty in crashing the ball into the net. The goal visibly affected the home side, who thereafter failed to mount a serious attack. In the end the superior fitness of the visitors told. Local fans in the 12,000 crowd mercilessly taunted Guimaraes for their second-half failure, in truth, although the end result was slender, they had been beaten over two legs by the better side.

FINAL SCORE: GUIMARAES 2. HIBERNIAN 1.

FAIRS CUP 2ND ROUND (2ND LEG), WEDNESDAY 28 OCTOBER 1970, STADIUM MUNICIPALE.
HIBERNIAN: BAINES, SHEVLANE, SCHAEDLER, BLACKLEY, BLACK, STANTON, HAMILTON, GRAHAM, MCBRIDE, HUNTER, DUNCAN.

A heavier than usual rainfall at the beginning of November caused the league game with Rangers at Easter Road to be cancelled on account of the waterlogged pitch – the Morton match the previous Saturday had been abandoned after only 35 minutes' play in driving rain, which had restricted the attendance at Cappielow to well under 3,000, and there had been few complaints when referee Jim Callaghan called a halt to proceedings in the first half, out of concern for the players' safety. It had not been a great day for full back Erich Schaedler. Running late, he had left his Penicuik home by taxi only to discover on arriving at Easter Road that he had missed the team coach. Making a mad dash for Waverley Station to catch a westbound train, he reached Glasgow with barely enough time to make the connection to Greenock, finally arriving at the ground just in time for the kick-off. His titanic efforts had all been for 35 minutes of farcical football.

Manager Willie Macfarlane was highly critical of referee Callaghan's decision even to start the game. Perhaps the first sign that all was not well behind the scenes at Easter Road came in an official statement released on the Monday said that that the club was distancing itself from the managers comments, 'wishing to abide by all referees' decisions in any circumstances, and keep in line with officialdom'.

Much of the fluency and consistency of the previous season had now gone and only two points were gathered from the following three games including a 2-1 defeat in the rearranged match against Morton. There was even more concern over the news that the exciting teenage discovery Kenny Davidson, who was being carefully nursed along with only the occasional first-team outing, had broken a bone in his ankle against St Johnstone reserves. Although the injury was not thought to be overly serious, it would mean the player missing several weeks of the season at a stage crucial to his development. There was better news for the supporters, however, when it was announced that John Blackley, who had been on the open-to-transfer list for some time, surprisingly, failing to attract any offers, now reopened negotiations with the club. That same day, goalkeeper Thomson Allan, who was now number three in contention for a first-team place, submitted a written request for a transfer.

Liverpool were to be Hibs' next Fairs Cup opponents and Bill Shankly took the opportunity to watch Hibs in action in the rearranged home game against Rangers. The Liverpool manager found the match 'very brutal, but interesting'. He would have been impressed by Hibs' tenacious 90-minute battle to record a well deserved victory. Twice behind, the home side had fought back bravely with two goals by Jim Blair to level the scores at 2-2, when with 15 minutes remaining, Willie Johnston of Rangers was sent off after an altercation with the centre forward in Hibs defensive line-up as the visitors were preparing to take a free kick. Blair was booked for his part in the incident. Six minutes before the end Johnny Graham scored from close range to seal a famous victory. It had taken two-goal Blair some time to settle at Easter Road. After almost four months at the club, apart from a goal in the 6-0 drubbing of Malmö in the Fairs Cup, the player had scored his first league goal in Hibs colours only seven days before in a 1-0 victory over Kilmarnock. Now, with three goals in two games under his belt, the former St Mirren player was beginning to live up to his early promise.

The profit and loss accounts for the 1969–70 season released at the AGM in November had again made obvious the necessity to transfer at least one player every season. Although the sale of Cormack and Marinello had raised almost £200,000, a profit of £24,777 was revealed for the 12 months ending 31 July – compared to £3,637 the previous year. Income during this time had increased substantially from £204,894 to £264,665, due in no small part to the rise in admission charges at the beginning of the season. Admission to the terracing now cost 6/-, with a proportionate increase for both the stand and the enclosure. Wages, administration costs and the acquisition of Blair, Duncan, Schaedler and Graham had seen expenditure rise from £202,304 to £244,670. Proceeds from the Development Club had doubled from the previous year to just over £8,000, and there was an excess at the bank of £54,000.

It was around this time that Hibs advertised for a full-time coach to assist manager Macfarlane. Confident that the attractive post and generous salary would attract a high calibre of applicant, both Hart and Younger motored to Carlisle on the final day of November to interview a prospective candidate. Despite some fanciful guesswork by the media suggesting that Tommy Docherty, then manager of Porto, might be in the running, the successful applicant was revealed as former Manchester City player Dave Ewing, who was a friend of Tommy Younger and a former colleague of Bobby Johnstone in both the 1955 and 1956 FA Cup Finals. After retiring from the playing side of the game, Ewing had been a coach at Manchester City under the guidance of Malcolm Allison, and had been an integral part of the backroom staff during the highly successful period that had seen City win the League Championship in 1967–68, and the FA Cup, and Cup Winners' Cup in successive seasons. Seeking a fresh challenge, he had joined Sheffield Wednesday as coach only at the beginning of the season. Although reportedly surprised at the speed of the appointment, he was nevertheless delighted to take up his new position at Easter Road.

The Scotland versus England Fairs Cup clash had created a colossal interest among the fans and stand tickets for the game at Easter Road had been quickly sold out. Liverpool requested as many tickets as possible in order to satisfy the demand on Merseyside, with thousands of supporters expected to make their way north by car, bus and special train, with at least six plane-loads of supporters planning to fly to Edinburgh for the game.

A printing mistake on the match tickets indicated that they were for a first-round tie, third leg, instead of the reverse, but with no time to reprint them, the tickets were pressed into use and are no doubt a prized collector's item today.

With excitement mounting by the day as the match approached, less than 24 hours before kick-off the Hibs fans were astonished to learn that Willie Macfarlane had been sacked. It transpired that the manager had refused to bow to a demand from Tom Hart that both Johnny Graham and Joe McBride be removed from the starting line-up for the game. Macfarlane included both players in the party that made its way to Hibs' pre-match retreat at Gullane, and had been asked to resign. Defiantly refusing to relinquish the post, Macfarlane was sacked on the spot and Dave Ewing appointed temporary manager. The following morning, after barely a week at the club, Ewing accepted the manager's position on a permanent basis.

Behind the scenes a personality clash between the chairman and Macfarlane had been evident for some time, and Macfarlane himself was convinced that Hart's interference in the team selection was no more than a thinly veiled attempt to force his resignation, with Ewing already signed as a replacement.

The decision to axe Macfarlane provoked outrage. Tom Hart could not be contacted, PR man Tommy Younger had no comment to make. *The Scotsman* commented: 'The club has become so much smaller because of this decision. Macfarlane has been sacked as a result of a judgment that was mishandled monumentally.' The *Daily Mail* admitted bewilderment: 'On the eve of one of the most important matches in the history of the club, Hibs have managed to behave as though they were intent on some sort of football suicide.' *The Daily Record* went further: 'Scottish soccer has seldom witnessed a sadder or more sickening scene than the self-humiliation of the once proud Hibs.'

The public and media alike were united in support of Willie Macfarlane who had walked away with his dignity intact and his head held high. He himself observed: 'A board of directors have the prerogative of choosing the manager and of sacking him if he is a failure, but while he is still in charge he must be allowed to exercise his judgement.'

In his first interview, the new manager promised to be his own man regarding team selection but for whatever reason, there was still no place for McBride in the starting 11, with Hibs' top European goalscorer having to settle for a place on the bench. There was no place for Graham in either. The decision to axe McBride was a monumental gamble. Only one goal behind top scorer Duncan in all games that season, the former Celtic player had clearly upset Hart in some way.

Since gaining promotion from the Second Division at the end of the 1961–62 season, the Anfield club under Bill Shankly had earned a fearsome reputation. Winners of the League Championship twice in the following four seasons, they had continued this successful run by defeating Leeds United in the 1965 FA Cup. Losing to Borussia Dortmund in the 1966 Cup Winners' Cup Final at Hampden after beating Celtic in the semi-final, Liverpool had since gone through a transitional period, but the current team were thought by many in the game to be even better than the previous side. Ever-present in the European competition for the past seven years, the side contained players of the calibre of 1966 World Cup winner Rodger Hunt, Emlyn Hughes, Ian Callaghan, Peter Thompson, Ron Yeats and John Toshack, who had been signed from Cardiff City for £100,000 just in time to take his place at Easter Road. As well as the established internationals, the side was packed with players who would soon make their name on the same stage such as Tommy Smith, Steve Heighway, Larry Lloyd and Ray Clemence. Eighteen-year-old Alun Evans, a £100,000 signing from Wolves, would miss the game in Edinburgh because of injury.

For several days before the game an industrial dispute by Electricity Board workers had paralysed the country with regional blackouts, and for a while it was thought that the game might be in danger. Although the Easter Road area had not been included in any cuts planned for that evening, there could be no guarantee that power would not be disrupted during the match. Consequently, the large crowd that was expected to attend the game were advised by the police to carry torches, as would their own officers in the vicinity of the stadium. Although the Hibs floodlighting system contained its own emergency back-up, the generator could not cope with the demand of also lighting the approaches to the ground. As it was, fears of a blackout proved unnecessary and the game proceeded uninterrupted.

Showing little indication that the disruption behind the scenes had affected them, and only too aware of the renowned attacking abilities of their opponents, Hibs took the game to Liverpool from the start and were denied a stonewall penalty in the opening minutes when Davidson was cynically pulled back in the box as he prepared to shoot.

During the opening period the home side held the upper-hand although most of their good play was restricted to the middle of the park, rarely troubling goalkeeper Clemence. Hibs failed to utilise the pace of Davidson and Stevenson on the flanks to pose a threat deep in their opponents' half and the home support were repeatedly frustrated at their persistence in sending high crosses into the opposing penalty area which were easily mopped up by Clemence and the giant Liverpool defenders.

As the game wore on, Hibs' over-cautious approach allowed the visitors to reassert themselves in midfield, and with Stanton in a less commanding mood than usual, Liverpool took control of the game.

The 30,296 crowd, a great number chanting for Macfarlane and McBride throughout the 90 minutes, helped to create a white-hot atmosphere inside the ground as they frantically urged their favourites to make the breakthrough, and Duncan almost scored with a header in one of Hibs' rare attacks on goal.

Showing little of their expected flair, Liverpool often seemed content merely to retain possession, although the pace of Heighway and Scots-born Brian Hall frequently posed a potential threat to Baines' goal. Conscious that at least one goal was needed to take to Merseyside, the home side tried all they knew to make the breakthrough as half time loomed, but were constantly denied by an experienced and confident Liverpool rearguard.

The second half continued in the same vein, with most of the play confined to midfield and Hibs perhaps guilty of showing their opponents far too much respect.

With little sign of the home side making a breakthrough, the fans got their wish when McBride replaced the ineffective Davidson on the hour mark. The youngster, now fully recovered from his ankle injury and making his first start in six games, had tried manfully, but it was asking too much of the slightly built attacker to make an impression against the rugged, red-shirted defenders, who were a totally different proposition from the non-physical continentals he had previously faced in the competition.

McBride took the field to a deafening roar from an expectant home support and made an immediate impact, with Hibs coming close on several occasions.

The big talking point of the game came in the 63rd minute. McBride started a move in the centre of the park, sweeping the ball out wide to Stevenson on the left. Stevenson's measured cross was met by Arthur Duncan, who rose majestically to head past Clemence, but the cheers of the huge crowd were silenced in mid-roar when the East German referee, who had had an otherwise impeccable game, disallowed the goal, indicating that Duncan had fouled the goalkeeper, a decision hotly disputed by the home side.

The power of McBride had given Hibs a new impetus, and spurred on by an excited and enthusiastic crowd it seemed almost certain that they would get at least the draw that their spirited performance deserved, when a simple mistake by Black, his first of the evening, cost the home side the game with just 14 minutes left to play. In attempting to clear a harmless ball, Black made a dreadful hash of the clearance and the ball fell straight at the feet of Heighway just inside Hibs half. Quickly sizing up the situation, the tricky Irishman set off at speed down the wing and his pin-point cross found Toshack, who was on the spot to nod past the helpless Baines to score his first goal for his new club.

With ten minutes remaining, Hamilton was introduced in place of Stevenson as Hibs attempted to take something from the game, but they were unable make the vital breakthrough and now faced an almost insurmountable task in the second leg against a side that had yet to concede a goal at home in the competition.

FINAL SCORE: HIBERNIAN 0. LIVERPOOL I.

FAIRS CUP 3RD ROUND (IST LEG), WEDNESDAY 9 DECEMBER 1970, EASTER ROAD.
HIBERNIAN: BAINES, BROWNLIE, SCHAEDLER, BLACKLEY BLACK, STANTON, DAVIDSON, MCEWAN, STEVENSON, BLAIR, DUNCAN.
LIVERPOOL: CLEMENCE, LAWLER, LINDSAY, SMITH, LLOYD, HUGHES, HALL, MCLAUGHLIN, HEIGHWAY, TOSHACK, THOMPSON.

A major concern for the new manager was the fact that Hibs had now gone four games without scoring a goal, but in front of just over 5,000 spectators against Dunfermline on the Saturday, Easter Road's smallest crowd of the season so far, Jim Blair scored what were to prove his last goals for the club. Despite a double by the former St Mirren player, Blackley put past his own keeper late in the game to earn the hard-working Fifers a well deserved 2-2 draw.

By this time the off-form Schaedler had been replaced by Mervyn Jones at left back, but with only two goals scored in the previous five games, it was obvious that Hibs' problems were not at the back, and a discouraging no-score draw in Glasgow against part-time Clyde seven days later provided little confidence for the trip to Merseyside in midweek.

John Hazel and Johnny Graham were added to the squad that made its way to Merseyside. There was a triple boost for Hibs with the news that three influential Liverpool players were fighting a fitness battle. World Cup winger Thomson and record signing Toshack were struggling with injuries received the previous Saturday, as was full back Lindsay, but in his own inimitable style Bill Shankly dismissed this as a reason for Hibs to be confident, stating that, 'Celtic came here five years ago a goal in front and still lost, and teams of the calibre of Juventus and Honved have also failed here. Hibs are one down, and are playing in front of the Kop. Need I say more?'

Thomson and Toshack failed a late fitness test, their places being taken by Boersma and the veteran Ian Callaghan. Future Liverpool manager Roy Evans replaced Alec Lindsay at left back in one of only 11 first-team appearances by Evans in over ten years as a player at Anfield.

Written off by the bookies and the press, and stung by Shankly's dismissive pre-match comments, Hibs fought with typical Scottish ferocity to prove the doubters wrong and within minutes of the start they had their opponents reeling when the lightning fast Duncan sped past full back Roy Evans before sending over a tantalising cross that McBride met with awesome power, only to see his goal-bound header saved magnificently by Clemence.

After a tense opening exchange, Liverpool, roared on by the Kop, shrugged off their early hesitancy, and as in the first game at Easter Road, quickly took control in the middle of the park.

Duncan and Stevenson, who had the beating of Lawler and Evans in the opening period, were creating problems down the flanks, but their distribution was woefully poor and consequently the moves provided little danger in the Liverpool penalty area.

The home side opened the scoring after 24 minutes and yet again it was defensive slackness that cost Hibs dear. Hughes easily dispossessed Blair deep inside the Liverpool half, to send a wonderful through ball to Heighway on the halfway line. As Heighway turned to make his way into the Hibs half, the ball struck him on the back, completely wrong-footing centre half Black. The centre forward took full advantage of this fortuitous break, proceeding at full speed towards his opponent's penalty area as the previously solid Hibs defence retreated in his path. Letting fly from just inside the box, Heighway's half-hit shot was blocked by Baines, but the keeper could only watch in agony as the ball trundled over the line and into the net. Living up to their manager's pre-match promise to attack, Hibs refused to let their heads go down, and Duncan had the best chance of the night just minutes after Heighway's goal when a McBride overhead kick created an opening, but again Clemence who on this performance looked a future England goalkeeper, produced yet another breathtaking save to deny the Hibs man.

The big support that had made their way from Scotland for the game saw Hibs play their best football of the season, finding gaps in the Liverpool defence time and again, but on reaching the danger area they came up against a goalkeeper in defiant mood.

Liverpool had been the better side in the first half – more compact, faster, and deserving of the lead – but Hibs had been far from disgraced. Had they taken their chances, they may well have gone in at the interval ahead.

Inspired by skipper Stanton, Hibs started the second half in positive mood, but within five minutes of the restart the game was as good as over and yet again it was down to a terrible blunder by the defence. Full back Boersma, wide on the right, sent over a speculative lob that appeared the goalkeeper's ball all the way. Drawn to his near post, Baines remained rooted to the spot and could only watch helplessly as the ball sailed over his head and into the far corner of the net.

With the game now seemingly well beyond Hibs, Liverpool could relax. Urged on by the majority of the 37,815 crowd, they attempted to play some neat, clever football, but the visitors were having none of it. At the back, Brownlie was combining well with Stanton and Blackley to prevent the home side from increasing their lead, but once again Hibs' main problem was in front of goal. McBride tried manfully but was left on his own too often, and when a chance was created, the wide men persisted, as in the first game in Edinburgh, in sending high balls into the Liverpool penalty area that were easily swept up by the giant defenders.

The introduction of Graham and Hamilton for Blair and Stevenson saw an improvement, but by then it was far too late. With the saving of the game now well behind them, a persistent Duncan had two great efforts scrambled to safety by the keeper, and in the closing minutes a Graham effort rebounded from the left-hand post, with Clemence beaten.

FINAL SCORE: LIVERPOOL 2. HIBERNIAN 0.

FAIRS CUP 3RD ROUND (2ND LEG), TUESDAY 22 DECEMBER 1970, ANFIELD.
LIVERPOOL: CLEMENCE, LAWLER, EVANS, SMITH, LLOYD, HUGHES, HALL, MCLAUGHLIN, HEIGHWAY, BOERSMA, CALLAGHAN.
HIBERNIAN: BAINES, BROWNLIE, JONES, BLACKLEY, BLACK, STANTON, DUNCAN, MCEWAN, MCBRIDE, BLAIR, STEVENSON.

The game at Anfield was Joe McBride's last for Hibs. Only a few weeks before, an initial bid from Dunfermline for the centre forward had been rejected, but incredibly, with Hibs now in the middle of a severe goal drought, having scored only twice in the previous six games, one of the most prolific goalscorers in the country was allowed to cross the Forth for a fee in the region of £4,000. As if to prove Hibs wrong, McBride was on target for his new side on the Saturday, in a 5-0 whitewash of Ayr United; meanwhile, his former teammates were going down 1-0 to Dundee United at Easter Road.

More transfer speculation surrounded the club at this time. Only weeks after accepting a new deal, the unsettled John Blackley again asked for a transfer, and it was also rumoured that Newcastle United would be sending a delegation to watch Pat Stanton at Tynecastle on New Year's Day.

The on-field unrest was mirrored by apathy on the terracing. With the exception of the matches against Rangers and Liverpool, the previous five home games had been played before an average of less than 6,000 spectators, well below the season's overall average of just under 16,000. It was now imperative that both Ewing and Tom Hart made winning back the missing fans their top priority.

For a third consecutive year the New Year's Day derby was to end goalless, and for Hibs in particular, the saga continued. With the exception of the two scored against Dunfermline in mid-December, it was now 720 minutes since they had found the net, and both themselves and Hearts could have played for a week and still not have broken the deadlock. The fans on both sides of the Edinburgh divide were united for once as they showed their displeasure at the dreadful fare on offer by jeering the respective combatants throughout the entire 90 minutes. Hearts were slightly the better side for most of the game, but during the final 20 minutes, still fortunate to be level, Hibs created three golden chances to steal the points but were again found lacking in front of goal. The first came after 73 minutes of abject boredom, Hibs' first effort on-target all afternoon. A sadistically heartless referee extended the match by adding three minutes of injury time, which was more than enough for those that had already suffered the previous 90, and the final whistle came as an overdue relief for all concerned.

In the match against Cowdenbeath at Easter Road the following day, Saturday 2 January 1971, Hibs were attempting to secure their first double of the season. A crowd of only 7,267 could be bothered to turn up for the traditional holiday fixture and once again, those that stayed away were the lucky ones. A Blackley penalty in the second half ended Hibs' goal famine and silenced the slow handclapping for a while, but it required a goal three minutes from time by the recalled Davidson, the best player afield, to earn his side a 2-2 draw against a team that had been rooted to the foot of the table since the opening day of the season and would be relegated after just one term in the top division. As the depressed Hibs fans made their way from the ground, the disappointment of the poor result paled into insignificance with the breaking news that 66 people had lost their lives at Ibrox that afternoon when a barrier at stairway 13 had collapsed during a Rangers-Celtic game.

It was first thought that a last-minute equalising goal for Rangers scored by former Hibs player Colin Stein had brought the thousands of fans already leaving the ground at the fateful stairway hurrying back up towards the pitch, only to be met by a rush of jubilant spectators exiting the stadium at the final whistle, resulting in a massive crush. However, it is now believed that a youngster being carried down the stairway on the shoulders of an adult had fallen, causing hundreds of fans to collapse on top of each other. The death toll made it Britain's most costly football disaster and one that deeply affected the entire population, including football supporters of every persuasion.

A disaster fund was set up, and in line with countless other organisations throughout the country, the Hibs Supporters Club sent a cheque for £100 and Hibernian FC sent a substantial donation plus the proceeds from a match.

On the following Saturday at Parkhead both Celtic and Hibs took the field wearing black armbands in respect of the fans who had tragically lost their lives only five days before. A minute's silence was meticulously observed by everyone inside the ground. Played out in an almost surreal atmosphere, a Celtic side rarely needing to find top gear secured both points with a 2-1 victory that meant it was now ten games since a win for the Edinburgh men, although in the circumstances the result on the day meant little after the terrible tragedy at Ibrox earlier in the week. Stanton had put an air of respectability on the scoreline when netting right on the final whistle, but in reality the game was never as close as the scoreline would suggest, the result meaning that Hibs had now dropped to 11th place in the table.

The urgent need for a goalscorer was now an obvious priority and in a move that was as surprising as it was sudden, Dave Ewing travelled to Sunderland to sign former Easter Road favourite Joe Baker. Since leaving Edinburgh almost exactly ten years before, Baker had done the rounds at Torino, Arsenal and Nottingham Forest before settling with Sunderland, scoring goals galore along the way. Baker's return to Edinburgh was far removed from his less that elegant departure from Easter Road in 1961. At that time his teammate John Fraser's father-in-law ran a small pig farm on the outskirts of the city. With plenty of time on his hands in the afternoons it was Fraser's job to collect the pigswill from numerous locations around the city in a small van. The van was also often used to transport colleagues to and from the railway station on training days, some having to be squashed into the space normally reserved for the collection of the discarded and often odious foodstuff. Baker had asked Fraser to collect him from the station and take him to meet a deputation from Torino at an Edinburgh hotel to conclude the transfer negotiations that had been ongoing for some time. In what could be considered the modern equivalent of a million-pound transfer deal, not many players nowadays would arrive for negotiations in a pigswill van. After the deal had been concluded Baker left the hotel carrying a small bag containing his part of the signing-on fee... in cash. How things have changed.

Cult hero Baker made his home debut the second time around against Eddie Turnbull's Aberdeen who were sitting proudly at the top of the League Championship table, four points ahead of nearest challengers Celtic. The Dons had gone 15 games without dropping a single point and goalkeeper Bobby Clark had not conceded a goal for 1,093 minutes – more than 12 games, a Scottish record. Baker replaced Blair in the Hibs attack with the former St Mirren player relegated to the substitutes' bench. Blair had not lived up to expectations at Easter Road, scoring only five times in the championship and another in the Fairs Cup. Placed on the open-to-transfer list, within a few weeks he would return to St Mirren in a cut-price deal.

The return of Joe Baker guaranteed a big turnout and a well above average crowd of 23,402 saw captain-for-the-day Baker, resplendent in new white boots, lead the team onto the field. When told of Baker's return to Easter Road, former teammate Eddie Turnbull's reply had been characteristic: 'Joe will be welcomed back by the Hibs fans and will add to the crowd, but he doesn't worry us at all.'

A hard-fought game remained goalless at half time, but only thanks to a fantastic goal-line clearance by Blackley. Centre forward Harper beat Baines with a low shot and had already turned away to celebrate the goal, when somehow Blackley managed to get back to clear off the line as the ball slowed in the mud.

With the pace at times frantic, a goal just had to come and when it did it was scored by Hibs. In the space of a few minutes in the second half, Clark's 12-games-unbeaten record was shattered twice, first when a raging shot by Stanton screamed past the helpless keeper to give Hibs the lead, and four minutes later when Baker himself scored with a header to cap a fairytale return to the club. Hibs had to endure a few nervous moments after Robb scored for Aberdeen late in the game, but overall it was a deserved and welcome victory for the home side, their first since defeating Rangers ten games before, and one that lifted them three places up the table. Since losing to Liverpool the forward line had undergone a complete transformation. Only Duncan remained from the front line at Anfield, the others replaced by O'Rourke, Baker, Hamilton and Davidson.

Failing to be registered in time to take part in the first round of the Scottish Cup, Baker was forced to sit out the game against Forfar at Easter Road, but even without their new signing, Hibs were still far too good for the Second Division side. Three goals by O'Rourke and a double from Stevenson on his return from injury sent Hibs on their way to an emphatic 8-1 victory and a meeting with rivals Hearts at Tynecastle in the next round.

Before then, Baker celebrated his first away league match in Scotland for almost a decade by being sent off late in the game in a 3-1 defeat at Love Street. The mist that hung over the ground all afternoon closed in, making visibility extremely difficult, but not enough to cloud the view of referee Crawley who clearly saw Baker tangle with Ian Munro in the Saints penalty area.

Scottish Cup fever had gripped Edinburgh since the city's bitter rivals had been drawn together in the competition for the first time since 1966, and on a sunny afternoon at Tynecastle a well above average crowd of 30,450 awaited the start with mounting excitement. John Hazel gave Hibs the lead when he opened the scoring in the first half, only for Hegarty to level after the break, but a magnificent second-half goal by Arthur Duncan, who raced fully 40 yards with the ball, brushing aside the despairing tackles of three Hearts defenders on the way, before crashing a great left-foot shot high into the corner of the net past the helpless Jim Cruickshank to give Hibs their second Scottish Cup win at Tynecastle since 1910. Centre forward Joe Baker had had the satisfaction of playing in both victories, with his own special memories of Hibs' last Scottish triumph at the ground in 1958 when he had scored all four of their goals. Apart from victory in the Scottish Cup five years before, Hearts had now failed to overcome their city rivals at their own ground since 1963.

Only two championship wins from their previous 13 starts were statistics that made it unlikely that Hibs could secure a Fairs Cup place by virtue of a league placing, leaving only the Scottish Cup as a possible avenue into Europe, a fact that would evoke no great confidence among the supporters, who were well aware that it had now been 69 years since Hibs last success in the competition.

Third-round opponents Dundee stood between the Easter Road side and a place in the semi-final at Hampden. The Dark Blues made their intention of taking Hibs back to Dens Park for a replay crystal clear: in a bruising struggle against a side listing only two forwards, they were prepared to employ negative spoiling tactics throughout. Only a Jimmy O'Rourke goal from the penalty spot in the first half, after Baker had been sent crashing to the ground by centre half George Stewart, separated the sides, and Hibs were through to face Rangers in the semi-final at Hampden, their ninth Scottish Cup encounter since the war.

During the match a policeman was injured when trouble erupted between rival fans at the Hawkhill end of the ground, an outbreak that culminated in over 20 arrests. The management were quick to condemn the violence. Throughout the history of the game there had been the occasional outbreak of trouble, but the recent alarming increase in hooliganism was a trend that was set to blight the game in the UK for over two decades. In certain Latin South American countries where it had been endemic for years, moats and high fences were standard crowd control features. The steady rise in the number of incidents of violence at matches throughout Europe had prompted UEFA to remind member clubs at the start of the previous season of their responsibility for the behaviour of their fans. The disciplinary committee had since been given sweeping new powers to order a match to be forfeited by up to a 3-0 scoreline if it had to be abandoned due to a pitch invasion or similar outbreak, with potential further punishment such as ground closure for UEFA competitions. Manchester United, AC Milan and Glasgow Rangers had already been warned that more trouble involving their supporters at home (or away, in the case of Rangers), could lead to banishment from the competition. During the Ibrox side's Fairs Cup semi-final against Newcastle United at St James Park two seasons before, the Glasgow fans had run riot after Newcastle doubled their one-goal lead. Missiles had been hurled and a pitch invasion had delayed proceedings until the police managed to restore order.

Perhaps guilty of ignoring the league to concentrate solely on European qualification by way of the Cup, all four championship games in the run up to the semi-final had ended in defeat with Eric Stevenson sent off at Kilmarnock along the way. Dismissed for retaliation after being fouled for the umpteenth time, Stevenson had never before been booked in ten years since signing as a professional. The poor run of results meant that Hibs were now anchored firmly in 13th position in the table, dangerously close to the relegation zone.

For a third consecutive season Hibs were drawn against Rangers in the Scottish Cup. Played at the national stadium, both sides contested a torrid and rough semi-final. In a game sometimes degenerating into a kicking match, the Edinburgh side more than held their own in that particular department. Matching the expected physical challenge of the Ibrox side, Hibs possibly surprised Rangers with their tigerish application and for a period they had the Light Blues on the back foot. But with Hibs continuing their inadequacy in their opponent's penalty area, it was no surprise when the game finished goalless, meaning the replay would take place at Hampden five days later.

In the dressing room after the game, a reporter hovering about outside the changing rooms overheard Dave Ewing describe Rangers as 'rubbish', and the next morning the comment was plastered all over the back pages of the newspapers, much to Rangers' fury. Not everyone disagreed, however. One reporter asked three neutral managers watching from the stand their off-the-record opinion, and all agreed with Ewing. Furthermore, added the scribe, the majority of Rangers supporters exiting the stadium at full time were of the same opinion as the Hibs manager.

Ewing's outburst did nothing to improve relations between the teams in the replay, another torrid game. While Hibs were the better side for spells, Rangers scored the goals that took them through to the final and yet another meeting with Celtic. With the scores level at 1-1 midway through the second half, Johnny Graham missed a golden opportunity to give his side the lead – after beautifully beating two opponents, he shot weakly into the goalkeeper's arms with the goal gaping. It was to prove an expensive miss. Just minutes later, Henderson scored the winner for the Ibrox side.

Yet another season of disappointment can be summed up perfectly by the outcome of the final three league games for Hibs: winning one, drawing one and losing the other. Hibs fans were surprised to say the least to discover that Erich Schaedler would be at centre forward against Dunfermline in the penultimate game at East End Park, the full back's inclusion in the forward line supposedly intended to put pressure on centre half Cushley. Whether the experiment worked or not is open to question, with the match finishing 3-3. In the final game against Clyde, Hibs recorded their biggest victory of the season, winning 5-1 in front of just 3,800 spectators, the lowest crowd at Easter Road for several years.

Meanwhile, Hearts had fought their way through to the final of the inaugural Texaco Cup, losing over two legs to Wolverhampton Wanderers. But regardless of the mickey-taking inflicted on the Tynecastle fans by their Hibs counterparts over the Maroons' participation in what was seen as a joke cup, the fact is that Hibs couldn't even qualify for this consolation Cup, finishing 12th in the table. Neither could Hearts, who finished only one place better off.

In a season that had started so promisingly, only 47 goals had been scored in 34 league games – the same number as in the near relegation campaign of 1962–63 – while 53 had been conceded. Of the 34 games played, only ten had ended in victory, with ten drawn, Hibs ending the season a massive 26 points behind the 56 recorded by champions Celtic who, under Jock Stein, were winning the league for a sixth consecutive season. Although featuring in only a third of Hibs games since returning to Easter Road in January, Joe Baker ended the season as top league marksman with eight goals, two ahead of O'Rourke. Both Blair and McBride, neither of them still at the club, came next with five.

Gordon Marshall, Thomson Allan, Bobby Duncan, Colin Grant and Mervyn Jones were among the free transfers announced by Ewing. The inclusion of Jones was a surprise as he had been the man in possession when the season ended. John Murphy and Johnny Hamilton were placed on the open-to-transfer list.

A proposed close-season tour of America, Canada and Bermuda was cancelled almost at the last minute because of trouble with travel arrangements relating to the stay in Bermuda – the visit to the Caribbean island had been the main attraction and so Hibs decided to withdraw completely. A 14-day visit to Majorca was hurriedly arranged, including a game against the island's top side Real Majorca that ended in a 2-1 victory for the visitors.

One of Dave Ewing's last duties at Easter Road was to pay a £50 fine after he mistakenly submitted an incorrect team sheet before a game, listing Davidson's name instead of Eric Stevenson. Although he was understood to have signed a five-year contract after succeeding Macfarlane, on 7 July, just weeks before the start of the new season, he offered his resignation, stating a preference to return to coaching in England. Whether it was his own decision or that of Tom Hart, the resignation left the way clear for the people's choice to make his return to Easter Road.

11

Turnbull Comes Home
and Disaster in the Scottish Cup Final

1971–72

FOR JOHN BROWNLIE, what had already been an exciting summer was about to improve beyond the youngster's wildest imagination. Arriving home from the trip to Majorca contemplating a restful few weeks before the start of a new season, the full back was staggered to be notified that he had been selected for the Scotland party to tour Denmark and Russia. Although the squad had been severely depleted by injuries and withdrawals, it was nevertheless still an incredible honour for a player who had been a full-time regular for less than a year and had yet to feature in the Under-23 set-up. Expecting to go along only to make up the numbers, he was delighted to be right back for the game against Russia. The 19-year-old, who had already proved that he had the temperament for the big occasion, emerged from the 1-0 defeat as one of Scotland's top performers with a bright international future ahead of him.

Dave Ewing's surprise resignation had brought the usual lobbying of replacements in the media, including a far-fetched rumour that Tommy Docherty had been spotted in the vicinity of Easter Road several times. But only one name was seriously in the frame: that of former Hibs legend, Eddie Turnbull.

After leaving Easter Road abruptly in March 1963, Turnbull had spent a short spell as trainer at Queen's Park and had made an immediate impression at Hampden. Since their relegation from the top division at the end of the 1957–58 season, Queen's had drifted around the bottom few places in the table, once finishing second-bottom, but the amateurs had finished seventh in Turnbull's first season and fourth the following year, gaining him a reputation as a deep and revolutionary thinker on all aspects of the game and it seemed certain even then that the former Hibs player would not remain in the Second Division for long.

In March 1965 a prominent newspaper reporter had suggested that Turnbull would be well in the running to take over from the recently sacked Tommy Pearson if he applied for the manager's job at Aberdeen. At the interview, however, Turnbull had been dismayed at the lack of ambition that seemed to permeate a club that had won the championship and the League Cup only ten years before. Giving his prospective employers an indication of his forthright personality, he enquired as to the level of success that would be expected of him. He was met by a mystified silence, and when informed that he would be notified once the other interviews had been completed, Turnbull said that the train back to Glasgow was at six o'clock and if he had not heard by then, he was off. Soon after, he was told that his application had been successful.

Aberdeen had been drifting aimlessly in the lower reaches of the league since winning the championship in 1955 and finishing runners-up the following year, occasionally managing to finish only as high as 6th in the table and generally failing to achieve their crowd-pulling potential. Like Willie McCartney at Easter Road before the war, Turnbull had inherited a team that was in the doldrums. Within a short time he had cleared out the dead wood and brought in his own players, many of them youngsters signed on the recommendation of the legendary talent scout Bobby Calder. Although the transformation took some time to effect, Turnbull's talents as a coach, strict disciplinarian and, above all, supreme tactician, were soon in evidence and there was a marked rise in the club's fortunes, culminating in Scottish Cup success over Celtic in 1970. Under his management, with the team almost unbeatable at home, Pittodrie became a virtual fortress and Aberdeen gained a reputation as a tough, disciplined and skilful side. There is no doubt that Eddie Turnbull was responsible for laying the foundations for their incredible success in the late '70s and early '80s.

As far as Tom Hart was concerned there was only one man to lead his new revolution at Easter Road, but the matter was complicated by the fact that he and Turnbull had fallen out many years before. The shrewd Hart approached Stewart Brown of the *Edinburgh Evening News* to act as an intermediary. Brown contacted Turnbull's wife, Carol, to discover that she had failed to settle in the Granite City and that Turnbull might just be receptive to a move back to the capital. A meeting was arranged in a St Andrews hotel, and it is now history that he accepted Tom Hart's proposition and motored south to take up his new appointment in Edinburgh on 13 July 1971, only 24 hours before training was due to start for the new season.

At Pittodrie, preparations for the new season were already well under way and there was widespread disbelief that Turnbull could even consider leaving to join a club ten places and 24 points below them in the table. One of Turnbull's last duties there was to rubber-stamp the signing of a very young Willie Miller, a player who was destined to become an Aberdeen legend in the not too distant future.

It is difficult to fully convey the excitement generated in Edinburgh at the news of Turnbull's return. As far as Lawrie Reilly was concerned, Turnbull was Hibs' best signing in years. Gordon Smith was even more to the point: 'There are three good reasons for welcoming him back. He has the confidence of the directors, he knows football from A-Z, but thirdly and most importantly, he is a Hibs supporter.' The fans saw the signing as a masterstroke, a sentiment reflected by the secretary of the Hibs Supporters Association, who had no doubt that every one of his members would be ecstatic at the appointment.

Turnbull himself, pleased to be 'home', stated in his first interview that he believed he could achieve the same success at Easter Road that he had at Pittodrie: 'Aberdeen may have better gates at the moment, but Edinburgh has more potential and I have lots of promising talent to work with at Hibs.' Tom Hart commented, 'We have always seen Eddie Turnbull as a Hibs man.'

As Turnbull prepared to take his first training session at the Hawkhill sports ground, two other newcomers were meeting their teammates for the first time. European Cup winner Bertie Auld had been Dave Ewing's last signing, had come in the close season from Celtic and was joined at Easter Road by goalkeeper Eddie Pryce, a Scottish Junior international signed from Kirkintilloch Rob Roy.

As part of his strategy to make Hibs one of the top teams in the country, Tom Hart decided to resurrect the third team, which had been discontinued for financial reasons in the early '50s. Former player Stan Vincent was appointed to take charge of the youngsters, who would once again play in the East of Scotland League. At the same time, Cecil Graham, who would give many years of loyal service to the club, replaced Dan McKay as secretary.

One of Turnbull's first decisions was to select a seat for himself in the directors' box, from which vantage point he felt a clearer understanding of the proceedings could be obtained than at the trackside. On the first day's training, he was handed a shabby tracksuit with holes in the knees, and just as he had done when taking over at Aberdeen, he immediately ordered the substandard training gear to be thrown on the boiler-room fire and replaced with the existing playing kit. Brand new strips were then ordered for the players. A lesson he had learned from Harry Swan, in whose time Hibs had been the smartest side in the country, was the psychological importance of players being smartly turned out. On the Friday afternoon before every home game, Swan had inspected the playing kit hanging in the dressing room, ordering replacement or repair as necessary – a practice Turnbull would continue.

His first game in charge, a pre-season friendly at Easter Road against Middlesbrough on Saturday 31 July 1971, gave an indication of just how lax discipline had become when, instructed to be at the stadium no later than two o'clock, the players drifted into the ground, several arriving after the allotted time. The wrath of the keenly disciplinarian manager left them in no doubt as to what would be required of them in future. They were informed that from now on two o'clock *meant* two o'clock. The players would become accustomed to the inflexibility and commitment of the new boss. Once, when Aberdeen had been playing in Glasgow, he had ordered the Danes, Petersen, Mortensen and Ravn, who had made arrangements to meet up with their wives at a party organised for them by some of their fellow countrymen, to travel back to Aberdeen by coach as per club rules, only to hire a taxi to take them the 100 or so miles back to Glasgow. In fairness, Turnbull himself in later years would concede that he had been far too strict on this occasion, but it showed the measure of the man and his single-minded determination to succeed.

Days after the 0-0 draw with Middlesbrough, Hibs played host to German side Schalke in another pre-season friendly. Before the game, 79-year-old Jimmy McColl was presented with a gold watch by Hibernian Football Club as a token of appreciation for his years of loyal service at Easter Road. It seems fitting that the presentation was made by Gordon Smith, often described by McColl as the best player he had ever seen. Although no longer required to do anything over-strenuous, McColl was still officially part of the set-up. He was the only man in the history of the club to be associated with what is now recognised as the three great sides: that of the Harper, McGinnigle, Dornan, era; the Famous Five period; and Turnbull's Tornadoes, whose emergence lay a few months in the future. Joining McColl on the pitch before the game was a former teammate from the '20s, Johnny Halligan; perhaps to whet the appetite of the supporters for better things to come, the pair were joined by the Famous Five, all of them receiving tremendous applause from the supporters.

Gordon Marshall and Thomson Allan had both been freed during the summer, leaving Hibs short-handed in the goalkeeping department. First-choice Roy Baines had been injured during pre-season training, leaving Eddie Pryce as the only goalkeeper. The youngster was pitched into the first three friendlies – against Middlesbrough, Schalke and the return fixture against Middlesbrough at Ayresome Park. Although he had acquitted himself reasonably well, Turnbull felt it was unfair on the inexperienced player, and he looked around for a more seasoned campaigner. Jim Herriot had played for Dunfermline against Hibs in the 1965 Scottish Cup semi-final before joining Birmingham City and winning several international caps with the English First Division side; another claim to fame was that Reg White, a fanatical blues fan, used his name as a nom de plume for his highly successful 'It Shouldn't Happen to a Vet' books and television series. The goalkeeper had been in dispute with Birmingham and had had loan spells with Aston Villa and Mansfield, but was now a free agent playing for South African side Durban City on a short-term contract. Turnbull realised that the experienced 31-year-old would be a solid signing and Herriot wasted little time contemplating the move to Edinburgh, making his debut for Hibs in a 2-1 defeat in a friendly against York City at Bootham Crescent. Although he had signed, he had not yet been officially registered and the wily Turnbull took a chance, playing him under the name of second-team goalkeeper, Pryce – given that Herriot was a Scottish international, it is extremely surprising that few people realised who he was.

At that time a 14-year-old Craigroyston schoolboy named Gordon Strachan had been signed on an s-Form registration during the summer. Hibs fanatic Strachan would not be at the club long. Just weeks after signing, a financial dispute arose between the manager, who knew nothing about the youngster, and Strachan's father, suggesting that it would perhaps be best if he continued his football education away from Easter Road.

On the competitive front, the impact of Turnbull's guidance was immediate with a League Cup section involving Motherwell, Dundee United and Kilmarnock won, with two games still to play. The 4-1 victory at Tannadice meant that after four games, Hibs were now the top scorers in the competition and the only side in the country with maximum points. Only one point was eventually dropped from the 12, the setback coming in the final section game against Kilmarnock in Ayrshire, a venue that traditionally gave the Edinburgh men great difficulty. Apart from an impressive display by goalkeeper Herriot, the only thing of note in a dull, no-score draw was the first appearance of what was to become the recognised defence for some time to come: Herriot, Brownlie, Schaedler, Stanton, Black and Blackley, although on this particular occasion Blackley was at right half, Stanton on the left.

Fourteen goals scored in the six section games, with only three conceded, was testimony, even this early, to the many hours spent by the defence on the practice pitch. Only too well aware that all good sides were based on a solid defensive set-up, Turnbull had taken the players, particularly the back four and goalkeeper Herriot, for specialised defensive tactical training until they were totally conversant with each other's play. Afternoon after afternoon there were games of four against two, six against three and numerous other permutations. Every single move that it was possible to encounter on a football pitch was explored and practised. On match days the players began to demonstrate what would be an almost telepathic understanding of each others play.

The 1971–72 league campaign kicked off at Tynecastle. In brilliant sunshine, the drabbest Edinburgh derby match for many a year, and there had been plenty recently, was decided when Cropley and Hamilton both scored for the visitors in the final six minutes of the game. The 2-0 scoreline meant that Hearts had failed to beat their city rivals in the league at Tynecastle for eight seasons, and had now gone six games against the Greens failing to score a single goal.

In the quarter-finals of the League Cup, Hibs were drawn against Turnbull's hometown side, Falkirk. Despite being a goal behind at the interval at Brockville after a 'soft' penalty kick award had been converted by former Hearts captain George Miller, the Greens looked in a comfortable position with the second leg still to come, until conceding a farcical second goal late in the game when Herriot and Black collided going for the same ball, leaving Young an easy task to double the inspired Bairns lead.

The return leg at Easter Road was an uncompromising affair as Falkirk, perhaps understandably, employed spoiling tactics in an effort to preserve their two-goal lead. O'Rourke celebrated his 25th birthday by opening the scoring early in the second half, but try as they might, the elusive second goal that would have taken the tie into extra time proved beyond Hibs. The experience of Baker, who had been injured in the section game against Motherwell in Edinburgh nearly a month before, was again badly missed, and although Hibs had a couple of penalty claims turned down by referee Bobby Davidson, Falkirk – who, according to Turnbull 'had come to do a job and achieved their aim' – deserved due credit. Pat Stanton, however, was more to the point when he stated, rightly, that the damage had been done in the first game at Brockville.

Hibs' 100 per cent league record was surrendered at Motherwell at the beginning of October when they could only manage to draw 1-1 in front of a disappointingly low crowd of 5,757. Johnny Hamilton gave the Greens a first-half lead, but Dixie Deans, who would prove to be a thorn in the side of the Edinburgh club over the next few years, equalised late in the game.

Seven days after Celtic had inflicted their first championship defeat of the season, Hibs visited Aberdeen. Prior to the kick-off, Eddie Turnbull, who was making his first appearance at Pittodrie since moving to Easter Road, received a presentation from the Aberdeen players in recognition of his services to the club. There would be no more gifts, and goals from Joe Harper and Edinburgh-born Willie Young cancelled out an earlier goal by Arthur Duncan to ensure that Hibs made the long journey back to Edinburgh pointless.

Johnny Graham was not considered to be part of the new manager's long-term plans, and he was transferred to Ayr United. Graham was joined at Somerset Park several weeks later by Eric Stevenson, at that time the longest serving player at Easter Road. Turnbull, who had been instrumental in securing Stevenson's move from Tynecastle to Easter Road in 1960, had made several attempts to sign him while at Aberdeen, only to be turned down flat by Bob Shankly. Although Stevenson had not figured in the first team except as a substitute since the victory at Tynecastle six weeks before, Turnbull was keen to retain his services at Easter Road. Stevenson, perhaps feeling that his best years were behind him, insisted on the move to Ayr – a huge mistake. Within a few short months the wing wizard with the mesmerising ball control would retire from the game almost obscenely prematurely.

As Stevenson was making his way to Ayrshire, Alex Edwards was signed from Dunfermline for a bargain fee of £13,000. Edwards, who had something of a 'bad boy' reputation in the game, was at the time currently suspended for four weeks after a dismissal, but was also in dispute with the club and working on a building site. It was against the rules to sign a player while he was under suspension, but the shrewd Turnbull pleaded ignorance to the infringement, for which he was admonished with a caution. Capped for Scotland at amateur, youth, Under-23, and inter-league levels, the tricky Edwards had earned a tremendous reputation for skill and there were few others capable of matching his reading of a game and his passing ability. He was to play a major part in the transformation of Hibs and their success during the following few seasons.

In other transfer activity around this time, Chris Shevlane joined Morton on a free transfer and goalkeeper Eddie Pryce was released.

October proved to be a bad month, Hibs managing to take only three points from five games. One of the few bright spots was the comprehensive 6-0 drubbing of Falkirk at Easter Road. Joe Baker made his long awaited comeback from injury, but the day belonged to Arthur Duncan, who ran riot, scoring four of the goals and laying on another.

At the beginning of October a Golden Goal competition designed to raise funds for improvements to the stadium was launched by the Development Club, the winning ticket corresponding exactly in minutes and seconds to the time of the first goal scored at that day's game. By an incredible coincidence, Pat Stanton's wife Margaret purchased a ticket before the home game against Dunfermline at the beginning of November and duly won herself £50 when her husband scored Hibs' first goal at the time stated on the ticket. The 2-0 victory saw Hibs rise to third place in the table.

With his suspension now completed, Alex Edwards made his eagerly awaited debut at Broomfield in a two-each draw. Former Hibs player Derek Whiteford scored both Airdrie goals in the first half after Hibs had taken an early lead. After the interval, stubborn persistence by the Greens earned due reward when Blackley equalised with a spectacular drive that gave goalkeeper Roddy McKenzie no chance. Edwards had made an impressive first start for his new side, doing more than enough to suggest that he would be a valuable acquisition in the months ahead.

At a ceremony in the clubrooms in midweek, Stanton once again proved a popular winner when previous recipient Chris Shevlane travelled through from Greenock to present him with the Hibernian Supporters Association Player of the Year award for a second time.

Something big was about to happen at Easter Road and people were starting to sit up and take notice. Ian McNiven, writing in the *Edinburgh Evening News*, could not recall any Hibs team moving out of defence and into attack at such pace: 'The Turnbull stamp is already showing clearly in the teams style, and in a triumph for teamwork every man plays his part as the games are won playing controlled and skilful football.'

Alex Edwards scored his first goal the club in a 3-2 victory against Kilmarnock at Easter Road on 27 November, and it was one to remember. Collecting the ball near the halfway line, the diminutive midfielder let fly with a tremendous drive from all of 30 yards that bent just inside the post before bulging the back of the net to the obvious satisfaction of the 9,000 Hibs fans.

A run of four straight wins was brought to an end against Morton at Cappielow when Erich Schaedler turned the ball into his own net after just three minutes. Thereafter, inspired goalkeeping by Eric Sorensen, particularly in the second period, made it difficult for the Edinburgh men, who had to be content with a share of the points after O'Rourke levelled the scoring midway through the half.

For only the fourth time since the war, Hibs were involved in a game played on Christmas day. Coincidentally Rangers would be the Yuletide visitors to Edinburgh for a second time, but there was to be little Xmas cheer for Hibs. Nine wins from their previous ten games suggested that the Glasgow side would be difficult adversaries, but Alex Edwards hit top form and Hibs totally dominated a 90 minutes that should have been over by half time had it not been for poor marksmanship in front of goal. Cropley missed the best chance of the game when he blasted wide with the goal gaping as Hibs carried on where they had left off after the interval, with McCloy in the Rangers goal repeatedly keeping his side in the game with several outstanding saves as Hibs turned on the pressure in an attempt to turn their dominance into goals. With just seconds remaining and the game still goalless, Rangers scored what was to prove the winning goal in one of their rare excursions into Hibs' half. Goalkeeper Herriot, defending at the Dunbar end of the ground, appeared to be deliberately nudged by Johnston as he came to collect a cross from the right, allowing Stein to score from close range. Despite furious protests that the keeper had been impeded, the referee allowed the goal to stand, Rangers leap-frogging Hibs into third place in the table.

As usual the new year started with the traditional fixture against Hearts, this time at Easter Road, but for a fourth consecutive year the holiday game ended goalless. Every player gave his all to break the deadlock, but although the game was exciting for the spectators it was mostly all effort with little skill. In the opinion of one newspaper reporter, the ball was in danger of ending up black and blue from the hammering it received. Hearts had now failed to score against their great rivals in seven derby games, although Hibs themselves had scored just four times against the Gorgie men during the same period. Four Hibs goalkeepers had shared the honours of having kept a clean sheet in the seven games – Gordon Marshall, Roy Baines, Thomson Allan and now Jim Herriot. Willie Wilson had been in goal the last time Hearts had breached the Hibs rearguard in September 1968.

In the other holiday game a few days later, East Fife, who would finish the season just one place above the relegation zone, achieved what Hearts had failed to do in over three seasons when they scored twice to defeat Hibs 2-1 at Bayview. As against Rangers on Christmas day and Hearts seven days later, the Greens would be left to rue a host of missed chances that had now cost them five championship points. The defeat was to prove even more disappointing when Alex Edwards, who had promised Turnbull on signing that his days of indiscipline on the football field were over, was sent off for retaliation just after the restart after being fouled by John Love. John Brownlie would join Edwards at the next sitting of the SFA disciplinary panel, after receiving his fourth booking of the season in the same game.

Speculation that an Everton bid for Alex Cropley was imminent was rife in the city. Just before Christmas, Everton had sold 1966 World Cup winner Alan Ball to Arsenal for £250,000; according to unconfirmed reports, Arsenal manager Bertie Mee had been on his way to Edinburgh to sign Cropley when he heard of Ball's availability and had diverted to Merseyside instead.

After the barren holiday spell, Stanton scored Hibs' first goal of 1972 in a 3-0 home victory over Dundee United. Arthur Duncan and John Brownlie were Hibs' other marksmen, with the full back in particular delighted with his first league goal from a spectacular drive. His only other counter had been in a friendly match against Elgin City. Taking charge of United in one of his first games for the club after replacing the long-serving Jerry Kerr in the Tannadice hot seat was the recently appointed former Kilmarnock and Dundee player Jim McLean, a long-time admirer of Eddie Turnbull's managerial methods.

The traditional annual dinner dance, which had been reintroduced by Eddie Turnbull, took place in the North British Hotel in mid-January. The event, popular with players, guests and dignitaries alike, had been allowed to lapse since Harry Swan's death. But Turnbull recalled that in his playing days the social gathering had performed a significant part in fostering team spirit and camaraderie, and its revival was viewed as an important step in the further rebuilding of a club whose exciting, fast-flowing football was beginning to draw the crowds back to Easter Road where the average gate was now well over the 17,000 mark.

At the beginning of the year, Aberdeen's Joe Harper topped the goalscoring charts with 20 goals; Donald Ford of Hearts was in fourth place with 15. The highest-placed Hibs players were in ninth position, with O'Rourke, Duncan and Hamilton all on eight. Since the injury to Joe Baker earlier in the season and his operation just before Christmas, Hibs had lacked a natural goalscorer. Turnbull now travelled to Tannadice to sign Alan Gordon from Dundee United for the bargain price of £12,000, which was to prove a shrewd bit of business for Hibs, the player being the final piece of the jigsaw in a side that would soon gain fame as Turnbull's Tornadoes. After the deal had been concluded, a bemused Jim McLean confided to the Hibs manager that he felt he had been 'done' in letting Gordon go so cheaply. Since making his debut for Hearts as a 17-year-old schoolboy in 1961, Gordon had developed into a prolific goalscorer with particularly lethal prowess in the air. Perhaps unfairly, the fondest memory retained by Hibs supporters of Alan in a maroon shirt came on the last day of the 1964–65 season at Tynecastle, with Hearts needing to score just one goal to win the League Championship on goal average from their opponents that day, Kilmarnock. With Hearts trailing 2-0 and just minutes of the match remaining, Gordon struck an accurate shot that appeared net bound all the way, but at the very last second Kilmarnock goalkeeper Bobby Ferguson somehow managed to get a fingertip to the ball to divert it to safety. The save denied Hearts the League Championship and gave Gordon nightmares for years to come.

By season 1966–67, no longer an automatic first choice at Tynecastle, he had decided on a short-term move to South Africa to play for Durban United. Scoring almost a goal per game in Durban, things were going well on the field for him, but with his family homesick they soon decided to return to Scotland and Hearts. A move to Dundee United quickly followed. In his three seasons at Tannadice Gordon had scored more than 50 goals, hence the interest from Eddie Turnbull.

Gordon made his Hibs debut in a home defeat by Motherwell at the end of January 1972. Although he failed to figure on the scoresheet, he linked up well with his new teammates and generally did enough to suggest that Hibs had made yet another exciting capture.

By now the fans were well aware that a club like Hibs needed to sell at least one player each year, and this again became apparent when it was revealed that a loss of £40,500 had been incurred during the latest financial year, compared to a profit of £7,200 in 1970. Good runs in the Fairs, League and Scottish Cups had seen gate receipts rise by over £4,000 in the previous 12 months, but this was counterbalanced by a £7,000 drop in revenue for league games. Wages had increased by £15,000 and Turnbull's insistence that Hibs players should be well rewarded for their efforts suggested the problem would only get worse. Input from the Development Club had doubled from the previous year's donation, to £16,000, but even allowing for the expense incurred in the refurbishment of the new offices and gymnasium in the Main Stand, the figures were extremely concerning and there was little guarantee that things would improve the following year, when VAT would be levied on admission charge for the first time.

Away from the financial worries, even the most pessimistic Easter Road supporter began to think that this just might be Hibs' year in the Scottish Cup. Paired against League Cup holders Partick Thistle at Firhill in the first round, Alan Gordon scored his first goal for the club in a 2-0 victory. Erich Schaedler scored the other, also his first for the club, and it had been worth the wait. Taking a throw-in just level with the 18-yard line on the left, the full back found Gordon with the ball. Receiving a headed return from the centre forward, Schaedler met the ball on the volley and his tremendous 25-yard thunderbolt screamed past the helpless Alan Rough in the Thistle goal to safeguard Hibs' place in the next round.

Alex Edwards was missing from the Firhill line-up after being banned for eight weeks and fined £60 in midweek after his dismissal against East Fife. As he had been sent off five times and booked on 15 other occasions, his disciplinary record was difficult to defend. However, another player appearing before the same committee for the sixth time in his career had been suspended for only seven days. This lack of consistency was extremely frustrating. It was difficult to fathom just how each individual case was dealt with and the savage sentence received by Edwards caused many to wonder if the player was a marked man. At the same meeting, Brownlie was suspended for a week and fined £25 for his four bookings.

In mid-February Joe Baker made his long-awaited return from injury when he was listed as substitute for the league game at Brockville. Johnny Hamilton stunned the Falkirk defence and the many supporters still attempting to gain admission to the ground when he opened the scoring inside the first ten seconds with what many thought to have been the fastest ever goal scored in Scotland – but that record was actually held by Willie Sharp of Partick Thistle, who had scored against Queen of the South in only seven seconds in 1947. In a rough and often stormy game fought out at a frantic pace by both sides right from the start, the refereeing fell far short of the required standard. In the 35th minute Cropley was involved in an incident with Alec Ferguson which left the Hibs man crumpled on the ground. As the game raged on, the referee repeatedly signalled to Cropley to get on with things and eventually the diminutive Hibs forward managed to limp to the touchline for treatment. Although he was keen to return to the fray, he was immediately replaced by Baker. It was later discovered that Cropley had broken his ankle; he would not play again that season. As the player received treatment in the dressing room, the bad-tempered and bruising encounter continued. Ferguson, who had been a persistent offender all afternoon, was sent off in the second half after yet another foul on Schaedler. Baker set up Hibs' second goal for Alan Gordon before scoring the winning goal himself, diving full length to head home a spectacular cross from a suspiciously offside-looking position to give his team a hard fought 3-2 victory.

A brilliant goal by Alan Gordon and a tap in by Baker were enough to see off Texaco Cup finalists Airdrie in the second round of the Cup. The first was a beauty. Collecting a pass from Stanton 25 yards from goal, Gordon beat three defenders as he made his way into the penalty area before smashing an unstoppable left-foot drive high into the net. Baker's goal, after good work by Gordon had created the opportunity, was the centre forward's first Scottish Cup strike for the club since scoring against Hamilton exactly 11 years before all but a day.

It was around this time that Turnbull's unique style of management came to the fore. Immediately after a league victory over Clyde, the entire first-team squad was taken to Turnberry for a week's holiday. There was to be no training, with golf and relaxation the order of the day. The players were encouraged to take it easy after what had been a hard season, with the culmination still to come.

In the third round of the Cup, Hibs and Aberdeen were drawn together for the 14th time in the past 50 years, Hibs trailing 9-4 in the series. In the days leading up to the game, Easter Road season ticket holders were furious to discover that the briefs, with the exception of those held by debenture holders, would not be applicable for the game, a decision that resulted in a multitude of letters of complaint both to the newspapers and to the club itself. Previously, a season ticket had always guaranteed admission to all domestic matches and it was felt that the directors were exploiting the expected huge demand for the game. One supporter complained, 'The powers that be seem to forget that when the team weren't doing as well as at present, with attendances around the 5,000 mark, it was the season ticket holders who helped make up the numbers paying in advance for the privilege.' Another said, 'As a ticket holder of over 20 years, I protest at the lack of thought the present management have for the loyal support that have paid the price of a season ticket year after year without knowing how the team would play.' He finished by complaining that with the concessions for the game also suspended, 'old age pensioners were being ruthlessly written off, and future loyal supporters too'.

The Hibs Supporters Association joined in the protest. Secretary O'Donnell voiced his concern over the closure of the boys and OAPs gate for the game, insisting that young fans in particular should be encouraged in every way possible, not forced away.

At that time, many First Division clubs claimed that, solely in the interest of safety, there would be no OAPs' or boys' gates for the big games – in Hibs' case, those involving the Old Firm or Hearts – but if a youngster or pensioner was willing to pay full price, these safety concerns were conveniently overlooked. Completely missing the point, a statement released by the club suggested that the Easter Road fans more than received value for their season ticket money, pointing out that Aberdeen supporters were charged £11 and Hearts supporters £12, so at £9 Hibs were easily the cheapest of the big clubs. Whether the pricing structure influenced the turnout or not, a disappointingly low crowd of only 25,736 watched a game expected to attract at least 40,000. Eight days later the Hearts and Celtic Scottish Cup replay at Tynecastle would attract a crowd of 40,029.

As to the game itself, the road to the semi-final beckoned when Jimmy O'Rourke gave Hibs a dream start after just 17 seconds, and the Edinburgh side's first Scottish Cup win over the Dons for 24 years was assured when Joe Baker scored a second goal shortly after the interval. The speed and trickery of Arthur Duncan constantly troubled the Aberdeen defence, but by far the best player afield was John Blackley who helped blot out the danger of Harper while still finding time to assist his front men.

Around this time, Kenny Davidson made a rare first-team appearance against Dunfermline, and Dennis Nelson, top goalscorer for the reserves, made his debut against Airdrie. Both of these games ended in defeat. With the new manager still finding his feet, league results were inconsistent, with the team hovering just outside the top three places in the table.

Confidence for the forthcoming Scottish Cup tie against Rangers at Hampden was boosted considerably when St Johnstone were defeated 7-1 at Easter Road seven days before the semi-final. Hibs' lowest crowd of the season – just 6,358 – watched the game, but those who decided to stay away were the losers. With all the forwards getting their names on the scoresheet – Gordon twice – Hibs recorded their biggest win of the season. Rangers manager Willie Waddell, watching from the stand, would no doubt have been impressed, even concerned, by the free-flowing football on display, particularly from Edwards and Stanton in midfield.

For a fourth consecutive season Hibs and Rangers met in the Scottish Cup, for a second time at semi-final stage. Although only 12 months had elapsed since the last cup meeting between the sides, Hibs had undergone a considerable change in personnel. Only five of the side that lost after a replay in 1970–71 were involved this time around. Marshall, Jones, Graham and Stevenson had all moved on, Pringle was in the reserves and Cropley was recovering from the broken ankle received at Brockville.

Once the match was underway, the Edinburgh side struggled to find any kind of fluency during the first 45 minutes and deservedly trailed to an Alec McDonald goal at the interval. O'Rourke equalised soon after the restart and the goal injected new life into the Edinburgh team, who improved the longer the game went on, and Rangers were relieved to hear the final whistle.

HIBERNIAN: HERRIOT, BROWNLIE, SCHAEDLER, STANTON, BLACK, BLACKLEY, EDWARDS, O'ROURKE, BAKER, GORDON, DUNCAN. SUB: MCEWAN.

Before the semi-final there had been an outcry by supporters from the east of Scotland regarding the allocation of tickets for the game. Both sides received the normal 20 per cent of the available briefs for the stands and enclosure, about 3,200, with the remainder going on general sale – but only in the Glasgow area. Admission could be gained to the Hampden terracing on the day by paying at the gate, but an Edinburgh supporter wishing to guarantee a seat had had to make the return trip to the west coast, clearly a most unfair situation.

The replay took place nine days later on Monday 24 April, 1972. John Hazel replaced Baker, who dropped to the substitutes' bench, with Gordon moving into the centre forward position. Straight from the start Hibs were by far the more aggressive and determined side. With Edwards and Stanton, in superb form, dictating play from the middle of the park, Rangers quite simply just didn't have an answer. Captain Pat Stanton scored before half time and Alex Edwards settled matters when he stroked home the second goal in 66 minutes after Hazel headed on a beautifully measured cross from Gordon. In no way did the scoreline reflect the balance of play and only poor finishing and some desperate defending by Rangers prevented the Light Blues from suffering their worst cup defeat since being murdered 7-1 by Celtic in the 1957 League Cup Final. Rangers centre half Jackson was reduced to stopping Gordon by any means, fair or foul, and the large, travelling Hibs support were furious that the referee often failed to punish the defender for his at times blatant indiscretions.

HIBERNIAN: HERRIOT, BROWNLIE, SCHAEDLER, STANTON, BLACK, BLACKLEY, EDWARDS, HAZEL, GORDON, O'ROURKE, DUNCAN. SUB: BAKER.

Three days after the semi-final, Hibs' last league game of the season, the fickleness of the football fan was demonstrated when a crowd of less than 9,000, many from the Edinburgh area, were inside Ibrox to watch both teams in action. Considering that the match, just prior to Rangers' victory over Moscow Dynamo in Barcelona, was between both the Cup Winners' Cup and Scottish Cup finalists, it would be a major understatement to describe the attendance as disappointing. Hibs took the opportunity to give 16-year-old Alec McGhee his first start at outside left, but even without the rested Edwards and Duncan they were still far too good for Rangers and the small home support started to melt away long before the end. Bertie Auld, making a rare appearance in the first team, scored the winner, only his third league goal of the season after Rangers equalised O'Rourke's opening goal from the penalty spot. The win temporarily lifted Hibs into third place in the table, but they had to be satisfied with fourth place on goal average when Rangers defeated Ayr United at Ibrox in their final league fixture a few days later, before another very small crowd.

With doubts over his long-term fitness after his serious injury earlier in the season, Joe Baker had been handed a free transfer just 24 hours before the league encounter at Ibrox. He was joined on the list by goalkeeper Baines, Nelson, Pringle, Gillett, Mathieson and half a dozen youngsters.

After a promising start far too many points had been surrendered to teams in the lower half of the table,. The manager's first priority was to ensure more consistency in the coming season. On the brighter side, the younger players in the first team would have benefited from having another year's experience under their belts, but they would be hard pushed by an influx of new talent including Bobby Smith, Derek Spalding, Willie Murray, Alec McGhee, John Minford and the recently signed 17-year-old Tony Higgins. Seemingly well out of the picture at Easter Road just a few, short months before, Jimmy O'Rourke's qualities had been quickly recognised by Turnbull and the stocky inside forward ended the season as top scorer with 15 goals, 11 of them in the league. He too would have a major part to play at Easter Road in the seasons ahead.

During the lead-up to the Cup Final, Hibs' first appearance at the ultimate stage of the competition for 14 years, one half of Edinburgh was awash with intense excitement. Impatient anticipation of the meeting with Celtic, who were chasing a League and Cup double, spread through the city and an overnight queue formed outside the ground to purchase the few coveted stand tickets released by the club. In the morning those at the front of the line were provided with tea by the staff at the adjacent Norton Park School, all hoping that former pupil Alex Cropley would help bring the Cup back to Edinburgh.

On the morning of the match the road to Glasgow was jammed with a seemingly endless convoy of buses and cars bedecked in the green and white of Hibs as perhaps the club's biggest ever travelling support for a Cup Final made their way to Glasgow.

Among the thousands making the trip west, desperate to see an end to the 70-year Scottish Cup drought, were many former players, including the remaining four members of the Famous Five. Gordon Smith, now a regular spectator at most of the home games, had watched all of the cup-ties so far that season. Bobby Johnstone, who had intended to attend the Centenary FA Cup Final between Leeds and Arsenal at Wembley, quickly changed his plans on learning that his former side had made it through to their sixth final since last winning the trophy in 1902. Ormond, who had an important football engagement in the north of Scotland, revealed that nothing would prevent him from making it to Hampden in time for the kick-off. For golf fanatic Lawrie Reilly there was an even bigger sacrifice. Despite winning through to the qualifying stages of the Lothians Golf Tournament, Reilly had withdrawn from the competition to watch his only senior club in the Cup Final instead.

In all reality, the 1972 Scottish Cup Final between Hibs and Celtic was over almost before it had really started. Turnbull's final instruction before the players left the dressing room, had been to remind Alan Gordon to pick up the dangerous Celtic centre half McNeil at corners and free kicks.

Within two minutes of the start John Hazel was harshly penalised for a foul on Johnstone wide on the right-hand side of the pitch. The resultant free kick deep into Hibs penalty area was met by the unmarked McNeil, who swept it past the helpless Herriot and into the net, with Alan Gordon caught ball-watching. The centre forward partly atoned for his mistake by equalising midway through the half as Hibs briefly threatened to make a game of it, but Man of the Match Dixie Deans put his side ahead for a second time from another poorly defended free kick just before half time and the game was already all but over.

After the break Celtic turned on the style, scoring another four times, greatly assisted by poor defending by the Edinburgh side who were quite clearly overawed by the occasion. The third and decisive goal was scored nine minutes into the second half when Deans collected a mis-headed clearance by Brownlie. The former Motherwell player beat Herriot to the ball at the edge of the box, eluded tackles from Blackley and Brownlie and dribbled round the goalkeeper again, before dispatching a right-foot shot into the empty net to the utter despair of the huge Hibs support. Johnstone was in magical form as he continually tore the Hibs defence to shreds, and the final whistle couldn't come fast enough for Hibs and the few Easter Road faithful who had remained to the end.

Eddie Turnbull admitted later that the final had come too soon for his team. Fearing a tongue-lashing from the manager in the dressing room after the game, the shell-shocked players were surprised when told to lift their heads. They would be back, he said, and the next time they would emerge victorious.

SATURDAY 6 MAY 1972, HAMPDEN PARK. ATTENDANCE: 106,000.
HIBERNIAN: HERRIOT, BROWNLIE, SCHAEDLER, STANTON, BLACK, BLACKLEY, EDWARDS, HAZEL, GORDON, O'ROURKE, DUNCAN. SUB: AULD.
CELTIC: WILLIAMS, CRAIG, BROGAN, MURDOCH, MCNEIL, CONNOLLY, JOHNSTONE, DEANS, MACARI, DALGLISH, CALLAGHAN. SUB: LENNOX.
REFEREE: A MCKENZIE (LARBERT).

While in no way compensating for the embarrassing defeat – a record equalling score for a Scottish Cup Final – the cup run had proved lucrative for Hibs. From the semi-final and final alone, they had received £43,000, nearly £10,000 more than winners Celtic. The semi-final gates had been shared equally between the four participating teams, but Hibs had the benefit of the replayed semi-final against Rangers, that gate being divided only between the two sides. However, much more important than the immediate financial reward, was qualification for Europe the following season. Champions Celtic would again take their place in the European Cup, with Hibs as losing cup finalists making their first appearance in the Cup Winners' Cup. For Bertie Auld, his appearance as substitute late in the game would be his last in top-flight football after a career spanning 17 seasons.

12

Tornadoes, League Cup Final Success and the Magnificent Seven

1972–73

EDDIE TURNBULL'S SECOND SEASON as manager at Easter Road was one of high expectation. The cataclysmic Cup Final demolition in May apart, there had been more than enough evidence over the past 12 months to suggest that better days lay just ahead. The inspirational signing of Edwards, Gordon and Herriot had been the catalyst in unveiling hidden depths in the players already at the club, and optimism was high among the supporters that this could at last be Hibs' year, although perhaps understandably the manager would make no predictions regarding the coming season.

In England the unsettled Peter Cormack, who had no wish to play in the Second Division with relegated Nottingham Forest, had been placed on the transfer list at his own request. In recent months there had been rumours that a move back to Scotland could be on the cards, with some talk of a return to Easter Road, but the reported £150,000 transfer fee made this scenario highly unlikely. Within a few weeks Cormack would join Liverpool for £110,000, but he would return to his native Edinburgh before his playing days were over.

In a short pre-season tour of Eire, a no-score draw against Irish Cup winners Cork City denied Hibs a 100 per cent record. Former Hibs goalkeeper Roy Baines was to have lined up against his former colleagues in Cork, but unfortunately he was forced to withdraw at the last minute because of illness. A victory against Home Farm opened the tour and Willie Murray celebrated his first-team debut by scoring two minutes after coming on as a substitute in a victory against league champions Waterford.

The former St Mirren manager Wilson Humphries had been invited by Tom Hart to accompany the team to Ireland, and on his return to Edinburgh he was offered the position of first-team coach at Easter Road. Humphries, a member of the Motherwell side that defeated Hibs in the 1950 League Cup Final and won the Scottish Cup victory against Celtic in 1952, had been manager of St Mirren until January that year, before resigning after a spate of poor results. Delighted to accept Hart's offer, Humphries openly admitted that only the opportunity to work with Eddie Turnbull would have drawn him back into football. Turnbull's reputation within the game was such that the new coach considered it 'an honour to work beside the manager, having been a disciple of his methods for years'.

For a second consecutive season, the 1972–73 campaign kicked off with the sponsored Drybrough Cup, a competition contested by the four top scoring sides in each division. Hibs had qualified for the competition by scoring 62 goals the previous year compared to Celtic's 96, Aberdeen's 80, and Rangers' 71. The games were played under experimental rules that decreed that players could only be offside inside a line drawn the width of the pitch, touchline to touchline, along the 18-yard line. The inaugural tournament had been won by Turnbull's former side Aberdeen, who defeated Celtic in the final at Pittodrie 12 months before. The exciting new competition proved immediately popular with the fans and, perhaps predictably, the final had now been moved to Glasgow.

By this time the green-and-white-hooped collar on the jerseys had been replaced by the more distinctive all-white crewe neck, with the socks reverting back to the more traditional all-green, topped by a broad white band. Wearing the new kit for the first time, Stanton, Hamilton, Gordon and Duncan saw off the challenge of a stuffy Montrose side in the first round at Easter Road to set up a semi-final meeting with Rangers. Unlike the First Division sides, who had all finished in the top four, Montrose had ended the previous season in tenth position in the Second Division but had qualified for the competition by scoring more goals than half-a-dozen of the sides above them in the table.

At Easter Road on the Wednesday evening, Rangers attempted to nullify the speedy, positive, skilful football of Hibs with a typically physical and aggressive performance, but failed miserably. There was only one team in it, and although it took until first-half injury time for Stanton to open the scoring by blasting home an Edwards chip, there was never any doubt that the Edinburgh side would contest the final.

Alan Gordon scored twice in the second half and although Rangers had their chances, so did Hibs. The 3-0 scoreline failed to adequately reflect to the huge gulf between the sides. Rival fans clashed in the covered enclosure behind the Albion Road goal, the bad-tempered, foul-packed game doing little to calm the situation. In the few years since its construction, the covered enclosure had already gained an unwelcome reputation as a trouble spot between rival factions, and the area was fast becoming a major source of concern for the club and the police.

After the victory against Rangers, Scottish Cup holders Celtic awaited Hibs in the final at Hampden. There was a pre-match disappointment for the huge contingent from Edinburgh when it was announced that Alex Edwards had been excluded from the line-up. When asked why the midfield maestro would not be playing, Turnbull replied 'He's just not, that's all.'

Despite initial concern among the Hibs fans, once the game was underway there was little sign of the team suffering from an inferiority complex about facing Celtic so soon after the Cup Final mauling of just a few months before. Gordon opened the scoring as early as the fourth minute when Williams had failed to hold a shot from Stanton. Another strike by the centre forward, added to an own goal by centre half McNeill, gave the Edinburgh men a commanding 3-0 lead with just 30 minutes to play. Although it was not covered in the television highlights later that evening, and was hardly mentioned in any of the newspaper match reports, trouble had flared among the Celtic fans shortly after Hibs scored the third goal and the game was held up for several minutes as the fans spilled onto the pitch.

The break in play seemed to rob Hibs of the cohesion and rhythm of the previous hour. Losing the initiative as Celtic came back strongly to level the score in the dying seconds, Hibs held on grimly under relentless pressure from Celtic to force extra time. In fairness to the Parkhead side, they were so much on top during the closing stages, with Jimmy Johnstone in particularly scintillating form, that it seemed certain they would have won if the game had gone on any longer.

The interval gave Turnbull the opportunity to reorganise the side tactically, and the Celtic fans, who were perhaps expecting a goal rout in extra time, were stunned when substitute O'Rourke, who had replaced Hamilton, renewed Hibs' lead with a magnificent 25-yard thunderbolt in the opening half of added-on time. With just seconds remaining, Duncan put the game beyond doubt when he scored from an impossible angle. True to the manager's vow after the Scottish Cup Final, Hibs had returned, and just as he had predicted, this time they had emerged victorious.

DRYBROUGH CUP FINAL, SATURDAY 5 AUGUST 1972, HAMPDEN PARK.
HIBERNIAN 5. CELTIC 3.
HIBERNIAN: HERRIOT, BROWNLIE, SCHAEDLER, STANTON, BLACK, BLACKLEY,
HAMILTON, HAZEL, GORDON, CROPLEY, DUNCAN. SUBS: O'ROURKE, ROBERTSON.
(G.K.).
CELTIC: WILLIAMS, MCGRAIN, BROGAN, MURDOCH, MCNEIL, CONNOLLY, JOHNSTONE,
DEANS, DALGLISH, MACARI, CONNOLLY. SUBS: WILSON, CONNAGHAN. (G.K.).
REFEREE: W. MULLEN (DALKEITH).

For the second time inside the space of a few days, a game involving the Edinburgh side had been blighted by crowd trouble, and although the bother had appeared to be sparked by the opposition fans on both occasions, Hibs were asked by the SFA for a detailed report on both incidents. The media, particularly in the east, felt that it was time for the authorities to take action against the louts who were driving decent fans from the game.

The Drybrough Cup was paraded around Easter Road before the friendly match with West Bromwich Albion the following Tuesday, Hibs' final game before the season kicked off in earnest. The lustre on the silverware, however, failed to rub off on the proceedings, and the home side's distinct lack of shine allowed the English visitors to leave with a 2-0 victory.

Only that morning Hibs had announced that they would shortly be installing seats in the covered enclosure. In the few years since its construction the 'Cow Shed' had become a magnet for troublemakers and it was felt that seating the spectators would reduce any opportunity for violence, while also making it easier for the police to spot any offenders.

Around this time the manager dismissed newspaper reports that Stoke City and Everton had tabled bids for full back John Brownlie. It was obvious that any team playing well would attract the attention of predators, but Turnbull made it crystal clear that he was building a side at Easter Road, not breaking one up, and neither Brownlie, nor anyone else for that matter, was for sale.

For the first time in many years there had been no new faces at pre-season training, apart from Gerry Adair and John McGregor who had both been signed at the end of the previous campaign, although goalkeeper Bobby Robertson would join the club from Whitburn Juniors later in the month. Robertson had been on the books at Ibrox, but with little opportunity to make the breakthrough he had been released. The 19-year-old would not have long to wait for a first-team opportunity at Easter Road. With Jim Herriot injured, the youngster, a full-time professional for only a few weeks, made his debut against Queen's Park in the League Cup at Easter Road on the opening day of the season.

The amateurs surprised Hibs by taking a first-half lead, and again late in the game when they levelled things to make it 2-2. But with just two minutes remaining, Hamilton scored from the penalty spot and Gordon notched another with the last kick of the ball to give the home side a deserved but mightily relieved 4-2 victory.

On the Wednesday at Pittodrie, with young Tony Higgins making his first-team debut in place of the injured Alan Gordon, Aberdeen took a 3-0 lead into the interval. Hibs managed to pull one back with a fortuitous deflection off Edwards early in the second half, but the big talking point occurred in the 62nd minute, just as the visitors were making a determined attempt at a comeback. Centre forward Harper collected a long through ball deep into the Hibs half but drew up immediately on realising that he was yards offside, and the ball was collected by Herriot. The Hibs goalkeeper side-footed the ball upfield for the free kick to be taken, but at the same moment Harper realised that the referee had not blown for offside and promptly lobbed it over the stranded keeper and into the net. Despite irate protests by the entire Hibs team, the goal was allowed to stand, the 4-1 victory allowing Aberdeen to top the section.

Seventeen-year-old Tony Higgins, a former provisional signing, had joined the full-time staff that summer. He had considered quitting football to study Engineering at university, but had been talked out of the idea by the manager, who was convinced that he had a bright future as a professional footballer. The former Kilsyth St Pat's player, one of the tallest and heaviest in the Scottish League, was not a bruiser, but a cultured ball player with a delicate touch and a good football brain.

On Wednesday 23 August 1972 Hibs gained revenge for the League Cup defeat at Pittodrie by defeating Aberdeen 2-1 in the return at Easter Road. Positively brilliant in the first half and well ahead of anything Aberdeen could muster, the home side went into the halfway break only one goal ahead. Both sides scored in the second period, with Aberdeen hitting the bar in the dying seconds. An equaliser would have been totally undeserved. Although the Hibs fans were not to know it at the time, they had just witnessed the very first competitive outing as a unit of an 11 who were soon destined to become part of club folklore. Very soon their names would trip of the tongue as easily, even today, as those of the famous sides of the '20s and '50s, Herriot, Brownlie, Schaedler, Stanton, Black, Blackley, Edwards, O'Rourke, Gordon, Cropley and Duncan. Hibs, though, were much more than 11 players. Hazel, Hamilton, Higgins, McEwan and Robertson were all vital members of a rapidly improving squad, with McArthur, Smith and Spalding making an appearance as the season progressed.

Aberdeen would eventually top the section on goal difference, but it was immaterial as far as Hibs were concerned, with both teams progressing into the later stages of the tournament. The supporters had become bored by the old League Cup format, and in a bid to entice back the missing fans it was decided that the top two sides in each section should qualify for the next round instead of one. Seeding had also been introduced for the first time. Initially this was to have been for Rangers and Celtic only, but after furious protests it was stretched to include the top four sides of the previous season. The new format initially failed to have the desired success, with attendance figures lower in the earlier stages of the competition than before, but things gradually improved as the competition progressed.

On the opening day of the league campaign, a single flash of genius by Harper was enough to secure both points for Aberdeen when the teams met at Pittodrie for the third time in 17 days.

Seven days later, much to the surprise of the 21,221 spectators packed inside Easter Road, Hibs took the field for the first Edinburgh derby of the season wearing all-green jerseys with white collars and cuffs. The new attire was designed to combat Hearts' Ajax-style strip that featured more white than normal, having just a broad band of maroon down the middle. After discussions with the police, the Hibs board had taken positive steps to combat troublemakers by closing the covered enclosure behind the Albion Road goal. The enclosure would remain closed until seats had been installed.

As to the game itself, Hibs led by a Cropley goal at the interval, but were denied from adding to their lead until late in the game thanks to a magnificent performance by visiting keeper Kenny Garland. Although there was never any real doubt that Hibs would win in the end, a decisive second goal by Stanton helped seal the result. It was now four years since Hearts had scored against their local rivals.

Hibs had already been notified that they would be facing Portuguese side Sporting Lisbon in their inaugural appearance in the Cup Winners' Cup, and immediately after the final whistle against Hearts, both Tom Hart and Eddie Turnbull flew to Lisbon to watch the local side in action. The Cup Winners' Cup was the most recent of the three main European tournaments. Played on a home and away knockout basis, the competition had been inaugurated in 1958, but it was only with the demise yet again of the Mitropa Cup in 1960 that the tournament had finally got off the ground. Italian side Fiorentina had won the first competition, beating Glasgow Rangers 4-1 on aggregate over the two-legged Final, but British teams had been reasonably successful in the tournament since, winning five of the 12 finals so far and supplying the losing finalists in three of the others. Rangers were the holders of the trophy after beating Moscow Dynamo 3-2 in Barcelona the previous year, but had since been banned from European competition for two years by UEFA (a ban that was later reduced to one on appeal) after their fans had invaded the pitch towards the end of the game. In the interests of safety, Rangers captain John Greig had been presented with the trophy in the security of the dressing room after the game.

Like Hibs, Sporting Lisbon had entered the first European Cup in 1955, although they had been eliminated in the first round. Like Hibs, they had also qualified for the competition as runners-up after losing to Benfica the previous season. Then, managed by former West Bromwich Albion and England centre forward Ronnie Allen, they had made a good start to their league campaign by winning the opening game of the season the previous Sunday, watched by Hart and Turnbull.

Although plagued by injuries that severely limited his selection for the game against Hibs, Allen had 16 former or current internationals at his disposal when all were fully fit. An enquiry about how Sporting would fare against Hibs in Lisbon drew a distinct lack of concern from Allen who 'wasn't really bothered how his team played at home, because they were so formidable away'.

For the first time Hibs chartered their own aircraft for the trip to Portugal, and to help defray the cost of the hire, supporters were invited to travel with the official party. The flight, leaving from Abbotsinch, would cost the 80 or so fare-paying passengers approximately £50 each, a saving of around £20 on the normal price.

All of the competing sides in the three European competitions had now been warned as to their conduct, and that of their fans, in a strongly worded letter from UEFA reminding them that the organisers were determined to ensure good behaviour at all grounds through measures that could include declaring matches forfeit, closing stadiums, or excluding clubs entirely from any tournament under their authority. Trouble, however, was the last thing on the minds of the Hibs players, and the 17 who travelled to Portugal all stripped for action apart from youngster John Minford, who had been taken on the trip mainly for the experience.

Both teams took the field at the Estádio José Alvalade in Lisbon to the unlikely strains of Hector Nicol and 'Glory Glory to the Hibees'. The Portuguese officials had somehow managed to obtain a copy of the record from Edinburgh, and the gesture was much appreciated by the players and the travelling fans. Hibs once again sported an unfamiliar strip, this time all-purple jerseys with white trim, white shorts, and purple socks, chosen to contrast with Sporting's normal attire of green-and-white hooped jerseys and black shorts. As Turnbull had promised in his pre-match interview, Hibs attacked straight from the start and Cropley gave the home fans an early scare when his left-foot shot struck the post inside the very first minute. The sheer pace and aggression of the Scots repeatedly created panic among the stunned Lisbon defenders, who clearly had expected Hibs to employ the accustomed negative and defensive tactics in the away leg of a European tie.

For the first 20 minutes or so it was all Hibs. The home-side defenders were left chasing shadows as the Edinburgh side gave a brilliant exhibition of the fast and intelligent play that had become their hallmark in recent months. Only on rare occasions did Sporting Lisbon threaten Herriot's goal, and when they did, they found Black and Blackley in commanding and uncompromising mood. O'Rourke twice had good opportunities to give his side an interval lead, but both times the danger was averted at the last second and the ball scrambled to safety. Urged on by a noisy home support, Sporting tried everything they knew to break the deadlock, but against a disciplined defence the nearest the Portuguese came to threatening Hibs' goal was when Herriot had to look lively and save with his feet after a promising move by the home forwards. Immediately on the restart there was a scare for the visitors when Sporting seemed certain to open the scoring after some good interplay in Hibs' penalty area, but Black somehow managed to clear off the line with the keeper beaten.

So far the game had been played mainly in a fair and sporting manner, but 15 minutes into the second half Herriot was punched in the face by right half Manaca in full view of the referee. To the amazement of the Hibs players, the incident was completely ignored by the referee, who otherwise was having a fine game. Herriot required attention from trainer McNiven. Possibly still concussed by the blow, in a spell of defensive suicide almost immediately afterwards the goalkeeper conceded two goals inside two minutes. Fraguito opened the scoring when he shot home with Herriot stranded, and before Hibs could recover their composure, the home side doubled their lead when the goalkeeper slipped as he went to collect a harmless looking through ball, giving Manaca the easiest of chances to net.

Up until then the Scots had given every bit as good as they got and hardly deserved to be behind, but if the home fans expected Hibs to wilt then they were disappointed. Although Lisbon came close to adding to their lead, Hibs redoubled their efforts to score the vitally important away goal, and in the 66th minute they succeeded when Duncan, utilising his phenomenal pace, darted past his marker, Gomez, to collect a superb through ball from Brownlie before neatly shooting past Damas to score his fourth European goal in seven starts.

FINAL SCORE: SPORTING LISBON 2. HIBERNIAN 1.

CUP WINNERS' CUP 1ST ROUND (1ST LEG), WEDNESDAY 13 SEPTEMBER 1972, ESTÁDIO JOSÉ ALVALADE.

HIBERNIAN: HERRIOT, BROWNLIE, SCHAEDLER, STANTON, BLACK, BLACKLEY, EDWARDS, O'ROURKE, GORDON, CROPLEY, DUNCAN.

Despite surrendering two bad goals inside a chaotic two-minute spell, Hibs' fighting spirit and the goal by Duncan appeared to have given the Edinburgh side an excellent opportunity to progress into the second round. Every man had played his part, but centre half Black had been head and shoulders above the rest. Against a tricky forward line, the defender had looked sharp and decisive, particularly in the air, totally dominating centre forward Yazalde.

After the game, Pat Stanton advised the Portuguese not to make any plans for the next round, backed up by full back Brownlie who warned: 'Wait till we get them at Easter Road, they won't know what's hit them.'

Sportingly, manager Ronnie Allen was full of praise for Hibs' attacking play, decsribing the game as 'a cracking tie', one of the best he had ever seen in Europe. His view was that the end result 'might easily have gone either way'.

Turnbull was justifiably pleased with his side coming back so strongly after conceding two bad goals, but less than pleased with the comments made later by chairman Sir John Bruce who criticised the performance of the team, causing Turnbull to complain furiously to Tom Hart regarding the surgeon's ill-judged remarks. According to the vastly experienced Turnbull, it had been the best away display he had ever witnessed by a Hibs team in all his years at Easter Road, and Bruce's comment was not only unnecessary but also totally inaccurate.

In the dressing room after the game, all the players, backroom staff and officials were presented with wristwatches by their opponents. Turnbull, who smoked at the time, burned his hand on his cigarette as he was talking to his players. Throwing back his arms in pain, he inadvertently knocked the tray of watches that were being carried into the room up in the air. At this, the cheeky Glaswegian Johnny Hamilton had everyone in hysterics when he piped up, 'Time flies, eh boss.' According to legend, the manager then ordered the players to pick up the watches, with the instruction that any broken ones were to be handed over to the directors.

On yet another occasion the chirpy Hamilton had been less than reverent to Turnbull during a training session and the manager had decided to teach him a lesson. With the session ended and his teammates making for the showers, Hamilton was 'invited' to take part in a further training session. Put through the mill with punishing runs up and down the huge main terracing and various other forms of torture, the player, to give him his due, completed his tasks without complaint, although at the end he was almost on the point of collapse. Eventually deciding that Hamilton had learned his lesson, Turnbull brought the session to an end. As the player showered, Turnbull returned to his office to attend to some paperwork. A short while later there was a knock at the office door and the irrepressible Hamilton peeking in to thank the 'Boss' for the extra training, adding that it had been 'great'.

An Alan Gordon goal was enough to give Hibs both points against East Fife at Bayview before facing Dundee United twice in four days. In the League Cup tie at Tannadice, Hibs were a goal behind at the interval, and two down within a minute of the restart, but in a magnificent turnaround the Easter Road side proceeded to turn on the style to run up a convincing 5-2 victory that did not flatter United; in all probability, Hibs had already booked their place in the quarter-finals even before the return leg at Easter Road. Three times inside the final few minutes they should have added to the lead, including a goal-line clearance from a Gordon effort. At the end United manager Jim McLean gave due credit, asserting that there was no disgrace in losing to the best side in Scotland. The game was Erich Schaedler's 100th in a Hibs jersey, and the full back celebrated the occasion by being carried off with concussion midway through the second half. Although he soon returned to the fray, in the dressing room afterwards he could remember nothing of the game.

The sides met again in the league three days later at Easter Road. Level at the interval thanks to a strike by Gordon, two goals in the final two minutes of the match, courtesy of another strike by Gordon, and an own goal by Copeland, lifted Hibs to the top of the table and set them up for the return leg of the Cup Winners' Cup.

Sporting Lisbon had followed their opening-day victory with a further two wins and now shared top spot in the table with Benfica. Arriving in Scotland on the Monday evening they trained at Meadowbank on the Tuesday morning before embarking on a sightseeing tour of Edinburgh, always a popular excursion for visitors to the beautiful capital city. Sporting were of the opinion that any British side that beat them would go on to win the cup. When they themselves had won the trophy back in 1964, they had defeated Manchester United along the way. Since then they had lost to Arsenal, Newcastle United and Rangers, all of them going on to success in the final.

The covered enclosure behind the Albion Road goal was reopened on a one-off basis for the game. With the absence of opposition fans in any numbers, the police were reasonably satisfied that there would be little chance of trouble, and the decision was welcome news for a section of the support who were able to watch the action from their favourite spot, even if only for the one night.

With the side again wearing all-green jerseys, the midfield trio of Stanton, O'Rourke and Cropley initially had difficulty in getting to grips with the game, their hesitancy allowing Fraquito to give Sporting an early lead with a flashing shot that went only narrowly past.

After 28 minutes Alan Gordon gave the 28,000 fans cause for celebration when he opened the scoring. A typical Edwards' cross from the right to the far post was met by Gordon, whose header gave Damas no chance. Hibs were now ahead on the away-goals ruling.

Although in front, the home side were still struggling to find cohesion, and three minutes before half time Sporting equalised to take an overall lead. A Portuguese attack threatened little danger when, unluckily for Hibs, the ball accidentally struck the referee and diverted into the path of Marinho. Reacting quickly to the situation, the outside right pounced and, evading a challenge from Black, he sent over an inch-perfect cross that allowed Yazalde to beat Herriot easily from close range.

Turnbull's particular forte was the ability to change the pattern of play to his team's advantage, and the half-time break allowed him to reorganise the side. Kicking down the slope in the second half, Hibs attacked, firing on all cylinders, and the fast and direct wing play of both Edwards and Duncan began to cause all kinds of bother in the visitors' penalty area.

A fantastic solo run by Duncan deserved to put his side ahead, before a Stanton header was brilliantly turned away by Damas, but the non-stop pressure was beginning to tell and eventually the visitors wilted.

Five minutes before the hour mark, the home side took the lead when a Gordon head flick was calmly lobbed over the advancing keeper by O'Rourke, and just seconds after the restart, Brownlie crashed a tremendous effort that was well worthy of a goal off the foot of the post and behind, to safety.

It was now all Hibs, with the excited fans in an exuberant and expectant mood. The keeper had another fantastic save, this time from Duncan, but such was Hibs' dominance that it was almost impossible for Sporting to hold out and Gordon scored Hibs' third goal from a Schaedler cross in the 59th minute.

Four minutes later a Brownlie pass was finished off by O'Rourke, and it was now a question of just how many Hibs would score.

Sporting Lisbon made a double substitution but it made no difference to the pattern of play, and with ten minutes remaining O'Rourke scored again, this time from the penalty spot after Duncan had been brought down inside the box.

In the very last minute of the game a Gordon move set up Duncan and the outside left's shot was deflected into the net by the unfortunate Manaca.

FINAL SCORE: HIBERNIAN 6. SPORTING LISBON I.

CUP WINNERS' CUP IST ROUND (2ND LEG), WEDNESDAY 27 SEPTEMBER 1972, EASTER ROAD.
HIBERNIAN: HERRIOT, BROWNLIE, SCHAEDLER, STANTON, BLACK, BLACKLEY, EDWARDS, O'ROURKE, GORDON, CROPLEY, DUNCAN.

For a second successive midweek Hibs had scored five goals during the second half; the final scoreline was Sporting Lisbon's heaviest ever defeat in Europe, and a result that was certain to reverberate around the continent. Hat-trick hero Alan Gordon, and two-goal Jimmy O'Rourke had been the goalscorers, with a little assistance from an own goal by Manaca, but it had been a real team effort with no failures in the home side. As could perhaps be expected, Ronnie Allen put the blame for the loss of at least four of the goals down to defensive lapses, but he was man enough to admit that Hibs could now win the cup.

Before the game Turnbull had asked the fans to get behind the side and in the end he could not praise them highly enough for their magnificent backing. The exciting football being played was drawing the crowds back to Easter Road in ever increasing numbers, many of them neutrals, including a number of Hearts fans, who were turning up at Easter Road to watch Hibs in midweek European action while their own side was inactive.

Controversy between the season ticket holders and the board was never far away. The cost of admission to the Main Stand for the Sporting game had been increased to £1, which was thought by many to be far too expensive, but that was the least of the management's problems. Following the furore over the ticketing arrangements for the cup-tie with Aberdeen the previous season, the club had now promised that in future a season ticket would guarantee entry to all domestic games, excluding European matches. For the Sporting Lisbon game, season ticket holders were denied their customary first option for their regular seat as all were sold on a first come, first served basis. Consequently, a petition was sent to Tom Hart from about 150 irate season ticket holders in protest at the new arrangement. Councillor Hastie of the Central Leith Ward, a Hibs supporter for over 25 years, was also of the opinion that they should have been given the opportunity to purchase their desired seat before tickets went on general sale. He observed, 'This is the first time to my knowledge that loyal fans have not been given the opportunity to do so. Hibs have been appealing for more fans recently, but they did not deserve them.' Neither club secretary Cecil Graham, the chairman, or any other insider was available for comment.

At the beginning of October John Brownlie was selected for the Scotland squad to face Denmark in the forthcoming international at Hampden. Pat Stanton, once rated by Tommy Docherty as a better player than England's Bobby Moore, was a notable absentee. Acting on the advice of his family doctor, during the close season Stanton had decided to take his wife on holiday instead of travelling to South America with the touring Scottish party, and consequently he had been excluded from the squad playing the Danes. Asked to appear before the International Selection Committee to explain why the player had been dropped, Docherty claimed that it had all been a misunderstanding and the matter eventually resolved amicably, allowing Stanton to resume his international career.

It was also around this time that an article appeared in a Manchester-based newspaper suggesting that Manchester City were about to bid £170,000 for Pat Stanton. The rumour was immediately dismissed out of hand by Turnbull, who insisted that Stanton would end his career at Easter Road.

Hibs' next opponents in the Cup Winners' Cup would be Albanian side FC Besa, but the matter had been complicated by the fact that Danish side Fremad Amager had lodged a protest with UEFA after their first-round defeat to the Albanian side on the away-goals ruling after drawing 0-0 in Albania and 1-1 in Denmark.

The basis of the complaint was that, contrary to a UEFA ruling, the venue for the away game in Albania had been changed from Tirana to Durres at the last minute, and also that the condition of the pitch fell far short of the standard required for a European competition. They had only been notified on the morning of the game that the kick-off had been brought forward from 3pm to 11am, and that they were to be out of the country by early afternoon. The Danes had demanded a replay, but their appeal was eventually thrown out, leaving Hibs to contemplate a journey into the unknown.

Before the European game there was the eagerly awaited second leg of the League Cup tie against Dundee United. With a 5-2 lead from the first game at Tannadice, a large crowd turned up at Easter Road in anticipation of yet another goal feast, but sadly, they were to be disappointed. With the tie all but won, perhaps understandably the home side lacked urgency, but nevertheless the no score draw was more than enough to see them safely through to a quarter-final meeting with Airdrie.

As in the previous round, Hibs hit top form in the first leg at Broomfield, and once again it was a vintage second-half performance that accounted for most of the damage. Trailing 2-1 at the interval, five second-half goals by Hibs, four in a scintillating 14-minute spell, more than suggested even at this early stage that a semi-final place beckoned. Arthur Duncan notched a notable hat-trick, but the real goalscoring honours fell to defender John Brownlie, at that time the best attacking full back in the country by far. Brownlie, a former Airdrie ball boy, was as usual more than willing to help his colleagues up front, and two of his cavalier forays up the right wing ended with him scoring in spectacular fashion, both thunderbolt shots from well outside the area that simply screamed past goalkeeper Roddy McKenzie. It was Brownlie's first ever double for the club. O'Rourke was Hibs' other goalscorer, from the penalty spot. Poor Airdrie had more than held their own in the first 45 minutes, but they just couldn't live with Hibs on that second-half display, leaving dazed former Hibs player Derek Whiteford to confess after the game, 'In the second half, we simply didn't know what had hit us.'

The teams met again on league business at Easter Road on the Saturday, with Hibs continuing where they had left off three days earlier. This time it was O'Rourke's turn to score a hat-trick in the 5-2 romp, but it was the magical display of Edwards that caught the eye as he dictated play from midfield with lethal incisiveness and accuracy. The goal spree continued at Firhill, and another brilliant performance by Edwards orchestrated a vital 3-1 championship win to set his side up nicely for the FC Besa's midweek visit.

Hibs had added another goalkeeper to the pool when they paid Cowdenbeath £10,000 for 20-year-old PT teacher Jim McArthur. Turnbull had been following the career of the 6ft Fifer from Halbeath with some interest after a particularly impressive performance against Aberdeen in a league game at Central Park 18 months before. McArthur, who had also been attracting the interest of both Everton and Celtic, was thought by the Hibs manager to be a much better prospect than Bobby Clark, at that time Scotland's regular goalkeeper, had been at the same age.

FC Besa arrived in Edinburgh on the Sunday evening before the game and trained at Meadowbank Stadium the following morning before being taken on the now traditional sightseeing tour of the city. The Albanian party had been well satisfied by the warm hospitality provided by their Scottish hosts and assured Hibs that the gesture would be reciprocated in the return fixture.

For this game the season ticket holders had now been given first opportunity to purchase tickets for their usual seats. Within minutes of the start it was obvious that the home side were far too good for the keen, but clearly inferior, visiting side. A fast, direct, confident display by the Scots pulverised the opposition right from the opening whistle, and it was evident that the Albanians were out of their depth.

Jimmy O'Rourke led the rout with his fourth hat-trick of the season, a personal best for the stocky inside forward, and the opening period became little more than shooting practice for the home side, with Besa unable to get the ball out of their own half for long spells of the game. It was only a question of how long the Albanians could hold out, and it came as no surprise when Cropley opened the scoring from close range in the 12th minute after a left-foot drive by Gordon had rebounded from the cross bar. Before the visitors had fully recovered from the blow, less than two minutes later Hibs increased their lead when O'Rourke scored a second. It was still mainly one-way traffic until the interval, but although a Duncan shot came crashing back off the bar there was no more scoring in the opening 45 minutes.

The 22,000 crowd, who waited impatiently during the interval for the anticipated second-half goal avalanche, were not disappointed. Storming down the slope, Hibs once again scored five goals, all inside a blistering 12-minute period.

The tie was all but over, notwithstanding the trip to Albania yet to come, but with 20 minutes left to play the home supporters were stunned when Besa scored on one of their rare forays upfield when Kariqui beat Herriot, who had been a virtual spectator all evening, with a well directed shot.

In the remaining 20 minutes of the match there were several near things, all in the visitors' penalty area, but try as they might there was to be no more scoring and the home side were rapturously and deservedly applauded from the field at the final whistle by the delighted fans.

FULL TIME: HIBERNIAN 7. FC BESA 1.

CUP WINNERS' CUP 2ND ROUND (1ST LEG), WEDNESDAY 25 OCTOBER 1972, EASTER ROAD.

HIBERNIAN: HERRIOT, BROWNLIE, SCHAEDLER, STANTON, BLACK, BLACKLEY, EDWARDS, O'ROURKE, GORDON, CROPLEY, DUNCAN.

It was now becoming almost a habit, with most of the goals in the convincing win scored during the second half, leaving the fans to wonder just what the manager said to the players during the interval. Turnbull later explained that, contrary to general belief, there was rarely any shouting and screaming. After the players had been allowed to relax with a cup of tea, he would set about pointing out just where they had gone wrong and how they were going to rectify matters, and invariably he got it right.

Obviously satisfied with a result that represented Hibs' biggest ever win in Europe, Turnbull was of the opinion that the players 'achieved the victory in brilliant style'. Yet again he found time to congratulate the crowd for their pivotal part in giving the side the encouragement they needed. An official statement after the game by a FC Besa spokesman was short and to the point: 'This is a very black day for us.'

Jim Herriot had picked up a slight injury against Besa, allowing Jim McArthur to make his first-team debut in a 2-2 draw with Dumbarton at Boghead on the Saturday. Despite taking the lead after only three minutes, it required a last-minute goal by Alan Gordon to save Hibs from the humiliation of defeat by a side only recently promoted from the Second Division and currently lying near the foot of the table. It was not the greatest of starts for McArthur. Badly at fault at Dumbarton's equalising goal when he failed to collect a pass back from Black, the goalkeeper injured his hand during the second half, although he managed to finish the game.

With both Herriot and McArthur injured for the second leg of the League Cup tie against Airdrie in Edinburgh, teenager Bobby Robertson was called upon to make his second appearance in the competition. Already assured of a place in the semi-final after the resounding first-leg victory at Broomfield, the performance from the home side was somewhat erratic, but they were still far too good for an Airdrie side whose 4-1 defeat meant that they had now conceded 15 goals to Hibs in the three games between the sides that season.

High flying Hibs, now considered by many to be the most attractive side in the country, regained second spot in the league table with an emphatic 4-1 home win over Kilmarnock three days later before they were due to fly to Albania in a chartered aircraft. The flight was direct from Turnhouse to Tirana, but unlike the trip to Portugal, this time there would be no fans on board, only a handful of newspaper reporters. The flight was delayed, and things went downhill from there. The landing at the military airport outside the Albanian capital was made even more precarious due to the high mountains surrounding both sides of a runway that was liberally lined with gun emplacements. Ramshackle coaches awaited the players to transport them to their hotel.

Hibs had come well prepared, bringing not only their own food but also their own chef, hired from the North British Hotel on Princes Street. Officious airport officials at first refused permission for the food to be loaded onto the coaches, and only conceded after a heated intervention by Tom Hart. At the hotel the party were disappointed to be allocated shabby rooms of extremely basic quality. Again the food situation became a problem when the Hibs chef was refused permission to use the kitchen, the hotel staff insisting that only local food was to be consumed. However, the players found the local dishes impossible to stomach, and again it was only after a long and heated protest that their own food was allowed to be used.

The warning that it was against regulations for any visitor to leave the premises without an official guide proved unnecessary as there was absolutely nowhere to go and nothing to do in the desperately poor city. In the morning a request for a bus to take the squad to training was initially refused, the authorities only relenting after another argument, and there was yet another totally unnecessary altercation when the Albanian authorities refused to allow the press to accompanying the team. As with the Danes in the first round, Hibs had been assured that the game would take place in Tirana, but at short notice the venue was moved to Durres, 25 miles away. Unwilling to remain in the country a minute longer than necessary, the Easter Road officials lodged a request for the kick-off time to be moved forward to enable them to return to Edinburgh immediately after the game – the airport closed for the evening at 4.30pm. Their request was refused, forcing them to spend a second night in Albania.

Arriving at Durres to find that they would be playing on a threadbare and badly rutted pitch that featured goalposts of dubious dimensions, the players were alarmed to find a low concrete wall surrounding the playing area only a few inches from the touchline that presented a dangerous hazard to the participants. Hibs, like the Danes before them, felt that the conditions fell far short of the standard expected in a European Competition, and even before a ball had been kicked an official protest was lodged with the neutral UEFA observer who was expected to follow up Hibs' three main complaints: the conditions of the playing surface fell below the required standard; the concrete edging round the pitch was dangerous; accommodation and facilities were unsatisfactory.

In his pre-match talk, Turnbull urged his players to ignore the setbacks and concentrate on the game in hand. With Herriot back from injury, in front of just under 20,000 highly volatile local fans, Hibs were in control of the game for almost the entire 90 minutes. However, the bumpy pitch, the worst playing surface ever experienced by most of the visiting players, made accurate use of the ball nearly impossible.

Besa were keen and competed well, but it was obvious from the start that they were fighting an uphill battle, and Hibs should have gone in at the interval at least a couple of goals ahead. O'Rourke squandered a good chance to open the scoring when he shot narrowly past, as did Duncan a short while later, before the goalkeeper did well to save a net-bound Stanton header. Despite this almost relentless pressure, Hibs failed to turn their possession into goals and the teams went in at the interval level.

The opening period of the second half saw the visitors again well in command, but with just under an hour of the game played, Pagria gave the excitable Besa fans a rare opportunity for celebration when he opened the scoring from close range after taking advantage of a defensive error. Barely six minutes later, Gordon restored the status quo when he fired home a left-foot drive. In the circumstances, a draw was perhaps acceptable to both sides. Jim Herriot's return from injury was cut short when he suffered a badly gashed knee midway through the second half. He was replaced by Robertson, who again proved himself a capable understudy on his European debut, pulling off several good saves near the end.

FULL TIME: FC BESA I. HIBERNIAN I.

CUP WINNERS' CUP 2ND ROUND (2ND LEG), WEDNESDAY 8 NOVEMBER 1972, DURRES. HIBERNIAN: HERIOT, BROWNLIE, SCHAEDLER, STANTON, BLACK, BLACKLEY, EDWARDS, O'ROURKE, GORDON, CROPLEY, DUNCAN.

The attitude of the Albanians thawed somewhat at the post-match reception, but as a final footnote to what had truly been a trip to hell and back, the aircraft carrying Hibs to Edinburgh the following day was diverted to Glasgow because of high winds, and the team made the final leg of the journey by coach.

Once again Hibs had been drawn against Rangers, this time in the League Cup semi-final at Hampden. There was a dress rehearsal at Easter Road on the Saturday. Hibs made two changes to the side that played in Albania, with McArthur and Hazel replacing the injured Herriot and Gordon. Stanton gave Hibs a deserved first-half lead in a thrilling match, the Glasgow side equalising nine minutes later against the run of play. Future Hibs player Graeme Fyfe gave the visitors both points early in the second half from what appeared to be an offside position – where have we heard that before? It was Hibs' first home defeat of the season and gave Rangers their first win over the Edinburgh side in five starts and confidence for the forthcoming cup-tie.

The main talking point before the game had been Tom Hart's refusal to allow the STV cameras into the ground to record highlights of the match for transmission later that evening. No official explanation was forthcoming, but the consensus was that the increasing coverage of football on television was having a detrimental effect on attendance figures. However, with both of Hibs' home games in the Cup Winners' Cup being totally ignored by both STV and BBC, those of a more cynical nature wondered if this was Tom Hart's revenge for being snubbed.

Four days later the sides met again, this time at Hampden. In a foul-packed game overflowing with stoppages, Hibs found it difficult to establish any kind of rhythm, but they were still far too good for Rangers. The only goal of the game came midway through the second half after a brilliant solo run from deep in his own half by Brownlie. Evading several tackles on a magnificent foray into his opponents' half, the right back unleashed a tremendous shot from just outside the penalty area that screamed past the Rangers keeper to silence the thousands of Light Blue fans gathered behind McCloy at the traditional Rangers end of the ground. The composed Hibs defence managed to hold out comfortably until the end to earn yet another crack at Celtic in the League Cup Final, although there was a scare when a scrambled shot by Mathieson went narrowly past the post. Blackley, Edwards and goalscorer Brownlie stood head and shoulders above every player on the pitch, oozing class and quality. Rangers had no one to compare with them on the night.

Twenty-four hours before facing Celtic, Hibs signed defender Des Bremner from Highland League side Deverondale. Originally seen as one for the future, Bremner, who could play either full back or centre half, had first come to Turnbull's attention while he was still manager at Pittodrie and he had kept track of the player's progress. The signing of Bremner, who had been training at Easter Road for several weeks, taking part in several games as a trialist for the reserves, would become even more relevant in the coming weeks.

Hibs' victory over Celtic in the Drybrough Cup at the beginning of the season and the enthralling form shown by the team since, had helped to erase most of the painful memories of the heavy Scottish Cup Final defeat only seven months before, and once again a mass exodus of coaches and cars left Edinburgh carrying thousands of supporters along the M8 to Glasgow on Saturday 9 December 1972. Thousands more from all over the central belt, particularly the Borders and Fife, traditional hotbeds of Hibs support, made their way to Hampden for the League Cup Final, convinced that this was finally to be Hibs' year.

During the build-up to the final, a major doubt over John Brownlie's fitness had been kept a closely guarded secret. An ankle injury sustained by the inspirational defender during the match against Falkirk the previous Saturday had been examined by orthopaedic surgeons twice during the week, but fortunately the full back had recovered sufficiently to take his place as the teams took the field on a dreich winter's afternoon.

A pretty unexciting first half ended goalless with Hibs perhaps just shading it, having had the best of the few real chances, none better than when McNeil almost put through his own goal while attempting to pass back to his keeper in the closing minutes of the half, with Williams saving a brilliant header from Stanton from the resulting corner. But after the interval there was always only going to be one winner. Two goals in six minutes midway though the second half failed to reflect Hibs' superiority accurately, and although Dalglish pulled one back late in the game, Hibs held out comfortably to win their first trophy for 21 years, and their first national cup for 70 years.

The opening goal came after McNeil barged Gordon off the ball just outside the penalty area in the centre of the goals. In an obviously well planned move, Edwards cheekily lofted the free kick over the Celtic defensive wall to find Stanton in space. It first appeared that Stanton had missed his opportunity as he took a step to the right to evade a tackle – from Jimmy Johnstone, of all people – but as he fell the Hibs captain struck a beautiful right-foot shot past the despairing dive of Williams, high into the Celtic net. At this point Celtic didn't have an answer and six minutes later Hibs went two ahead. O'Rourke, running through at full speed from the inside right position, headed an absolutely magnificent Stanton cross from the right wing, high into the net from just outside the six-yard box. Minutes later, Gordon had an opportunity to settle things when he found himself in front of goal with the keeper stranded. It seemed easier to score, but somehow the centre forward managed to drive his shot against McNeil, who was standing on the goal line, before the ball was cleared to safety. It was all Hibs now, and a powerful Stanton shot from just outside the box struck the outside of the left-hand post with the goalkeeper beaten.

With 13 minutes of the match remaining, Dalglish pulled one back for Celtic with a brilliant drive after a breakaway from deep in his own half after Duncan had been dispossessed, making the tension near the end almost unbearable for the huge Hibs support. Their relief at the final whistle was unmistakable.

Before receiving the cup from Glasgow's Lord Provost, Sir William Gray, the overjoyed Hibs players ran to face the enormous Edinburgh support that had mainly congregated behind the end to the left of the dugouts. The team were received rapturously by the Hibs fans, who had been incredibly supportive throughout the entire 90 minutes, and by far the more vocal, as Jimmy O'Rourke would later relate. Although the game remained goalless as the teams left the field at half time, the ovation given to the capital side convinced O'Rourke that Hibs would eventually emerge victorious.

HIBERNIAN: HERRIOT, BROWNLIE, SCHAEDLER, STANTON, BLACK, BLACKLEY, EDWARDS, O'ROURKE, GORDON, CROPLEY, DUNCAN. SUB: HAMILTON.
CELTIC: WILLIAMS, MCGRAIN, BROGAN, MCCLUSKEY, MCNEIL, HAY, JOHNSTONE, CONNELLY, DALGLISH, HOOD, AND MACARI. SUB: CALLAGHAN.
REFEREE: A. MCKENZIE (LARBERT).

In Edinburgh later that evening the streets were lined with jubilant supporters to watch the open top bus, so often not required after cup finals involving Hibs, packed with players and officials all proudly taking turns to display the cup to the masses, make its way along the allotted route through Corstorphine to the West End, along the length of Princes Street and down to the foot of Leith Walk, before returning to the North British Hotel for the celebrations later that evening. Hibs fans of all ages, delirious with joy, surrounded the bus carrying the victorious party throughout the entire journey, making progress difficult. Later they cheered from the street as the triumphant players and officials emerged onto the hotel balcony to display the coveted silverware to the hordes blocking the thoroughfare at the junction of Princes Street and North Bridge. Even those who were not football fans joined in, for this was a momentous occasion for the city.

Back at the North British Hotel, Gordon Smith, who had been unable to attend the match because of illness, was the first person to telephone Eddie Turnbull to offer his congratulations. Another of the fabulous forward line of the '50s, Bobby Johnstone, who had travelled up from his home in Oldham for the match, thought that it was now time for the people to forget about the Famous Five and start talking about the Famous 11 instead. The jubilant party were met inside the hotel by the rest of the playing staff, most of who had, incredibly, not even been at Hampden for the final, but had played for either the reserves against Motherwell at Easter Road that afternoon, or for the third team against Edinburgh University.

The Saturday after the Cup Final, over 17,000 crowded into Easter Road to see both the Drybrough and League Cups paraded around the ground before the league game against Ayr United. Before the silverware had disappeared down the tunnel, Hibs went a goal ahead, scored after only 11 seconds by Cropley, and in what must rank as Hibs' best, albeit not the most important, performance of the season up to that point; Gordon scored his own hat-trick and Hibs' fourth, before 35 minutes had been played. Gordon's third goal was Hibs' 100th of the season, and it was still only mid-December. Poor Ayr were quite simply not at the races as the home side provided a demonstration of scintillating exhibition football. The final 8-1 scoreline was the Easter Road side's highest of the season. By this time Jimmy O'Rourke led the league goalscoring charts with 19, level with Dalglish of Celtic and Duncan of Dundee. Alan Gordon was on 14 and Arthur Duncan 12.

A magnificent Gordon header gave Hibs a half-time lead in a thrilling game at Parkhead between the League Cup finalists seven days later. Heavy rain had reduced the expected 65,000-plus crowd, but there were still far in excess of 45,000 spectators packed inside the stadium to see the top two teams in Scotland. The Glasgow giants gave their all in a desperate bid to avoid a hat-trick of defeats, but both sides were happy to settle for a draw after a strike by Dalglish cancelled out Gordon's opener, the game ending 1-1. At that stage of the season Celtic led the table with 28 points; Hibs were in in second place with 24. In the corresponding reserve fixture between the sides at Easter Road on Christmas Day, Kenny Davidson, who had been on the bench against Ayr United and was now attempting to re-establish himself in the first team after an absence of many months due to injury, tragically suffered a compound fracture to his leg in the dying minutes of the game. This new setback would seriously curtail Davidson's career at Easter Road, and his ambition to make a name for himself in the game.

The government-ordained price freeze of winter 1972 led the Department of Trade and Industry to query why Hibs had increased the stand and enclosure prices for a game against Aberdeen during the Christmas period. The ruling was that prices could only be raised in special circumstances, and as there had been no increase for the previous games against Aberdeen that season, the club was summoned to attend a meeting at New St Andrew's House with representatives from the Department of Education, which, strange as it may seem, held responsibility for sport in this country. Hibs explained that their pricing structure was flexible and that therefore they had no standard rate that could be applied. Surprisingly, this explanation appeared to pass muster, and consequently stand prices for the Aberdeen match were raised from 6/- to £1, and ticket prices for the wing stands and enclosure accordingly.

Although home attendances had been improving, the average gate at the time was only 14,600. Turnbull and Tom Hart both thought that the football then being played by Hibs deserved a far bigger audience. The League Cup run, excluding the final, had cost the club in excess of £3,000, and in line with the other leading clubs at the time, Tom Hart once again raised the subject of reconstruction. Echoing the words of Harry Swan 20 years before, he was emphatic that there had to be a reconstruction of some kind, and that the bigger clubs had to push it through. In his opinion it was unfair that 'small-minded people' were standing in the way of progress. As far as Hart was concerned the game would suffer in the long run if changes were not made. A step in the right direction according to the Hibs supremo would be to allow the home side to keep its own gate. As talk of reconstruction had surfaced many times to no consequence, there was little optimism that things would change in the near future.

Hibs maintained their tremendous recent form with a 3-2 victory over Aberdeen at Easter Road, a scoreline that failed to demonstrate their superiority, particularly in the second half, and it was now on to Tynecastle for the New Year's Day derby.

In recent months Hearts had been playing their best football for years and now sat fourth in the table. An article in the *Pink News* the previous day highlighted the fact that the Maroons fancied their chances of reversing the recent dismal record against their Edinburgh neighbours that had seen them go 13 league games without a win, eight without even scoring a goal. So far that season at Tynecastle, Hearts had conceded just three goals in league games, and it seemed likely that the free-scoring Hibs would get little change out of the mean Gorgie defence.

Bill Mullen of Dalkeith, Scotland's top referee, was to have taken charge of his first ever league game between the sides, but just before the match the whistler was involved in a car accident and he was replaced by J. Gordon of Newport.

As expected, a huge crowd greeted the teams as they took the field at Tynecastle on January 1 1973 – incidentally, Britain's first day as an official member of the European Union, or the Common Market as it was then known.

With the crowds still streaming into the ground, Hearts missed two great chances to take the lead inside the first few minutes, the better of them when Donald Park dragged his shot wide from near the penalty spot when it seemed easier to score. But from then on Hearts had no answer to Hibs' almost total domination as the majestic green machine moved into top gear, harassing the Gorgie side into a state of total demoralisation.

Left back Schaedler had Hibs' first attempt at goal but his 22-yard right-foot drive sailed well over the bar. This was just a taste of things to come. A few minutes later O'Rourke opened the scoring when he ghosted between two static Hearts defenders at the Gorgie Road end of the ground to blast a left-foot rocket high into the roof of the net from six yards. Gordon scored number two a few minutes later when he evaded two Hearts defenders to brilliantly chest the ball and fire past Garland all in one movement after a delightful diagonal midfield cross by Edwards.

Although Duncan scored a third a little later after a solo run, the Hearts fans were still in fairly good voice with taunts of 'We hate the Hibees' reverberating around the ground, but a magnificent left-foot volley by Cropley from outside the penalty area in the 34th minute silenced the Gorgie faithful.

Duncan put the Greens five ahead with a fortuitous header from a corner kick on the left. Shortly after, a cheeky Edwards chip over Hearts' defensive wall at a free kick found the quick-thinking O'Rourke unmarked, but the inside forward's right-foot effort went narrowly past Garland's right-hand post, the audacious effort fully deserving of a goal. At half time the score stood at 5-0 for Hibernian.

Seconds after the interval, in one of their few ventures into Hibs' penalty area, Hearts had the ball in the net, but the by now almost muted cheers from the Hearts fans were totally silenced when referee Gordon blew for offside.

For a short time the home side enjoyed a period of pressure without seriously managing to trouble Herriot, and it was Hibs who scored again when an interception and mazy run by Stanton from just inside his own half was finished off by O'Rourke for goal number six. The goal knocked any remaining fight from the Maroons, and their supporters, many of whom had left during the first half, now began to desert the stadium in droves.

With 15 minutes remaining, Gordon completed the scoring when he bulleted a header into the net off Garland's left-hand post from a precision Duncan cross. The move had been set up after a typical bone-crushing tackle by Schaedler on right back Clunie allowed Hibs to take possession. At the final whistle Hibs topped the table on goal average over Celtic, who still had two games in hand.

The scintillating football displayed by the Easter Road side had totally bamboozled their city rivals throughout almost the entire 90 minutes, and only good goalkeeping by Garland and the Hearts players' contentment to play out time in the later stages of the game deprived Hibs of an even bigger victory.

It had been the 100th league meeting between the sides in the 50 years since season 1921–22, Hibs' victory levelling the series at 36 wins each. By coincidence, the programme editorial, featuring previous high scoring games between the sides, speculated as to whether Hearts could keep up their slender lead over their rivals and asked, 'Can Hibs even score?' Both questions had now been emphatically answered.

It had been Hearts centre forward Donald Ford's 300th game in a maroon jersey, and incredibly he was still to score against Hibs. At left back, a young Jim Jefferies, who was not listed in the programme, was making only his second first-team appearance.

The past few months had been the most exciting experienced by the Hibs fans for many years, and the delirious Easter Road supporters leaving Tynecastle at the end of the match could be forgiven if they were dreaming of better things to come. Sadly, the 7-0 victory, the widest margin ever between the sides in a league game, was the supreme pinnacle of Turnbull's time at Easter Road, and things would never quite be the same again.

HEARTS: GARLAND, CLUNIE, JEFFERIES, THOMSON, ANDERSON, WOOD, PARK, BROWN, FORD, CARRUTHERS, MURRAY. SUB: LYNCH.
HIBERNIAN: HERRIOT, BROWNLIE, SCHAEDLER, STANTON, BLACK, BLACKLEY, EDWARDS, O'ROURKE, GORDON, CROPLEY, DUNCAN. SUB: HAMILTON.
REFEREE: J. GORDON (NEWPORT).

Six days after the Tynecastle victory, in what would prove to be an ominous afternoon for the club, only a last-minute goal by Alan Gordon in a nasty, niggling game against East Fife, gave the home side a narrow win at Easter Road. Willie Ormond, recently appointed national team manager, watched from the stand, probably to cast an eye over the potential Scotland candidates Stanton and Brownlie.

Shortly before the interval, right back Brownlie was involved in an accidental tackle with East Fife left back Printy just in front of the tunnel, and was stretchered off with his leg broken in two places. The injury was a terrible blow, not only for the youngster, at that time possibly the most exciting and influential defender in Britain, if not Europe, but also for Hibs and the Scottish international side.

In what appeared to be a continuation of a long-running feud between Love of East Fife and Alex Edwards, it had taken the visiting inside forward only two minutes to earn a warning from the referee for a bad challenge on the Hibs player. Love, booked after 15 minutes for another terrible tackle on Edwards, was joined in the book by teammate Borthwick later in the game after further rash challenges on the same player. It seemed obvious that the East Fife manager Pat Quinn had pinpointed the Hibs number seven as the danger man, and the wing wizard became the victim of a series of cynical fouls throughout the match. The ongoing vendetta between Love and Edwards boiled over near the end: after yet another foul, the patience of the Hibs outside right snapped and he threw the ball – away, according to some, and at Love, according to others. Either way, Edwards was booked for his part in the incident, his fourth caution of the season and one that would prove expensive for him and the his teammates. Although there could be little excuse for the behaviour of the Hibs player, as often happens on these occasions the main offenders had escaped almost scot-free.

After only a few weeks at the club, 20-year-old Des Bremner made a premature first-team debut when he replaced the injured Brownlie at right back in a 1-0 defeat at Tannadice, Hibs' first defeat in eight games. Lacking the sparkle of the previous few months, the Greens produced little in the way of excitement for their travelling fans, although Bremner had made a satisfactory start to his Hibs career. United's winning goal was heatedly disputed by the visitors, who claimed that the ball had not crossed the line, but referee Greenlees disagreed and the points remained in Dundee.

Hibs' championship aspirations were further dented the following week when they could only manage to draw 1-1 with Dundee at Easter Road, a result that saw them drop to third place. Although Bremner had again performed well, the team clearly missed the panache of the injured Brownlie and the leadership of Pat Stanton, who had been banned in midweek for 14 days after picking up four bookings.

The disappointment of recent weeks was forgotten, for the evening at least, when on 15 January 1973 Lord Provost Jack Kane paid tribute to the team at a Civic Reception in the City Chambers to celebrate the League Cup win. Edinburgh's first citizen paid tribute to the great honour and prestige that the current side had brought to the city, adding, 'There have been great teams at Easter Road before, but the present team outshines even the Famous Five. The players are a tribute to their manager, and are destined to get even better.' Praise indeed.

Meanwhile, the subject of league reconstruction refused to go away. Tom Hart led a delegation of clubs that included both Edinburgh and Dundee sides and representatives from Aberdeen and Celtic at a meeting in Glasgow to discuss the subject further. Although they had been invited, Rangers did not attend the meeting.

Opinion varied as to the best way to take Scottish football forward. A major stumbling block to any future move to streamline the game was the fact that only three clubs were in favour of the three divisions advocated by Hart, all the others were happy with the status quo. All were agreed, however, that a review of the guaranteed payment made to visiting sides was necessary, or better still, that the home side be allowed to keep all the gate receipts. Other topics discussed included a return to the original format of the League Cup, with perhaps some seeding, and sponsorship of the tournament, a move long opposed by the authorities. Also on the agenda was the usual demand for more revenue from the pools companies, and a continuing debate over the potential damage of radio and television to the game. A further meeting was arranged to discuss the proposals further.

Despite a reasonably successful 1971–72 season, the club reaching a major cup final, a shortfall of £29,071 was declared at the AGM. Gates had risen by more than 11,000 during the campaign and the donation from the Development Club by £5,000, but the final figures made disappointing reading, and again it was abundantly clear that if the top players were to be retained at Easter Road there would have to be a drastic rise in the number of paying customers.

The first step on the seemingly eternal quest for Scottish Cup glory was successfully overcome at the beginning of February with a 2-0 home victory over Greenock Morton. In a vintage performance reminiscent of the form displayed earlier in the season, first-half goals by Higgins, his first for the league side, and a glorious 25-yard drive by Cropley ensured Hibs' entry into the second-round draw.

Alex Edwards had complained of feeling unwell for some time, but the following week he had recovered sufficiently to put his case to the disciplinary panel in Glasgow regarding his fourth booking of the season picked up against East Fife at the beginning of the year. Unfortunately, the pint-sized Fifer's version of events fell on deaf ears and he was suspended for eight weeks, a harsh sentence that provoked one scribe to suggest that 'the decision of the panel had effectively destroyed Hibs' championship hopes'. Edwards's last game before starting what was seen by most as a savage ban, was against Airdrie at Broomfield. In Hibs fourth victory of the season against the Diamonds, Blackley, Bremner and Edwards, were all in top form, but there was no question as to the game's star performer when Alan Gordon scored all four Hibs goals in a 4-0 whitewash, taking his league tally for the season to 24. The centre forward was now the leading scorer in the country and a front-runner in the race for the 'Golden Boot', an award presented annually to Europe's top goalscorer.

Hearts had already made a Scottish Cup exit at the hands of Airdrie in the first round, leaving Hibs as Edinburgh's sole representatives in the competition. Almost predictably the Easter Road side were drawn against Rangers for a fifth consecutive season, the match to be played in Glasgow at the end of February.

Hibs had been informed that the Yugoslavian side Hajduk from Split would be their next Cup Winners' Cup opponents. After flying to Scotland to cast an eye over his future cup opponents, Hajduk coach Branco Zebec made his way through to Ibrox on the Hibs team bus to spy on the Edinburgh side.

Watched by an extremely interested Zebec, the visitors were in unimpressive form until an Alan Gordon goal on the hour mark cancelled out a first-half strike by centre half Johnstone. From then until the final whistle the Greens were the better side and could – should – have scored the goals that would have prevented a replay.

In the rematch at Easter Road, the rugged and robust Rangers adopted spoiling tactics specifically designed to prevent Hibs from settling into any sort of rhythm. Content to concede free kick after free kick, the game-plan worked perfectly and Hibs made an exit from the Scottish Cup on home soil for the first time in 11 years. After opening the scoring as early as the sixth minute, the Ibrox side spent the rest of the half on the defensive. Duncan levelled things just after the interval, but Rangers regained the initiative from the penalty spot, a correct decision by referee Davidson, but the official enraged the large home support by denying Hibs an equally clear-cut penalty after Forsyth had blatantly fouled Gordon inside the box. From then until full time, only the brilliance of McCloy in the Rangers goal prevented Hibs from equalising for a second time, and at the final whistle the match official was forced to endure a barrage of jeers from the home support as he left the field.

There was to be no cup hangover. On the Saturday at Easter Road, poor Dumbarton who had won only one of their 17 games so far were ruthlessly dispatched 5-0, to set Hibs up for the forthcoming European game against Hajduk Split on the Wednesday. The victory kept Hibs in contention with the league leaders, but things were not so rosy on the other side of the city. The Hearts supporters were now wondering just what was going on at Tynecastle after lowly Arbroath had defeated the Maroons 3-0 in Angus that same afternoon. Like Hibs, the Gorgie side had enjoyed a successful start to the season but they had failed to recover from the New Year's Day mauling by Hibs, and there were now demands for the resignation of both manager Bobby Seith and chairman Lindsay. In an attempt to pacify the fans, an audacious bid to sign Dennis Law from Manchester United failed when the player refused to even consider a move to Tynecastle, and they turned their attention towards Kenny Aird of St Johnstone instead.

Hajduk Split was the oldest team in Yugoslavia, and had once supplied all 11 players for the Yugoslavian national side in a match against Czechoslovakia in 1924. Founded in 1911, they had finished as champions six times, the most recent at the end of the 1970–71 season when they had completed the entire league programme without defeat. Their previous solitary outing in the Cup Winners' Cup had been during the successful 1970–71 season when they had exited the competition at the hands of another British club, Tottenham Hotspur.

Nineteen-year-old John Salton was added to the Hibs squad for the game, but by far the biggest surprise was the inclusion of the suspended Alex Edwards. The midfielder had not featured since his eight-week suspension nearly a month before, but because the domestic ban did not apply to European games he was eligible to play against Split. Des Bremner would be taking part in his first ever European tie only weeks after becoming a full-time professional.

Tom Hart's wife, Sheila, had written the words for a Hibs song and earlier in the year the players had spent several hours under the direction of Hibs fanatic and composer of the famous Z Cars theme, Johnny Keating, recording what would eventually be titled 'Hibernian – Give us a Goal!/ The Hibs Song'. The flip-side featured a Keating/McPherson version of the John Lennon classic 'Happy Xmas (War is Over)' entitled 'Turnbull's Tornadoes'. Reviewing the recording for the first time, the management team at the mighty EMI Studios, under whose umbrella the disc had been produced, were reportedly impressed by the end product, some thinking it one of the best football songs they had ever heard. Performed for the first time at the club's annual dinner dance at the North British Hotel in January, the record had only recently been released for sale to the general public, and both Hibs and Hajduk Split took the field at Easter Road to the strains of 'Hibernian – Give us a Goal!'

In the early stages, the home side, again wearing all-green jerseys, adopted their usual and expected forceful attacking football style that was geared to knocking their opponents out of their stride, but they found the Slavs a difficult side to subdue. However, inspired by the large enthusiastic and vocal crowd, Hibs raced into an early lead. The re-called Edwards took a free kick from the left, his perfectly flighted cross finding the head of Gordon who powered the ball into the net through a gap in the crowded penalty area.

Although the visitors were dangerous on the break, Hibs scored again after 25 minutes and again it was Gordon who inflicted the damage. Kicking up the slope, Duncan started the move with a powerful run up the left-hand side. His pass to Cropley looked too strong but the Hibs inside left just beat Sirkovic in a race to the ball. Rounding the stranded keeper, Cropley cut the ball back into the path of the inrushing Gordon, who blasted it high into the unguarded net.

For a while it was all Hibs, but just when Hajduk looked in danger of being completely overrun, the home side lost an unexpected away goal. With just eight minutes remaining before the interval, Surjak collected the ball on the left-hand side of midfield. He raced up the left wing, his beautifully measured cross was met by Hlevnjac who headed spectacularly past the helpless Herriot, the goal stunning the large home support into silence.

During the interval Alex Edwards and left back Muzinic were called to the referee's room to receive a warning after a confrontation between the pair shortly before half time; the fiery Edwards was lucky to escape further punishment for his part in the incident.

The loss of the important away goal made it imperative that Hibs score again and they regained their two-goal cushion almost immediately after the break. A Stanton shot was blocked by a defender. The rebound broke kindly to Duncan whose first attempt hit the keeper, but again the rebound fell perfectly for the outside left, who was on the spot to run the ball into the net. It was a scrappy but nonetheless vitally important goal.

Almost on the restart Hibs had had a remarkable double escape. A dangerous cross from the right eluded the Easter Road defence, only for the inrushing Hlevnjac to completely miss his kick a few yards from goal. The ball ran through to teammate Surjak bearing down from the left, but fortunately for Hibs, with the goal gaping, he blasted his shot into the side netting. Hibs continued with their all-out attacking policy, but regardless of the pressure, Hajduk refused to retreat into a totally defensive policy and it was imperative that the home kept their concentration at the back.

It was now mainly all Hibs, but with their opponents leaving three men up front the visitors proved to be a continual threat on the break. There was a scare when a Boskovic header was cleared for a corner, and from the resultant kick Bremner was forced to clear off the line.

Midway through the second half, a spell of almost incessant pressure by Hibs paid off when Schaedler intercepted a pass in his own half. The full back went on a run deep into the Split half before thundering a tremendous drive that was brilliantly parried by the keeper. The ball spun free, but Gordon, reacting quickest, prodded the ball over the line from close range to score his own hat-trick and give his side a three-goal advantage.

With 15 minutes remaining, Hibs had yet another amazing escape when

Jerkovic hit the post, the ball fortunately rebounding into the arms of the stranded Herriot. The warning went unheeded, however, and 60 seconds later, amid complete shambles in the home penalty area, Hajduk scored a vitally important second goal after Bremner failed to clear a corner on the right, allowing Hlevnjac to beat Herriot from close range after evading a couple of despairing tackles. With a seemingly unassailable lead to take into the second leg, Hibs had been the architects of their own downfall due to slack marking, and there was no mistaking the delight on the faces of the Split players at the final whistle who were now confident of reversing the result in Yugoslavia thanks to that late goal.

An air of gloom and trepidation hung over the stadium as the Hibs fans among the 28,469 crowd slowly filed out of the ground at the end, fully aware how important the late strike by Hajduk had been. At 4-1, the tie had perhaps been won, but the crucial late and avoidable second goal had put a completely different complexion on the result.

FINAL SCORE: HIBERNIAN 4. HAJDUK SPLIT 2.

CUP WINNERS' CUP, 3RD ROUND (1ST LEG), WEDNESDAY 7 MARCH 1973, EASTER ROAD.
HIBERNIAN: HERRIOT, BREMNER, SCHAEDLER, STANTON, BLACK, BLACKLEY, EDWARDS, HIGGINS, GORDON, CROPLEY, DUNCAN.

Leading goalscorer Alan Gordon had been Hibs' top performer on the night, his hat-trick bringing his total for the season to 41, but it was the two goals conceded that were the main concern for manager Turnbull. Not since drawing 3-3 with Belenenses in 1961 had Hibs lost two goals at home in a competitive European game.

Johnny Hamilton replaced the still suspended Edwards for the trip to Kilmarnock on the Saturday. Despite controlling most of the game, another important championship point was dropped when the Greens failed to capitalise on a host of chances and in the end they had to be satisfied with a point. Rugby Park had long proved a difficult venue for Hibs, and the 2-2 draw meant that Hibs had now not won at the Ayrshire ground for 16 years. Home victories over Partick Thistle and Morton put Hibs back on the winning trail, boosting confidence for the forthcoming return leg in Yugoslavia, but before then there had been a managers' meeting in a Bridge of Allan hotel. As mentioned earlier, there was general dissatisfaction at the direction that the game was taking, particularly the financial side, and among the items on the agenda was a call for the pools companies to set aside ten per cent of their profits to be shared amongst the clubs. Sunday football was also discussed, and again the possible detrimental effect on attendances by the cameras. A novel proposal that clubs be limited to a pool of 18 full-time players at the beginning of each season gained little support.

Five Hibs players had been selected for the Scottish League squad to face the Football League at Hampden later in the month. The inclusion of

Stanton, Blackley, Schaedler, Duncan and Gordon was testimony to the calibre of player then at Easter Road, but, unbelievably, once again there was no place for Alex Edwards, who at that time was playing the best football of his career. Turnbull had called upon his former teammate to select Edwards for the full international side, reminding the Scotland manager that there was not a finer player in the country at that time. Sadly, Edwards would finish his career without that elusive full or inter-league cap to go with his minor representative honours, which was nothing short of a scandal considering the many ordinary players that had won international esteem through the years, more than a few of them wearing either the blue of Rangers or the green of Celtic. For newcomer Des Bremner, however, there had been quick promotion to the international scene. After less than three months as a first-team player at Easter Road, the full back was named in the Scotland Under-23 squad to face Wales in Swansea later in the month.

Since resuming after the winter shutdown in Yugoslavia, Hajduk Split's results had been poor, managing to take only one point from a possible six, and for the first time since the war they were in grave danger of relegation from the top division. Turnbull, paid scant heed to reports of the poor form of the Slavs and insisted that Hibs, who had been now been installed as third-favourites after Leeds and AC Milan to lift the trophy, would play their normal attacking game.

Although still in plaster, to boost his moral, double-leg-break victim John Brownlie was included in the party that made its way to Yugoslavia. A pre-match comment by Eddie Turnbull that few teams were capable of defeating Hibs 2-0 proved to be only partly correct. Hibs beat themselves – in this case, 'surrendered' would be a far more apt description of the Edinburgh side's exit from the competition.

Both teams took the field at the Plinada Stadium amid a backdrop of cheering from the 25,000 excited fans and the deafening noise of firecrackers and rockets helped to create an electric atmosphere inside the tight arena. Set in a densely built-up area, the stadium was surrounded by houses and several hundred fans took the opportunity to enjoy a free view of the proceeding from nearby rooftops.

Against a struggling side that had conceded 13 goals in their last four games, a disastrous six-minute spell in the first half put paid to Hibs' hopes of a place in the semi-finals and another meeting with Leeds United. The away penalty area at times resembled a disaster zone as goalkeeper Herriot failed to cut out two relatively simple crosses and the visitors found themselves trailing on the away goals ruling.

From the first blast of the referee's whistle, Hibs were unusually hesitant, allowing the enthusiastic and determined Hajduk Split to dominate the crucial midfield area of the pitch. The central trio of Stanton, Cropley and Higgins were second to every ball, failing miserably to stamp any sort of authority on proceedings. Although having the bulk of the pressure, Hajduk rarely showed any real signs of causing danger until Herriot's double blunder. Both the rugged Schaedler and the inexperienced Bremner struggled to contain the clever runs of Surjak and Hlevnjac. Both wide men scored from crosses, one from each wing, in the 17th and 23rd minutes, after Herriot had failed to cut out what appeared both times to be an easy goalkeeper's ball. Afterwards Herriot would claim to have been blinded by the strong sun at the first goal, but nevertheless the former international would have been expected to have done better.

The two-goal cushion had put the Slavs ahead over the two legs, the away goals scored in Edinburgh counting double in the event of a draw, and their superiority was confirmed seven minutes into the second half when Herriot again failed to collect an easy ball driven across the face of the six-yard box by Surjak. In attempting to clear the danger, the inrushing Blackley deflected the ball into his own net and the game was as good as over.

Of the forwards only Edwards showed any real determination, with Gordon and Duncan completely subdued by their markers, although O'Rourke demonstrated his usual industry after replacing Higgins for the second half.

Major concerns over the fitness of goalkeeper Vukcevic before the game had been unnecessary. The custodian, rarely troubled by the Hibs forward line, was called upon to deal with only two or three harmless efforts in the entire 90 minutes.

With five minutes remaining Schaedler was injured in a heavy tackle and was carried off with what was later diagnosed as a dislocated right shoulder and it looked likely he would miss the remainder of the season.

Edwards apart, Jim Black, who had battled manfully against the odds, had been the only other Hibs player exempt from criticism, although young Bobby Smith, making his first-team debut replacing Cropley during the second half, showed a fight lacking in his more experienced colleagues.

In reality, the game had been lost at Easter Road when Hajduk scored the important late away goal, but Herriot's indecision played a major part in the defeat in Yugoslavia. The poor display would prove an expensive one for the goalkeeper: he never again played for the first team.

FINAL SCORE: HAJDUK SPLIT 3. HIBERNIAN 0.

CUP WINNERS' CUP 3RD ROUND (2ND LEG), WEDNESDAY 21 MARCH 1973, PLINADA STADIUM.
HIBERNIAN: HERRIOT, BREMNER, SCHAEDLER, STANTON, BLACK, BLACKLEY, EDWARDS, HIGGINS, GORDON, CROPLEY, DUNCAN.

After the match a devastated Turnbull revealed that he had been extremely concerned that his team had shaded off in recent weeks: 'The key players had not been doing well of late, and we rely heavily on their experience to help the youngsters.' In later years he would confess that he had fully expected Hibs to reach the Cup Winners' Cup Final in Salonika later that year and the manner of the defeat in Split had caused him to contemplate his future in the game. Things would never be quite the same for him after that evening in Yugoslavia.

Jim McArthur replaced Herriot for the trip to Ibrox on the Saturday, with Bobby Smith making his league debut. A controversial winning goal by Tommy McLean late in the second half appeared to have all but ended any lingering ambitions still held by Hibs of winning the title. Appearing yards offside when he collected a long through ball from Greig, McLean was allowed to proceed by referee Davidson, and the former Kilmarnock player took full advantage of the situation to score the only goal of the game. Blackley, who had already been booked, protested the decision too vigorously and was ordered off. Near the end, Tony Higgins, Hibs' top performer on the day, beat goalkeeper McCloy with a lob from all of 45 yards, but typical of the luck being enjoyed by the Easter Road side, the ball rebounded from the bar to safety leaving Hibs five points behind leaders Rangers with a game in hand.

At the beginning of April John Blackley appeared in front of the disciplinary committee and was suspended for 22 days. Facing a double charge, he was banned for 14 days for the accumulation of four bookings, and eight days plus a £50 fine for the ordering off at Ibrox. During the interval between the defeat at Ibrox and the tempestuous defender's suspension, Hibs had dropped yet another three precious league points when they could only draw 0-0 with lowly Arbroath at Easter Road and the players were forced to endure 90 minutes of derision from a highly critical crowd who now expected better. Things were even worse seven days later when Falkirk collected both points in a narrow 1-0 home victory. Schaedler made an early return to the side at Brockville after his injury in Split. The rugged defender had made a near miraculous recovery and missed only two matches after dislocating his shoulder.

In mid-April any lingering hopes of winning the championship disappeared completely after two games against Motherwell within four days. Blackley started his suspension before the game at Fir Park, which coincided with the return of Alex Edwards to the side. The scoring touch that had deserted the side in the previous four games was rediscovered briefly, but only enough to secure a share of the spoils in a 1-1 draw.

For the first time VAT was to be levied on admission charges to football matches, and supporters attending the home game against Motherwell were requested to have the correct change ready to cover the 8 per cent increase, from 30p to the princely sum of 33p with equivalent increases to other parts of the stadium. Hibs, who were fielding three 18-year-olds in Smith, Higgins and Tom Stevens (making his first-team debut), were the better side, particularly during the first half, but their recent habit of scorning numerous scoring opportunities continued and they paid the price when Motherwell scored the only goal from the penalty spot late in the game, an award that had been conceded by the otherwise impeccable Stanton.

To bring what had been a pretty magnificent season to an end, at least one point was required from the final two league games to be sure of finishing third in the table. Shortly after the interval, former Rangers player George McLean, now with Ayr United, scored again from a position that looked suspiciously like offside, but O'Rourke had already notched the goal that secured Hibs third-place position and qualification for next season's UEFA Cup.

Underlining his faith in Hibs' youth policy, Turnbull gave 19-year-old Derek Spalding his debut at Somerset Park in place of the suspended Blackley, the youngster making an impressive start to his top-team career.

The title was won at Easter Road on the final day of the season, but unfortunately for the home fans it was not by Hibs. Over 47,000 crammed into the stadium to see Celtic secure their eighth championship in a row with a 3-0 victory that flattered the visitors, the first time that season that Hibs had conceded more than one goal in a league game at Easter Road. The champions were matched all the way by a Hibs side that should have scored on several occasions, but nevertheless, the defeat meant that the home side had now concluded their league programme without a victory in their final eight games, six without even scoring a goal, statistics which were obviously far removed from title winning form.

Although they were highly disappointed to finish in third place behind Celtic and Rangers, this represented an improvement from the previous season's fourth, but the 11-point gap between them and Celtic was much wider than it should have been for a team with real title aspirations. There could be little doubt that the injury to Brownlie had proved particularly costly, as had the long suspensions meted out to Edwards. And with Stanton and Blackley both missing the latter part of the season, the situation further highlighted the difference in depth of squad between the Old Firm and the others. The future seemed bright, however, with the baptism of several talented, although largely inexperienced, youngsters. McArthur, Bremner, Spalding, Stevens, Smith, Murray and Higgins all made their debuts during the season just ended, and as a further bonus for the club, the home attendances had increased substantially during the past year.

For Alan Gordon in particular it had been a tremendous 12 months, his best ever. Apart from collecting Drybrough Cup and League Cup winner's medals, the centre forward had been a contender for Scotland's 'Football Writers' Player of the Year' award, only to lose out narrowly to George Connolly of Celtic. Only injury had deprived him of international honours when he was forced to withdraw from the Scottish League side to face the English League at Hampden in March. His 42 goals, 27 of them in league games, had kept him in the running for the prestigious 'Golden Boot' award until the very late stages of the season. Finally having to settle for seventh place, Gordon at one point had been in illustrious company, sharing first place with Eusebio of Benfica and Gerd Muller of Bayern Munich for an honour that was eventually won by Eusebio.

Although only a small compensation, the fair-haired striker was presented with a crystal decanter for winning the Scottish Player of the Year award by *Inside Football* magazine, but an even bigger honour came his way when he was invited to take part in a star-studded testimonial match for the former Hamburg and West Germany centre half, Willi Schulz. Gordon came on as a second-half substitute for an International XI versus a Hamburg Select, and didn't look out of place in the distinguished company of such greats as Law, Charlton and Moore. The legendary Pelé was to have taken part in the match, but was forced to withdraw due to injury at the last minute.

Top scorer Gordon's 42 goals in all competitions, allied to the 34 scored by O'Rourke and the 23 by Duncan, meant that the trio of marksmen finished only one goal short of a total of 100 goals, an astonishing total unsurpassed in the history of the club.

At the end of the season, goalkeeper Herriot, McEwan, Auld and Hamilton were handed free transfers. Auld, whose last appearance had been as a substitute in the Scottish Cup Final 12 months before, was retained on the coaching staff. Hamilton, a surprise 'free', had featured in the first team 20 times during the season and was quickly snapped up by Rangers. McEwan would later join Blackpool.

Defender Gerry Adair, released by West Bromwich Albion at his own request, was signed near the end of the season, with Alex McGregor, a free transfer from Ayr United, added to the squad at the beginning of May. Turnbull had been a huge admirer of the skilful McGregor and had been keeping tabs on him for some months. Ian Munro, who could play either at full back or in midfield, was yet another close season acquisition. Recommended to Turnbull by ex-Love Street manager Wilson Humphries, the former youth international, who would go on to play for the full international side, was signed from St Mirren at the end of the season for a fee in the region of £20,000. Munro was so keen to sign for the club that he didn't even bother to ask about terms. There was a further end-of-season boost for the club when Stanton and Schaedler were both selected to join the Scotland squad for the forthcoming Home International series. Schaedler failed to feature in any of the three games, but Stanton captained the side to victory against Wales in Wrexham and defeat by Ireland at Hampden, and only an injury received against Ireland would prevent him from playing against England at Wembley.

13

Enter Joe Harper
and Penalty Kick Heartache in Europe
1973–74

BY NOW, KENNY DAVIDSON had fully recovered from the broken leg received during the previous season and was ready to stake a claim for a regular first-team place. As yet, there would be no comeback for defender John Brownlie, who had undergone another operation on his injured leg during the summer, although it was anticipated that his eagerly awaited return would be not too far in the future.

Hibs took advantage of a three-game, pre-season tour of Scandinavia to sharpen their fitness but none of the matches – in Denmark, Sweden and Norway – ended in victory. These were seen only as training games and the results were considered unimportant – it's funny how results are only important when you win! A surprise inclusion in the party was full back Dave McMillan, an ever-present in the reserves during the past 12 months, although the youngster failed to feature in any of the games.

It had originally been planned to take the players on a five-match tour of Australia during the summer as a reward for their efforts during the cup winning season just ended, but the trip had been cancelled by the Australian authorities almost at the last minute. It then emerged that Stoke City had been invited in Hibs' place, prompting a furious Tom Hart to threaten legal action against the Australian FA for breach of contract. It later turned out that an invitation to tour New Zealand had been turned down in favour of the Australian trip and Hibs felt entitled to 'handsome' compensation. Although the matter was reported to the SFA, it was decided not to continue with the complaint.

Once again the Drybrough Cup competition heralded the start of a new season, the holders again qualifying as one of the four top-scoring sides in the First Division during the previous campaign. Aberdeen, winners of the inaugural competition, had ended in fourth place but were overlooked in favour of Dundee, lying one place below, who qualified by scoring seven goals more.

In the opening game at Easter Road, played along the usual experimental rules with no offside outside of an extended 18-yard line running the width of the pitch, Ian Munro scored his first goal for the cup holders in a 2-1 victory against his former Love Street colleagues when he put the ball past Jim Herriot, who was facing Hibs for the first time since his free transfer during the summer. The win set up yet another semi-final meeting with Rangers in Edinburgh.

Yet again, extra time was required, and once again Rangers came off second-best in a match that was far more decisive than the 2-1 scoreline would suggest. Hibs rarely looked in too much danger as the Ibrox men suffered their first defeat in 27 matches to set the Easter Road side up with another meeting against who else but Celtic in the final. New signing Munro had quickly endeared himself to the Easter Road support, when with one of his first touches of the ball he cleverly 'nutmegged' Ibrox iron man John Greig and left the defender floundering. The visitors employed their usual power tactics, but were well beaten by a side determined to play fast, attractive football. Trouble erupted on the terracing during the second half, but the trouble on the field happened much earlier. The referee was guilty of ignoring a multitude of illegal challenges, most perpetrated by the visiting side, and the nasty nature of the game did much to inflame the violence between rival supporters.

The Drybrough Cup was retained after yet another gruelling match against Celtic in the final at Hampden, and yet again extra time was needed to separate the sides. Celtic had the better of the early exchanges, a promising move ending with Dalglish hitting the bar, but the Easter Road men finished the first 45 minutes the stronger side. After the break Hibs continued where they had left off and held the upper hand for most of the half, but the 90 minutes ended without a goal. Despite intensive efforts by the Glasgow side, extra time was almost all one-way traffic towards the Celtic goal, but try as they might, Hibs just could not force the breakthrough. With only one minute of the 120 remaining and penalties looming, Alan Gordon broke the deadlock when he finished off good leading-up play by Cropley and Higgins to smash the ball past Williams from 18 yards, despite the close attention of McNeill, to ensure that the trophy would remain in Edinburgh for at least another 12 months.

The ghost of the Scottish Cup Final defeat by Celtic had now been well and truly put to rest. In the 14 months since the 6-1 humiliation, Hibs had defeated their Glasgow counterparts in three cup finals. Although the Drybrough Cup was considered by some to be an unimportant tournament, usually by supporters of sides that had failed to qualify, let there be no mistake, Celtic and Rangers had been desperately keen to win the trophy, and in Hibs' case both of the Old Firm teams had to be overcome twice to earn the consecutive victories.

DRYBROUGH CUP FINAL, SATURDAY 4 AUGUST 1973, HAMPDEN PARK, GLASGOW.
HIBERNIAN: MCARTHUR, BREMNER, SCHAEDLER, STANTON, BLACK, BLACKLEY, EDWARDS, HIGGINS, GORDON, MUNRO, AND DUNCAN. SUBS: CROPLEY, SMITH.
CELTIC: HUNTER, MCGRAIN, HAY, MURRAY, MCNEILL, CONNOLLY, MCLAUGHLIN, DALGLISH, LENNOX, CALLAGHAN, AND LYNCH. SUBS: HOOD, BROGAN.
REFEREE: A. MCKENZIE (LARBERT).

The defence of the League Cup got off to a flying start with a 4-1 win at Greenock. Morton manager Hal Stewart, who had watched the Hampden final, described Hibs as 'an absolutely brilliant side, without a single weakness'. Ex-Hibs goalkeeper Roy Baines faced the visitors at Greenock, one of five former Easter Road goalkeepers then playing in the Scottish League. As well as Herriot at Paisley, Marshall was now at Arbroath, Allan at Dundee and Wilson with Berwick Rangers.

For one season only, the authorities had decided that the League Cup should continue with the experimental no offside ruling used for the Drybrough Cup. For some time now there had been an alarming drop in attendances at many section games and it was hoped that this would encourage more goals to be scored. Unfortunately, the move proved unsuccessful in its aims until the later stages of the tournament. The Scottish League management committee had instructed referees, managers and directors to submit a report at the end of each game to allow the experiment to be evaluated, but somewhat surprisingly – or there again, perhaps not – they failed to consult the opinions of the people who probably mattered most, the players and the fans. There was also to be a change to the ruling regarding substitutes. Now, two extra players could be used instead of one.

Against Ayr united at Easter Road in midweek only a late goal by Bremner, his first for the club, separated the sides in a scrappy affair, but it was one well worth waiting for. Starting the move in his own half, the full back used Edwards and Higgins in turn. Receiving the return for a second time, he crashed an unstoppable shot into the net from just outside the penalty area to send Hibs to the top the section.

Three days later Pat Stanton celebrated his 500th appearance in a Hibs jersey by leading his side to a narrow 1-0 win over Dumbarton at home, the victory maintaining Hibs' lead at the top of the group.

In the return game against Ayr United at Somerset Park, the visitors were struggling until half-time changes again demonstrated Turnbull's tactical acumen. Replacing Duncan and Edwards with Higgins and Cropley, the manager got it just right; both players scored within two minutes of each other to maintain Hibs' 100 per cent League Cup record. Jim McArthur was injured during the second half, but although clearly in some discomfort the goalkeeper managed to finish the game.

McArthur's injury, later diagnosed as a fractured thumb, meant he would miss several weeks of the season and Turnbull lost no time in signing 27-year-old Roddy McKenzie from Airdrie for a fee in the region of £8,000. Currently under club suspension following a dispute over a benefit payment, the Irish international goalkeeper had not played for some time. Signed on the morning of the game, McKenzie made his debut in Hibs penultimate group game against Dumbarton at the aptly named Boghead. Taking full advantage of defensive slackness in the Hibs rearguard, bottom-placed Dumbarton ran riot against the beleaguered Greens, eventually winning 4-1 to inflict Hibs' first defeat in eight games. The final whistle came as a huge relief to the visiting players and the travelling support. It was perhaps just as well that the section had already been won.

In the league Hearts gained sweet revenge for the New Year's Day ignominy with a thoroughly deserved and comprehensive 4-1 victory at Tynecastle. Erich Schaedler gave the Maroons a first-half lead when heading past a startled McKenzie in attempting to clear. Two goals inside two minutes in the second half by Aird and Ford sandwiched a Cropley strike during the same period, Busby ensuring Hearts' first league win at Tynecastle for ten years over their deadly rivals when he scored a fourth late in the game. The goal scored by Donald Ford was the centre forward's first ever against Hibs in well over 300 appearances for Hearts, and until that afternoon, Hibs had scored more goals at Tynecastle in the nine months since the New Year's Day thrashing than the home side.

Fans' favourite Joe Baker returned to Easter Road in the colours of Raith Rovers for the second round of the League Cup. It was his first visit to the ground since being freed almost 17 months before, and he received a rapturous welcome. The Second Division side, then managed by former Hibs and Blackpool goalkeeper George Farm, gave a good account of themselves and the slender 3-2 Hibs victory left the tie finely balanced for the return leg. A Bobby Smith header levelled an early own goal by Bremner, Hibs' second own goal in two games, before Baker earned the applause of both sets of supporters when he gave his side the lead for a second time with a typical striker's goal. Stanton pulled the home side level with a header before Higgins scored the winner in the final few minutes of the match.

In the opening round of the UEFA Cup Hibs were paired against Keflavik. The Icelandic side had drawn their final league game of the season on the Saturday before travelling to Scotland, giving them the Icelandic League Championship by four clear points. Formed as recently as 1956, they had now secured the premier trophy for the fourth time in their short history. Joe Hooley, Keflavic's English manager, made no secret of the fact that his team intended to play a tight defensive game designed to contain Hibs, both in Edinburgh and at home. It would be a new experience for the Scots, who had never faced a team from Iceland before, although manager Turnbull had visited the country during his time with Aberdeen.

Alan Gordon, still receiving treatment for a muscle injury received at Tynecastle nearly two weeks before, missed the game and his place was taken by Jimmy O'Rourke. Signed after the European deadline, goalkeeper McKenzie was ineligible and with McArthur still injured, once again the capable understudy Bobby Robertson took over between the posts.

UEFA had issued a new directive at the start of the season. Now five substitutes could be stripped, any two of whom could play.

The Icelandic minnows could hardly be classed as attractive European opposition, and a disappointingly small crowd of 13,652, were inside Easter Road at kick-off, most expecting to see Hibs score their 100th European goal during the course of the evening. At present the total stood at 94, and the fans, by now spoiled by several high scoring encounters in recent years, saw the part-time amateurs merely as bit players as Hibs endeavoured to reach the century.

Keflavic, however, had not been informed of these plans, and the enthusiastic Icelanders hassled and harried their more experienced opponents for the entire 90 minutes. The constant time-wasting the numerous petty fouls by the part-timers infuriated the crowd, but more importantly it totally disrupted their opponents' rhythm, Hibs struggling to find cohesion.

Cropley should have opened the scoring midway through the first half, but Olafsson was his equal, producing a brilliant save to deny the inside left. A few minutes later O'Rourke shot high over the bar from a dangerous position, These chances apart, Hibs were finding it incredibly difficult to pierce the nine-man defensive set-up of Keflavic. With four minutes of the first half remaining, Jim Black, Hibs' top player on the night, scored the goal that his perseverance deserved. Finding himself with little to do defensively and driving forward to assist the attack, the centre half unexpectedly decided to have a shot, his right-foot effort off the left-hand upright, only his second goal for the club, beating the keeper.

If the part-time amateurs were expected to run out of steam in the second half, the fans were to be disappointed. Although they were yet to mount their first real attack on Hibs goal, the visitors proved to be an extremely fit side that refused to buckle and managed to keep up the fierce pace until the end.

After 64 minutes Higgins scored a second for Hibs. Stanton created the opening by nodding a Schaedler cross into the path of the giant forward, who wasted no time in smashing a right-foot volley past Olafsson. It was Higgins' first goal for Hibs on the European stage, and he was now top scorer so far that season, with seven goals. A few minutes later Duncan replaced Munro, who had had a fairly innocuous baptism in Europe, and the dangerous runs of the outside left brought an almost immediate improvement. Inspired by the former Partick Thistle player, Hibs turned on the pressure in the later stages of the match, but again found goalkeeper Olafsson in brilliant form – two of his saves, from O'Rourke and Stanton, were in the spectacular class.

FINAL SCORE: HIBERNIAN 2. KEFLAVIC 0.

UEFA CUP 1ST ROUND (1ST LEG), WEDNESDAY 19 SEPTEMBER 1973, EASTER ROAD.
HIBERNIAN: ROBERTSON, BREMNER, SCHAEDLER, STANTON, BLACK, BLACKLEY, EDWARDS, O'ROURKE, HIGGINS, CROPLEY, MUNRO.

Although disappointed at failing to secure a more emphatic victory over the Icelanders, who had contributed absolutely nothing of note as an attacking force, most observers were of the opinion that the two goals from the first leg would be more than enough in Keflavik to earn Hibs a passage into the next round.

On the Saturday, Alan Gordon made his return to the side at the expense of Higgins in a 4-2 victory over Ayr United at Easter Road, Hibs' third win of the season so far against the Somerset Park club. A four-minute purple patch in the first half saw the home side score three goals, a result that lifted them into third place in the table.

It was a time of conflicting fortunes for Hibs' two regular full backs. As Schaedler was preparing to join his Scotland colleagues for the forthcoming World Cup qualifying game against Czechoslovakia at Hampden, where he would watch from the bench as goals from Holton, and substitute Jordan gave Scotland a famous 2-1 victory that set them on the road to Munich, John Brownlie was preparing to make his comeback from injury in the third team. Watched by managing director Tom Hart, the defender made his return, after a nine-month absence, against East of Scotland side Spartans at Canal Field, Meggetland, as his teammates were defeating Ayr 4-2 at Easter Road. Brownlie played for only the first 45 minutes. At half time Hart made a speedy return to Easter Road and was just in time to see Ayr score two late goals.

Hibs had decided not to use a charter aircraft for the trip to Iceland, preferring instead to travel by scheduled flight As there was no direct flight from Edinburgh, the party made its way to Glasgow for the connection. Getting back, however, wound create a far bigger problem. As there was no direct flight from Iceland to Scotland on Thursdays, special arrangements were made to divert the Reykjavik to London flight to Glasgow, the Hibs party completing the journey back to Edinburgh by coach.

Incessant rain the day before the match had made the game extremely doubtful. With a trip to Pittodrie on the Saturday, the last thing Hibs needed was a cancellation and an enforcement of the UEFA ruling that compelled an away side to remain for another 24 hours in the hope of completing the fixture. Their fears were allayed when the referee declared the game would go ahead as scheduled. The pitch was heavily sanded, which made the goalmouths in particular extremely treacherous and good football for both sides all but impossible.

In relation to the 6,000 population of the town, what must be called a huge crowd of over 4,000 watched the game, Hibs' 50th in European competition. Because the Keflavic Stadium lacked floodlights, an early evening kick-off time of 5.15pm had been arranged to allow supporters to attend straight from work.

Playing in front of his own fans, goalkeeper Olafsson continued where he had left off at Easter Road and was in magnificent form when he was brought into action almost immediately by producing a good save from a promising O'Rourke effort. Ignoring the treacherous conditions, Hibs went into concerted attack to secure the goal that would to all intents and purposes settle the tie and the home keeper again saved a net bound effort from O'Rourke before diving to tip a Gordon drive over the bar.

Midway through the first half a Gordon goal had been rightly chalked off by the referee, but for the wrong reason. The official declared that Black had fouled an opponent in the home penalty area, a decision hotly disputed by the centre half, but after the game Gordon confessed that the ball had not crossed the line anyway.

Duncan's pace was causing all kinds of bother among the Keflavic defenders, but somewhat surprisingly it was the amateurs who took the lead, well against the run of play. In a rare attack on Robertson's goal, Zakariasson scored from a corner in the 35th minute. Bremner, standing on the goal line, cleared the ball from under the bar, but the referee correctly signalled that the ball had crossed the line.

Although they were trailing at the interval, there was never the slightest doubt that Hibs would go through to the next round. The home side threatened only sporadically, and even Olafsson's fine form could not deny Stanton from scoring an equaliser in 64 minutes. From an indirect free kick in the home penalty area, Gordon's drive was blasted into the heavily packed six-yard box and Stanton was on the spot to drive the ball home from close range.

The pace of full-time Hibs was really troubling the home side now, particularly the thrusts of Edwards and Duncan on the flanks. Because of the heavy conditions that saw boots sinking up to the ankles in mud in some parts of the ground, the part-timers were rapidly tiring and the remainder of the game was all one-way traffic towards the home goal.

Only Olafsson's heroics prevented O'Rourke from extending Hibs' lead, and the keeper made the best save of the evening from a Black effort, the centre half taking full advantage of his opponent's fatigue to support his teammates at every opportunity.

FINAL SCORE: KEFLAVIC I. HIBERNIAN I.

UEFA CUP 1ST ROUND (2ND LEG), WEDNESDAY 3 OCTOBER 1973, KEFLAVIC STADIUM.
HIBERNIAN: ROBERTSON, BREMNER, SCHAEDLER, STANTON, BLACK, BLACKLEY, EDWARDS, O'ROURKE, GORDON, CROPLEY, DUNCAN.

Although it had not been one of Hibs' most impressive performances in Europe, nonetheless the result was acceptable considering the atrocious conditions, prompting Turnbull to ask any of the watching journalists if they had ever seen a pitch quite like it.

Hopes of avoiding any of the favourites, or any fixture that involved logistical travelling problems in the next round of the UEFA Cup were dashed when the draw paired Hibs with a revenge match against their old adversaries, Leeds United, at that time well out on their own at the top of the English League and one of the best sides in Europe.

In the five and a half years since their last meeting, Leeds had realised their potential, winning the UEFA Cup twice when defeating Ferencvaros in 1968, after knocking out Hibs in the third round, and Juventus in 1971. League Cup winners in 1968, they had become league champions for the first ever time in 1969, and FA Cup winners in 1972 – an altogether impressive pedigree.

As usual Revie had left nothing to chance. Having watched Hibs several times in recent weeks, he described them as 'a very good and exciting side'.

There was to be yet more controversy over the ticket pricing when Hibs released the staggering news that a Centre Stand ticket for the Leeds game would rise from the usual 75p to £2.00, and tickets for other areas of the ground in proportion. Admission to the terracing would now be 50p instead of the usual 35p.

The reaction from the fans was swift. A spokesman for the Hibs Supporters Association described the rise as 'savage, fantastic, unfair and unjustifiable'. Honorary President Willie O'Donnell went further, declaring that the club was 'just not looking to the future at all'. He had expected the prices to go up, but not by such a 'savage amount', and 'in particular the incredible increase was bound to annoy the terracing fans who support the club loyally from one year to the other'. Unsurprisingly, when contacted by the media no one at the club had any comment to make. In comparison, at that time Leeds United's top prices were cheaper, but admission to the terracing more expensive.

Since the last meeting of the sides seven years before, Scotland cap David Harvey had replaced Sprake in goal for Leeds. Jack Charlton had retired, to be replaced by another Scottish international in Gordon McQueen, although McQueen would miss the first game at Elland Road due to injury. As some indication of the daunting task facing Hibs, nine current or future internationals would take the field against the Easter Road side at Elland Road.

Five of the Leeds side from the last game were still first-team regulars at Elland Road; in direct contrast, only Pat Stanton remained from the team defeated by the English side in 1968, although Jimmy O'Rourke was still at the club.

A newspaper article written by the Middlesbrough manager, former Leeds centre half Jack Charlton, advising the Edinburgh team to save the expense of their bus travel, was pinned on the Hibs dressing room wall prior to the game, and it had the desired effect.

As usual Hibs had promised to attack and once again they were as good as their word. Only a magnificent display by Scotland's World Cup keeper Harvey prevented the Greens from turning round at the interval one or even two goals ahead as the trio of Stanton, Higgins and Cropley dominated and outclassed Leeds in the middle of the park. A magnificent display by the captain was particularly inspiring.

Scotland manager Willie Ormond could not fail to have been impressed by the form of his Scottish-based players in a Hibs team that was without a weakness. From McArthur, who had little to do but performed brilliantly when required, right through the side to Duncan, whose pace on the left flank caused England international Reaney all kinds of problems throughout the 90 minutes, every Hibs man played his part. Magnificently led by Stanton, the midfield trio defied all that the opposition could throw at them and still found time to assist their front men.

Inside the opening minutes Yorath tackled Gordon in the box with a ferocity almost bordering on criminal assault, but to the amazement, not to say the fury, of the large crowd, the referee somehow managed to ignore the incident.

Goalkeeper Harvey, who was unaccustomed to visiting sides attacking with such ferocity at Elland Road, had his busiest 90 minutes for some time and only several brilliant saves – the highlight a marvellous stop from a Cropley effort just before half time – kept his side in the game.

Just before the break Lorimer came close for Leeds with a typical thunderbolt, but the alert McArthur turned the ball away for a corner.

Such had been the dominance of Black and Blackley in the heart of the Hibs defence, that the home side were forced to substitute Jones, who had been ineffectual all evening, for Scot Joe Jordan, but it made absolutely no difference to the pattern of play.

The Scotland skipper Billy Bremner worked tigerishly to stem the tide of green-shirted attackers, but several attempts by Tony Higgins, having his best game yet for the club, were deserving of a goal. Hibs' best effort came late in the game when Higgins, inside the six-yard box, shouted for Gordon to leave a Duncan cross from the right; unfortunately, the giant forward mistimed his header, and the ball glanced off the top of his head and high over the bar to safety.

Hazel replaced Smith for the last 20 minutes, but this had no effect on the design of the game, the visitors sensing that they could score the vital away goal, remained on top until the final whistle.

FINAL SCORE: LEEDS UNITED 0. HIBERNIAN 0.

UEFA CUP 2ND ROUND (1ST LEG), WEDNESDAY 24 OCTOBER 1973, ELLAND ROAD.
LEEDS UNITED: HARVEY, CHERRY, MADELEY, BREMNER, ELLAM, YORATH, LORIMER, CLARKE, JONES, BATES, GRAY.
HIBERNIAN: MCARTHUR, BREMNER, SCHAEDLER, STANTON, BLACK, BLACKLEY, SMITH, HIGGINS, GORDON, CROPLEY, DUNCAN.

Let there be no doubt, the English champions elect had been let off the hook. An inspired, cavalier, yet disciplined Hibs' performance had been well worthy of a two- or three-goal victory. After the game Leeds boss Don Revie admitted, 'I always thought that Hibs were a good team, and they proved it here. They should have won on the night.' Asked how his team would play in the return at Easter Road, Revie would only add, 'If we can nick a goal in Edinburgh, Hibs would have to score twice, so it should be interesting.'

Pat Stanton was deeply disappointed that, despite having the bulk of the pressure and the majority of chances, some of them fairly easy, the teams were still level. Jack Charlton, displaying a distinct lack of magnanimity, declared that it had not been the real Leeds that had faced Hibs. He did concede, however, that the Edinburgh side had been deserving of a victory on the night, having murdered the English team in midfield, and mentioned that he had been particularly impressed with the performance of Pat Stanton.

In the dressing room after the game, Eddie Turnbull was informed that a friend was waiting to see him. The friend turned out to be none other that former teammate Bobby Johnstone who could not believe just how well Hibs had played. Turnbull could be justifiably proud of the high quality of football displayed by his players, and paid tribute to the thousands of 'absolutely fabulous' fans who had travelled down from Scotland. Sadly, the evening would end in tragic circumstances when shortly after the game a Hibs supporter was knocked down by a car and killed.

A 2-0 second-leg victory over Raith Rovers at Starks Park saw the Easter Road side progress into the quarter-finals of the League Cup and yet another meeting with Rangers, but a double visit to Ibrox inside the space of five days would end in defeat, the first a mauling by the Light Blues that saw the visitors lose two points and four goals without reply. Jim McArthur was Hibs' top performer in a disappointing display by the Edinburgh side which produced little in the 90 minutes. Losing 4-0, Hibs, in the words of the old saying, were 'lucky to get nothing!'

In the League Cup at Ibrox on the Wednesday, the visitors, trailing by a goal at the interval looked the likeliest to score, and Schaedler underlined the fact by heading into his own net in trying to clear. Alex McDonald, always the consummate sportsman, was warned for his over-zealousness in congratulating the full back for his efforts, when perhaps a booking may well have been warranted. The double victories inside the space of a few days gave the Glasgow side confidence for the return. Although a reversal would not be beyond Hibs, they would have to play to their full potential in the second leg at Easter Road.

A Pat Stanton treble, his first in senior football, inspired Hibs to a comprehensive 5-0 home win against the Bully Wee, the first goals scored by the Greens since drawing with Celtic four games before. The score did not flatter the home side, who were applauded from the field at the end by supporters who were confident that their favourites could inflict the same punishment on Leeds four days later.

Just a few days before the second leg at Easter Road, Leeds were rocked by the news that six first-team regulars – Giles, Jones, McQueen, Hunter, Madeley and Harvey, all full internationals – would miss the game in Edinburgh because of injury. Worse still, second-team goalkeeper Dave Stewart, a recent signing from Ayr United, was ineligible, forcing 19-year-old third-choice keeper Shaw to make a European debut. Even with such a horrendous catalogue of injuries, Leeds could still field a team containing eight current or future internationals in Edinburgh.

Hibs, on the other hand, had no injury worries. Blackley had fully recovered from the thigh strain that had meant him missing the end of the Clyde game the previous Saturday, and the home team would be along the normal lines.

A crowd of just over 36,000, well below the expected 45,000 capacity, were inside the ground at the kick-off, the draconian pricing structure no doubt a major factor in the less than expected attendance.

The weakened Leeds took the field with a totally negative attitude and their time-wasting tactics, possession football, petty fouling and gamesmanship did little to endear them to the large home support.

In one of the most one-sided games at Easter Road in living memory, the visitors had Billy Bremner to thank for preventing a rout. Withdrawn into the sweeper's role, Bremner had a quite magnificent match, using every ounce of his experience and football acumen to thwart a rampant Hibs side, even clearing the ball from his line on four or five occasions.

Emulating Harvey in the first game at Elland Road, goalkeeper Shaw was in immense form, saving brilliantly, first from Blackley, then from Cropley a few minutes later.

Despite all their pressure, there was a let-off for the home side in the 20th minute when centre half Ellam hit the bar following a corner on the right, but fortunately for Hibs the danger was cleared.

As an early sign of their intentions to perhaps settle for penalty kicks, danger man Peter Lorimer was withdrawn into a deep-lying position, and Leeds' ultra-defensive tactics annoyed the large crowd, who were not slow in voicing their disapproval.

Keeper Shaw, who had done his reputation no harm with a quite outstanding first-half performance, was forced to retire with a hand injury at half time and was replaced by fourth-choice goalkeeper Letheren.

The second half resumed where the first had left off with one-way traffic towards the Leeds goal. Cropley was guilty of wasting a couple of gilt-edged chances to give Hibs the lead when he might have passed to a teammate in a better position rather than having a go himself.

The keeper was kept busy and he distinguished himself with a double save from Hazel, who had replaced Higgins at the interval.

The big talking point of the 90 minutes came early in the second half when Gordon cut through the Leeds defence to head a Stanton knock on high into the net past the helpless Letheren. Easter Road went wild with delight as the referee pointed to the centre circle, but the cheers soon turned to despair when the official spotted the stand-side linesman with his flag raised. After a brief consultation with his assistant, the referee disallowed the goal, judging Gordon to have been offside. The linesman had been the only person inside Easter Road to think Gordon offside and according to the Hibs manager after the game it had been a ridiculous decision.

The arrogance and gamesmanship of Bremner, who had contested every decision by the referee, was clearly upsetting the Hibs support, but this seemed to inspire the red-head to even greater heights. Leeds had rarely been seen as an attacking force and the 90 minutes ended with Bremner displaying an impudent nonchalance as he trapped the ball on the goal line before clearing it to safety.

FULL TIME: HIBERNIAN 0. LEEDS UNITED 0.

The 30 minutes of extra time passed in similar vein to the first 90, with Hibs on the ascendancy but still failing to make the vital breakthrough and it was on to penalties.

Penalty kicks had been introduced in European games only at the beginning of the season, replacing the highly unpopular method of separating teams who were still equal at the end, by the toss of a coin. It was the first time that either side had faced such a situation in a competitive game. It had been decided beforehand that in the event of the tie still being goalless at the end of 120 minutes, that the penalties would be taken at the 'top' goals, or Dunbar end of the ground. Hibs won the toss and elected to go first.

Pat Stanton stepped forward to take the first kick, but even before the ball had been placed on the spot, Eddie Turnbull insisted that Tom Hart make an immediate formal protest to the official UEFA observer, claiming the tie on the grounds that in clear contravention of the rules, the Leeds manager Don Revie and trainer Les Cocker were still on the field in the vicinity of the centre circle, and in direct contact with the Leeds players as the spot-kick procedure was about to begin. Revie remained on the field throughout. Turnbull, as the rules required, stood trackside.

Stanton sent goalkeeper Letheren the wrong way with his spot-kick but could only watch in anguish as his shot rebounded back off the upright.

Successful strikes by Cropley, Blackley, Des Bremner and Hazel and the remainder of the Leeds players meant that it was left to Billy Bremner to cap a brilliant personal performance by scoring from the final kick to send his team through to the third round.

Although it had been a tremendous feat to prevent one of the best sides in Europe from scoring in both legs, Hibs had been by far the better side in both games and had fully deserved to go through to the next round. Turnbull was devastated for his players who had put so much into the game only to go out in that manner, but in truth the game was lost at Elland Road, where Hibs had been even more dominant but had failed to take their chances. The result, however, would do little to harm the reputation of the Scottish side in Europe.

As advised by Turnbull, the chairman protested to the UEFA observer attending the game regarding Don Revie's blatant disregard for the rules during the penalty kick situation, and on the back of an official telegram of complaint, the following day both Hart and Younger flew to Switzerland to personally put Hibs' case before the European Disciplinary Committee. Besides the fact that both the Leeds officials had remained on the pitch throughout the entire penalty kick procedure to coach their players, a clear infringement of the rules, Billy Bremner had also broken the rules by leaving the field of play before returning to play his part in the proceedings. Hart had every confidence in the appeal succeeding, believing that the least Hibs could expect would be a replay, but he was to be proved wrong. After a wait of several days while the case was deliberated, it was announced that although Leeds had been found guilty of deliberately infringing the rules, and Revie

consequently banished from the dugout for the home leg against Setubal at
Elland Road, the disciplinary committee had decided that the manager had
not influenced his players, and therefore the incident did not warrant the
game being replayed. Incredibly, despite their case being technically upheld,
Hibs were forced to forfeit the bond of 500 Swiss francs required upon receipt
of the protest.

HIBERNIAN LOSE TO LEEDS UNITED 5-4 ON PENALTIES.

UEFA CUP 2ND ROUND (2ND LEG), WEDNESDAY 7 NOVEMBER 1973, EASTER ROAD.
HIBERNIAN: MCARTHUR, BREMNER, SCHAEDLER, STANTON, BLACK, BLACKLEY,
EDWARDS, HIGGINS, GORDON, CROPLEY, DUNCAN.
LEEDS UNITED: SHAW REANEY, CHERRY, BREMNER, ELLAM, YORATH, LORIMER, CLARK,
JORDAN, BATES, GRAY.

At the end of the month, two-goal Jim O'Rourke missed the chance to
score a hat-trick in Hibs' 2-1 victory over Dundee at Easter Road when
he missed a first-half penalty. The main talking point, however, was John
Brownlie, making his first appearance for the league side since his injury over
ten months before. The full back soon showed that he had lost little of his
former cavalier approach and was given resounding encouragement on his
overlapping forages up the wing by an appreciative crowd.

The return leg of the League Cup quarter-final against Rangers in
Edinburgh four days later was unusual for the fact that it was played in the
afternoon. Because of industrial action, random areas of the country were
liable to be affected by 'surprise blackouts' and, in the interests of safety,
games under floodlight had been prohibited. The unusually early kick-off
time of 1.30pm attracted a crowd of just under 20,000, far less than would
normally have been expected to attend the game, many of those present no
doubt taking advantage of the by then almost obsolete excuse from work
that they were attending their granny's funeral.

Although far from their best, the attack-minded Hibs were constantly
thwarted by a Rangers side totally committed to the negative, defensive play
that was geared to protect their 2-0 lead from the first leg. In a compliment
of a kind, Rangers outside left Ally Scott spent much of the game preventing
John Brownlie from making his trademark forays up the park, and this close
attention became too much for Brownlie, who was booked after foolishly
throwing the ball at his opponent. Although they had been the better side
for large parts of the game, Hibs had found it extremely difficult to breach a
Rangers ten-man 'Iron Curtain' defence and the game finished goalless, the
holders relinquishing their grip on the League Cup.

Before the game Eddie Turnbull had asked referee Alistair McKenzie to
clamp down on bad language from the Rangers players, which had been
directed towards the official during the first match at Ibrox – the request
earning the Hibs manager a £20 fine at the next meeting of the disciplinary
committee.

At the end of November Hibs were still seeking their first away win of the season, a situation rectified with a 2-0 victory against St Johnstone at Muirton. A second away win in the space of seven days, this time at East End Park, was enough to see the Edinburgh side move to second place in the table. Strikes by Duncan, Stanton and Gordon, earned the Greens a narrow 3-2 win against a stuffy Dunfermline side, one of whose goals was scored by a young Jim Leishman. Both teams had taken the field wearing black armbands as a mark of respect for Dunfermline defender John Lunn, who had died of leukaemia earlier in the week.

In a 5-0 whitewash of Morton, yet another hat-trick by O'Rourke, his tenth for the club, helped Hibs consolidate second place in the championship race. They were now only three points behind leaders Celtic, but had the advantage of a game in hand; furthermore, the champions were still to visit Easter Road.

A meaningless, but nevertheless interesting survey carried out in a local newspaper just before the turn of the year regarding the number of penalty kicks for and against all the First Division sides that season, revealed that only two of the 18 teams had not had a penalty awarded against them. It is left to the reader to form their own conclusions as to the identity of these Glasgow-based sides. Surprisingly, although both Rangers and Celtic were amongst the leaders as to the number of spot-kicks awarded with five, Hearts topped the list with six, all of them converted.

On New Year's Day 1974, Hearts celebrated the start of their centenary year by losing yet again to their city rivals at Tynecastle. A healthy crowd of over 35,000 saw Alex Cropley cap a scintillating display by scoring both goals in Hibs' 2-0 victory. Cropley's outstanding performances had been earning rave reviews for some time and it was no secret that observers from a number of English First Division sides were at the game to run the rule over the midfielder, who did his chances of a move to England no harm.

In mid-January, representatives of the so-called 'big six' – Hibs, Hearts, Rangers, Celtic, Dundee and Aberdeen – met yet again to discuss proposals for the formation of a new league set-up, but this time with the approval of the league management committee. Their perseverance paid dividends of a sort when it was announced that the committee were now prepared to canvas all the sides in Scotland regarding a proposal for three leagues of ten and one of 18 that had been suggested by the six, a package designed to entice back the missing fans. Nearly everyone in the game acknowledged that a change was necessary, but the problem still remained of getting the two-thirds majority required to implement any change. The six were even prepared to give the new set-up a two-year trial period that could be changed back if unsuccessful, but one way or another change would have to come.

In the first round of the mystical Scottish Cup, Hibs were favoured with a home draw against Second Division Kilmarnock, their odds at the bookies shortened from 10-1 to 4-1 to win the trophy. For those not familiar with gambling odds, it meant that for every ten pounds placed on Hibs winning the cup, the punter had little chance of receiving anything back. Kilmarnock shocked their First Division counterparts by taking an early 2-0 lead, but the home side stepped up a gear to lead 3-2 at the interval, Hibs eventually crushing the Ayrshire side 5-2 to run out more than worthy winners. Once again, a number of representatives from England, including Spurs, Nottingham Forest, Arsenal and Everton, were in the Main Stand, their target believed to be either Cropley or Blackley.

After his horrific injury almost 12 months before, Brownlie was being gradually nursed back to full fitness and he had again been replaced in the league side by Des Bremner. Turnbull, however, had thrown down the gauntlet, telling Brownlie that it was up to him to replace the Deveronvale man who was then playing the best football of his career and on the verge of international honours. Unfortunately, Bremner was involved in a collision during the cup-tie against Kilmarnock and broke his collarbone, the injury proving severe enough to keep him out of action for six weeks.

On the final day of the month Turnbull motored south to sign the unsettled centre forward Joe Harper from Everton for a Scottish record fee of £120,000. A £100,000 bid for the player had earlier been agreed by both clubs, but a late attempt by Aberdeen to lure a player they had earlier sold to the Liverpool club for £180,000 back to Pittodrie, meant that an improved offer from Hibs was had been required to secure Harper's services at Easter Road.

The big question of who would drop out of the Hibs line-up to make way for the record buy was postponed temporarily when it was discovered that Harper was still serving a two-match suspension imposed by the FA. The striker, who looked decidedly overweight, watched from the stand as his new side defeated his former Aberdeen teammates 3-1 at Easter Road, the Hibs goals ironically enough scored by Gordon, and O'Rourke, both possible candidates to be replaced by the new signing.

Harper made his debut at Brockville seven days later, on 9 February 1974. He stepped into the side as a direct replacement for fans favourite Alan Gordon who was on the bench, but he did little to impress in a dour and unimaginative game that ended 0-0. Falkirk's keeper, Donaldson, was not called upon to make one single save throughout the entire 90 minutes, but Harper might well have opened his account for his new club near the end, only to see his scuffed shot from close range cleared to safety.

Alan Gordon was recalled for the Scottish cup-tie against St Johnstone at Muirton the following week, replacing Harper who took his place on the bench. The tried-and-tested pairing of O'Rourke and Gordon proved immediately successful, O'Rourke scoring all three goals in a fine 3-1 victory.

For a third successive year a heavy loss was declared at the AGM, proof yet again, if it was still needed, that many clubs were finding it impossible to break even on just income alone. Although the gate receipts had soared by more than £52,000 during the previous year, mainly due to another rise in admission charges, wages and expenses had soared by a colossal £63,000. It

Hibernian season 1965–66. Back row left to right: Blackley, Simpson, Stein, Duncan, (J.) Stevenson, Reilly, Allan, Wilson, Whiteford, Falconer, Murphy, Martin, Baxter. Middle row: Stanton, Fraser, Vincent, Cullerton, McNamee, Wilkinson, (C.) Grant, McNeill, Gartshore, Hamilton. Front row: (B.) Hogg, O'Rourke, Quinn, Cormack, Brown, Scott, (D.) Hogg, (E.) Stevenson, Davis.

Action from the Scotland versus Brazil international at Hampden in 1966, Peter Cormack's first full cap.

Jim Scott sends a header narrowly past Montgomery of Sunderland. North American Tournament, 1967.

Hibs' line-up before the ill-fated pre-season friendly at Blackpool 1967. Back row left to right: Simpson, Davis, Duncan, Allan, Madsen, McGraw, (D.) Hogg, Marinello. Front row: O'Rourke, Quinn, (C.) Grant, Stein, Cormack, (E.) Stevenson, Murphy.

Hibernian, season 1968–69. Back row left to right: Brownlie, Fraser, Madsen, Wilkinson, Allan, Wilson, Duncan, McGraw, Simpson, (D.) Hogg. Middle: Shankly (manager), Stanton, McEwan, – , Cormack, O'Rourke, Murphy, Grant, Blackley, McNeill, McNiven (physio). Front row: Jones, Quinn, McCabe, Marinello, Davis, Pringle, Stein, (E.) Stevenson.

Action shot from an almost deserted Easter Road. Late 1960s.

Chairman Tom Hart.

Manager Willie Macfarlane pictured as a player during the 1950s.

Joe Baker opens the scoring in Hibs' 3-1 win against Airdrie at Easter Road in 1971.

Johnny Graham scores Hibs' third goal in the same game.

'Mr Hibs', Pat Stanton.

Team Photo 1971–72. Back row left to right: Shevlane, Stanton, Black, Baines, Blackley, Brownlie, McEwan, O'Rourke. Front row: Baker, Graham, Auld, Duncan, Turnbull, Hazel, Pringle, Davidson, Cropley. Sitting: McNiven, Stevenson, Hamilton, Fraser.

Programme for the 1972 Drybrough Cup Final.

CELTIC *VERSUS* HIBERNIAN

LEAGUE CUP FINAL

5p OFFICIAL PROGRAMME

HAMPDEN PARK
Saturday
9th December 1972
KICK·OFF 3·00 p.m.

Programme for the victorious 1972 League Cup Final.

The Hampden dressing room after the 1972 League Cup Final. From left: Black,
O'Rourke, Brownlie, Hamilton, Cropley, Duncan, Stanton, Herriot.

Turnbull's Tornadoes. Back row left to right: Smith, Spalding, McArthur, Bremner,
O'Rourke. Middle row: Turnbull (manager), Humphries (trainer), Blackley, McGregor,
Higgins, Brownlie, Black, Fraser (coach), Auld (coach). Front row: Edwards, Schaedler,
Munro, Stanton, Gordon, Cropley, Duncan, McNiven (physio).

Manager Eddie Turnbull (pictured as a member of the Famous Five in the mid-'50s).

Physio Tom McNiven.

Alan Gordon scoring the last minute winner against Celtic in the 1973 Drybrough Cup.

Hibernian season 1975–76. Back row left to right: MacLeod, Barry, McArthur, Brownlie, Blackley, Schaedler. Middle row: Muir, Stanton, Higgins, Munro, Spalding, Carroll. Front row: Murray, Duncan, Harper, Bremner, Edwards, Smith.

Jackie McNamara.

Programme for the 1979
Scottish Cup Final.

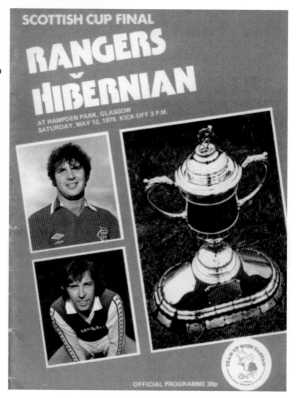

Hibs' 1979 Scottish Cup Final squad. Back row left to right: McNamara, Macleod, McArthur, (D.) Lambie, Duncan. Middle: Turnbull (manager), (J.) Lambie (coach), Callaghan, Higgins, Farmer, Brazil, Fraser (coach). Front: Campbell, Bremner, Hutchison, Stewart, Rae, Brown.

George Best on his first day in Edinburgh.

Left: Best with his new teammates.
Back from left: Ward, McNamara.
Front: Higgins, Best, Campbell.

Below: Willie Ormond, who replaced
Eddie Turnbull as manager after the heavy
semi-final defeat by Celtic.

was now imperative for ambitious full-time clubs like Hibs that a new league structure be implemented as soon as possible, and also that clubs be allowed to retain a larger share of the gate money. After major consultations with all the clubs, in mid-February the SFA management committee at last recommended that league reconstruction be implemented. Now, a new Premier League of ten teams playing each other four times a season would be in place for the start of the season after next.

Meanwhile, the keenly anticipated showdown with league leaders Celtic in the capital ended in a 4-2 defeat for the Edinburgh Greens. Harper was still on the bench, as was Celtic's new signing, Jimmy Bone. Once again Hibs had no answer to the danger of Dixie Deans, who opened the scoring in the first minute, capitalising on a mistake by Black. He scored again in the final minute of the match to put the result beyond the Edinburgh men and increase his side's lead at the top of the table to five points.

Seven days later Joe Harper made his home debut against Rangers in a new-look line-up with Pat Stanton at inside right and Spalding at right half. It proved to be a winning combination. Two goals from Gordon and another by Bremner gave Hibs a comfortable victory to consolidate their second place position and set them up for the forthcoming Scottish Cup quarter-final against Dundee at Easter Road.

In bright sunshine, the same 11 that had started against Rangers recovered from a poor first-half performance against the Angus side to earn a Scottish Cup replay at Dens Park. Gordon continued his recent good form by scoring all Hibs' goals in an exciting 3-3 draw. The striker even missed a great chance to win the game in the dying seconds, his header from close range just clipping the post, and it was on to Dundee on the Wednesday evening.

Torrential rain, however, gave the referee no option but to cancel both the cup replay and the home game against Motherwell a few days later. For some time now the condition of the Easter Road playing surface had been causing concern and plans were already underway to invest a four-figure sum to upgrade the pitch at the end of the season.

In the eventual cup replay at Dens Park, Hibs blundered out of the competition in what one leading newspaper dubbed 'A nightmare at Dundee.' All three Dundee goals were scored in a 15-minute spell in the first half as the visitors surrendered with barely a fight. Earlier in the proceedings, O'Rourke, encouraged by the huge support that had made its way from Edinburgh, twice had the opportunity to open the scoring, but after the Dark Blues took the lead after a mistake by McArthur, the roof fell in and the fans would now have to wait at least another year before the Scottish Cup made a return to Easter Road.

After being involved in the periphery of the Scotland set-up for some time, at the end of March Erich Schaedler won his first – and only, as it would turn out – full cap, against West Germany, the country of his father's birth. The game in Frankfurt would be a particularly unhappy one for teammate Pat Stanton, who had a torrid time in the 2-1 defeat. After conceding the penalty that had allowed the Germans to open the scoring, late in the game he was dispossessed in midfield, the mistake leading directly to Germany's winning goal. It was to be Stanton's last cap. He would not feature in the full side again.

The game against Motherwell postponed earlier because of the waterlogged pitch was rescheduled for Wednesday 3 April. Thick fog had hung over the area all afternoon, but the referee decided that visibility was good enough to allow the game to proceed; 17 minutes later, and the home side leading by a goal from the penalty spot after Motherwell had missed from a similar award, the fog thickened leaving the referee with no alternative but to send the players to the dressing rooms. After a five-minute wait, consultation with the Met Office confirmed that the fog was unlikely to lift and a tannoy announcement informed the spectators that the match had been cancelled. If the 11,000 fans were dismayed at the game being abandoned, they were furious to learn that there would be no refund, nor even a voucher entitling them to free entry when the game did eventually go ahead. Apparently, there was nothing in the rules to stipulate that the paying customers should be reimbursed in these circumstances.

Draws against St Johnstone and Dumbarton saw Hibs drop to fourth place, but a 3-1 win at Dens enabled the Easter Road men to arrest the slide and also gain revenge for the earlier cup defeat by Dundee. Gerry Adair, making his first-team debut impressed on his first outing. McKenzie replaced McArthur who had again injured his hand, and on a night that witnessed what was possibly Scotland's first football streaker, Hibs recovered from a first-half deficit to record an impressive 3-1 win. Apart from Adair, Brownlie and Hazel had also been in brilliant form, but it was Man of the Match Harper who did most to earn the victory, capping a brilliant performance by lobbing former Hibs goalkeeper Thomson Allan for Hibs' third goal in the very last minute.

Just three days later at Gayfield, Hibs' league title aspirations came off the rails when lowly Arbroath stormed back to win 3-2 after trailing by two goals at the interval. A penalty just after the break inspired the Red Lichties, who went on to totally dominate the second half, scoring the winner four minutes from time, much to the embarrassment of the Easter Road side and to the fury of the travelling fans.

Hibs had now dropped in fourth place, behind Celtic, Rangers and Aberdeen, but although they still had two games in hand, they trailed the leaders by eight points, and second-placed Rangers by two.

The twice-cancelled game against Motherwell finally went ahead in mid-April. Hibs had now decided to allow the fans into the ground at reduced rates, but the suggestion was immediately vetoed by the Scottish League who insisted that the gesture, while admirable, was contrary to the rules. Common sense prevailed and with the agreement of their opponents, prices were drastically reduced for the stands and the enclosure, over which the authorities had no jurisdiction, with the admission charges for the terracing remaining as normal. A Bobby Smith goal gave the home side a slender win, but after conceding 22 goals in their last nine matches, goalkeeper Jim McArthur would have taken great satisfaction at achieving Hibs first shut-out in ten games.

A few days later Alan Gordon scored all Hibs' goals in a 3-0 win over Dumbarton at Easter Road, his fifth and last hat-trick for the club. The first was scored after just 67 seconds, and his second, just before the interval, was Hibs' 100th goal of the season. Although Stanton had not been at his best for some weeks, it was still a huge shock when the fans discovered that the captain had been left out of the side, his place taken by Adair, and was not even on the bench.

With Rangers dropping a point at Pittodrie, the Edinburgh side now had second place all to themselves.

Hibs gained revenge for the earlier defeat by Arbroath, when in an astonishing final three minutes of a previously drab and goalless game, they first took the lead, then lost it, within seconds, before Harper sealed the vital points with a fine solo goal just before the final whistle. After an absence of only two games, the recalled Pat Stanton was in his usual place at right half.

An easy 3-0 win at Cappielow with a goal by Stanton and two from Harper meant that Hibs now needed just three points from their final two games to ensure finishing in second place for the first time since 1953. A 1-1 draw against Clyde at Shawfield, where, incredibly, Hibs hadn't won since October 1965 when goals by John Baxter, and John McNamee had given the capital side a 2-1 victory, meant that even a draw at Tannadice against Dundee United would be enough.

In the final game of the season, the 4-1 win had flattered Hibs somewhat against a hard-working United team, but a strong finish gave them the necessary points to finish ahead of third-placed Rangers to qualify yet again for UEFA Cup. Chelsea manager Dave Sexton was in the crowd to cast an eye over Alex Cropley who scored Hibs' opening goal, but it now seemed that Arsenal would be the favourites to sign the diminutive inside forward.

A major surprise for the Hibs fans who had made their way to Tannadice was the exclusion of favourite Alan Gordon from the line-up. There would be even more astounding news after the game, when the club revealed that Gordon had been placed on the open-to-transfer list along with centre half Black who had not featured in the side since losing his place first to Adair and then to Spalding, after the 3-3 draw with Dumbarton nine games before.

Gordon had scored ten goals including two hat-tricks since the signing of Joe Harper, compared to the former Everton players nine, and had again ended the season as the club's top scorer, with 25 goals in all games, 16 in the league. Gordon had been an almost ever-present all season, missing just a handful of games, and the announcement that he would be allowed to leave was received with utter astonishment.

John Hazel had failed to command a regular first-team place recently, making just six league appearances during the past two seasons and another five as a substitute, and he was transferred to Morton just before the seasons end, teaming up again with former Easter Road colleagues Roy Baines and Alec McGhee at Cappielow.

14

A Disastrous Eight Days
and Centenary Celebrations
1974-75

FOR JOHN BLACKLEY and Erich Schaedler there had been little time for rest during the summer. Both had been included in the Scotland squad for the Home Internationals in May, Blackley winning his second full cap in the 2-0 defeat of England at Hampden, before joining up with the Scotland squad that made its way to Germany for the World Cup finals. Blackley would play in Scotland's opening game, a 2-0 victory over Zaire in Dortmund, Denis Law's first and last in a World Cup Final. Schaedler would take no part in the competition and watched from the sidelines as Scotland gave a good account of themselves, failing only narrowly to qualify for the second round despite ending the group stages unbeaten.

A few days after the start of pre-season training, Hibs chairman Sir John Bruce had been seriously injured in a road accident when his car was in a collision at the junction of Arboretum Road and Inverleith Place in Edinburgh. The surgeon suffered severe injuries to the head and ribs and was taken to the Royal Infirmary where he was detained for some time. He never fully recovered. His wife, a passenger in the car, was also hurt but escaped serious injury.

A bid by Blackpool for the popular Jimmy O'Rourke, placed on the transfer list at his own request, was rejected. Although O'Rourke had scored 14 goals from only 16 league starts the previous season, he was finding it extremely difficult to command a regular first-team place and now saw his future away from his beloved Easter Road.

Attempting to secure a third successive Drybrough Cup success, Hibs relaxed their hold on the trophy at the semi-final stage when Rangers won a close game 3-2. Goals from Duncan and Harper had seen of the challenge of newly promoted Kilmarnock in the first round, but in the semi-final at Easter Road the Ibrox side were found to be a much tougher proposition. After dominating the opening 30 minutes of the match, the home side found themselves two down at half time. Two late goals by Harper gave them an opportunity to save the game, but the 3-2 defeat meant the end of Hibs' eight-game unbeaten run in the competition.

On the eve of the League Cup campaign Hibs played Dutch side NEC Nijmegen in a challenge match at Easter Road. The programme underlined the fact that Joe Harper had already averaged a goal a game that season, with five in five games. Against Nijmegan the centre forward took his tally to ten when he scored all the Hibs goals in a totally one-sided 5-0 victory. The loudest cheer of the night, however, was reserved for the introduction of fans' favourite Alan Gordon when he came on as a second-half substitute. There were already dissenting signs among large sections of the support, who blamed the introduction of Harper as the catalyst for the breaking up of the hugely popular pairing of Gordon and O'Rourke, and in later years Harper would often state light-heartedly that in the Nijmegen game he scored five goals and was booed off the park. In fact Turnbull had signed Harper to play alongside O'Rourke and Gordon in a three-pronged attack, but it had never quite worked out. Gordon would drop back to play a few games in midfield, but both he and O'Rourke would soon be on their way, Harper handed the role of recognised striker.

Off the field, the Players' Union were once again demanding a share of the television revenues received by both the SFA and Scottish League. A similar request near the end of the previous season had fallen on deaf ears, but now the Union were stipulating that unless 15 per cent of any television money was forwarded to the Benevolent Fund, the players would refuse to take part in any game played in front of the cameras. Scotland was one of the few major European footballing nations not to have a benevolent scheme in place for its members, but once again the appeal fell on deaf ears and both the SFA and Scottish League refused point-blank to bow to their demands. As often happens, the promised strike action failed to materialise.

For a second successive season the League Cup was again played under the experimental offside ruling, but the format that had allowed the two top teams from each section qualifying for the later stages the previous season had proved both unpopular and time-consuming, and it had reverted back to only the top side going forward to the quarter-finals. Hibs had been drawn in a tough and uncompromising section. As well as the by now almost mandatory meeting with Rangers at some stage in the competition, they would face holders Dundee who had beaten Celtic 1-0 in the previous year's final, as well as the 1973–74 semi-finalists, St Johnstone.

In a dispute of a different kind regarding the televising of games, Tom Hart had banned the cameras from covering the opening League Cup tie against Rangers at Easter Road. For some time Hart had been gravely concerned that football was in danger of being seriously over exposed on the TV screens, and had been unhappy at the previous two Drybrough Cup Finals being broadcast live. Barred from covering Rangers at Easter Road, the cameras would in all probability have turned their attentions to the Celtic game at Parkhead that same afternoon.

Dropping only two points from the six League Cup games, the section had been won far more easily than would have been expected, the Drybrough Cup defeat by Rangers well and truly avenged by Hibs taking all four points from the Ibrox side. Alan Gordon had been recalled for the opening fixture and both he and Harper were among the goalscorers in Hibs 3-1 victory. On the morning of the game, Jim Black, who had lost his place near the end of the previous season, rejoined his former club Airdrie for a fee in the region of £8,000.

Hibs' solitary reverse in the opening rounds of the League Cup came in a 2-1 defeat at Dens Park, when only a superb display of goalkeeping by Thomson Allan had denied his former teammates the reward a magnificent second-half performance had probably deserved. That same day, Jimmy O'Rourke became the third of the legendary Tornadoes to leave Easter Road when he was transferred to St Johnstone for a fee in the region of £15,000. O'Rourke would make his first start for his new club against his former colleagues in Hibs 3-1 win at Muirton seven days later. After more than 12 years at Easter Road, Hibs' longest-serving player admitted that it was a huge wrench to leave the club he had supported all his life, and could not leave 'without making reference to the wonderful treatment received from the supporters over the years.'

The ever-popular O'Rourke received a rousing reception from the visiting fans when he took the field before the start of the game wearing the familiar number eight jersey, but despite his valiant efforts he could do little to prevent his former teammates from consolidating their position at the top of the section. So far that season, including friendly games, Joe Harper had scored 14 goals, but in Perth the former Everton player failed to score for the first time since the opening game of the season, the role of match winners falling to Stanton, Gordon, and Edwards.

The serious business of attempting to win the championship began in earnest at Pittodrie. Alan Gordon, playing in an unfamiliar midfield role, was carried off, injured, midway through the second half, with Aberdeen leading 2-1. In a marvellous fightback, Harper equalised with a tremendous 20-yard volley from a free kick with just four minutes remaining. Cropley, who was then attracting even more interest from south of the border, scored his second goal of the afternoon to secure both points in the final seconds of the game.

A look through the record books just before the first Edinburgh derby of the season would have revealed that of the 20 league games between the sides over the previous ten years, ten had been won by Hibs compared to Hearts' four. Six had ended all square, amazingly all by the same 0-0 scoreline. At Easter Road it was a game of three penalties when Hearts goalkeeper Garland saved spot-kicks from both Cropley and Harper. Donald Ford scored after a similar award for the visitors, but an own goal by Hearts full back Clunie, and a late winner from Arthur Duncan allowed Hibs to maintain their recent dominance over their Gorgie rivals.

At Firhill, seven days after the victory against Hearts, according to press reports an Alan Gordon solo goal was almost worth the admission money alone. Collecting the ball on the halfway line Gordon stormed through the middle of the park leaving a trail of Partick defenders sprawling in his wake before firing an unstoppable shot past goalkeeper Arrol from just inside the penalty area. The convincing 5-1 win gave the visitors maximum points so far, and although it was early days, Hibs now topped the table.

As part of their warm-up for the new season, the Edinburgh side had taken in a three-game tour of Norway. After drawing with OPE Ostersund, they wound up the trip by beating both Nesse Gutten and Rosenberg, the latter by a 3-1 scoreline. In an incredible coincidence, 24 hours after the victory over Rosenberg Tom Hart and Tommy Younger, both attending the draw in Zurich, were amazed to discover that the Norwegian side would be Hibs' next UEFA Cup opponents.

After a light training session at Easter Road in the forenoon, the players and officials embarked at Turnhouse on the flight to Trondhheim. After the somewhat awkward travel arrangements on the journey to Keflavik the previous year, the club had reverted to hiring a privately chartered aircraft, and several dozen supporters accompanied the team to Norway.

When Turnbull had watched Rosenberg draw 1-1 on the Sunday against bottom-of-the-table Raufoss, he had been very impressed by centre forward Iversen who was prepared to shoot from any angle, and it was evident on this showing that he would pose the main threat to the Edinburgh side. Arthur Duncan, who had not missed a European tie since joining the club, had been carried off late in the game at Firhill on the Saturday and was still in hospital under observation. He was replaced in the party that made its way to Norway by young centre forward Laurie Dunn, taken along just for the experience, in line with the chairman's current policy. Ian Munro would take Duncan's place in the unfamiliar outside left position. Before the game it had been decided, that in the event of Hibs being awarded a penalty kick, Alex Cropley would replace regular taker Harper, who already had missed three times from the spot that season.

In a game far more one-sided than the scoreline would suggest, goals from Stanton, Gordon and Cropley gave Hibs what appeared to be a commanding lead, but in a thrilling late fightback, danger man Iversen scored twice to give the part-timers what was seen as a slight chance at Easter Road. The visitor's third goal, scored by Cropley just after the interval, was Hibs' 100th in European Competition.

The wet and blustery conditions had made things difficult for both sides but the small crowd of spectators, including the few who had travelled from Edinburgh, huddled together for protection from the driving rain, saw Hibs play some clever exciting football irrespective of the slippery underfoot conditions. Man of the Match Stanton was involved in nearly every Hibs move, and it was the skipper who put his side ahead after 18 minutes. A good run and intelligent anticipation of the situation allowed the captain to collect a clever pass from Munro before calmly slipping the ball past Thunshelle in the home goal. Rosenberg were now struggling to compete with the tempo of the game, and Gordon gave Hibs a deserved two-goal lead, when he scored with a perfectly placed header from an accurate Harper cross eight minutes before the break.

The second leg at Easter Road seemed a mere formality for the players and the small group of Hibs fans when Cropley finished off another clever Munro move on the hour mark when he volleyed home a right-foot shot, but almost immediately Iversen pulled one back for the home side. The striker seemed to obstruct goalkeeper McArthur as he came to collect a cross, forcing him to drop the ball, the Norwegian reacting quickest to drive the ball into the Hibs net. Despite furious protests by the visitors that the goalkeeper had been fouled, the referee allowed the goal to stand. The official, who had not performed badly throughout the 90 minutes, was involved in yet more controversy in the final minute when he ignored a linesman's raised flag to allow Iversen, who looked at least five yards offside, to score a second goal.

FINAL SCORE: ROSENBERG 2. HIBERNIAN 3.

UEFA CUP 1ST ROUND (1ST LEG), WEDNESDAY 18 SEPTEMBER 1974, ROSENBERG.
HIBERNIAN: MCARTHUR, BROWNLIE, SCHAEDLER, STANTON, SPALDING, BLACKLEY, EDWARDS, CROPLEY, HARPER, GORDON, MUNRO.

To his credit, after the match the Belgian referee apologised to Hibs, admitting that he had not seen the raised flag when Iverson scored the Norwegians' second goal, but by then it was far too late and the damage had been done. Although disappointed at the two goals conceded, Turnbull was pleased with the overall form shown by Hibs, who had dominated the game from start to finish in treacherous conditions, and he did not visualise Rosenberg causing much of a problem in the return fixture in Edinburgh.

Hibs had been drawn against Second Division Kilmarnock in the quarter-finals of the League Cup. The first leg, at Rugby Park, ended all square at three goals apiece to set the stage for an exciting second game in Edinburgh.

The return leg was the first game to be played under the improved Easter Road floodlights. Some time before, UEFA had issued a directive that any side wishing to participate in any of the three major European tournaments must have lighting of a sufficient standard. The state-of-the-art floodlighting system, which still utilised the original pylons, had cost Hibs over £27,000. As far as the supporters were concerned, the existing 20-year-old Easter Road lights had been more than adequate, but those attending the Kilmarnock game were impressed by the new system, which made it much easier for the home fans to see their side progress into the semi-finals with a 4-1 victory, a late three-goal burst demoralising a gritty and industrious Kilmarnock side.

Arsenal manager Bertie Mee watched the game from the stand, presumably once again to cast an eye over Cropley, who had performed well, but he left immediately after the match and no contact was made with the Hibs directors. Cropley, who had been keen on a move to Highbury, would later confess that he had been in unofficial talks with the London club for nearly a year and that Hibs had already turned down a hush-hush bid for him. The fans knew nothing about this at the time, but rumours were circulating the city that certain players, including Cropley, might just be available for transfer. Turnbull was quick to scotch these rumours by stating categorically that he was 'building a side not dismantling one, and that no player at Easter Road was for sale'. He acknowledged that Cropley, then playing the best football of his career, was an important and valuable part of his plans and there was no way he would be allowed to leave.

The new lighting system was not the only improvement being made to the stadium. The poor condition of the pitch had been causing concern, and so during the close season major drainage and resurfacing work was carried out in an attempt to prevent postponements caused by bad weather, which had interrupted the league programme the previous season.

Three days after the victory over Kilmarnock, Jimmy O'Rourke made his first appearance at Easter Road since his transfer to St Johnstone in the summer. An editorial in the club programme welcomed him back to his ancestral home, paying tribute to his years of loyal service to the club. O'Rourke celebrated the return by scoring the only goal of the game after just four minutes, inflicting Hibs' first league defeat of the season.

Although they had failed to score against St Johnstone, their first blank of the season, a large crowd was expected at Easter Road on the Wednesday in anticipation of watching their favourites run up a huge score against the part-time Norwegian side. They were not to be disappointed.

Heavy rain before the game reduced the expected attendance to less than 12,000, but the hardy souls who braved the miserable weather saw Hibs run up both their biggest ever competitive European win, and a record aggregate score.

The visitors stunned the sodden home support by taking an early lead to level the overall score when danger man Iversen expertly curled a free kick beyond the grasping reach of McArthur from outside the box in the 16th minute, but that was almost their last involvement as an attacking force as Hibs stepped up a gear to score three times inside a four-minute spell.

Even before the amateurs had taken the lead, goalkeeper Thunshelle had produced three great saves to deny the Greens, and the end result was never seriously in doubt. In 19 minutes, good leading up play by Gordon created an opening for Harper whose right-foot shot flashed past Thunshelle to give Hibs the overall lead.

Three minutes later, an intelligent Harper head flick was collected by Munro, whose left-foot shot beat the keeper from a narrow angle, and almost directly from the re-centre, Hibs scored their second inside 60 seconds when Munro reciprocated by laying on a chance for Harper, who himself scored with a header.

A fortunate fourth was scored when goalkeeper Thunshelle misjudged an angled cross from Munro that curled into the unprotected net, and eight minutes before the break, Stanton took advantage of a rebound from a Harper shot to give Hibs an unassailable 5-1 interval lead.

The opening 45 minutes were little more than a shooting match and in the second half Hibs picked up where they had left off. With Edwards pulling the strings in was now no more than an exhibition match, precision passing by the diminutive midfielder produced almost constant danger for Rosenberg.

Cropley scored from the spot after Munro had been brought down in the box, and eight minutes later Edwards flighted over a precision cross for Gordon to score with a delightful head flick. Cropley scored his second of the night from the spot after the cavalier Brownlie had been brought down inside the penalty area with ten minutes remaining, before Stanton completed the scoring in the dying minutes when heading home a Schaedler cross. Brownlie, who had taken a knock, was substituted with two minutes remaining, but despite the predictable clamour by the fans for number ten, there was no more scoring.

FINAL SCORE: HIBERNIAN 9. ROSENBERG 1.

UEFA CUP 1ST ROUND (2ND LEG), WEDNESDAY 2 OCTOBER 1974, EASTER ROAD.
HIBERNIAN: MCARTHUR, BROWNLIE, SCHAEDLER, STANTON, SPALDING, BLACKLEY, EDWARDS, CROPLEY, HARPER, GORDON, MUNRO.

Falkirk, who had defeated Hearts over two legs in the quarter-finals, returned to Tynecastle on Wednesday 9 October to face the other half of Edinburgh's big two in the League Cup semi-final. A crowd of over 22,000 saw Hibs win a lacklustre game against a dour and negative Falkirk side, Joe Harper scoring the only goal of the game with a tremendous 20-yard drive 19 minutes from the end. The same player went on to smash a powerful header against the bar, but one goal was always going to be enough. Interviewed before the game, Falkirk's manager, John Prentice, stated that Hibs were without doubt the best side in Scotland, which was underlined by his team's dreary, defensive tactics, designed solely to frustrate both Hibs and their support. In the other semi-final, a slender 1-0 win over Airdrie at Hampden brought Hibs face to face for the fifth time in just over two and a half years in a Cup Final with who else but Celtic?

Bolstered by the confidence of reaching yet another Cup Final, Turnbull's men were in unbeatable form three days later when they dispatched Motherwell 6-2 at Easter Road. A brilliant display of fast, attacking football completely demoralised their opponents, and the game was well and truly over by half time with the home side leading 5-1. The pace understandably slackened in the second half, but the Steelmen quite simply had no answer to Man of the Match Ian Munro, who had a hand in the first four goals, setting up two before scoring two himself.

On the other side of the city things weren't going quite so well. A 5-0 defeat at Dens Park that same afternoon left the Maroons marooned at the foot of the table. Under fire, the Hearts manager Bobby Seith resigned later in the week.

Hibs' visit to Parkhead on Saturday 19 October marked the start of a momentous eight days for the club. Lying third in the table before the game, they would go top equal on goal difference if they managed to overcome Celtic and beat Rangers' results that same afternoon. It was not to be, however, and the Edinburgh side's championship hopes were severely dented when Celtic scored three times in a nine-minute spell during the first half. Any slight hopes of a recovery were shattered when Dixie Deans scored a fourth just minutes after the restart, and a woeful display by Hibs allowed Celtic to run out easy 5-0 winners, Deans scoring his, by now, almost standard hat-trick.

On the Wednesday evening the Edinburgh side faced the celebrated Juventus at Easter Road. In the role of interpreter, Gigi Peronace, the famous agent who had been instrumental in taking Joe Baker to Italy in 1961, was among the Italian party that arrived at Turnhouse Airport the day before the game.

Also in the Juventus party were two well known players who were making their second appearance against the Easter Road side – the legendary Altafini and Dino Zoff, now the regular Italian international goalkeeper. Both had played for Napoli against Hibs in 1967 although Altafini had not featured in the return game at Easter Road.

Turnbull had no injury worries for the game, nor had Juventus, whose only concern was the omission of goalscoring midfielder Fabio Capello, who had been forced to sit out the match after receiving two cautions in the previous round.

Hibs started well, their efforts earning them a series of corners in the opening minutes, but unfortunately they came to nothing.

It was obvious that Juventus were well aware of the danger of John Brownlie and his cavalier overlaps up the wing, and in the opening minutes Longobucco was booked for a cynical foul on the defender.

Hibs' first real chance of the night came after 35 minutes when Brownlie sent over a great cross from the right, but Harper was unable to connect properly and the chance was missed.

Two minutes before the break, the roars of the large Easter Road crowd of just under 30,000 were stifled when Juventus took the lead. Bettega beat Brownlie in a race down Hibs' right-hand side, his incisive pass inside finding the inrushing Gentile, who easily beat the advancing McArthur.

Spurred on by the late goal, Juventus pushed forward from the restart and almost immediately McArthur had to be alert to prevent his side going two down from a Cuccureddo effort.

Hibs equalised on the hour mark. From a short corner on the right, Brownlie found Edwards. The quick-thinking number seven spotted Stanton making an intelligent run through the middle between two defenders, and his perfectly measured cross was headed powerfully past Zoff from close range.

Now spurred on by an enthusiastic support, the home side took the lead five minutes later. After a good move, Duncan crashed a Harper deflection against the underside of the bar, but the relief of the Italian defenders was only momentary as the handily placed Cropley side-footed the rebound into the net.

Hibs' advantage lasted only a few minutes. The veteran Altafini, who had come on as a substitute at the start of the second half, tried a shot at goal. His half-hit shot was stopped by McArthur, but the keeper could only look on in agony as the ball trundled over the line.

The goal knocked the heart from the home side and renewed the flagging spirits of the visitors; it was no surprise when Cuccureddo gave the Italians the lead ten minutes from the end.

The ageing but ever-dangerous Altafini, scored his second goal of the night with just three minutes remaining, after his shot had deflected off McArthur's left-hand post, rolling along the goal line to hit the other upright before squirming over the line.

FINAL SCORE: HIBERNIAN 2. JUVENTUS 4.

UEFA CUP 2ND ROUND (1ST LEG), WEDNESDAY 23 OCTOBER 1974, EASTER ROAD. HIBERNIAN: MCARTHUR, BROWNLIE, SCHAEDLER, STANTON, SPALDING, BLACKLEY, EDWARDS, CROPLEY, HARPER, GORDON, DUNCAN.

Just a few weeks after registering their largest ever European victory against Rosenberg, the roles were reversed as Hibs suffered their heaviest home defeat in 27 European games. They were now left with the seemingly impossible task of having to score at least three goals in Turin to overturn the result.

Altafini, wearing the number 13 shirt that had proved so unlucky for Hibs on the night, was the main difference between the sides. He was rarely called upon to over-exert himself, but his accurate and precise shooting had troubled McArthur on numerous occasions throughout the second half.

On the morning of the Juventus game it had been announced that, in an attempt to curb the hooligan problem, a three-foot high fence was soon to be erected on the perimeter wall to prevent fans from entering the pitch. Hibs was the first club in Scotland to make such a move. A high fence was also to be erected at each end of the main terracing to separate the home support from the supporters in the Dunbar End, the traditional away end of the ground.

Just three days after the midweek European disappointment, it was on to Hampden for Hibs' second League Cup Final inside three years, and their third in six, all against the same side. Once again, a huge armada of fans left the capital to support their favourites, but for the second time in just over a week a leaky Hibs defence failed to curtail a rampant Celtic forward line, particularly Dixie Deans, who scored yet another treble. Slack defending allowed the Hoops to score twice in the first 45 minutes, but a Harper goal made the interval score a respectable-looking 2-1. After the break Hibs were again a poor second best and despite Harper scoring twice more, it was yet another afternoon of abject embarrassment for the Easter Road side, who finally succumbed to a humiliating 6-3 defeat.

The final whistle brought the curtain down on one of the most disastrous eight days for the club in many a year, but by that time most of the large Hibs support had already started to make their way home.

Alex Edwards and Ian Munro were among the better performers along with Joe Harper, who scored all three Hibs goals to finish as probably the only player ever to score a hat-trick in a national Cup Final and still finish on the losing side.

LEAGUE CUP FINAL, SATURDAY 26 OCTOBER 1974, HAMPDEN PARK, GLASGOW.
HIBERNIAN: MCARTHUR, BROWNLIE, BREMNER, STANTON, SPALDING, BLACKLEY, EDWARDS, CROPLEY, HARPER, MUNRO, DUNCAN. SUBS: SMITH, MURRAY.
CELTIC: HUNTER, MCGRAIN, BROGAN, MURRAY, MCNEIL, MCCLUSKEY, JOHNSTONE, DALGLISH, DEANS, HOOD, AND WILSON. SUBS: LENNOX, MCDONALD.
REFEREE: J. GORDON (NEWPORT ON TAY).

Seven days after the Hampden debacle, Morton were trounced 5-0 in Edinburgh, restoring some semblance of confidence before the forthcoming trip to Italy for the return leg of the UEFA Cup. But after the events of the past few weeks, there was little real hope of the 4-0 deficit being overcome.

On their arrival in Italy on the Tuesday, the team followed a short training session with a relaxing afternoon tour of the Turin Motor Show courtesy of Italian car giants Fiat, the main sponsors of the Italian club.

Although they would have to be prepared to go at Juventus from the start if they hoped to take anything from the game, in his pre-match team talk Turnbull warned of the dangers of being over-adventurous. At Easter Road they had been forced to attack freely in the search of goals, but they would now adopt a more cautious approach, aiming to hit Juventus on the break, hopefully assisted by overconfidence and lack of urgency on the part of the home side.

Because of their commanding lead from the first leg, the majority of the home fans considered the tie to be effectively over and a well below average crowd paid the equivalent of between £1.50 and £6 to take their place at the start. Built during the Fascist regime, the Stadio Comunale had originally been named after the dictator Benito Mussolini when it opened in 1933. Sharing the 70,000 capacity stadium with great rivals Torino since 1960, Juventus – who, incidentally, had adopted their famous black and white striped jerseys in 1906 when a member of the club returned from a trip to England with a Notts County shirt – had become one of the top teams in Italy with numerous championship successes. At that time they were still to realise their dream of winning either of the main European trophies, but they went on to become the first side in Europe to win all three.

Abandoning their usual cavalier but disciplined approach to European games, Hibs, as planned, started the game playing intelligent football but with an uncharacteristically slow build-up. It almost paid off.

Hibs were magnificently led by Pat Stanton who with a bit of luck could have scored a hat-trick himself inside the opening quarter of an hour. Instead, against the run of play, a terrible refereeing decision allowed Bettega to score from what looked an obvious offside position. Despite vigorous appeals by the Hibs players, the goal was allowed to stand.

During the first half, Harper had complained of stomach pains and a lack of energy and did not resume after the interval. His place was taken by Edwards. On the restart it was still Hibs who looked the better side, although Bettega's goal had killed off any real chance of an upset by the visitors. Hopes of a comeback by Hibs were killed stone dead on the hour mark when an absolutely sensational goal by Anastasi gave the Italians an overall 6-2 lead. With his back to Hibs' goal, the centre forward collected a pass from a colleague fully 25 yards out, and all in one movement, before any Hibs defender could even react, he sent an incredible hitch kick screaming past the helpless McArthur and into the back of the net.

The visitors were not finished, however, and midway through the half Duncan, who had been on the receiving end of several crude tackles by Longobucco, including being punched in the face (all ignored by the official), crashed a thunderous shot against the bar, before Zoff had another great save from yet another effort by Stanton.

From the first whistle the wildly partisan crowd had been demanding the appearance of substitute Altafini, and his entrance with 25 minutes remaining was greeted by tumultuous cheering.

The legendary Altafini had scored half of the 14 goals scored by Juventus in the last four games and once again he managed to get on the scoresheet when he headed a third goal past the despairing dive of the Hibs goalkeeper after 73 minutes. The veteran had the ball in the net again a few minutes later, but this time it was ruled offside by the referee.

For some time the game had been a mere formality and it mattered little when Anastasi scored a fourth six minutes from time with a shot that went in off the post.

Although the 4-0 win had flattered Juventus, the 8-2 aggregate score was now Hibs' biggest ever defeat over two legs in a European competition.

FINAL SCORE: JUVENTUS 4. HIBERNIAN 0.

UEFA CUP 2ND ROUND (2ND LEG), WEDNESDAY 6 NOVEMBER 1974, STADIO COMUNALE.
HIBERNIAN: MCARTHUR, BREMNER, SCHAEDLER, STANTON, SPALDING, BLACKLEY, DUNCAN, CROPLEY, HARPER, GORDON, MUNRO.

Meanwhile, a Joe Harper goal at Ibrox at the end of November gave Hibs a narrow 1-0 win to bring Rangers' unbeaten league run to an end, wrecked by a superb display of skilful and entertaining football with the midfield trio of Stanton, Munro and Smith in devastating form. The victory had been vital in keeping Hibs' championship hopes alive. Defeat would have meant dropping seven points behind leaders Rangers and Celtic.

As they had demonstrated so positively at Ibrox, the Easter Road side were still capable of producing magnificent football. Since the start of the season, 18 of the 28 games played in all competitions had been won, with four drawn, scoring 71 goals while conceding 42, but the recent calamitous results against Celtic and Juventus showed that the side would now have to be rebuilt.

In a surprise move at the beginning of December, Ally MacLeod was signed from Southampton for a fee believed to be in the region of £25,000. The former Renfrew Juniors player had joined the English club from St Mirren 19 months before for £40,000 but had since found difficulty in securing a first team place at the Dell. MacLeod had come to prominence when he scored all four St Mirren goals in a shock 4-0 League Cup victory over Rangers in 1972. In the habit of trying to buy any player who had performed well against them, the Ibrox side attempted to sign the player, but MacLeod elected to try his luck in England instead. Alec Ferguson, then manager of Second Division St Mirren, had tried to lure the player back to Love Street, but MacLeod, not unnaturally, preferred First Division football in the capital.

Conjecture among the fans as to who Macleod would replace in the Hibs side ended later that evening when it was announced that Alex Cropley had joined Arsenal for a club record fee of £150,000. The twice-capped Cropley, while reportedly disappointed to be leaving his boyhood favourites, was pleased that the transfer speculation that had dragged on for so long was finally over. He was now, in his own words, 'looking forward to life at a bigger club'.

MacLeod made his debut in Hibs colours against Airdrie at Broomfield on the Saturday in a fairly drab 0-0 draw. On as a half-time substitute for Derek Spalding, his first contribution to the game was to be booked for jersey pulling. Apart from that, he showed his undoubted ability and it seemed certain that he would be a huge favourite with the Hibs fans for some time to come.

Alan Gordon, who had not featured in the first team since scoring Hibs' goal in a 1-1 draw with Dunfermline at the beginning of November, had since turned down a move to Motherwell in an exchange deal with Jim McCabe. However, realising that his prospects at Easter Road were limited, he agreed to join Dundee in a £13,000 deal a few weeks later, becoming one of the few players to serve all four Edinburgh and Dundee clubs. Signed as a direct replacement for John Duncan, who had joined Spurs in a big-money move shortly before, he had also interested St Johnstone, keen to reunite him with goalscoring partner O'Rourke, and Partick Thistle, whose manager Bertie Auld well knew the capabilities of the striker from his time at Easter Road both as a player and coach. By his own reckoning, Gordon had scored 83 goals for Hibs in 153 appearances, three more than his during time at Hearts, but his Easter Road goals had been scored over a much shorter period of time. Gordon's exit from Easter Road meant that in the just over two years since Turnbull's Tornadoes had won the League Cup at Hampden, only six from the squad of 13 still remained at the club.

Alex Edwards, who had been suspended for 28 days and fined £50 after the accumulation of yet another four bookings, made his return to the first team against Dumbarton 11 days before Christmas. He was sent off for the sixth time in his career two weeks later in a 1-0 defeat by Aberdeen at Easter Road. Fouled towards the end of the game by full back McClelland, Edwards foolishly retaliated, and both players were dismissed by referee Marshall, who had a bad day throughout. During the game Munro missed the chance to give his side a sixth-minute lead from the penalty spot, and thereafter goalkeeper Clark was in top form to deny Hibs a deserved equaliser as the Dons became the first side to inflict defeat on the home side since losing to Juventus in Turin nine games before.

On 1 January 1975 Hibs celebrated the start of their centenary year with the traditional New Year's derby against Hearts at Tynecastle. The last ever First Division League game between the great Edinburgh rivals was watched by a huge crowd of 36,500 who were treated to a dreary and uninspiring typical local derby that again ended goalless. With just four minutes remaining, Hearts missed the best chance of the game, one of the very few created by either side in the entire 90 minutes, when Ford struck the post with McArthur well beaten, both sides having to content themselves with a share of the spoils.

Like Cropley before him, Blackley had watched a procession of players leave Easter Road on the journey down south. Also keen to sample life in England, at the beginning of the month he submitted yet another written transfer request, the demand resulting in him missing most of remaining season.

It did not require a financial genius to predict that the accounts for the year ending July 1974 would again give major cause for concern. At the AGM a huge pre-tax loss of £149,827 was declared. This followed the £40,000 shortfall of the previous fiscal year. Of considerable concern, the figures did not include the £120,000 paid for Joe Harper. Although transfer fees, wages and running costs had again increased substantially, income had decreased significantly owing to a poor run in both domestic cups. Tom Hart felt it necessary to explain publicly that in the region of £4,000 each week was needed to keep Hibs in the black, but in several instances already that season they had received a guarantee of as little as £650 at some away grounds. Worse still, some of the recent home games had ended with the club losing money. Like some of the other 'bigger' teams, Hibs were being forced to rely on the large gates that were generated by games against Rangers, Celtic, Hearts and, to a lesser extent, both Dundee clubs. It was hoped that the advent of the Premier League in the summer, with the home club allowed to retain all the gate revenue, would go some way in solving the financial problems.

Goalkeeper Hugh Whyte and Pat Carroll made their debut against Dundee United at Tannadice in a hard won a 3-1 victory, Whyte keeping his place against Celtic in the Scottish Cup at Easter Road a few weeks later. It was now 73 years since Hibs had won the famous trophy, but who was counting? Before the game the fans yet again had cause for outrage after admission charges had been raised substantially. The highly critical supporters were advised by a club spokesman that they should be prepared for this happening more often in future with the forthcoming arrival of the Premier League. As to the game itself, Hibs' old nemesis Dixie Deans was once again the villain of the piece when he scored Celtic's opening goal after Whyte, who performed well otherwise, made a mess of collecting a corner in the 12th minute. The young goalkeeper allowed the ball to rebound from his chest and the Celtic man was lying handy to head home. Spalding was in inspirational form to otherwise mark Dalglish out of the game, while at the other end Hibs created plenty of chances. A second Celtic goal after the interval put paid to their Scottish Cup hopes for yet another year.

Hibs moved into the transfer market at the beginning of February to sign 32-year-old centre half Roy Barry from Crystal Palace for a nominal fee. The short-term signing was geared to restoring some of the much needed steel at the heart of the defence that had been missing in recent months. Since the departure of Jim Black six months before Spalding had held the number five shirt, but following his injury against Airdrie Bremner and Stanton had shared the position.

The resolute defender began his Hibs career badly when he needlessly handled the ball to concede a first half penalty in a 4-1 reverse against Motherwell at Fir Park, former Hibs s-form signing Willie Pettigrew scoring twice against his old side as the Steel Men overran the visitors after the interval. Barry, who had won a Scottish Cup medal for Dunfermline against his first senior club, Hearts, in the 1968 final, proved his worth seven days later when he totally subdued Dixie Deans in Hibs' 2-1 win over champions Celtic. Goalkeeper Jim McArthur, who had lost his place to Whyte five games before, was recalled for the match. The Easter Road side's first victory of the season over the reigning champions was achieved by sheer aggression. In a victory for teamwork, Hibs took a firm grip of the game right from the first whistle and never relinquished it until the last.

Hibs were now lying handily in third place behind Rangers and Celtic, but any lingering hopes of winning the championship disappeared completely just days later, with a surprise 2-0 home defeat at the hands of Kilmarnock. The side with the best home record in the entire country just 12 months before had dropped nine points from the last nine games and were now a huge seven points behind Rangers at the top of the table.

Among the many reasons behind Hibs' unpredictable form had been the absence of midfield maestro Alex Edwards for much of the season, first due to injury and then to suspension. The Fifer was suspended yet again, this time for 20 days, and fined £150 for his dismissal against Aberdeen at Christmas. Given his history in front of the disciplinary panel, the sentence was lighter than many – including perhaps Edwards himself – had expected.

Back-to-back wins against Dunfermline and Clyde set the Greens up for the visit of Rangers to Edinburgh at the end of March. Rangers needed just one point to secure the championship, and a second-half strike by former Hibs player Colin Stein cancelled out an earlier goal by Ally MacLeod to enable the Ibrox side to end Celtic's nine-year domination of the championship. The ill-tempered game was more rugged and physical than the provider of quality football, but that would be of little consequence to Rangers as they collected their first League Championship in 11 years, with four games still to play. The discerning Hibs fan, however disappointed at losing out in the title race, would soberly consider that they had won three and drawn one of the five games against the champions that season.

At the beginning of April, a mystery consortium of Edinburgh businessmen, dissatisfied at Tom Hart's handling of the club, made an offer to buy the managing director's shares in Hibernian. Stating, somewhat diplomatically, that they believed it to be unhealthy that the majority of shares were held by only three main shareholders, the unnamed group made an offer for Hart's 1,305 shares, a 65 per cent stake in the club. The remaining 35 per cent was distributed among 21 other shareholders, only one of whom, Tom Hartland junior, son of the former director, who owned 205 shares, was directly involved in the running of the club. The remaining leading shareholder was Joe Croan, a member of the well known Newhaven fishing family, who owned 202.

Hart ended any speculation of a possible takeover by declaring he had requested a meeting with the 'faceless people', as he described them, and that the consortium had refused to reveal the identity of the individuals involved. Up till then the only contact had been between rival lawyers and the straight-talking Hart was not prepared to deal with anyone who was not prepared to show their hand in public.

With three games still to play, a Joe Harper treble in a 6-1 demolition of Airdrie left Hibs needing only one point from their final two games to guarantee entry to the UEFA Cup. Airdrie centre half Jim Black could do little to prevent former colleague Joe Harper from opening the scoring in the very first minute, and for the next 89, he and his teammates, who would be defeated by Celtic in the Scottish Cup Final a few weeks later, could do little to stem the tide of green-shirted marauders. Edwards made his return to the side after suspension, incredibly only his second start in four months, and he was to be the difference between the sides. His intelligent prompting from midfield eventually helped Harper to claim his 11th league goal of the season, his 22nd in all games.

UEFA Cup qualification was secured at the aptly named 'Boghead' the following Saturday, but not without some difficulty. On a badly waterlogged and heavy pitch, confident Dumbarton raced into a two-goal lead. After the interval, goals by Smith and Duncan added to a tremendous strike by Schaedler which was deflected into his own net by full back Ruddy, gave the visitors the victory that guaranteed European football for a fourth consecutive season.

The final game of the campaign against Arbroath at Easter Road was meaningless as far as the league table was concerned, but the main talking point was a delightful match-winning strike by right back John Brownlie.

Collecting the ball in the opposing penalty area, the Scottish international beat three defenders before unleashing an unstoppable shot from an acute angle past Gordon Marshall in the Arbroath goal. His teammates – and everyone on the ground, for that matter – could do little but stand back and applaud the magnificent solo goal that brought the curtain down on the season.

Reflecting on a championship race that had ended with the Easter Road side once again finishing in second place, but seven points behind champions Rangers, Eddie Turnbull could only ponder the reason for the post-Christmas depression that had proved so expensive. It had taken Hibs far too long to recover from an unexpected defeat at the turn of the year by an Aberdeen side that had failed to win any of their previous eight games, with seven points dropped from Hibs' following seven fixtures.

Among those making an exit from Easter Road as part of an ever-revolving conveyor belt were goalkeeper Roddie McKenzie, Laurie Dunn and Gerry Adair, just three of the seven freed by Turnbull at the end of the season.

15

Nightmare at Montrose
and a (Very) Late Goal at Tynecastle
1975–76

ON THE EVE of the 1975–76 season, an important one for the future of Scottish football, the former Hibs manager Jock Stein was involved in a serious car crash on the A74 near Lockerbie. Surgeons battled for over an hour to save the life of the Celtic manager. In the car with Stein, and fortunate to receive only minor injuries, were his great friend Bob Shankly (who he had recommended as his successor at Easter Road), their wives and a family friend.

Less serious, but of no less concern to the club, was the news that Eddie Turnbull had taken ill during the summer break with an abdominal complaint which required immediate surgery, causing the manager to miss the start of the new season.

Starting earlier than usual, all talk at the opening session was regarding the forthcoming plum UEFA Cup tie against English giants Liverpool for the second time in five years. Although the manager was absent from ground, Turnbull's influence was still in evidence. Flouting the code Turnbull had instituted, Joe Harper turned up for training on the opening day sporting a full beard and he refused to remove the offending growth when confronted by stand-in manager Wilson Humphries, who referred the matter to chairman Hart on his return from holiday. Hart pronounced that while Harper was perfectly entitled to grow a beard, he would not play for the club with one. He pointed out that Eddie Turnbull set the rules without interference from the board. However, in this case the directors were unanimously in agreement with him.

Several players had attempted to grow full facial hair during Turnbull's time in charge, but all had removed the offending hair when requested to do so. The dispute dragged on for several days, but was resolved when Harper appeared for training that morning clean-shaven, just in time to join his colleagues for a three-game tour of the Emerald Isle. The centre forward would score three of Hibs' nine goals without loss in victories over Cork Hibs, Waterford and Bohemians.

Near the end of the previous season Hart and Turnbull had attended the European Cup semi-final between Leeds United and Barcelona at Elland Road, hoping to invite the Spanish club to Easter Road as part of Hibs' centenary celebrations, but neither they nor Real Madrid were able to fit a game into their busy schedule. Consequently, English champions Derby

County accepted an invitation to take part in what was billed as a glamour pre-season friendly. The match turned out to be a less than glamorous affair, however. The still recuperating Eddie Turnbull and a more than reasonable crowd for that time of 17,000 saw the English side completely dominate a dull and lifeless 90 minutes, their solitary match-winning goal scored just after the interval.

A League Cup section containing Dundee, Ayr United, and Dunfermline was won comfortably enough with only a 2-1 defeat at Somerset Park spoiling an otherwise 100 per cent record, to set up a meeting with lowly Montrose in the quarter-finals.

In the home game against Dunfermline, the suspended pair of Brownlie and Edwards were welcomed back to first-team action, but Hibs finished the match with ten men when Pat Stanton was ordered off for only the second time in his career. Referee Brian McGinley saw nothing wrong in a challenge by the Hibs captain, but acting on his linesman's advice that Stanton had been guilty of violent conduct, the player was ordered off. The harsh decision angered both the home crowd and the player, who protested that he had only put his hands up to protect himself.

Meanwhile, Alex Edwards had posted yet another transfer request, one that was again quickly refused. He had started only a dozen games during the previous season although suspension accounted for much of this, but in reality he was far too good a player to be watching from the sidelines.

The traditional annual cricket match against Leith Franklin, discontinued some years before, was resurrected as a one-off fundraiser; the game, which ended in a draw, drew plenty of laughs, and the fund to purchase a bus for the Eastern General Hospital was substantially enhanced by a collection taken among the spectators. Several guest players were transferred back to Hibs for the day, including Tommy Preston, Lawrie Reilly, Bobby Kinloch, director Tommy Younger and Jimmy O'Rourke, who ended the afternoon as top scorer with 63 runs. They were joined by Stanton, Brownlie, Smith, Bremner and several others from the current squad.

Hibs played their first ever Premier League match on Saturday 30 August 1975. A brilliant 20-yard drive by Joe Harper just before half time, kept the striker's goal-per-game ratio intact to give his side victory over Hearts at Easter Road. Turnbull, recently returned from holiday, was given a warm reception from the fans as he took his seat in the directors' box. Well on top throughout, the home side should have turned their dominance into goals, but Hearts, while inferior in skill on the day, were in determined mood and Hibs had to be content with the slender but satisfying 1-0 victory.

The teams for Edinburgh's first ever Premier League match were:

HIBS: MCARTHUR, BROWNLIE, SCHAEDLER, STANTON, BARRY, BLACKLEY, EDWARDS, BREMNER, HARPER, MUNRO, AND DUNCAN. SUBS: SMITH, MACLEOD.

HEARTS: CRUIKSHANK, KAY, CLUNIE, JEFFERIES, ANDERSON, MURRAY, BROWN, BUSBY, HANCOCK, CALLAGHAN, PRENTICE. SUBS: PARK, GIBSON.

That same afternoon, trouble had erupted between rival fans during and after the first Old Firm game of the season at Ibrox, prompting Ian McNiven of the *Edinburgh Evening News* to predict that there would be no future for the Premier League if the morons who supported Celtic and Rangers continued to display this type of disgraceful behaviour. He added, 'These thugs are continually referred to as "a small minority" when quite clearly they are much more than that.'

The impressive form of Joe Harper and Arthur Duncan had not gone unnoticed by the international selectors. Both players were called into the Scotland squad for the forthcoming European championship game against Denmark in Copenhagen. Harper, who had already been capped twice with Aberdeen, would win his first cap in Hibs colours against the Danes. Incredibly, his previous Scotland outings had also been against Denmark. The player recalls a humorous incident during his Scotland baptism in the 4-1 victory in Copenhagen in 1972. Assured by manager Ormond that he would only be on the substitutes' bench for experience and not be called upon, Joe was surprised to be told to get stripped during the second half as he would be replacing Jimmy Bone. In consternation, he realised that he was desperate for the toilet. Running inside the unfamiliar ground, he quickly relieved himself, then walked through a door to find himself outside in the street in his football kit. An extremely embarrassed Harper was forced to bang on the door to gain the attention of a steward for readmittance to the stadium.

This time, however, the trip to Copenhagen would not end in humorous circumstances for the Hibs man. On from the start, Harper kept Scotland's championship hopes alive when he scored his side's solitary goal in a 1-0 win. Team-mate Arthur Duncan replaced Tommy Hutchinson late in the game. In exuberant spirits after an important victory, some of the players decided to visit a discotheque in the city. In the early hours of the morning, several of the Scotland players were involved in a dispute with some locals that quickly got out of hand. The police were called and the players expelled from the club. After a thorough SFA investigation, Joe Harper, Billy Bremner, Pat McCluskey of Celtic, and Willie Young and Arthur Graham of Aberdeen, were banned for life from playing for their country. The suspensions were lifted several years later, but too late to benefit most of the miscreants.

In the first leg of the League Cup quarter-finals in Edinburgh, a no-nonsense approach by Second Division Montrose kept the Premier side at bay until the dying minutes of the game, when who else but Harper scored to secure a slender and nail-biting win. Pathetic Hibs would soon have cause to regret their failure to win by a bigger margin.

With European experience with both Hearts and Dunfermline, centre half Roy Barry would be vital in the game against Liverpool. Injured against Ayr on the Saturday he had recovered sufficiently after treatment to be included in the Hibs line-up. Of even more concern for Turnbull was the recent lack of goals by the Hibs forwards. In the three league games played so far, only two goals had been scored, one of them from the penalty spot by Brownlie.

Liverpool had selection worries of their own, with centre half Phil Thompson failing a late fitness test. The hard-tackling Tommy Smith would also miss the match because of a two-match ban received after he had been ordered off against Ferencevaros in the Merseysider's last European game. Kevin Keegan had been earmarked by Turnbull as the main threat to Hibs, but Liverpool were full of dangerous opponents in all areas of the pitch, none more than former Hibs player Peter Cormack, making his first return to the capital as a player. Although wearing the number five jersey, Cormack was the midfield inspiration of the side and would later be included in former Liverpool manager Bill Shankly's list of the 11 all-time best Liverpool players. The vastly experienced Liverpool could count on seven current internationals, three Under-23 caps, and young players of the calibre of Phil Neal and Kevin Keegan who would represent their country at the top level in the very near future.

They were indeed formidable opponents and it was no surprise when manager Paisley, interviewed after a training session at Meadowbank regarding his team's chances against Hibs, answered only that, 'Liverpool respect all teams, but fear none.' Somewhat surprisingly, although the English side were almost unbeatable at home in European ties, having lost just three of the 33 games played, they had only managed to win nine of their 35 matches away from home and Turnbull was extremely confident that his side could record their first ever victory over an English club in Europe.

Seeking revenge for the defeat five seasons before, Hibs started the game much the slicker side. A crowd of just under 20,000 braved the elements. Driving rain had fallen all afternoon, rendering underfoot conditions treacherous. The players – let alone the fans huddled together on the terracing – soon found it difficult to distinguish the pitch markings, which were in danger of being completely washed away.

Hibs were well aware of just how important it was to keep a clean sheet at home. Liverpool's sporadic attacks found a Hibs back four in determined mood with Brownlie as always prepared to reinforce Smith, Harper and Duncan up front.

In the heavy conditions, the speed of Smith and Duncan on the flanks were causing full backs Neal and Jones all kinds of problems and it was from a Duncan cross that Hibs scored the only goal of the game after 20 minutes. The move started with the outstanding Munro playing a long ball down the left wing for the fleet-footed Duncan to chase. Duncan's hard and low cross on the run was met by the inrushing Harper, who crashed an unsaveable first-time volley past Clemence from 12 yards.

Although Liverpool were dangerous on the break, with the incisive passing of Cormack behind most of their moves it was the home side who came nearest to scoring again when a brilliant Stanton header almost doubled Hibs' lead. Just before the interval a Smith effort troubled Clemence, who was mightily relieved to see the ball slip past the post to safety.

Toshack replaced Kennedy at the interval and it was soon evident that the patient first-half build-up by Liverpool, which had proved ineffectual, had been replaced by the long ball to the Welsh striker.

Neal scored what Liverpool thought was the equalising goal midway through the half, but the referee, correctly as would later be proved by television footage, disallowed the goal for offside.

Now playing up the famous slope, Hibs were producing some intelligent, slick football, a remarkable feat in the terrible conditions. The important second goal, however, had so far proved elusive. Wth ten minutes remaining, Duncan was brought crashing down in the box by Neal and the referee had no hesitation in pointing to the spot, despite the heated appeals of the red-shirted defenders. As he prepared to take the kick, Brownlie, who had been successful with his last four efforts from the spot, appeared to change his mind at the last second and ended up placing a weak shot to Clemence's right-hand side that allowed the keeper to gather at the second attempt. It would prove a costly miss.

FINAL SCORE: HIBERNIAN 1. LIVERPOOL 0.

UEFA CUP 1ST ROUND (1ST LEG), WEDNESDAY 17 SEPTEMBER 1975, EASTER ROAD.
HIBERNIAN: MCARTHUR, BROWNLIE, SCHAEDLER, STANTON, BARRY, BLACKLEY,
EDWARDS, SMITH, HARPER, MUNRO, DUNCAN.
LIVERPOOL: CLEMENCE, NEAL, JONES, LAWLER, CORMACK, HUGHES, KEEGAN HALL
HIGHWAY KENNEDY, CALLAGHAN.

Hibs made their way to Links Park for the return leg of the League Cup quarter-final against Montrose. They were 1-0 ahead from the first game at Easter Road, and a place in the semi-finals looked a mere formality when Arthur Duncan gave his side a two-goal aggregate lead after only 30 seconds. Against all the odds, however, the lower league side staged a remarkable comeback to hand the visitors one of the most embarrassing results in the long history of the club. Two goals in the second half by Montrose levelled the overall score, forcing extra time, a freak goal by right back Barr sealing the visitors' fate. With the strong wind at his back, right back Barr lobbed a speculative clearance deep into Hibs' penalty area from the halfway line. Caught in the wind, the bounce completely deceived goalkeeper McArthur, who otherwise had played well, and the ball flew over his head and into the net for the winning goal. Overall it had been a poor performance by Hibs, with only Barry and Blackley exempt from criticism, and as the Montrose players celebrated at the final whistle the green-shirted players left the field with their heads hung low.

On the Saturday, club captain Pat Stanton was left out of the line-up against St Johnstone – he was not even on the bench. His place was taken by Bremner. Stanton, at that time Hibs' longest-serving player, upset at appearing to be made a scapegoat for the humiliating midweek defeat, promptly handed in a transfer request. The demotion was possibly the first public sign of a rift between the player and the manager that had been simmering behind the scenes for some time. Higgins, who had also played at Links Park on the Wednesday, was on the bench, his place taken by Ally MacLeod in a 4-2 win over the Saints that restored a modicum of pride before the return trip to Merseyside in midweek.

With the exception of the still-suspended Smith, Liverpool manager Paisley had a full squad at his disposal. Phil Thomson had now recovered from injury and was added to the side, with Kennedy replacing full back Jones who had endured a torrid 90 minutes at the hands of Bobby Smith in the first match at Easter Road.

The main talking point before the match among the large Hibs support that made its way to Merseyside was whether Stanton would play or not. Since making his European debut against Valencia ten years before, the vastly experienced Stanton had featured in 36 consecutive continental games and it seemed inconceivable that he could be left out of one of the biggest games in the club's long history.

Although he had made his way to Merseyside with the team, Pat Stanton watched from the bench as Hibs, as was their style, made no attempt to sit back and defend their slender lead. Adopting their by now customary tactics in the away leg of a European tie, they attacked straight from the first whistle and there were several near things at either end.

The energetic Keegan again proved to be the main danger to Hibs and the future England cap set up the opening goal for teammate Toshack after 20 minutes. Squirming free from the attentions of the Hibs defenders on the right, Keegan's measured cross found the head of the inrushing Toshack who had no difficulty in directing the ball past the helpless McArthur in the Hibs goal. Roared on by the majority of the 30,000 crowd, Liverpool pushed forward in search of more goals and Brownlie was booked for one foul too many on Highway midway through the half.

It was far from all Liverpool, however, and the huge Anfield crowd were silenced 12 minutes before half time when the visitors regained the overall lead. Accepting a return pass from Bremner, the magnificent Alex Edwards smashed the ball past the oncoming Clemence for a rare but vitally important goal. The away goals ruling now meant that there could not be extra time, with the home side now needing at least two to win. As the whistle blew for half time, the huge crowd on the Kop were left to visualise exit from Europe at the first hurdle as the teams left the field, while the sizeable Hibs support made themselves heard above their eerie silence.

As expected, Liverpool went into all-out attack from the restart. It was vitally important that the Greens hold out for the opening ten minutes of the second half, and they were within 60 seconds of the target when disaster struck. Hibs once again gave away possession on the left and it was who else but Keegan who supplied the pinpoint cross that enabled Toshack to score his second goal of the night with another accurate header.

Ten minutes later, another bad defensive blunder by Hibs meant the match was all but over. Blackley was easily dispossessed by Keegan near the visiting side's left-hand corner flag and another pinpoint cross found the head of Toshack whose effort passed under the despairing arms of diving McArthur to bulge the net for the winning goal. It was the Welsh international's first ever hat-trick for Liverpool.

Hibs renewed their efforts to score the goal that would put them into the next round but it was not to be, and it was the English side that came nearest to scoring when Toshack missed a chance to score a fourth in the closing seconds.

FINAL SCORE: LIVERPOOL 3. HIBERNIAN 1.

UEFA CUP 1ST ROUND (2ND LEG), TUESDAY 30 SEPTEMBER 1975, ANFIELD.

LIVERPOOL: CLEMENCE, NEAL, LINDSAY, THOMPSON, CORMACK, HUGHES, KEEGAN, HALL, HIGHWAY, TOSHACK, CALLAGHAN.

HIBERNIAN: MCARTHUR, BROWNLIE, SCHAEDLER, BREMNER, BARRY, BLACKLEY, EDWARDS, MACLEOD, HARPER, MUNRO, DUNCAN.

Although they had been beaten, after the match there was lavish praise for the performance of the Edinburgh side that had once again done Scotland proud, but the financial implications of an exit from Europe in the first round, for the first time since losing to Valencia in 1965, would be significant.

Even before the game it had seemed obvious that the aerial dominance of Toshack would provide the main goalscoring threat to Hibs, leaving the manager to contemplate the loss of three bad goals that had all been engineered from similar moves on Hibs' left, and the fans to wonder if it had been a mistake to leave out Stanton, whose height and experience in the middle of the park might just have proved crucial defensively.

Stanton's omission from the side did not go down well with the supporters, most of whom shared the view that the captain's presence might have countered the danger of Toshack. Numerous letters of complaint were received by the newspapers, most expressing the view that Stanton's only fault was in being too loyal to the club.

Calling an emergency meeting to discuss the situation, the board of directors surprisingly, but apparently unanimously, agreed to accept the captain's request for a move, and the player was notified of the decision immediately after training that same day.

Alex Edwards had posted a transfer request of his own some weeks before, and after being dropped for the 2-1 defeat by Motherwell on the Saturday, demanded a meeting with the manager to discuss developments. At the meeting, Edwards, who had only recently been voted player of the year by the Hibs Supporters Association, confirmed his desire for a move.

After missing four matches, including the game against Liverpool, only one of them ending in victory, Stanton was recalled to the side for a controversial meeting with Celtic in Glasgow on Saturday 18 October 1975. A magnificent performance by Hibs saw them cruising to their first win at Parkhead for six years, when the game was dramatically abandoned by the referee five minutes from time because of the poor visibility effected by a blanket of fog that had threatened the proceedings all afternoon. Leading by a Bremner goal at the interval, Hibs totally outplayed Celtic in the second half. The game was held up for several minutes when home fans in the Jungle spilled onto the pitch shortly after Harper had given his side a two-goal lead.

Order was eventually restored by the police only for the referee to decide that visibility was insufficient and although there were only a few minutes left to play, the game was abandoned. The decision was met unfavourably by the Hibs officials and the travelling support, who were also angry at the 'invasion' by the home supporters. Eddie Turnbull took little consolation from being informed by Celtic coach Sean Fallon that it was 'God's will' that the game had been called to a premature halt. Ironically, only a few minutes after the teams left the field, the fog lifted, but by then it was far too late.

A centenary dinner to celebrate the illustrious, though often turbulent first 100 years of the club was held in the North British Hotel on Princes Street on Monday 27 of October 1975. Almost 200 guests and dignitaries were in attendance, including representatives from every Scottish side. Willie Bauld and Jimmy Wardhaugh represented Hearts, with Alfie Conn unable to attend. From the Famous Five, only Ormond was missing. Jimmy McColl and 79-year-old Willie Harper represented the famous '20s team, but the oldest former player was 84-year-old Johnny Lamb who had signed for the club in 1909. Many others, including Jock Weir, looking resplendent in the kilt, Bobby Combe, Peter Aird and Bobby Kinloch mingled with former colleagues for the first time in many years, reminiscing of bygone glories. To mark the prestigious occasion, each guest received an inscribed commemorative pewter tankard.

The players and officials were also invited to the City Chambers by Lord Provost John Millar, acting on behalf of the citizens of Edinburgh, for a celebration dinner to mark the centenary. The Hibs Supporters Association celebrated the occasion some weeks later with a centenary rally in Leith Town Hall. The demand for tickets for the rally had been so overwhelming that it had been decided to switch the venue from their own clubrooms to an outside arena capable of holding well over a thousand people. The evening, headlined by the well known impressionist Janet Brown, proved to be yet another successful undertaking by an enterprising and ambitious committee.

An excellent book entitled *100 Years of Hibs*, co-written by lifelong supporters Gerry Docherty and Phil Thomson, was released to coincide with the centenary celebrations. Believed to be the first ever history of the club, it was an immediate hit with the fans and sold out almost at once. The publication is now keenly sought after by collectors of football memorabilia. During the glory days of the early '50s Joe McMurray, a Manchester-based Hibs supporter and regular contributor to the official match programme, had started to write a history of the club in co-ordination with programme editor Magnus Williamson. With Williamson's then heavy workload and the paper restrictions that were still in force after the Second World War, the project was never completed. Later both McMurray and Williamson would be only too pleased to allow Docherty and Thomson access to their original manuscript and notes containing a mountain of useful information about the early days.

Controversy surrounded Hibs' visit to Tynecastle on 1 November 1975. In a presentation in the boardroom before the game, Tom Hart was presented with a magnificent silver rose bowl by the Hearts directors to commemorate their 100th birthday. The bowl was just one of many gifts received from football clubs and organisations the length and breadth of the country.

On the field an impressive Hearts side dominated an opening goalless 45 minutes and fully deserved to be ahead at the interval. After the break Hibs began to assert themselves, when on the hour mark, the Maroons took the lead through a Ralph Callaghan goal. Retaking the initiative, Hearts were denied a victory when Stanton headed home a glorious equaliser deep into injury time. In a rare late attack towards the School End, Brownlie sent over a cross for Stanton to score a typical headed goal from close range as the Hearts players appealed vainly for offside. Television coverage later that evening suggested that Stanton was indeed offside, but the result stood, and the dropped point prevented Hearts from joining Celtic as joint leaders at the top of the table. The main point of contention among the Gorgie faithful, however, was the timing of the goal. In those days, injury time was rarely added by the referee, and if it was, it was generally only a few seconds. Stanton's goal, even according to the Hibs supporters inside Tynecastle, appeared to be well after the game should have been over. There was no all-day drinking then – pubs opened at five in the afternoon – and Hearts fans will swear to this day that the first pints were being poured in Gorgie when the Hibs captain scored what has now become a famous goal.

The ecstatic Hibs fans streamed from Tynecastle, delighted that their heroes had preserved their unbeaten status in Premier League games against their rivals, even if somewhat undeservedly. They had even more reason to be pleased in midweek when Stanton withdrew his recent transfer request. The player would later say that in no way had he wanted to leave Easter Road, but that he had demanded a transfer in protest at being made the scapegoat for the cup exit at Montrose.

Alex Edwards, missing from the side for almost two months, made a return to the first team against Rangers at the end of November. At Easter Road the then league leaders were completely outplayed by a rampant Hibs side inspired from midfield by a two-goal Stanton. The Light Blues' physical approach proved totally ineffective against the fast-flowing football served up by Hibs, particularly in the second half, and the 2-1 final scoreline flattered the Glasgow side.

In their infinite wisdom, the Scottish League had decided that the game abandoned at Parkhead in mid-October should be replayed, even though Hibs had been leading 2-0 with only minutes of the match remaining. According to the League Management Committee, if the game had been abandoned on account of the pitch invasion by the Celtic fans, the result would have stood. However, as there was no mention of the incident in the referee's official report, which stated merely that the game had been called off because of the inclement weather conditions, it was only right, in the opinion of the committee, that the match should be replayed. Hibs were furious at the decision. Prepared to forfeit any potential gate money from any replayed game in favour of the points, immediately after the match Hibs had forwarded a protest detailing both the crowd 'break in' and the resultant cancellation. But a replay it was.

An Erich Schaedler strike from a free kick, his first goal for three years, gave Hibs a well deserved equaliser in the replayed game at Parkhead. The home side had taken the lead early in the second half when Dixie Deans escaped the attentions of the impressive Roy Barry for the only time in the game, but from then on Hibs were the better side, and as Turnbull would comment after the game, in the circumstances it would have been a travesty had they not taken something from the match. The result lifted Hibs into third place, two points behind leaders Celtic.

Joe Harper had lost his goalscoring touch since netting against Motherwell nine weeks earlier, and just before Christmas the centre forward found himself on the substitutes' bench for the first time since joining the club from Everton, for the corresponding game against Motherwell at Easter Road. Former Hibs player Peter Marinello, who had been signed from Portsmouth for £35,000 just three days before, was facing his former Easter Road teammates for the first time. The ex-Arsenal star lined up alongside former Hibs provisional signing Willie Pettigrew and former Liverpool star Bobby Graham, at that time one of the top goalscorers in Europe owing to his prolific partnership with Pettigrew. It was not, however, to prove a productive pairing on the day. Stanton swooped to place a strong header past Rennie for the only goal of the game from a perfectly flighted Edwards free kick.

Now back to something like his best, right back John Brownlie was selected for the Scotland side to play Romania at Hampden midweek. He celebrated his first international call-up since facing Denmark in November 1972 with a fantastic display of effervescent, attacking play from defence and his now customary eagerness to assist his forwards.

Just days before Christmas, the supporters were informed that from now on there would be no boys' gate for games involving the Old Firm and Hearts at Easter Road. Tom Hart explained that for some time a close check had been kept on the gates used by juveniles, and it was found that most of the supporters attempting to gain entry were over 16, and in many cases smelling strongly of drink. He pointed out, however, that there would still be the usual parent-child gates. This was not the first time that admission had been restricted for youngsters at the so-called bigger games. During the '40s, '50s, and well into the '60s, many of the top clubs had a policy in place, that in the interest of safety, there would be no OAP, juvenile or boys' gates. Some cynical fans were of the opinion that the policy was merely a ploy to extract extra money from the supporters, as a juvenile or an OAP could still gain admission on presentation of the appropriate adult fare, safety concerns or not.

Two days after Christmas Alex Edwards was sent off for the seventh time in his senior career during a 2-2 draw with Aberdeen at Pittodrie. The outside right had been booked by the over-zealous referee David Syme for attempting to take a throw-in that had been awarded to Aberdeen. The booking was to prove costly less than a minute later when Edwards saw red after an innocuous tackle on Eddie Thomson. To his credit, Thomson appealed in vain on behalf of the Hibs man, who now seemed to be a victim of his reputation. The ridiculous sending-off spoiled what was otherwise a tremendously exciting game, Aberdeen fighting back to share the points despite missing a penalty.

After two fairly even encounters between the sides already that season, Hearts had the misfortune to encounter a Hibs side in sparkling form when they first-footed Easter Road on the opening day of 1976. Two goals from Arthur Duncan and one from Bobby Smith inside the opening 25 minutes finished the game as a contest as magnificent Hibs totally outplayed their opponents. Hibs played out the remainder of the game at a rather more relaxed tempo, much to the relief of Hearts fans mostly well aware that the scoreline might well have been far greater.

On the morning of the game news had been received that former club chairman and president of the Royal College of Surgeons of Edinburgh, Sir John Bruce, had passed away. Sir John, who had never totally recovered from the effects of his car accident 18 months before, died peacefully in the Western General Hospital on the last day of the year, aged 70. The players of both sides wore black armbands as a mark of respect and observed the customary minute's silence before the kick-off.

In the middle of the month it was business as usual for the Hibs Fifty Club. Since losing their rented premises under the Main Stand the previous May, when founding member Tom Hart had cancelled the lease claiming that the space was needed by the football club for redevelopment, the members had been searching in vain for a new site. The search had come to an end when new clubrooms were acquired in the basement of a building directly opposite the stadium. Hart, invited to perform the opening ceremony, expressed a wish for continued good terms between both clubs. Some members, however, were still extremely unhappy at the way they had been forced to vacate their original premises, and it was rumoured that it had been members of the exclusive club that had been behind the failed attempt by a mystery consortium to acquire Hart's shares in Hibs the previous season.

The seemingly eternal trail for the elusive Scottish Cup began with a hard-fought battle against First Division Dunfermline in the capital. Twice behind, the courageous Fifers twice fought back to level the score, and with the prospect of a midweek replay at East End Park looming, Bobby Smith eased the fraying nerves of an edgy home support to ensure Hibs' entry into the second-round draw when he headed the winning goal past goalkeeper Barclay from a Duncan Cross late in the game. Only that morning Hibs had secured the services of 17-year-old Currie Hearts centre half Ally Brazil, who had been training at Tynecastle before finally opting on a move across the city. The gangly youngster, rated as a first-class prospect, had been attracting plenty of interest from clubs on both sides of the Border. Brazil would give many years of loyal service wearing the famous green and white jersey.

Goalkeeper Jim McArthur, who had been in inconsistent form in recent weeks, had been injured in the game against his hometown team, Dunfermline. Although he had managed to finish the match, the damage to his injured knee prompted Eddie Turnbull to travel south to sign 6 foot 3 former Clydebank goalkeeper Mike McDonald from Stoke City. Since joining Stoke for £25,000 some time before, the giant goalkeeper had been unable to establish a first-team position at the club and was now third choice, well behind first choice Peter Shilton. Delighted to have moved back to Scotland, McDonald made his debut in a 5-0 drubbing of St Johnstone in Edinburgh on the Saturday.

On Saturday 7 February 1976, the players of both Hibs and Dundee wore black armbands in respect for Hugh Shaw, who had died the previous Thursday, aged 80. Since leaving Easter Road in 1961, Shaw, Hibs' most successful manager ever, had been in charge at Raith Rovers for 18 months before finally deciding to retire from the game he had graced with distinction since joining Hibs in the final months of the First World War. Subsequently he concentrated on running his Edinburgh newspaper business. As well as leading Hibs to treble league championship success and entry into the inaugural European Cup, Shaw had also been trainer to the Scotland team on numerous occasions, and to the Great Britain side against Europe in 1947. He was buried in the Grange Cemetery in the city, a short distance from the final resting place of one of the founding fathers of Hibernian, Canon Edward Hannan.

Hibs' quest for Scottish Cup glory continued, but only after a replay at Tannadice. Dundee United, managed by the legendary Jim McLean, proved obstinate opponents in the first game, but encouraged by a huge support that had made its way from the capital, Spalding and Edwards both scored inside the first 30 minutes, more than enough to give the visiting side a comfortable victory. Pat Stanton was Hibs' top performer on a heavily sanded pitch that had been ankle deep in mud in places.

It was around this time that Alex Edwards once again demonstrated his adept agility in evading an opponent, but this time his adversities were officers of the Fife Constabulary who wished to interview him regarding an alleged road accident near his home – a motorist had complained that Edwards had slightly dented her car in passing. The minor incident was blown out of all proportion when the player decided he didn't wish to be interviewed and, in order to avoid taking a breathalyser test, escaped through a ground-floor window of his home and made his way across neighbouring fields.

Although Hibs were still lying handy in third place, a heavy 4-0 defeat by Celtic in Glasgow at the end of February put paid to their hopes of winning the title, leaving them marooned, for the want of a better word, six points behind the Parkhead side. The season was effectively ended two weeks later when, with Alec McGhee deputising for the injured Ally MacLeod, Hibs made their by now almost expected premature departure from the Scottish Cup, this time at the hands of Motherwell after a second replay. The first game at Fir Park had ended level at two goals each after a spirited Hibs had overcome a two-goal deficit to become favourites to progress into the semi-final, but on the Wednesday evening in Edinburgh, it required several brilliant saves by recent signing McDonald to ensure a third play-off at Ibrox after extra time had failed to separate the sides. Although they had been second-best for most of the game, Hibs had the best performer afield in John Brownlie, who was now back to his magical best, but unfortunately for the home side they had no one up front capable of taking advantage of the defenders intelligent, often brilliant, attacking play.

Before the game at Ibrox, Hibs made their way to Tynecastle on league business. An extremely disappointing crowd of less than 19,000 saw Arthur Duncan score the winner and his 100th goal for Hibs after just three minutes. Thereafter, only a stuffy rearguard action by a Hearts side who were still seeking their first Premier League victory over their rivals prevented an even more conclusive defeat, and the late goal by Stanton at Tynecastle in November now meant that Hibs had taken seven points from eight against the Gorgie side that season with the loss of only one goal.

Boosted by the derby win, on the Monday, Hibs travelled to Ibrox in optimistic mood, but once again their confidence was found wanting when Motherwell, who had looked down and out at the interval, overturned a one-goal deficit to win by the odd goal in three. Hibs' goal was scored by Joe Harper as the Edinburgh side spurned numerous chances to increase their lead in the second half. It would be the last Harper would score in a green and white jersey.

Never far from controversy or afraid to speak his mind, Tom Hart became embroiled in a war of words by accusing both Celtic and Rangers of cowardice when they refused to play each other. Both sides were separated by only one point at the top of the table when their game was postponed because of a 'flu epidemic'. Although no action was taken against Hart by the league management committee, who were empowered to act only in the case of a complaint from another club, the Hibs chairman was later forced to withdraw his comments after being informed that a rule existed that entitled the cancellation of a match if five or more players were absent owing to illness, providing of course that a doctor's certificate had been obtained.

Since signing for Hibs almost three years before, Ian Munro had proved a more than reliable acquisition. In brilliant form for most of the early part of the season, although he remained a valuable part of the first team squad, he had mainly been used as a substitute since losing his place to Bobby Smith after the defeat by Celtic in December. He was now attracting the attention of Rangers, who even then were not above weakening other sides by signing their best players. A deal was suggested that involved a swop with former

Hibs centre forward Colin Stein, at that time unable to command a regular first-team place at Ibrox. This was rejected out of hand by the Rangers player who, if anything, would rather have moved to England. The perseverance of the Ibrox side to get their man paid off, however, and Munro eventually joined the Light Blues in exchange for centre forward Ally Scott and outside right Graham Fyfe.

The move was seen as the first step of a major rebuilding programme at Easter Road that was now fairly obvious to all desperately needed. Because the move had been completed after the transfer deadline had passed, neither of the players involved in the deal could take part in any match involving promotion or relegation. Scott and Fyfe would subsequently play out the season in the reserves, the Ibrox side lending Munro to St Mirren for the remainder of the campaign.

A few days after Munro made the short journey through to Ibrox, Joe Harper rejoined his former club Aberdeen. Harper had been unsettled at Easter Road for some time and had never been fully accepted by the Hibs fans, who blamed him for breaking up the prolific goalscoring partnership of Jimmy O'Rourke and Alan Gordon. A swop deal involving Harper and forward Davie Robb was suggested, but although both clubs had agreed the move, Robb refused to leave Aberdeen and a straight cash deal was implemented instead. Harper had not consistently produced his best form during his time at Easter Road, although he had scored a fair number of important goals, 26 from 69 league appearances. Latterly he had dropped back into midfield, but had not figured on the team sheet at all in recent weeks and it was fairly obvious that his Easter Road career was nearing its end. Rumours abounded that Harper had been shunned by several of the established first-team players, who felt that apart from being seen as one of Eddie Turnbull's favourites, he was also being paid more than the rest. These claims, however, were quickly refuted by the manager.

With only four games remaining, Motherwell, rivals for the third-place spot and a UEFA Cup place, were defeated with the help of a second-half goal by MacLeod from the penalty spot. The 2-0 victory put the Greens two points ahead of the Lanarkshire men, who still had a game in hand. Alex McGhee, who scored the opening goal, replaced Harper as the spearhead of the attack in Turnbull's new-look side that also featured youngsters Willie Murray and Lindsay Muir. Bobby Smith deputised for the injured Brownlie at right back.

A 2-0 win against Celtic at Parkhead four days later kept Hibs well on track for a European place, the penultimate match of the season against relegation candidates Aberdeen at Pittodrie. Along with Rangers Celtic and Hearts, Aberdeen could boast of never having been relegated from the top division, but their record would be in extreme danger if they lost to Hibs. Perhaps predictably, any restless nights that had been suffered by either the Aberdeen players or their fans had proved to be entirely unnecessary and they made certain of Premier League survival against a charitable Hibs side whose performance never at any time reached that at Parkhead four days earlier or even looked as though it was an important European qualifier.

The curtain was drawn on yet another season of mixed fortunes for the Easter Road side with a fixture against relegation-haunted Dundee United at Easter Road. Like Aberdeen, the Tannadice side had endured a traumatic season and a win was absolutely vital if they were to remain in the top flight. An illuminated sign recording the fact that Hibs were a registered charity should have been erected above the entrance to Easter Road as Hibs once again failed to score against a troubled United, who managed to preserve their Premier League status at the expense of neighbours Dundee, although only on goal difference, with a comfortable 2-0 victory. United had now taken seven points from Hibs that season, while fellow relegation strugglers Aberdeen had taken three from eight.

In spite of the calamity of the final two games, Hibs had done enough in finishing in third place to qualify for the UEFA Cup for a fifth consecutive year, as had their Tynecastle neighbours Hearts, who qualified for the Cup Winners' Cup as losing finalists after defeat by treble winners Rangers. Hearts went into the history books as perhaps the only side ever to be a goal behind even before the kick-off time in a Cup Final. The referee had mistakenly started the game 60 seconds early, and by the time of the official starting time of three o'clock, Rangers, who went on to win 3-1, were already a goal ahead after Johnstone had opened the scoring in the first few seconds.

16

Shirt Sponsorship
and Stanton's Shock Move to Celtic
1976–77

DURING THE SUMMER 28-year-old centre half George Stewart was signed from Dundee for around £40,000. He would be the first brick in the rebuilding process at Easter Road. Edinburgh-born Stewart had been contemplating football in the First Division with the recently relegated Dens Park club when he was informed of Hibs' interest. It was a foregone conclusion that he would jump at the chance to sign for his boyhood heroes. Stewart was joined at Easter Road by former Falkirk and St Johnstone player John Lambie, who was taking over as second-team coach. Crossing paths at the SFA coaching classes at Largs over the past couple of years, Turnbull had been impressed both by Lambie's knowledge of the game and his unbridled enthusiasm. Lambie would replace John Fraser, who had been promoted to first-team coach in place of the popular Wilson Humphries who had unexpectedly resigned at the end of the previous season to return to his former occupation as a schoolteacher.

Graham Fyfe and Ally Scott both looked forward eagerly to the start the new campaign. Circumstances dictated that they featured only in minor games at the end of the previous season and they now welcomed the opportunity to display their talents on a bigger stage.

For a third successive year the start of the new season (1976–77) was preceded by a three-game tour of Ireland, and it was a major surprise to many that Pat Stanton failed to feature in the starting line-up in the wins against Bohemians, Dundalk and Drogheda. Stanton, who had been replaced as captain by John Blackley at the beginning of the season, made an appearance as a substitute in the final two games of the trip. Yet another indication that he would not now be an automatic first-team choice at Easter Road was provided when Hibs' longest-serving player at that time was on the bench against Montrose at Links Park for the opening game of the League Cup. Ally Scott celebrated his first-team debut by scoring the only goal of the game in the first half against a side that had proved so troublesome in the competition the previous season. During the game, supporters continually called for the introduction of Stanton, but to no avail.

Ally Scott and Ian Munro, central figures in the swap deal the previous season, both managed to score for their new sides in a 1-1 draw at Easter Road. But despite Hibs taking both points from St Johnstone at Muirton Park, a 3-0 defeat at Ibrox resulted in Hibs failing to reach the quarter-finals of the competition for the first time in seven years. Rangers, it must be said, fully deserved the victory, but yet again only the assistance of a soft penalty award had allowed the future Hibs manager Alex Miller to open the scoring early in the game.

Hibs ended the preliminary round in second place, although for a short time they had visions of topping the group after defeating St Johnstone 9-2 in Edinburgh, five of the goals scored in a magical 12-minute spell in the second half. Rangers, however, confirmed their lead at the top of the table when the Hibs could only manage to scrape a no score home draw against Montrose in the final game of the section. The disappointing result against the lowly Angus side would turn out to be the least of the supporters' worries. That morning news had started to filter through that the immensely popular Pat Stanton had been transferred to Celtic, and the disappointingly low crowd of 4,462 were not slow in venting their anger at the shock move. Hibs fans throughout the country were united in condemning the player's move to Glasgow in exchange for 23-year-old Jackie McNamara. Supporters Association secretary Bert Melrose echoing the frustration of the majority of his members, announced his disappointment at watching such a much admired and respected player leave Easter Road. Ryder Cup golfer Bernard Gallacher, a celebrated Hibs fan who still retained his season ticket although living 400 miles away in London, was also shocked and disgusted when he heard of the move. He commented, 'It would seem that the PR within the club is almost non-existent, and that the current management have no regard for the supporters.'

When questioned, Eddie Turnbull admitted that he and everyone else were 'quite aware of what a great servant Pat has been to the club,' adding, 'I am trying to rebuild a side, and no one can go on for ever.' As for the player himself, Stanton declared his great regret at leaving Easter Road and the fans that had always been so supportive, and he could not thank them enough for their wonderful backing throughout the years. Having played more than 650 games for Hibs, scoring his 75th goal for the club when coming on as a substitute against Dundalk in the pre-season tour of Ireland, he said he found it difficult to appreciate that he was no longer a Hibs player after all these years. He had 'fully expected to end his career at Easter Road'.

Glasgow-born Jackie McNamara had been at Parkhead for over five years since signing from Cumbernauld United. He had been handicapped for some time by a nagging knee injury, although managing to play through the pain, and it has been suggested that Jock Stein deviously tried to offload an injured player on the quiet. The wily Turnbull, however, was well aware of McNamara's injury, and had been assured by medical specialists that the player would recover fully after an operation to correct the problem.

During his nine seasons as manager at Easter Road, Turnbull received more criticism over the transfer of Stanton than of any other player, including Gordon and O'Rourke, but in truth the move was probably to the benefit of all three parties. For whatever reason, the high level of consistency Stanton had set himself over the years had been lacking in recent months, and the move to Glasgow would see him end the season as one of only two ever-presents as Celtic won the League and Scottish Cup double, the player completing a full set of domestic medals. The intelligent McNamara had been a near-regular at Parkhead the previous season with 23 starts plus four others as a substitute, but when he could only manage a second half place in one of Celtic's pre-season friendly matches in a tour of the Scottish Highlands, he had decided that his future probably lay anywhere but the east end of Glasgow. Finally, Hibs would benefit with ten years of solid service from a player Turnbull would describe as the last real tackler in the Scottish game. Highly popular with the fans, McNamara would become a Hibs legend in his own right.

As Stanton was helping his new teammates to a 2-2 draw with Rangers at Parkhead on Saturday 4 September 1976, McNamara was making his first appearance in a Hibs jersey at inside right in a 2-1 defeat by Dundee United at Tannadice in the first league game of the new season. Leading by a Brownlie goal from the penalty spot, the midweek signing could only watch helplessly as Blackley needlessly conceded a penalty that was duly converted by goalkeeper Hamish McAlpine, before Wallace scored the winning goal in the very last minute to leave Hibs anchored at the foot of the table.

The final word on the Stanton saga was left to manager Turnbull in an article that appeared in the *Pink News* that evening:

> The midweek deal with Celtic has brought Hibs a lot of adverse publicity due to Stanton's standing with the supporters, but the transfer was negotiated with the Hibs' best interests in mind. I am well aware that the fans would think that if he is good enough for Celtic, then he is good enough for us, which is fair comment, except that Celtic wanted an experienced man to play in the middle of defence, while I have Stewart and Blackley playing there for Hibs. We brought McNamara to Easter Road because he has skill, pace, and works willingly. He is a different type of player to Stanton and at eight years younger, he will have time to prove himself, and then the supporters will be better placed to pass judgement.

Turnbull finished by reassuring the supporters 'that the current rumours linking Bremner and Brownlie with Newcastle United are just paper talk'. In the same article, Tom Hart backed his manager: 'No one chased Pat from Easter Road. The player, who has benefited financially from the move, was told of Celtic's interest and asked if he wanted to go.'

Perhaps in an attempt to appease the supporters, the chairman revealed that the club were taking steps to introduce a season ticket for juveniles who were unable to take advantage of the parent-child gate, although this might not be available until the start of the following season. Consequently, the board were prepared to re-examine the policy, and reintroduce the boys' gate, except for matches involving Hearts and the Old Firm, presumably yet again, according to the cynics, only on the grounds of safety.

Just days before their meeting with French club Sochaux in the opening round of the UEFA Cup, a last-minute goal by Peter Marinello had denied Hibs a confidence boosting win at Fir Park. After an indifferent start to the season, this had been a much more encouraging performance by Hibs, and only a brilliant display by Rennie in the Motherwell goal had prevented the visitors from increasing their lead after Scott and Murray both figured on the scoresheet. Even then, the acquisition of both points seemed assured until Marinello's equaliser in the dying seconds.

Sochaux had finished third in the French League, behind champions St Etienne, and were relative newcomers to the European scene. After their merger with Montbéliard in 1930, their most successful spell had been during the pre-war years when they had won the championship twice. A sporting club in every sense of the word, they were in the enviable position of being backed financially by car giant Peugeot, who invested a considerable sum of money each year in the football, athletics, boxing, basketball and various other sections of the club.

There would be no place in the Hibs line-up for the experienced European campaigner Alex Edwards, out of the side since injuring his ankle against Rangers at the start of the season, but Erich Schaedler, who had lost his place to Bobby Smith, would be making his first start of the season, Smith moving forward to add more fire power to the attack.

Stewart, Fyfe and Scott had all sampled European football with Dundee and Rangers respectively, but for McDonald, Murray and young Lindsay Muir it would be a new experience. Signed after the European deadline, McNamara would watch from the stand.

Before the game Turnbull appealed for the fans to turn up in numbers to encourage the side to a victory that could make the second leg a mere formality, but on the night only 9,454 paid heed to his plea.

Sochaux's first-choice goalkeeper, Rust, had failed to recover sufficiently from a recent injury and so his place was taken by the unfortunately named Bats. The understudy, however, proved anything but crazy inside the first few minutes when he was called upon to deny Hibs on several occasions, as the home side set out on their traditional attempt to finish the match in the early stages. In the very first minute, the goalkeeper brilliantly denied Bremner the opportunity to open the scoring, before Smith had several near things that brought the crowd to its feet.

George Stewart hit the post with a header from a corner, and although Sochaux had clearly come to Edinburgh to defend in depth to frustrate Hibs, and were successful in their aims, it was not all one-way traffic by any means, and on three separate occasions McDonald in the home goal had to look lively to save from danger man Pintenat.

The referee and linesmen adhered to the fussy continental style of officiating that allowed very little tackling, and it was little surprise when the rusty Schaedler was booked after taking a wild swing at Dufour.

The only goal of the game came ten minutes before the break. Brownlie, as always eager to support his forwards, took a short corner on the right. Receiving the return pass, the full back sent over a left-foot shot that completely deceived the Sochaux defenders as it swirled in the wind before sailing over the despairing arms of the stranded goalkeeper and into the top corner of the net. The home side ended the first half in all-out assault and after the interval resumed where they had left off. Stretching Sochaux down both wings, the pace of Murray and Duncan caused constant danger and the French defenders were forced deep into their own half as the home side created chances galore that unfortunately came to nothing in a packed penalty area. Much to the disappointment of the fans, the anticipated second-half goal rush failed to materialise and a single goal was scant reward for almost 90 minutes of remorseless pressure by the home side.

FINAL SCORE: HIBERNIAN 1. SOCHAUX 0.

UEFA CUP 1ST ROUND (1ST LEG), WEDNESDAY 15 SEPTEMBER 1976, EASTER ROAD.
HIBERNIAN: MCDONALD, BROWNLIE, SCHAEDLER, BREMNER, STEWART, BLACKLEY, MURRAY, MUIR, SCOTT, SMITH, DUNCAN.

At the final whistle the delight of the visiting players and officials was unmistakable. They were evidently confident of overturning the scoreline in France, but Turnbull though thought differently. As far as he was concerned, with even a tiny bit of luck Hibs could well have scored many more goals and he was optimistic: 'We are ahead, and that's important at this stage. I would have liked a bigger lead but if Hibs can score in France, it will take three to beat us.'

Referee Reidel and stand-side linesman Rudi Gloeckner had both officiated at Easter Road before in the game against Liverpool in 1970, but in reversed roles. Gloeckner had gone on to referee the World Cup Final between Brazil and Italy in Mexico.

A tremendous 25-yard drive by Bobby Smith that was in the back of the net before Rangers keeper McCloy could even move, gave Hibs a share of the points on the Saturday at Easter Road. Three games into the season both sides were still seeking their first league win. Seven days later at Easter Road a win bonus was still an unknown quantity when a dismally small crowd watched an equally dismal no-score draw with Aberdeen, the sole highlight of the game being the referee's whistle to bring the proceedings to an end.

The return of Edwards after injury would be Hibs' only change in France, the outside right replacing Lindsay Muir who dropped to the bench. As well as his extensive European experience with Hibs, Edwards was an old campaigner from his Dunfermline days and his inclusion would be a timely boost for a side that had recently experienced great difficulty in the goalscoring department. Like their Scottish counterparts, Sochaux's results so far had been anything but impressive: they were in the lower half of the league, having taken just six points from seven games, and Hibs were quietly optimistic of making their way into the next round.

With the improvements in foreign travel, it was now no longer necessary to leave two days before the away leg of a European game, and the Easter Road party made their way to Edinburgh Airport early on the Tuesday afternoon for the journey to Sochaux. The Carlton Branch of the Hibs Supporters Club had organised a bus for the trip to France, something of a novelty at that time. A newspaper advert advised that the journey would cost the grand sum of £35, including two nights' bed and breakfast. Leaving from Easter Road at 8.30 on the Monday morning, they would arrive back in Edinburgh on the Friday. A second bus run by the Pentland Branch would leave the city at the same time.

Although having the bulk of the play, Hibs had to be satisfied with a no-score draw in the picturesque, tree-lined stadium situated inside the grounds of the giant Peugeot factory. Since losing to Hajduk Split in 1973, the Edinburgh side had failed to score in only two of their five away fixtures in Europe – against Leeds United and Juventus – but the solitary goal scored in the city two weeks previously was enough to ensure progress into the second round. Any thoughts that the 0-0 scoreline meant it was an unexciting game should be discounted: only good defending, poor finishing, and some bad luck prevented the visitors from scoring at least three or four.

Bats, retained in the home goal, had yet another impressive outing. He had to be at his very best as early as the opening minute to prevent Bremner from doubling Hibs' aggregate lead. In contrast, Hibs goalkeeper McDonald was a spectator throughout the entire proceedings as the recalled Alex Edwards dictated the Greens' every worthwhile move from midfield. The former Dunfermline player showed that he had lost none of his skill and cunning, and a string of telling passes set up chances galore for Bremner and Smith that unfortunately came to nothing.

At half time, Higgins, making his first top-team start since January, replaced Duncan who had taken a knock, and Fyfe replaced the ineffectual Scott, who had made little headway up front. The intelligent Higgins made an immediate impression, creating all kinds of difficulty in the French back division. With just a touch of luck, the giant forward might well have scored twice.

Try as they might, Hibs just could not force the breakthrough, but it was obvious even midway through the second half that Sochaux did not possess enough weaponry to breach their defence and that, barring a disastrous mistake, the goal scored in Edinburgh would be enough to take the visitors through to the next round. With 20 minutes left to play, Sochaux made a double substitution, but this made absolutely no difference to the pattern of the game, and Hibs finished the stronger side. The small band of Hibs supporters who had made the long journey by coach had been vocal throughout the game, giving their team tremendous encouragement, and their singing drowned out the local fans near the end when it became obvious which team would be progressing into the next round.

FINAL SCORE: SOCHAUX 0. HIBERNIAN 0.

UEFA CUP 1ST ROUND (2ND LEG), WEDNESDAY 29 SEPTEMBER 1976. STADE AUGUSTE
BONAL.
HIBERNIAN: MCDONALD, BROWNLIE, SCHAEDLER, BREMNER, STEWART, BLACKLEY,
MURRAY, EDWARDS, SCOTT, SMITH, DUNCAN.

Both the Old Firm teams had already made an exit from European
competition in the first round, Rangers at the hands of Zurich in the
Champions' Cup and Celtic by Wilsa Cracow in the UEFA Cup. Now, with
the Tynecastle side seeing off the challenge of Locomotiv Leipzig in the Cup
Winners' Cup, it was left to Hibs and Hearts to carry Scotland's hopes into
the next round, much to the dismay of many in the media with their well
established west of Scotland bias.

At the beginning of October Pat Stanton made his first appearance against
his former club as Hibs' four-game sequence of league draws at Parkhead
continued. Playing in his favoured back four position, Stanton could do little
to prevent Higgins giving Hibs a first-half lead, but after two solid penalty
claims by the visiting side, Dalglish equalised from the spot to make the final
score 1-1, and after five games Hibs were still seeking their first win bonus of
the season.

Stanton had not featured in the international set-up in any capacity since
Scotland's defeat by West Germany in March 1974, but only a few weeks
after joining Celtic he had been included as one of the two over-age players in
the Under-21 side for the game against Czechoslovakia in Pilsen.

Because of Scotland's friendly international against Czechoslovakia in
Prague the following week, the Premier League programme the previous
Saturday had been cancelled. Several sides took full advantage of the break
to play challenge matches in England whose own top league had also been
cancelled.

At St James' Park Hibs were defeated 2-1 by Newcastle United, Ally Scott
scoring for the visitors. An unsavoury incident occurred midway through the
second half when the referee was forced to stop the game for well over a
minute as police moved to prevent the fighting that had broken out between
rival fans from escalating. Things were much worse at Birmingham that same
afternoon. Rangers' fans attending a 'friendly' against Aston Villa at Villa
Park went on the rampage after Villa took a two-goal lead, forcing the referee
to abandon the game in the 53rd minute. Bottles were thrown before a full-
scale pitch invasion and fighting continued in and around the stadium until
police eventually managed to take control of the situation.

Although Rangers did not hold a monopoly on incidents of hooliganism,
this was not the first time that the Glasgow supporters had been involved in
serious mayhem at games both at home and abroad. Some Scottish journalists
were now asking if the Ibrox club were doing enough to rectify the situation,
speculating that religion rather than sheer animalism was behind the terrible
behaviour that was beginning to drive many decent fans from the game.
Some also suggested that it was time for the club to re-examine the bigotry

that clearly existed inside the boardroom. The outburst prompted general manager and vice chairman Willie Waddell, a former Rangers player, to pledge that the club were out to smash the idea that they were a sectarian organisation, and they would definitely sign a Roman Catholic if they could find one good enough who wished to join the club. Waddell was insistent that Rangers did employ Catholics, but declined an invitation to enlighten the public as to what position they held within Ibrox.

The sectarian antagonism between Rangers and Celtic dated back to the early days of the game. Following a home game against Dunfermline in 1967, Rangers chairman John Lawrence had been vociferous in his condemnation of those who were guilty of singing what he called the 'filthy songs that blighted the Ibrox scene'. In a statement released to the press, he had blasted:

> Rarely have I been so angry! Every man has a right to his religious beliefs, but the dirt that is coming from some of our supporters has no place whatsoever inside a football ground. Our heads are hanging in shame because of the outbursts of these lunatics. With the co-operation of the police we are absolutely determined to root them out.

Lawrence's verbal salvo was aimed at the section of the Rangers support that was 'more interested in chanting their vile slogans than in watching the match and it cannot be allowed to continue'. It is a problem that remains even now, 40 years later, despite the gestures that are regularly made, and many take the view that not nearly enough is being done by Rangers and Celtic to eradicate the religious bigotry that mainly emanates from the West of Scotland.

It must be said, however, that at the time of Lawrence's outburst, the 'Soldier Song' and similar protest anthems could often be heard at Easter Road and pro-Irish banners were sometimes seen during matches. Recently the occasional tricolour has again been in evidence.

An interesting article relating to the hooligan problem appeared in the *Pink News*, stimulated by the fact that John Swan, a Hibs shareholder, had sent FA secretary Ted Croker a 'blueprint for combating hooliganism'. The comprehensive dossier outlined various methods of preventing trouble on the terracing: breaking up gangs at an early stage; earlier starts for certain games, which might combat drunkenness; and the possibility of introducing all-seated stadiums. Many of these measures are now standard policy. Mr Swan took no personal credit for the ideas – all had been suggested by his brother, Harry, many years before.

Mid-October saw the passing of 60-year-old Davie Shaw, Hibs captain during their first post-war league championship success in 1948. Signed from Grange Rovers in 1939, 'Faither' made an almost immediate debut. Winning eight full Scotland caps, five of them in a full back partnership with clubmate Jock Govan, both he and brother 'Tiger' of Rangers had faced England in the Victory International in 1946. Although best known as a Hibs player, Shaw had transferred to Aberdeen in the summer of 1950, giving the Dons 17 years' loyal service as a player, trainer, then manager, before reverting back to trainer during Eddie Turnbull's early years at Pittodrie.

With Hibs still seeking their first league win of the season, an inspired performance from goalkeeper Alan Rough in the Partick Thistle goal denied the home side victory before facing Swedish club Oesters IF in the second round of the UEFA Cup. The game ended goalless, Hibs' fifth consecutive draw and the sixth in seven matches.

Like Sochaux in the previous round, Oesters were something of an unknown quantity. With only limited European experience, they had usually made an exit at first-round stage. Formed as a schoolboy team in the 1930s, gradual progression had been made through the lower leagues until they had finally clinched a place in the Swedish First Division in 1968, making history by becoming the first side to win the championship and a place in the European Cup at their very first attempt. Managed by the legendary Swedish international centre forward Gunnar Nordahl of AC Milan and Roma fame, Oesters were still in contention for the league championship, which was in its final stages.

As was their custom, Turnbull and Hart had watched their opponents in action. Impressed by their all-action, attacking style, the Hibs manager felt that the part-timers would have a real go in Edinburgh. A match between two sides committed to all-out attack promised a rare treat for the fans, who despite Hibs' current difficulty in scoring goals, made their way to Easter Road anticipating yet another goal feast against a side from one of Europe's weaker nations.

With Erich Schaedler retaining his top-team place, Hibs lined up along the usual lines. But if the fans had been expecting a thrill-packed contest between two attack-minded sides, they were to be disappointed. Contrary to the pre-match hype, Oesters immediately fell back into a deep defensive formation geared to stifling Hibs in midfield. In what turned out to be 90 minutes of one-way traffic toward the Swedish goal, the home defence had their easiest evening for some time, but although having the bulk of the play, the Easter Road side met with great difficulty in converting their overwhelming possession into goals.

With any sharpness at all up front, the struggling Hibs attack could well have helped themselves to several goals, but as it was, it was left to the defence to show the way with two goals inside a minute in the first half. With 34 minutes played, Smith out wide on the left cleverly beat two men before firing over a waist-high cross that was met by the inrushing Blackley, who threw himself at the ball to bullet a tremendous header past Hagbert in the Oesters goal from six yards. After 25 starts it was the red-haired defender's first ever goal in Europe.

Encouraged by the goal, Hibs showed renewed determination from the restart and within 60 seconds were two ahead. A brilliant run by Bremner from just inside the opposition half ended with the midfield player smashing a thunderbolt right-foot shot against the bar with the keeper rooted to the spot. The ricochet from the underside of the crossbar was handled by right back Berquavist, leaving referee Aldinger with little option other than to award a penalty, Brownlie duly scoring from the spot.

Lindsay Muir, who had been given the job of marking the dangerous Linderoth, made a shaky start, but the youngster gained in confidence the longer the game went on and the experienced Swedish international rarely got the better of him.

In an attempt to inject more pace into the game, Turnbull replaced Schaedler with Willie Murray after the break with Smith moving to full back, but the expected second-half goal avalanche again failed to materialise, much to the disappointment of the home fans among the 11,000 crowd. A Muir effort midway through the half was only inches away from increasing Hibs lead, a Bremner attempt several minutes later suffering the same fate, but the Swedes managed to hold out for the final whistle.

FINAL SCORE: HIBERNIAN 2. OESTERS 0.

UEFA CUP 2ND ROUND (1ST LEG), WEDNESDAY 20 OCTOBER 1976, EASTER ROAD.
HIBERNIAN: MCDONALD, BROWNLIE, SCHAEDLER, BREMNER, STEWART, BLACKLEY, EDWARDS, MUIR, HIGGINS, SMITH, DUNCAN.

After an amazing game of three penalties at Ayr on the Saturday, several journalists suggested that perhaps only the top officials should be allowed to handle Premier League games. Referee McFaul, who had a poor game throughout, had already awarded a penalty kick to each side when Ayr were awarded another in what was thought to be one of the worst decisions seen for many years. As Schaedler was chasing a loose ball inside Hibs' penalty area, he was challenged from behind by substitute McSherry, when, to the absolute astonishment of all the players and both sets of fans, McFaul awarded a penalty to Ayr. Justice was served, however, when McDonald saved the spot-kick, and Hibs went on win 3-2, their first league victory, and first win bonus of the season.

Only days after the passing of Davie Shaw, news was received from Canada of the sudden death from a heart attack of former midfield maestro Willie Hamilton, aged just 37. The Scottish international had starred with distinction for both Edinburgh sides, performing brilliantly in Hibs' defeat of the great Real Madrid in 1964 and the historic treble victories against Rangers that same season. Hamilton's at times outrageous lifestyle threatened to eclipse his fantastic ability on the field and it is no coincidence that perhaps the best football of his career had been played at Easter Road under the influence of manager Jock Stein. Indeed, it is rumoured that Hamilton was encouraged to stay overnight at the manager's home before a big game in an attempt to deter him from overindulging in the Edinburgh clubs. There is no doubt that Hamilton at his best was a true footballing genius and his passing left thousands of fans with sublime memories of his mercurial talents.

After five successive league defeats at Easter Road, Hearts salvaged some pride with a late equaliser when young Willie Paterson opened the scoring for Hibs with a header after only 35 seconds. Thereafter a fiercely fought game was contested evenly and a share of the spoils left both sides reasonably satisfied. Hibs were still to record their first home win of the new campaign, but amazingly, although they had lost to Dundee United on the opening day of the season, they had remained unbeaten since, drawing seven of the nine games played to leave them sitting in mid-table.

There were injury problems for Turnbull before Hibs' flight to Sweden for the return leg of the UEFA Cup. Centre half George Stewart, injured against Hearts on the Saturday, had failed to recover. His place at the centre of defence would be taken by Ally Brazil, making his European debut. With Duncan, McGhee Ally MacLeod and now Stewart unavailable, Hibs would be forced to field a much weakened team.

The Oesters ground in Vaxjo was one of the most modern in Europe. Undersoil heating had recently been installed, with a blanket costing an astronomical £10,000 used to cover the pitch for extra protection. The cost would not be a problem to Oesters. Like all the major stadia in Sweden it was under the control of the state, which covered all costs in exchange for a monthly rent.

Before only 1,175 supporters, by far the lowest ever to watch the Scottish club in a European competition, Hibs produced their worst ever performance in the 21 years that they had graced the continental stage. Unbeaten since the beginning of September, and failing to concede even a goal in their last three UEFA Cup games, this was Hibs at their most mediocre.

Somewhat surprisingly, the Swedish players retreated into a defensive formation straight from the kick-off. Although there was an unusual hesitancy in the play of Hibs in the opening stages, the Edinburgh side looked totally in command until a poor clearance by Spalding was capitalised upon by Linderoth, who smashed an unstoppable drive from an acute angle past the surprised McDonald.

There was now a nervousness about the visitors' play. Willie Murray should have restored Hibs' two-goal aggregate lead when presented with an easy chance. Encouraged by the hesitancy of their opponents, Oesters became more adventurous and were rewarded nine minutes before half time with an overall leveller that once again should have been avoided. With no threat of danger, Brownlie lost his footing not far from goal. Ejderstedts took full advantage of the slip to crash in a drive that came back of the body of the diving McDonald but unfortunately for the Scots the ball fell kindly to the same player, who wasted no time in smashing it into the roof of the net.

Wilson replaced Muir at the interval. Within minutes of resumption of play, Hibs appealed for a penalty when Fyfe went down in the box, but the referee correctly waved away the claims.

On the hour mark, Johansson replaced Evesson and the substitute's first touch set up a third goal for Oesters. Schaedler opted to clear the ball instead of conceding a corner and the clearance was charged down by Johansson, whose chip into the danger area was headed home by Ejderstedts to give the Swedes an overall lead.

Ejderstedts missed an absolute gift with Hibs creating little of note at this stage, but still a goal for the Easter Road side would change the whole complexion of the match courtesy of the away goals ruling.

Minutes later a goal did come, but unfortunately for Hibs it was another strike by Linderoth, who put the result beyond all doubt when he beat the diving McDonald to score off the right-hand post.

The Edinburgh side were now a totally disjointed unit, but against the odds Smith managed to score a late scrappy goal that momentary increased the hope that they could still save the game but there was little belief behind their play, and the home side took advantage of every opportunity to waste time, eventually holding out comfortably for a victory that had seemed well beyond them in the early stages of the game.

FINAL SCORE: OESTERS 4. HIBERNIAN I.

UEFA CUP 2ND ROUND (2ND LEG), WEDNESDAY 3 NOVEMBER 1976, VAXJO STADIUM.
HIBERNIAN: MCDONALD, BROWNLIE, SCHAEDLER, BREMNER, SPALDING, BLACKLEY, MURRAY, EDWARDS, SMITH, MUIR, FYFE.

At the end of what had been a disastrous and humiliating 90 minutes, the Hibs players trooped dejectedly from the pitch. In a post-match statement a shell-shocked Turnbull could only confess to disappointment – a disappointment that would become even more acute at the news that the defeat had prevented a money-spinning repeat of the famous 1960–61 quarter-final clash with Barcelona. As it turned out, Oesters were soundly thrashed 8-1 on aggregate by the Spanish giants and Barcelona were defeated at the semi-final stage by the losing finalists and yet another of Hibs' former European adversaries, Juventus. Who is to say that Hibs would not have suffered a similar fate to Oesters.

The Edinburgh fans were given the opportunity to see a genuine football legend in action when Stoke City visited Easter Road for a friendly match in mid-November. Former England World Cup winning goalkeeper Gordon Banks had been forced to retire from competitive football near the peak of his career after losing an eye in a car crash in 1972. Although he was prevented from taking part in competitive games, he continued to play in benefit matches and friendlies. Banks demonstrated why he had been named Footballer of the Year just before the accident and why at one time he had been considered the greatest goalkeeper in the world. He produced a string of top-class saves to deny Hibs an equaliser after a young Garth Crooks scored the only goal of the game. John Blackley, recently voted Player of the Year by the Hibs Supporters Association, was with the Scotland party preparing for the following night's victory over Wales at Hampden, and missed the game.

The New Fifty Club, situated just across the road from the stadium, was officially opened with a dinner attended by the Hibs manager, chairman and board of directors. Former and present players were invited to the function including Pat Stanton, Jim Black and Alan Gordon, now club treasurer. Tom Hart presented the committee of the exclusive club with a pennant, declaring his delight that they had overcome their difficulties and were once again under way. A desire to maintain a good relationship with the supporters was reiterated.

A Joe Harper goal at Pittodrie was the difference between the sides as the Christmas period approached. Hibs were then lying in sixth place, just above city rivals Hearts, a far cry from the halcyon days at the beginning of the decade. Stewart Brown, writing in the *Edinburgh Evening News* on the day of the game, suggested that the Easter Road troubles had started with the acquisition of Joe Harper from Everton two years before. It was a view shared by many Hibs supporters at the time. Although it had been an ambitious move made in the best interests of the club, Harper had failed to live up to the goalscoring reputation of his earlier years; and the departure of both Gordon and O'Rourke to make way for him had further upset the balance of the side. According to Brown, the £120,000 transfer fee had been far too much for Hibs or any other Scottish team to pay in relation to the size of the gates and the club was now paying the penalty by being unable to add to their present pool.

Chairman Tom Hart disclosed that the football club still owed his family a substantial sum, rumoured to be as much as £200,000. It was no secret that Turnbull, renowned for his admiration for the skilful side of the game, had recently changed this strategy to introduce more backbone into the side, but this had been to the detriment of ability and the side now bore no resemblance to the team of just a few seasons before.

At the beginning of December Hibs fans were rocked by the announcement that Jackie McNamara required a cartilage operation. This was quickly followed by the news that young Willie Paterson, who had only just broken in to the first team, having scored his first top-team goal against Hearts a few weeks before, had injured an eye in a car accident. Paterson had been a passenger in a car driven by McNamara. Soon after dropping John Blackley off at his home in the central belt, the vehicle was involved in a collision with an articulated lorry on the Kilsyth road. There was initial concern that the player might lose his sight, but fortunately an operation proved successful.

Incredibly, it was now the end of December and the Easter Road side were still seeking their first home win of the season. On Christmas eve Hibs met Ayr United at Easter Road with an eye on a league double. So far that season United had been the only side to lose to Hibs in a league game. A decision to open the enclosure at terracing prices was not a sufficient enticement to attract the majority of the home support, who preferred to spend the evening with their families, and only a paltry 3,875 saw an own goal by Ayr's Joe Filippi after an hour, end an unwanted and truly pitiful home record. Hibs' victory now meant that only Forfar, of the 129 league clubs on both sides of the Border, were still without a home win.

Although there was little to choose between both Edinburgh sides at that time, Hearts were confident of ending a 22-year hoodoo, having failed to savour victory in the New Year's Day fixture at Tynecastle since 1955. In the intervening years Hibs had gained ample revenge for the 5-1 defeat inflicted by Hearts that day, the Gorgie side's last New Year's Day victory coming 12 years earlier when the visitors had overcome a 2-0 deficit to win 3-2 at Easter Road in 1966. Of the 22 players who played that day, only Hearts' goalkeeper Jim Cruickshank was still in contention for a first-team start, although at that time he was featuring mostly in the second team. Unfortunately, bad weather caused the postponement not only of the holiday match, but also of the Hibs game against Dundee United on the Monday. The latter game was rearranged for two days later after a sudden improvement in the weather. The exciting but goalless match was Hibs' tenth draw from 16 games as they attempted to overcome the negative tactics and petty fouling that at that time had become Dundee United's standard practice.

Although they had been playing well enough, for Hibs, goals were still proving difficult to come by and their following two games, against Motherwell away and Aberdeen at home, also ended in deadlock. At Fir Park a Brownlie strike gave Hibs a first-half lead, but an O'Rourke goal against his former teammates just after the restart resulted in the sides sharing the points. Against league leaders Aberdeen, the play of an all-out attacking Hibs side with Edwards in inspirational form, was deserving of both points but again they just could not break down the stuffy Dons' defence and had to be satisfied with a share of the honours after yet another no-scoring encounter.

Blizzards that were sweeping the country wrought havoc with the fixtures list. There was yet another postponement of the rearranged Ne'er Day game against Hearts, which finally took place in the middle of the month. Murrayfield had been suggested as a possible venue for the game if the extreme conditions continued, but despite ten hours of almost non-stop rain that had again threatened the fixture, it went ahead in conditions that were not conducive to good football. The pools panel, set up as an emergency measure during the big freeze in 1963 and continued since, had originally predicted a no-score draw, but one flash of genius from Ally MacLeod, making his first appearance since his injury in September, was the difference between the sides in a boring derby. Starting the move himself from midfield, MacLeod's pass out wide to McGhee was returned for the inside forward to smash the ball high into the net in match-winning style as Hibs recorded only their fourth championship victory after 19 starts.

In the past most of the crowd trouble at games in Scotland had been caused by sections of the huge Rangers and Celtic support, but as if to prove that the Old Firm held no monopoly over hooliganism, Edinburgh was now becoming more embroiled than ever before. During the game at Tynecastle the police had made 24 arrests, in itself was not all that unusual for a crowd of over 24,000, but taking into account the several dozen fans that had been ejected from the stadium during the game, it was clear that the problem in the city was intensifying.

Hibs had relaxed their once vehement opposition to Sunday football and just 24 hours after a 4-2 defeat by Celtic at Parkhead, they faced Partick Thistle in the first round of the Scottish Cup at Easter Road. Partick goalkeeper Alan Rough, who would spend several years as a player at Easter Road later in his career, was in splendid form as, almost single-handed, he repeatedly defied the thrusts of the home side during the first half, but he could do little to prevent Hibs three goals after the break as they sealed an emphatic win to set up a game against First Division Arbroath in the next round. Scoring his third goal in as many games since his return from injury, Ally MacLeod deserved much of the credit in an all-round brilliant performance. In common with most other grounds in the country, Easter Road attendances had been falling steadily, but the then healthy 14,000 turn-out suggested that the Sunday experiment had been a success.

MacLeod kept up his recent scoring sequence the following Saturday when he headed the only goal of the game in the 67th minute against Kilmarnock to give Hibs their first win at Rugby Park since 1957.

A further two draws, their 13th and 14th of the season so far, allowed Hibs to remain in fifth place. In the game against Rangers at Easter Road, a shocking performance by referee Muirhead, who had the proverbial nightmare, was the only talking point in a drab, goalless game watched by only 12,542, the dropped point severely denting the Ibrox championship challenge. The most controversial moment of the game came midway through the second half when Alec McDonald of Rangers, who had already been booked for persistently refusing to retreat ten yards at free kicks and corners, clashed with Edwards out wide near the stand-side touchline. As the Hibs player attempted to rise after the tackle, he was wrestled to the ground by McDonald. Referee Muirhead, quickly on the scene, gestured angrily at the still grounded McDonald, then, to the bewilderment of both sets of supporters, he booked Edwards while allowing the instigator of the incident to escape with a warning. The incredible decision, which betrayed a lack of courage on the official's part, provoked outrage among the Hibs support. The game deteriorated into a nasty, ill-tempered affair in the closing stages.

In the Scottish Cup at Gayfield it took a John Blackley goal late in the game to save Hibs' blushes. Arbroath took the lead ten minutes after the interval and thereafter numerous goalscoring chances were scorned by the Greens. They were almost made to pay the price as Arbroath themselves missed several opportunities to increase their lead. The late saver was enough, however, to earn the visitors a somewhat undeserved replay at Easter Road and another opportunity to set up an all Premier League meeting with Dundee in the next round.

With attendances still dropping, a decent run in the Cup was imperative, but an air of despondency lingered over Easter Road after a calamitous and embarrassing exit at the hands of lowly Arbroath. Giving their Premier

League opponents a goal of a start, Arbroath scored twice inside two minutes to inflict on Hibs yet another humiliating defeat by a lower league side. MacLeod appeared to have set Hibs well on the way to the plum third round tie when he opened the scoring after only five minutes, but that was as good as it got for the Premier League side as Arbroath stormed back to win the game in the second half. In reality Hibs were the architects of their own downfall, poor finishing allied to unbelievably slack defensive work at the back allowing their opponents their victory. MacLeod missed an easy chance with only former Hibs goalkeeper Marshall to beat, before Smith fell over a Duncan cross on the goal line when it appeared easier to score.

In the final few minutes, substitute Paterson missed an easy header in front of an open goal and it was obvious then that it was not to be Hibs' night. A stunned Turnbull, who was jeered at the final whistle by the Hibs fans who had bothered to stay until the end, was furious at the effort shown by a side that only started to play after going behind.

There had been several other embarrassing cup defeats at the hands of so-called inferior opposition in recent years, but they had all been away from home. This latest calamity was the first cup defeat by a lower league side at Easter Road since the humiliating 3-2 reverse by Edinburgh City during the 1937–38 season.

After the game, groups of rampaging thugs who found it difficult to stomach defeat embarked on a spree of wanton vandalism in the city centre, smashing the windows of several shops in the High Street. The incidents incensed Councillor James Cooke who intended to report the matter to a government working group then studying football and its behaviour. He called for the SFA and the Hibs directors to be held responsible for the £1,000 bill for the damage. The catastrophic defeat by Arbroath also prompted local newspaper columnist and fervent Hibs supporter John Gibson to jokingly suggest that perhaps a hypnotist would be of assistance at Easter Road. The publicity-conscious stage hypnotist Robert Halpern, then at the peak of his career, volunteered his services, but the offer was diplomatically refused. Perhaps Hibs had players who would be able to defeat the best efforts of the famous mesmeriser!

At the beginning of March Edinburgh lost two of its sporting stalwarts within a few days. Hearts' legendary centre forward Willie Bauld died at his home in Slateford aged 59. Often a thorn in the side of Hibs, particularly during the '40s and '50s, Bauld was a greatly respected figure even in the east side of the city, and his untimely demise was the passing of yet another legend from the golden years of Edinburgh's footballing heritage. Just days later, the news that John Harvey, trainer during the halcyon days at Tynecastle and later manager of the club, had also passed on, cast a giant shadow over the city's football fraternity.

Since the shock cup defeat by Arbroath, four points had been taken from the last six and at the end of the month Hibs extended their dominance over struggling Hearts. Goals by MacLeod, Smith and Scott gave the Greens a convincing 3-1 victory at Easter Road, leaving Hearts to wonder how a side that had experienced such difficulty in finding the net could score three goals for only the second time that season.

On Wednesday 30 March, Pat Stanton made his first competitive return to Easter Road as a player with league leaders Celtic in a 1-1 draw. Playing with the advantage of a strong wind, Hibs could well have been ahead at the interval. After the break it was expected that Celtic would take advantage of the elements to stroll to a commanding lead but a magnificent rearguard action by the Hibs defence, with Spalding particularly impressive, ensured a deserved share of the points.

At Tynecastle that same evening a home defeat by Ayr United saw Hearts deep in crisis. Lying fifth in the table at the beginning of February and above their Edinburgh rivals, Hearts had endured a torrid time since and their freewheel to second-bottom. A miracle was now required to stave off relegation for the first time in the club's history. Although they were six points clear of bottom side Kilmarnock, the Maroons were also six points behind seventh-placed Ayr. With only seven games remaining their Premier League survival looked precarious.

A 2-2 draw at Tynecastle in the last game between the sides that season, or the next two seasons, to be precise, saw Hibs record their 17th draw in just 32 games. It was a statistic that earned the Easter road side a place in the record books as the side with the most draws in any one season.

A brilliant 30-yard thunderbolt from Des Bremner cancelled out an early goal by Gibson to silence the Gorgie faithful and Hearts' Premier League status seemed in mortal danger when another Bremner goal gave Hibs a half-time advantage. This looked like being the final result, but with just seconds remaining, a controversial last-minute equaliser by full back and future Hibs player Jim Brown gave Hearts a slim chance of avoiding the drop into the First Division. The Hearts forwards in the Hibs penalty area were played offside by the retreating defenders. The linesman immediately raised his flag, but to the consternation of the now stranded Hibs players, the referee ignored his assistant and the frantic appeals of the visitors, allowing Brown to score the easiest of goals when he tapped the ball into the net for a surprise share of the points. Goalkeeper McDonald was so incensed that he pursued the referee as far as the halfway line, but the heated protests of the visiting players were waved away by the official. Less than 11,000 fans watched the game, making a total of fewer than 72,000 for the four Edinburgh derbies that season and an average of under 18,000 per game.

Pat Stanton was at the heart of the Celtic defence for the final clash of the Greens at Easter Road on Saturday 16 April, a game that would see the Parkhead side secure the league title for the first time in three years. In the days leading up to the fixture, Tom Hart had again banned television cameras from the ground 'for the good of the game'. The Hibs chairman had repeatedly claimed that the game was being overexposed on TV. Other clubs, including Celtic, had also spoken out against the TV menace, but only Hibs had taken action. Two years before, Hart had banned the cameras from the stadium for six months, and he now called upon the Scottish League to ban the televising of all games under their jurisdiction for a trial period of one year. The fee for broadcasting highlights during the evening was worth only £300 to the participating clubs, an insignificant figure even then. Hart was perhaps proved correct in his one-man campaign when a larger than normal travelling support from the west coast descended on the capital, as the BBC camera crews, somewhat predictably, travelled in the opposite direction to cover the Rangers game against Ayr United at Ibrox. A crowd of 22,036, which was good for those days but poor in comparison with the 40–50,000 which had been the norm for clashes between the sides in the halcyon years of the '40s and '50s, were inside Easter Road to see a second-half goal by Craig help win Stanton a league championship medal.

Seven days later a pathetic 2,835 – Hibs' lowest home crowd of the season – saw goals from Scott and Bremner give the Edinburgh side victory over Ayr United, their fourth of the season over the Somerset Park side. The following Saturday for Hibs' third home game in a row and their penultimate game of the current campaign, it was business as usual with a drab no-score draw against bottom-of-the-table Kilmarnock – Hibs' 18th draw in 35 games.

The end of the season just couldn't come quickly enough for everyone at Easter Road and it was no surprise when shot-shy Hibs were beaten 1-0 by Partick Thistle in the final game. The home side had sat in fifth place for the past few months, but the defeat allowed Thistle, who had yet another brilliant display by goalkeeper Alan Rough to thank for the victory, to overtake the Edinburgh side.

If things were bad in the east side of the city they were even worse over at Tynecastle. Although they had defeated fellow strugglers Motherwell 3-2 in the final game of the season, the victory was not enough to prevent Hearts from being relegated for the first time in the club's history. The veteran Rangers player John Greig was among the front-runners to replace sacked manger John Haggart, but the Hearts directors ultimately believed that the ex-Hibs legend and former Scotland manager Willie Ormond was the man to guide the club from the depths of the First Division at the first time of asking. Ormond would need all his vast managerial experience to revive a team that was in total disarray.

Finishing sixth behind champions Celtic, Rangers, Aberdeen, Dundee United and Partick Thistle would mean that for the first time in six years there would be no European games at Easter Road during the coming season. Instead, they could look forward with anticipation to playing in the now renamed Anglo-Scottish Cup.

In a season of highs and lows, the lowest point had undoubtedly been the disastrous defeat by lowly Arbroath. Only eight league games had been won, including all four against struggling Ayr United. The only other successes were the doubles over both relegated sides Kilmarnock and Hearts. Perhaps in an attempt to revive the flagging spirits of the supporters, Turnbull had praised the side's tremendous defensive record. In 36 games only 35 goals had been conceded, but the main problem was that only 34 had been scored, and the diminishing fall in attendances during the latter half of the season reflected the view that the majority of fans did not subscribe to the manager's confidence. Bobby Smith had ended the season as top scorer with a meagre eight championship goals. Ally MacLeod, who had missed a large part of the season owing to injury, was overall top marksman with 12 in all games. Again, several youngsters had made the breakthrough to the first team, including Paterson, Brazil, Wilson, and Muir, but only time would tell if they would compare to the blossoming talent that had broken through in the early years of the decade.

The inaugural Premier League had proved a massive disappointment. Instead of the anticipated substantial increase in attendances and the predicted increase in the level of skill and entertainment, not to mention finance, the reverse had been the case, with most sides having to contend with still drastically falling gates. The idea of a league featuring the ten best teams in the country had looked good on paper, but the predicted boom had failed to materialise. The standard of entertainment had also deteriorated as the league had become one ruled by fear. A relegation ratio of 20 per cent was far too high, particularly as the Old Firm could realistically be excluded from the equation, and already most managers had become resistant to introducing youngsters into first-team action.

At the end of the season seven players were freed, including Ian Campbell, John Murphy and Alec McGhee who had made several first-team appearances that season. Unable to command a regular first-team place in recent months, Tony Higgins was put on the open-to-transfer list. Also included in the list of 'frees' was young Gerry McCabe, who had featured regularly for the reserves during the season. McCabe would return to Easter Road as coach under manager Bobby Williamson 24 years later.

Like Higgins, centre half Derek Spalding had also found it difficult to establish himself in the first team. Since the signing of George Stewart, his top-team appearances had been few and far between and at the end of the season he married an American girl he had met in Scotland and decided to emigrate to the United States. After a lengthy dispute over a transfer fee for a player still registered to Hibs, the defender would eventually sign for the Chicago Stings; he ended his playing career with the Toronto Blizzards in 1984.

As for Pat Stanton, who had started the season in the green and white of Hibs, Celtic's 1-0 victory over Rangers in that years Scottish Cup Final allowed him to complete his set of domestic medals.

17

Anglo-Scottish Cup: Victory at Blackburn and Bust-up at Bristol
1977–78

THE SUMMER OF 1977 saw the dawn of a whole new era in Scottish football. In an exciting new age of advertising, Hibs became the first British side to feature a sponsor's name on their shirt. Throughout the years there had been stiff opposition to sponsorship within the game, but these firmly entrenched principles had gradually been eroded. With the formation of the privately promoted Drybrough and Texaco Cups a few years before, and now sponsorship of the Scottish Cup competition, it was only a matter of time before the logical progression to shirt advertising, all innovations that had been predicted by former Hibs chairman Harry Swan more than 25 years before.

For the first photoshoot, club captain John Blackley modelled the new v-neck strip bearing the name of the main sponsor – sportswear manufacturers Bukta – in four-inch-high white letters across the chest. For the first time the traditional all-white sleeves were emblazoned with broad green bands down each side featuring the sponsor's logo. The lucrative two-year deal had been sanctioned by both the SFA and Scottish League, and it was yet another first for the forward-looking Easter Road side, who had recognised the benefits of sponsorship well ahead of their competitors. Within a short space of time, shirt advertising would become common practice as others, realising the significance of the landmark move, joined a speeding bandwagon.

As well as a substantial cash payment from Bukta, Hibs received half a dozen strips and new dress tracksuits for players and staff, all featuring the sponsor's name.

The innovation was not welcomed by all. Both the BBC and STV were quick to show concern that the size of the lettering on the shirts was in clear contravention of their advertising codes, and hinted at a possible camera ban on all games involving the Easter Road club. The irony of this would not be lost on Tom Hart, who had been campaigning for such a blackout for years.

The threat by the television authorities provoked a commendable response from the delegates of the Scottish League who had approved shirt advertising for all the senior clubs, and they promised that any such veto against Hibs would lead to a blanket blackout of any game under their jurisdiction. Taking full advantage of the situation, both football associations again raised the thorny subject of remuneration for allowing match highlights to be transmitted. An offer made to the football authorities at the beginning of the season was described as derisory, with the broadcasting companies informed that unless the existing fees were substantially increased or even doubled, then there would be no football on television. Fees for repeat broadcasts also came under review. At that time both channels were at liberty to repeat the games as often as they wished, free of charge; a situation that was blatantly unfair as far as the clubs were concerned.

After flitting between several different training grounds in recent years, a smaller than normal Hibs squad reverted to the old favourite, Holyrood Park, for the first day of pre-season training. A new generation of players, under the watchful eye of trainer John Fraser, was encouraged to enjoy the experience of exhausting runs around Arthur's Seat that had been endured by countless hundreds of their predecessors during the previous 103 years. One player who had no complaint about the punishing schedule, however, was Jackie McNamara. Now back to full fitness, he was desperately keen to make his return to first-team action after sitting out the bulk of the previous season.

In an attempt to arrest the slump in attendances at football matches across Scotland, a new look League Cup format was now introduced. For the first time since its inception in 1946, the tired routine of starting a new season with qualifying sections of four, or sometimes five, teams, would be replaced by a straight knockout competition on a home and away basis, the games staggered in midweek throughout the opening months of the season.

A minor but important change was the advent of a new Premier Reserve League. Instead of a miscellaneous mixture of games against sides from various divisions, the second-team fixtures would mirror those of the first team, but obviously in reverse order.

In a behind-the-scenes shake-up, Tom Hart's youngest son, Alan, had been elected to the board. The 27-year-old quantity surveyor, like his father a lifelong Hibs supporter, was delighted to be joining the club as a director. With the addition of Hart Jnr and Eddie Turnbull, who had been co-opted on at the beginning of the centenary season, the board, under-strength since the death of Sir John Bruce, was once again at full strength.

In a change to the routine of previous years that had seen the club tour Ireland for their pre-season warm-up, Hibs embarked on three-game tour of the Highlands. Games against Deverondale, Inverness Thistle and Elgin were all won with the loss of only two goals. Ally MacLeod and Des Bremner finished the tour as joint top scorers with four goals apiece, Bremner notching a double in a 6-0 victory over his former club Deveronvale, who listed his brother Kevin in the line-up.

With the change to the League Cup format, Hibs' first three games of the new season were all at home. Intriguingly, all were in different competitions inside the space of eight days. The first was an Anglo-Scottish Cup match against Ayr United, which would be played on a home and away basis. In the first round all eight contesting Scottish sides played off, the winners of each game going forward to meet English opposition at the second stage, the matches to be played on the same evenings as the European fixtures. The previously named Texaco Cup competition had never proved overly popular with supporters on either side of the Border – they had recognised it as a second-rate tournament and had consequently failed to turn out in any great numbers. Its popularity declined even further when the petroleum giants withdrew their annual six-figure backing, leaving the competition, complete with name-change, appearing to have very little future.

In a bruising game, Hibs were forced to endure a torrid second half as Ayr proved a tougher obstacle than many expected. Scott scored the winner for the home side against the run of play to leave the second leg at Ayr finely balanced at 2-1.

On the Saturday, Motherwell were the visitors as Premier League football returned to the capital. In a scrappy and bad-tempered game with little to be seen in the way of flowing football, and not helped by a strong swirling wind, both sides were forced to settle for a point apiece in a goalless draw. The main talking point was the surprise inclusion of 19-year-old Gordon Rae, who took his place on the substitutes' bench alongside Alex Edwards. Signed from juvenile side Whitehill Welfare only 24 hours earlier, the strapping youngster was astonished to discover that he was to be included in the first-team pool the following day.

By now, Hibs had been officially informed by STV that according to IBA regulations, coverage of any match involving a club with shirt advertising was prohibited, but a month-long truce, in which Hibs games would not feature on either channel was agreed as attempts were made to find a solution to the issue. That same weekend, the BBC would show the highlights of the Celtic versus Dundee United game on their Saturday evening *Sportscene* programme, and to the surprise of no one, Scotsport were at Pittodrie covering Aberdeen's game with Rangers which would be shown on the Sunday afternoon. The dispute, which was financially harmful to both sides, continued for several weeks before Tom Hart came up with a temporary solution to the problem. After consultations with Bukta, Hibs agreed, for the time being at least, to wear an alternative strip for any matches covered by the cameras that would satisfy the broadcasting regulations, but let it be known that they planned to appeal to the House of Commons through MP Alex Fletcher, a supporter of the club. One anomaly that would be highlighted by Fletcher at Westminster was the fact that while Hibs were prohibited from wearing a sponsor's name on their jerseys, brewing giant Scottish and Newcastle had been permitted to sponsor the Scottish Cup to the tune of £250,000 that same season.

Four days after the Motherwell game and just five days after signing for the club, Gordon Rae made his debut as centre forward against First Division Queen of the South in the League Cup. The youngster was only denied his first goal in Hibs colours when his strike midway through the second half was mysteriously overruled by the referee. Just minutes later, things got much worse for the home side. With the scores level at one goal each, George

Stewart was harshly judged to have impeded a Queen's player inside the box, a decision that amazed the centre half. The penalty award allowed Dickson to score what would prove to be the winner from the spot. The final whistle was met by a barrage of jeering from the unhappy home support, whose attitude might well have been different had defeat by a side from a lower league been a new experience instead of a by now fairly regular occurrence.

Later that evening, angry Hibs fans again went on the rampage in the town centre, performing several acts of wanton vandalism in the Cockburn Street area. The windows of a shop on Leith Walk were also shattered. The incidents led to the chairman of the Hibs Supporters Club announcing that strong action would be taken if any of their members were found to have been involved.

Gordon Rae kept his place for the visit to Ibrox on the Saturday, and Turnbull's confidence in the youngster was rewarded when he opened the scoring in Hibs' 2-0 victory. After only four minutes, McCloy failed to gather a Smith cross and Rae was on the spot to prod the ball into the net off his knee. In the second half, Rangers went on all-out attack in a vain effort to secure an equaliser and the home support were absolutely stunned when Bremner added a another for the Edinburgh side with only seconds remaining.

In a week of mixed fortunes, another hard-fought, tough and bruising Anglo-Scottish Cup tie, this time at Somerset Park on the Monday evening, ended all square with goals from Bremner and Smith earning Hibs a second round tie against Blackburn Rovers.

Only two days later it was nothing short of disaster when the Greens made an exit from the League Cup at the first hurdle after a no-score draw in the return leg against Queen of the South at Palmerston. In a surprise move just before the game, the well respected physiotherapist Tom McNiven had tendered his resignation after 16 years at Easter Road. The former Scotland physio had not been under contract and refused to be drawn on his reasons for leaving, but it was widely believed that a longstanding personality clash between him and the manager had brought the situation to a head. On a saturated, muddy pitch, Hibs battled bravely for the goal that could have saved them, but as so often recently, their inability to take chances proved expensive. Relentless pressure, particularly in the final stages of the match, was to no avail, and it was the home side that came nearest to scoring when they missed a second-half penalty. The cold, wet and weary journey back from Dumfries was made even worse for many of the travelling fans when their buses were ambushed by rival supporters just outside the town, resulting in several smashed windows.

A 2-0 home victory over Clydebank, the visitors' first ever visit to Easter Road on league business, saw Hibs share top spot in the table for the first time in years, but only two points from the following five league games saw them plummet to seventh place, with the natives far from happy.

In the meantime, the inexperienced Gordon Rae had returned to the reserves, and in an attempt to solve the worrying goalscoring problem, centre forward Jim McKay was signed from Brora on a month's trial. A prolific goalscorer in Highland League football, McKay had impressed while training at Easter Road during the summer. He made his debut as a second-half substitute in Hibs' 3-0 victory over Newcastle United in a friendly at Easter Road, a game that also marked John Brownlie's first start of the season after injury.

McKay scored his first goal in Hibs colours the following week in a 2-1 Anglo-Cup home win against Blackburn Rovers. Two goals inside a minute early in the first half seemed to have put Hibs on easy street, but Rovers pulled one back and were only denied a late equaliser when Parkes, finding himself with only the goalkeeper to beat, allowed McDonald to smother the ball at his feet. In the return at Ewood Park, a tremendous 25-yard drive by Higgins, the only goal of the game, was enough to send Hibs into the semi-final and a meeting with Bristol Rovers and former Easter Road player Peter Cormack.

Back on league business, Hibs took the field at Parkhead on the first day of October, wearing an unfamiliar purple strip complete with white sleeves and the sponsor's name very much reduced in size to comply with the agreed regulations that allowed the television cameras to cover the game. Never a universally popular strip, the new attire was to prove unlucky when Edvaldsson headed past McDonald just before half time to give Celtic the lead. Irate Hibs players immediately surrounded the referee, claiming that he had blown the whistle before the ball had entered the net, but the official waved away their frantic appeals and the goal was allowed to stand. The decision appeared to unsettle the visitors who conceded two more in the second half, before McKay scored a consolation goal in the dying minutes, his second and final goal for Hibs. McKay's short-term contract expired after the game, and although Hibs were keen to keep a player who had looked a useful acquisition, the clubs were unable to reach agreement on a fee. According to reports, Brora were demanding £10,000 for his signature, with Hibs apparently only willing to pay half the amount, leaving the disappointed player with no other option but to return home.

Four days after the defeat at Parkhead, in a surprise move that stunned the majority of the home support by its lightning speed, wing half John Blackley was transferred to Newcastle United in a £100,000 deal. After 12 years at Easter Road and almost ten in the first team, the popular 29-year-old defender who had scored 12 goals in 424 appearances in a Hibs jersey, was desperately keen to try his luck in England. Capped seven times at full international level, Blackley had watched with envy as first one, then another of his teammates had made the journey south over the years. He described his move to Tyneside as a 'dream come true'. Regardless of the inevitable outcry by the supporters, it had been impossible in the financial situation, with attendances dropping alarmingly, for Hibs to turn down the substantial six-figure offer. Ally Brazil, or 'Benny' as he was popularly known by the fans, would take Blackley's place in the side.

With McKay back at Brora, former youth cap Martin Henderson was brought to Easter Road on a short-term-loan deal from Rangers, the striker going straight into the side that ended Aberdeen's unbeaten home record with a fine 2-1 victory. The result lifted the Edinburgh men into mid-table before the Anglo-Scottish Cup meeting with Bristol City.

The return of ex-Hibs player Peter Cormack had created plenty of interest in the city, but in the first leg at Easter Road, both former favourite Cormack and ex-Leeds United player Norman Hunter were sent off late in the game amid scenes of utter mayhem. Bristol had played on the weaknesses of the Hibs defence during the opening period and were deservedly leading at the interval. After the break it was a different story and Duncan drew Hibs level with a headed goal. From then until the final whistle, the English side was forced back on the defensive, often desperately, and things got completely out of hand in the closing stages when Hunter was sent packing for the latest in a series of crude tackles on MacLeod, all just outside the box. The decision seemed to affect Cormack, who in a rush of blood was red-carded for headbutting Bremner. Nine-man Bristol survived a late penalty scare when Higgins was sent sprawling inside the box with six minutes remaining, but the usually reliable Ally MacLeod missed from the spot, the match ending finely balanced at one goal each.

No sooner had the game ended than Tom Hart contacted the Scottish League for permission to withdraw from the competition. To his credit, Hart was concerned for the safety of his players after the at times over-zealous performance of the visiting side, particularly the wild scenes near the end, and he was prepared to pay a sizeable fine rather than allow his players to risk injury in Bristol. The clearly angered Bristol manager Alan Dicks and his board of directors were emphatic that they would vigorously pursue a demand for £12,000 compensation from the Scottish team if they failed to fulfil the return fixture at Ashton Gate.

Meanwhile, spectators crowding into Easter Road for the visit from Rangers at the end of the month were surprised to see the home side take the field wearing brand new jerseys, canary yellow with a green trim, their second change of strip that season. This was long before the days of regular third- or even fourth-choice options, and the change created quite a stir. It had been felt that the purple jerseys worn at Parkhead would clash with the dark blue of Rangers on the television screens, and after discussions with the manufacturers, Bukta had come up with the yellow shirt.

The on-loan Martin Henderson faced, for the moment at least, his former teammates as Hibs matched the league leaders all the way in a rugged and competitive contest. In a game of two penalty decisions, referee Paterson, wrongly in the opinion of most neutrals, ignored claims for a spot-kick by the home side when Higgins was scythed down inside the box by Forsyth in the first half, but the official had no hesitation in pointing to the spot after a similar incident at the other end when MacLeod tackled Russell, much to the fury of the home support. Sandy Jardine duly scored from 12 yards. The narrow defeat sent Hibs tumbling to third-bottom of the table, deep into the relegation dogfight.

Hibs had been informed by the authorities that they must play the second leg of the Anglo-Scottish Cup in Bristol. With no option, Hart reluctantly agreed, despite the controversy and bad feeling surrounding the affair.

In Bristol there was to be yet another change of kit by the visiting side when they were informed by the referee that the rules of the competition did not allow shorts off the same colour to be worn by both sides. With Bristol wearing white shorts along with their usual red shirts, Hibs took the field sporting their traditional green and white jerseys along with black shorts that had been borrowed from the hosts.

The torrential rain that had been falling in sheets all day had reduced the pitch to a field of mud, and the atrocious weather ruled out any chance of a large crowd, or for that matter skilful football. In front of 6,000 hardy, or foolhardy, souls, including many who had made their way from Edinburgh, both defences struggled in the slime, and only an unexpected late goal rush saw Bristol City go through to the final. 3-1 behind at the interval, Hibs staged a tremendous second-half fightback to trail 4-3 late in the game, thanks to two goals by MacLeod and a tremendous volley by Henderson, his first for the club. The visitors were looking the more likely to score the goal that would take the tie into extra time, when a last-minute Bristol strike put the tie beyond doubt.

Thankfully there had been little sign of any ill feeling from the terraces over the comments and threatened withdrawal by Hart. As a gesture of goodwill, the Hibs chairman was presented with a bottle of sherry by his Bristol counterpart in the boardroom after the game.

HIBERNIAN: MCDONALD, MCNAMARA, SCHAEDLER, BRAZIL, STEWART, HIGGINS, MACLEOD, CARROLL, HENDERSON, SMITH, AND DUNCAN. SUBS: MCARTHUR, SCOTT.

The league position now looked perilous for third-bottom Hibs, who needed to look no further than Tynecastle to appreciate the horrendous financial implications that relegation would bring. In an attempt to bolster their Premier League status, centre forward Bobby Hutchison was signed from Dundee in an exchange deal that saw full back Erich Schaedler moving to Dens Park. Schaedler had been unsettled at Easter Road for some time. Unable to secure a regular place in the side with Bobby Smith, now the preferred choice for the left back position, the defender had tabled a transfer request only weeks before. Twenty-four-year-old Hutchison had joined Dundee from Montrose in a £20,000 transaction four years before, and scored around 40 goals during his time in the Jute City. Schaedler's transfer would leave Arthur Duncan, John Brownlie and Alex Edwards as the only survivors from Turnbull's Tornadoes. An audacious move to bring back former fans' favourite Jimmy O'Rourke from Motherwell proved unsuccessful after the clubs failed to agree terms. Unhappy at having to travel from his Edinburgh home to Motherwell every day, O'Rourke had been desperate to return to his former stomping ground, but after protracted negotiations the deal collapsed. Motherwell, like Hibs, were in the bottom half of the table with only a precarious grip on Premier League survival, and were understandably reluctant to part with an important member of their squad to a fellow relegation struggler.

The signing of Hutchison made no immediate improvement to Hibs' dire league position. A 3-0 defeat at Paisley at the end of November meant the Greens had now taken only one point from their last six championship games, scoring only two goals in the process and conceding ten, a sequence of results that saw them slip to ninth place, or second-bottom.

Although it was still only December, Hibs' league position was now desperate. It was simply inconceivable that the visit to Ayr United, then only one place above in the table, should result in anything other than a victory for the visitors. The present run of bad results had all started with the shock defeat at Easter Road by the Ayrshire side two months before, but a solitary Arthur Duncan goal capped a fighting and determined Hibs performance as the Edinburgh side leapfrogged Ayr to sit third from bottom.

On the eve of the game, former Hibs legend Joe Baker had been highly critical of the Easter Road hierarchy in a hard-hitting article in a local newspaper. Baker put the blame for the current Easter Road crisis firmly at the feet of the management. According to the former England centre forward:

> Tom Hart is autocratic, remote, and completely out of touch with the supporters, and Easter Road has become a graveyard with most of the fans chased away. I am still in touch with some of the players at Easter Road, who confirm that the manager's attitude towards them had changed little since the days when Turnbull gave me a hard time, both in the dressing room and on the field.

Furthermore, Baker revealed that newspaper reporters had informed him that the manager's attitude towards them was abrasive to say the least, a demeanour that had no place in the modern game. Continuing in this outspoken vein, the former Torino, Arsenal and Nottingham Forest star said that it pained him to see the disintegration that had taken place at the stadium since his second stint with the club. Comparing the current squad with the team of only a few years back, he wondered why a potentially great forward line had been allowed to leave without adequate replacements being signed. He also pondered over the real reasons that Stanton, Gordon and O'Rourke had been allowed to leave, and why a talent like Edwards had been left on the bench for so long. Pulling no punches, Baker put the question, just why had physiotherapist Tom McNiven, described by many as the best in Britain, suddenly decided to quit one morning, and ended by wondering if a younger, more approachable manager – like Stanton, for instance – might bring back the fresh outlook that was desperately needed.

In that night's *Edinburgh Evening News*, Stewart Brown echoed Baker's sentiments. He too was bewildered at how Hibs could go from league runners-up to relegation candidates in three seasons, and why there had been no new additions in place at the beginning of the season after such a disappointing previous term.

Over the next few days, the newspaper was bombarded with letters from the fans, most agreeing with Baker. According to one: 'Tom Hart's lack of public relations with the supporters is painfully obvious, the chairman seeming to pursue a policy that is deliberately designed to antagonise and alienate the support.' Many complained at Hart's continual raising of admission prices for big games, and most were united in blaming the signing of Joe Harper for Hibs' current predicament.

A win against Aberdeen at Easter Road, Hibs' first double of the season, temporarily lifted the relegation gloom, and the good run continued with a victory over Motherwell and a no-score draw at Ibrox on New Year's Eve, results that saw a rise to sixth place in the table.

Just before Christmas, 18-year-old Craig Paterson, son of Hibs' post-war favourite, John Paterson, was signed from Bonnyrigg Rose after a series of trials for the reserve side. Like his father before him, the six footer was a centre half of considerable potential, and the coaching staff at Easter Road were in no doubt that he had a great future in front of him. Unfortunately, in his first game for the reserves as a signed player, he had the misfortune to crack a bone in his leg in a game against Ayr United at Easter Road, the injury requiring several weeks in plaster. He returned to claim a regular place in the second team well before the end of the season and a series of impressive performances put him in the running for a regular first team place.

With Hearts in the First Division, on 2 January 1978, Clydebank were the visitors to Easter Road for the traditional New Year holiday fixture. As Hibs were winning 2-0, that same afternoon, Hearts were facing East Fife at Methil. Former Hearts legend Jimmy Wardhaugh was covering the match for the *Daily Mail* when he took ill on his way home and died later that evening.

Hearts' sojourn in the lower division had denied the Edinburgh fans the drama of a local derby, and there was great anticipation by the supporters of both clubs regarding the East of Scotland Shield Final the following day at Easter Road. An overnight thaw left huge pools of water on the playing surface, leaving the referee with no option but to cancel the fixture, much to the frustration of the fans who would now have to wait until the end of the season for the rearranged meeting between the great rivals.

Throughout the month of January, persistent snowfalls played havoc with the entire fixture list. At the end of the month an attempt was made to save the Scottish Cup first-round tie with East Fife from the rigours of the enduring bad weather by the archaic remedy of covering the Easter Road pitch with straw. With no home game since the first Saturday of the year and an estimated £50,000 shortfall at the turnstiles during this period, Hibs were now desperate for revenue and an army of volunteers helped spread a liberal application of the material over the playing surface. Their efforts were rewarded when the game against the Fifers got the go-ahead from local referee Bill Mullen. On a still treacherous pitch, any hopes the Fifers had of producing a cup upset were quickly dispelled when the home side raced into a 2-0 lead after only 17 minutes, eventually running out 4-0 winners.

Although the continuing bad weather was not nearly as severe as the terrible winter of 1963, between the end of the month and 25 February only a friendly against Crystal Palace in London and another against Dundee at Dens four days later broke an extended period of competitive inactivity for Hibs.

A thaw during the final few days of February saw Hibs' winning streak brought to an abrupt end at Pittodrie, their first league defeat since losing 3-0 at Love Street over three months before. Including the friendly matches, seven games had been won and two drawn during this period, which in itself was championship form, but Hibs still hovered around seventh place in the table.

At Pittodrie, Aberdeen gained sweet revenge for the two earlier league defeats that season, but the majority of the spectators were unable to see much of the action because of a dense bank of fog that rolled in from the North Sea. Visibility was bad enough at times to threaten an early halt to the proceedings, but the game managed to run its course, much to the embarrassment of centre half George Stewart who, completely unaware that goalkeeper McDonald had come well off his line to collect an easy through ball in the first half, found the empty net with his 20-yard headed pass back.

Yet another postponement, but this time due to entirely different circumstances, led to an official letter of complaint being sent to the Scottish League. Somewhat controversially, the match against Ayr at Somerset Park had been called off only a few hours before kick-off. United claimed that a flu epidemic had decimated the side, striking down seven players, and in the circumstances they were unable to raise a team. Two years before, Motherwell had been unsuccessful in their attempt to postpone a game against Hibs for the same reason, and Tom Hart was now demanding clarification of the rules. Vehement protests by United that they had been unable to contact anyone at Easter Road the previous day, but had left a message, did little to placate the Hibs chairman, who was adamant that the league should adopt the SFA principle that if there were enough fit players to satisfy a full complement, the game should go ahead as planned. The outcome of Hart's protest, if any, is not known.

Jimmy McColl, the grand old man of Easter Road, died at Chalmers Hospital in Edinburgh on Monday 6 March 1978, aged 85. Few in the game had given such loyal service. McColl, connected with Hibs for over 56 years, was seldom seen without his trademark cigar. He had managed to attend to his daily duties as general assistant at the ground until only a few years before and was always willing to give a friendly word of advice if needed. Signed by

Celtic in 1913, Glasgow-born McColl had made one of his first starts in the replay of the 1914 Scottish Cup Final, against Hibs, of all teams, scoring two goals in Celtic's 4-1 victory. After a circuitous route that took him first to Stoke City, where his wife had failed to settle, and a short spell with Partick Thistle, McColl signed for Hibs well after the start of the 1922–23 campaign but still managed to finish the season as the club's top goalscorer. An integral part of the great Easter Road side of the '20s, he was the first player to score 100 goals in all competitions for Hibs. Tom Hart paid tribute to him, stating, 'Probably no one in the long history of Hibernian had had such a huge and valuable connection with the club.' McColl was laid to rest at Mount Vernon Cemetery in Edinburgh. His funeral was attended by many former players and dignitaries, and all the staff at Easter Road.

A potential all-Edinburgh third-round Scottish Cup clash was successfully circumvented when both Hibs and Hearts were defeated in the previous round. Partick Thistle successfully overcame Hibs 2-1 after a replay at Firhill, and according to press reports, during the first game at Easter Road, Thistle would easily have won widespread support as the most boring and predictable side in Britain.

Setting their stall out early for a draw and succeeding, they achieved their aims with possibly the most negative and unexciting no-score game ever witnessed at the stadium. The replay in Glasgow two days later was called off only 45 minutes before kick-off because the pitch was so waterlogged it was unplayable. The late decision infuriated the many hundreds of Hibs fans who travelled through from the capital. Conditions improved enough to allow the game to go ahead 24 hours later, but two goals by Melrose gave the home side a slender but sufficient one-goal lead. Forgotten man Ally Scott, making a rare appearance from the substitutes' bench, passed up an opportunity to level the score when he completely missed an open goal from eight yards. The forward held his head in his hands, but worse was to follow just minutes later when MacLeod missed an even easier chance, and Hibs were out of the cup for yet another year. It had been evident for some time where Hibs' problems lay. In the 22 league games played since the start of the season, only 20 goals had been scored. Eight different centre forwards had been tried – Rae, Duncan, Henderson, Hutchison, Scott, Higgins, Smith, and McKay – with only Rae and McKay managing to find the net, each scoring once.

Seven days after the cup exit at Firhill, Tony Higgins made his 100th appearance for the club in a vitally important relegation clash against St Mirren at Easter Road. Bobby Hutchison scored twice, his first goals for the club, after Saints had taken the lead in the sixth minute. Thereafter it was just like the old days as further strikes from Brazil, Higgins and MacLeod from the penalty spot saw the Greens go 'nap'. The victory was to prove the turning point in Hibs' season. The next four games all ended in wins, with 13 goals scored. Incredibly, during this period the Edinburgh side were the top goalscorers in the entire country, the amazing run propelling them from third-bottom of the table to third-top, and well in the running for a European place.

A 1-1 home draw against Rangers proved a mere setback to their progress, and revenge was gained for the Scottish Cup defeat by Partick Thistle three days later, despite a brilliant 90-minute performance by visiting goalkeeper Alan Rough. The game was evenly contested until Duncan, thundering down the left wing on the stand side, let fly a spectacular drive from all of 30 yards that Rough didn't even see until he was picking the ball from the net. MacLeod scored a third to put the result beyond doubt.

The magnificent run was brought to an abrupt halt with successive defeats at Parkhead and Paisley, but a 1-1 draw against mid-table Celtic at Easter Road before a paltry 10,902 crowd, the second meeting of the sides inside seven days, was enough to consolidate Hibs' third placed position.

The postponements caused by the Arctic conditions earlier in the year meant that the fixture list had been drastically and hurriedly rearranged, and just three days after the 1-1 draw with Celtic, the sides faced each other for the third time in ten days, again at Easter Road. This time the Hoops had no answer to a determined Hibs side hell bent on extracting revenge for the two away defeats that season, but their fans did. With just 13 minutes remaining and the home side leading by two goals to nil, the Celtic fans behind one of the goals invaded the pitch after an incident between Tom McAdam of Celtic and Hibs keeper McDonald, in what seemed no more than a cynical attempt to force abandonment. The proceedings were held up for more than four minutes as Celtic manager Jock Stein appealed for calm and the police struggled to gain control. Once order was restored, the game finally finished with a score of 4-2 in Hibs' favour, although McDonald did well to save a Burns penalty in the dying minutes.

Many felt that the pitch invasion had stemmed from an earlier display of weakness on the part of the football authorities. A few weeks before, an encroachment onto the playing surface by a large number of Rangers supporters during the game against Motherwell at Ibrox had caused the match to be held up for several minutes with the visitors leading. After an inquiry into the incident, the referees' committee recommended that Rangers, who eventually won 5-3, should either forfeit both points or the game be replayed. The decision was rubber-stamped by the SFA, who felt it important that the Scottish League, under whose jurisdiction the game fell, should ratify the decision in the interests of the fight against hooliganism. Not for the first time, the Scottish League totally shirked their responsibilities and merely fined the Ibrox club, a decision seen by many as a victory for the louts. The crowd trouble at Easter Road happened less than 24 hours after this judgement, or lack of it.

A 2-1 defeat by Partick Thistle at Firhill left Hibs walking a European tightrope, and another reverse seven days later against already relegated Ayr United, who even had to borrow a goalkeeper for the game because of injury to their regular custodians, left the Edinburgh side needing to take something from the final league game against Aberdeen at home if they were to qualify for a UEFA Cup place. Scanlon opened the scoring for Aberdeen, then managed by former Celtic favourite Billy McNeil, but an Arthur Duncan goal two minutes from time was enough to confirm Hibs place in next season's UEFA Cup draw.

It was a double celebration for Edinburgh. Hearts had won promotion from the First Division at the first time of asking when they finished second behind Champions Morton. Hibs pipped into third place by Dundee United, had to settle for fourth, one point ahead of fifth placed Celtic who failed to qualify for Europe for only the second time since 1963. Champions Rangers had secured the title for a third time in four seasons, two points ahead of the rapidly emerging Aberdeen, but it is interesting to note that had the Scottish League had the courage to forfeit Rangers the two points after the disputed match against Motherwell, then Aberdeen would have won their first League Championship since 1955 on goal difference. For Hibs, it was a quite incredible end to an otherwise undistinguished season. Almost certain relegation candidates at the turn of the year, the late burst had been nothing short of miraculous, leaving the players, officials and supporters at Easter Road to face the mid-season break with confidence for the future.

After a bright start, centre forward Ally Scott had been unable to pin down a regular first team place. He found himself amongst the handful of free transfers handed out by Turnbull and would shortly sign for Morton. Alex Edwards, on the other hand, who had featured mainly in the reserve side during the season, making only five appearances and another as substitute for the first team, was somewhat surprisingly among the players retained.

Twenty-four hours after clinching a European place, Easter Road was the venue for Pat Stanton's testimonial game between his former and present clubs. Torrential rain earlier in the day could not dampen the enthusiasm of the 25,000 crowd. The huge turnout was a testimony to the popularity of the 'Quiet Man'. Stanton himself, who played the first 45 minutes in the colours of Celtic, scored the winning goal from the penalty spot late in the game wearing the famous green and white of his beloved Hibernian. He and Peter Latchford had earlier agreed that if a second half penalty was awarded to Hibs, the goalkeeper would let Stanton score. Unfortunately, Latchford had already been substituted when Hibs were awarded a penalty near the end, but Stanton still managed to slot home the winner, despite Roy Baines' ignorance of the arrangement. Addressing the crowd by tannoy at the end of the match, Stanton joked that on awakening to torrential rain, he had been convinced that 'God is a Hearts supporter'. He was not disappointed at the size of the crowd that had turned out in large numbers in a genuine gesture of appreciation for the enjoyment given over the years by the player in his over 680 games for Hibs, and several dozen for the Glasgow side.

The season drew to a welcome conclusion the following Saturday at Easter Road with the final of the East of Scotland Shield which had been postponed from early January. The only meeting between the Edinburgh sides that season turned out to be an appalling advert for the game, with violence marring events both on and off the field. Gerry O'Brien, signed just a few days earlier from Clydebank in a near £10,000 deal, scored the only goal, but the big talking points were two terrible tackles by Drew Busby of Hearts that resulted in a red card for the player and ill feeling on the terraces. After being booked for a reckless tackle on Smith, Busby poleaxed Arthur Duncan in front of the dugouts only seconds later. Incensed, Hibs coach John Lambie had to be physically restrained from attacking Busby and skirmishes broke out in several areas of the ground. The final whistle brought the curtain down on a long, hard season.

18

Scottish Cup Final Controversy and an International Incident

1978–79

WILLIE TEMPERLEY HAD been signed from Celtic on a free transfer at the end of the previous season just in time for him to be included in the party of 16 players that made its way to Canada for what turned out to be a month-long, seven-game-unbeaten trip. After taking some time to adjust to playing on unfamiliar artificial surfaces, 36 goals were scored by the Easter Road side of only four conceded in the opening three games. The most difficult opponents turned out to be top North American side Vancouver Whitecaps, who were managed by former Blackpool and England goalkeeper Tony Waiters. Quickly coasting to a two-goal lead after goals from Murray and Duncan, a disputed penalty allowed the home side to equalise, before a contentious refereeing decision denied Hibs the winner when Macleod netted late on. Surprisingly, the incident made the front pages of the local newspapers and even national TV in a country not noted for its interest in soccer, and all were agreed that the visitors had been unfairly denied the victory. Although enjoyable, the tour was judged in retrospect to have been an unwise undertaking in view of the colossal amount of travelling involved, and hints were dropped to the organisers that the Scots would be reluctant to return the following season, if invited.

Centre half Rikki Fleming joined Hibs from Ayr United at the end of July in a £10,000 deal. The 29-year-old former Scottish League cap, who had been on Rangers books as a youngster, wasted no time in making the switch from part-time to full-time football. Colin Campbell, a 22-year-old student at Edinburgh University was signed on a two-month contract a few days after Fleming. Hibs had been aware of Campbell for some time and the Benbecula-born youngster had played several games for the second team during the previous season.

Newspaper rumours of an exchange deal between John Brownlie and Jimmy O'Rourke of Motherwell were rubbished by the manager, but within a few weeks both players would be involved in transfer moves, but in entirely different circumstances.

At the beginning of August 1978 Craig Paterson took the place of the unwell Fleming in what was now turning out to be the club's regular pre-season tour of the Scottish Highlands. It was an indication of the deterioration in the quality of the squad from only a few years before that inexperienced youngsters like Paterson, Temperley and Campbell were being given an opportunity to stake a claim for a first-team place during the coming season.

All three tour games, against Inverness Thistle, Elgin City and First Division Dundee, had been won comfortably, but the success of the trip was overshadowed by Bobby Hutchinson's back injury, received against his former teammates, which would keep him out of first-team action for some weeks. The injury was yet another setback for the unlucky player, who had spent eight weeks in plaster at the end of the previous season after cracking a bone in his back during a match against Celtic. The injury had prevented the player from taking part in any of the games in Canada, although he had travelled as part of the official party. This latest injury was as a major blow for the player. As well as limiting his first-team appearances for several months, it was potentially a serious threat to his career. Although Hutchison would eventually go on to make many appearances for Hibs, the injury handicapped his progress at Easter Road and the fans were probably denied seeing the best of the player in a Hibs jersey.

In a backroom shake-up, fans' favourite Jimmy O'Rourke, who was still a retained Motherwell player, retired from the playing side of the game to return to Easter Road as a coach, sharing his duties between the second team, and the part-time players in the evenings.

After a protracted on-off transfer fiasco, the highly talented former Hearts player Ralph Callaghan was signed from Newcastle United, ending a nightmare 18-month spell in England where he had failed to make an impact. The original £50,000 straight cash deal had changed dramatically to a player-plus-cash settlement in Hibs' favour, with full back John Brownlie moving to Tyneside. The deal had collapsed twice during a 24-hour period, with Callaghan unable to make up his mind. When terms were eventually agreed, the registration forms were hurried through to the Scottish League offices in Glasgow, allowing Callaghan to make his debut for Hibs against Rangers in the first home game of the season. Meanwhile, Brownlie made his way south to team up once again with John Blackley at Newcastle.

As well as centre forward Colin Campbell, several other promising youngsters had joined up at Easter Road around this time including Jim Farmer, Stevie Brown, and goalkeeper Dave Huggins. All would make an appearance for the first team. Also, Rab Kilgour from juvenile side Whitehill Welfare made a surprise debut against Rangers as a direct replacement for Brownlie after only a few weeks at the club. Both he and Callaghan made satisfactory first outings in a fiery, no-score draw whose main headlines revolved around bottle throwing and fighting on the terraces.

The trouble seemed to start after a clash between Hibs goalkeeper Mike McDonald and a Rangers player, the goalkeeper claiming later that he had been the target of several missiles thrown from the crowd. City councillor John Wilson offered a radical solution to the problem of rowdy supporters, suggesting that the troublemakers be herded into pens until the decent fans had gone home. Perhaps the authorities were by now so exasperated that they considered trying his suggestion.

In a new ruling introduced for a trial period, bookings would now earn the culprit penalty points, ten adding up to a one-match ban. Offences were penalised according to their level of seriousness: kicking, shoving, tripping etc were worth two points; handling and talking back to the referee, one. And in a seemingly never-ending change to the rules and regulations, Edinburgh whistlers Eddie Thomson and Bill Mullen became the first casualties of a new FIFA recommendation that referees should retire at 50. Designed to give younger officials a better chance of making the grade, the ruling would hopefully produce a better level of competence.

Hibs' Premier League dominance over their city rivals was severely threatened in the first derby of the season at Tynecastle. The Greens had won seven and drawn five of the 12 games since the inception of the new league, but against a Hearts side reduced to nine men after Park and Jefferies had been sent off in separate incidents, only a last-minute equalising goal by Arthur Duncan saved his side's blushes. In one of the most shameful matches between Hibs and Hearts in living memory, the police were hard pushed to contain the almost constant trouble on the terraces between rival supporters, making dozens of arrests. Many believed the time had come for Hearts to follow Hibs' lead and erect barriers to segregate the rival fans.

Hibs' reward for the astonishing late revival at the end of the previous campaign that had earned them a European place was a relatively easy game against Swedish side Norrkoping in the opening round of the UEFA Cup.

With key players Bremner and MacLeod injured during a 1-0 home victory over St Mirren on the Saturday, Turnbull was faced with a selection problem. As it turned out, the gifted MacLeod would be passed fit, but the veteran Arthur Duncan was a surprise replacement at right back for Bremner, who was suffering from a pulled hamstring. Recent signing Willie Temperley, who had made his first start against St Mirren only four days before, was making his European debut in a relatively inexperienced side, as were Fleming, Rae and Pat Carroll who replaced the ineligible Callaghan.

Experienced campaigners, Hibs were about to take part in their 63rd competitive European tie, far ahead in proficiency of the Swedish part-timers. Although Norrkoping had first featured on the Euro front as early as 1956–57 when they had been eliminated in the first round proper of that year's European Cup by Italian club Fiorentina, in the intervening 22 years they had only graced either of the three main tournaments on six occasions, never progressing further than the second round.

Although it would be Norrkoping's first ever trip to Scotland, the teams were old adversaries. In 1947, during Eddie Turnbull's time as a player, the Swedes had beaten the Scottish side 3-1 in a friendly match and the tie presented the perfect opportunity for revenge. There would be an even more significant incentive for Hibs and Scotland's other UEFA Cup representative, Dundee United, to do well in the competition: it had now been decided that from 1981, the number of UEFA Cup places allocated to each country would be dependant on results during the intervening five-year period, which could possibly mean the Scottish representation being reduced to one.

As for the game itself, goalkeeper Jonsson was called into action almost immediately when he was forced to divert a Murray effort to safety, and it was only the diligence of the custodian that prevented Norrkoping from conceding several goals in the opening phase as he defied efforts from Higgins, Rae and Murray before Hibs opened the scoring after 25 minutes. Little was seen of Norrkoping as an attacking force for the remainder of the first half, but despite the home side's almost monopolistic superiority they were unable to convert the numerous chances into the goals that their play deserved.

Hibs continued to dominate proceedings after the interval. A measured Duncan cross from the right after 50 minutes was cleverly flicked into the path of Temperley by Higgins for the former Bo'ness player to rifle home his first goal for the club. The strike eased both the growing pressure on the home side and the patience of the jittery home support.

In two minutes of recklessness, however, Hibs proceeded to throw away a seemingly guaranteed passage into the next round. One up from the first period, and now two ahead on the night, a couple of quite indefensible mistakes by the Easter Road rearguard allowed the amateurs from Sweden to draw level.

A game, indeed a tie, that should have been well beyond the visitors now hung in the balance with Hibs in grave danger of making another first round exit in Sweden on the away goals ruling. Hutchison replaced Carroll for the last 20 minutes and the pace of the lively former Dundee man upset the rapidly tiring Norrkoping. With the visitors desperately seeking the welcome final whistle, Duncan once again sped down the right-hand side on the overlap from the full-back position. His accurate cross found Higgins in space to head the winner past Jonsson, giving Hibs a slender lead for the second leg, a goal enthusiastically received by a mightily relieved home support. Hibs had been so much on top in the early stages that it looked as if they could score four or five; instead, they would travel to Sweden with only the narrowest of leads.
FINAL SCORE: HIBERNIAN 3. NORRKOPING 2.

UEFA CUP 1ST ROUND (1ST LEG), WEDNESDAY 13 SEPTEMBER 1978, EASTER ROAD.
HIBERNIAN: MCDONALD, DUNCAN, SMITH, RAE, FLEMING, MCNAMARA, MURRAY, MACLEOD, HIGGINS, CARROLL, TEMPERLEY.

Although furious that the defence had conceded two such basic goals after being so in command, Turnbull remained confident that the Swedish defence could be breached in the return leg. As a bonus, Hibs had discovered a full back: stand-in Arthur Duncan had been quite superb, his overlapping runs providing two goals. The former Scottish international outside left would spend the rest of his career at full back, either on the right, or more usually the left, and would from now on feature only rarely in an attacking role.

Temperley continued his scoring run with the only goal of the game against his former side at Parkhead on the Saturday. But although surrendering their unbeaten record to the visitors, who were also undefeated, Celtic still remained in top spot. The home side were the recipients of an unbelievably dubious opportunity to save the game when they were awarded a penalty kick, a decision that surprised even the most partisan Celtic supporters. While turning with the ball inside his own penalty area, Ally MacLeod ran into George McCluskey, who fell over. Unbelievably, referee Alexander immediately pointed to the spot. Justice was done, however, when the spot-kick was blasted against the post and out of play.

A 2-1 win over Aberdeen in Edinburgh seven days later meant that Hibs were now the only unbeaten side in the top division. Former Hibs player Joe Harper got little change from Rikki Fleming, while at the other end the inexperienced newcomers Leighton and McLeish were finding the home forwards a handful. In the post-match interview, the always sporting Dons manager Alex Ferguson, declared that Hibs were 'not a good side, but a well organised team that worked hard'. It had been an unhappy return to Easter Road for Pat Stanton. Forced into premature retiral through injury, he was now assistant to Ferguson at Pittodrie. Regardless of Ferguson's opinion of the quality of the Hibs side, the victory kept them well in touch with leaders Celtic and had been ideal preparation for the return trip to Sweden in midweek.

With Callaghan still ineligible, a squad comprising McDonald, McArthur, McNamara, Duncan, Smith, Stewart, Fleming, Bremner, Rae, Murray, O'Brien, MacLeod, Hutchison, Higgins, Temperley, Carroll and Campbell made the trip from Edinburgh to Copenhagen before catching a connection to Sweden. Shortly after arriving in Norrkoping, Tony Higgins came down with a bout of flu. Confined to bed, his roommate Mike McDonald was removed as a precaution in case the virus spread and further weakened an already injury-hit squad. Forced to rely on experience with a squad full of youngsters who were relatively untested at this level, Turnbull was taking a calculated risk with the fitness of McNamara, Bremner and Hutchison, all carrying injuries, and Higgins, who now felt well enough to take his place in the starting line-up.

Encouraged by a small but extremely vocal band of supporters who had made the trip from Scotland, Hibs produced a spirited and fighting performance to qualify for the second round of the competition.

Rain had fallen almost incessantly throughout the day and the waterlogged pitch presented a severe handicap to the tactical system employed by Turnbull, which required all-out effort and non-stop running, but the visitors did themselves and the country proud with an unfaltering exhibition of disciplined and selfless teamwork.

In front of a crowd numbering less than 2,000, Duncan and Smith totally subdued the threat of Hellberg and Ohlson on the flanks, while the central pairing of Stewart and Fleming effectively thwarted any danger through the middle. Sterling work by an enthusiastic and compact midline negated every effort by Norrkoping to get back into the game and the home side were forced to rely on long-range efforts that produced little danger, except on one occasion when goalkeeper McDonald had to look sharp to deal with an Erixon attempt midway through the first half.

The directness of the Scots helped to create numerous chances to score the goal that would have put the tie beyond the Swedish side, none better than a breathtaking first-half run by MacLeod, who left a trail of stranded defenders in his wake before firing narrowly past. But try as they might, they were unable to force the vital breakthrough.

On the resumption, it was again all Hibs and the unrelenting pressure created several near things in the home penalty area including a goal-line clearance from a Rae header. As expected in the heavy conditions, the part-timers tired in the second half, allowing the pace of the overlapping Duncan to cause all kinds of problems from the right, but somehow the Norrkoping goal still remained intact.

On the final whistle, Hibs were rightly cheered from the field by the small pocket of Scottish supporters huddled in one corner of the ground who had been more vocal than the larger home support throughout the entire 90 minutes, justly proud of a team effort that had been more noted for its resolve than good football.

FINAL SCORE: NORRKOPING 0. HIBERNIAN 0.

UEFA CUP 1ST ROUND (2ND LEG), WEDNESDAY 27 SEPTEMBER 1978, NORRKOPING.
HIBERNIAN: MCDONALD, DUNCAN, SMITH, FLEMING, STEWART, MCNAMARA, RAE,
MACLEOD, HUTCHISON, BREMNER, HIGGINS.

Claiming the result as an achievement of the fantastic team spirit among the players at Easter Road at that time, Turnbull also found time to express the club's gratitude for the tremendous backing received from the small band of travelling Hibs supporters, most of whom unable to secure accommodation in the town and had been forced to spend the previous night in the local railway station.

After an earlier bye, an easy 6-1 aggregate victory over Montrose in the second round of the League Cup created little difficulty and set up a meeting with First Division Clydebank in the next round. Cheered from the field in Sweden only a few days before, the Hibs players received a reception of a different kind from the fans during and after the first game in Edinburgh. A sluggish performance against an enthusiastic but fairly poor lower league side earned them a barracking in the later stages from the fans, who were unimpressed with only a late MacLeod goal from the penalty spot to show for the side's efforts.

Manager Turnbull missed the return game at Kilbowie, having travelled to France to spy on Hibs' next European opponents, Strasbourg, in a home game against former UEFA Cup adversaries Sochaux. At Kilbowie, the Edinburgh side cruised into the quarter-finals of the competition more easily than the 1-1 scoreline would suggest. A rare, headed goal by centre half Stewart just seconds before the interval gave the Greens a 2-0 overall lead and they were never in any danger until the Bankies pulled one back from the spot two minutes from the end. In an evening of mixed fortunes, Turnbull was delighted to learn that Hibs had qualified for the later stages of the League Cup, but he was less than pleased to discover that his journey to France had been in vain after the Strasbourg game had been called off less that an hour before kick-off due to thick fog, with hundreds of fans already inside the stadium.

Four days later Hibs' six-month unbeaten run came to end in Glasgow when they were beaten by the odd goal in three by the unpredictable Partick Thistle. After a reasonable first 45 minutes, the visitors, who were still to record their first Premier League win over their opponents at Firhill, were put through the mill in the second half and were fortunate to escape with such a narrow defeat. It was Hibs' first reverse in any game since losing 2-0 to Ayr United at Somerset Park at the end of April, a total of 26 games including the summer tour of Canada.

UEFA Cup opponents Strasbourg had made a great start to the season. Promoted to the top league just two years before, after spending 12 months in the Second Division, at that time they were unbeaten in the league and topped the table.

Like all major French clubs Strasbourg were heavily sponsored, in their case by a leading bank, but European rules prohibited them from displaying the sponsor's logo on the jerseys for the game, a rule that also applied to Hibs. Formed in 1906, Strasbourg had not featured in the European arena since exiting the Cup Winners' Cup at the second-round stage in the 1966–67 season. Like Hibs, they too had faced Swedish opposition in the opening round, beating Elfsberg 4-3 on aggregate. The better-known players in a relatively small squad of only 15 full-timers included full internationalists Albert Gemmrich, who consistently topped the goalscoring charts at the club, top midfielder Francis Piasecki, and the delightful but somewhat unfortunately named goalkeeper Dominique Dropsy, who had starred for France against Hungary at that year's World Cup in Argentina.

Jackie McNamara had injured a knee against Partick Thistle on the Saturday and had missed his first game of the season after the knock failed to respond to treatment. There was some good news for the manager, however, when Hutchison and MacLeod, who had both been rated as doubtful, passed a late fitness test. For the inexperienced Colin Campbell it would be his first European start.

Both teams took the field at the Meinau Stadium to a deafening backdrop of firecrackers and rockets set off by the vociferous and boisterous home support who made up the majority of the 30,000 crowd.

Strasbourg started the match well and for the first 30 minutes or so had Hibs on the back foot, although they had failed to put McDonald under any undue pressure. With the Hibs back four dealing comfortably with most of their probing attacks, like Norrkoping in the previous round the French side was forced to resort to shooting from long range and it was from one of these shots that they took the lead after 21 minutes. Centre forward Tanter tried his luck with a speculative shot from well outside the penalty area that McDonald could only parry, but unfortunately for the Scots the ball broke kindly for the lurking Gemmrich who tapped it home from close range. The goal encouraged Strasbourg and for a while the visitors were reduced to backs-to-the-wall defending, but gradually the Greens recovered their composure and finished the half the better side.

On the restart Hibs were once again forced into a defensive formation and had to fight to stay in the game as the blue-shirted home side, encouraged by the huge crowd, threw everything at the Scots in an effort to secure the vital second goal that they knew would be so important in Edinburgh. As in the first half, resolute defending and dogged determination by the visitors saw them recover their composure and they were well on top when disaster struck for a second time. After a solid but fair tackle by Rae, Gemmrich was rising from the ground when he seemed to fall over as the youngster cleared the ball. The unsighted referee, who had frustrated the visitors with many of his decisions, hesitated before appearing to react to the roar of the partisan crowd and, to the horror of the Hibs players, pointed to the penalty spot. The referee was immediately surrounded by a pack of protesting green-shirted players but refused to change his decision, leaving Piasecki to score a crucial second goal from 12 yards.

The final 15 minutes belonged almost entirely to Hibs as they endeavoured to score the vital away goal, nobody performing better than Gordon Rae, playing in only his third European tie. Although failing to find the net, the youngster capped a magnificent performance with a goal-saving tackle on Gemmrich shortly after Strasbourg increased their lead.

The tricky MacLeod, who had been on the receiving end of some heavy-handed treatment from the French defenders, caused all kinds of bother in the home ranks, particularly in the later stages, with several tantalising runs, one of which ended with the inside man being upended inside the box, but after his erratic performance all evening there was little surprise when the referee waved aside Hibs' appeals for a penalty.

FINAL SCORE: STRASBOURG 2. HIBERNIAN 0.

UEFA CUP 2ND ROUND (1ST LEG), WEDNESDAY 18 OCTOBER 1978, STADE MEINAU.
HIBERNIAN: MCDONALD, DUNCAN, SMITH, BREMNER, STEWART, FLEMING, CAMPBELL, MACLEOD, HUTCHISON, RAE, HIGGINS.

Although defeated, Hibs had performed admirably and confidence was high that the result could be overturned in Edinburgh. Ally MacLeod promised Strasbourg, reckoned to be the best team in France, all that they could handle in the second leg at Easter Road.

Jackie McNamara, who had watched the game in Strasbourg from the stand, had overcome both his earlier cartilage problems and the initial resentment by some narrow-minded fans angry at what they saw as his part in Pat Stanton's departure from the club, to become one of Hibs' most consistent performers. His consistency would be rewarded when he was voted Player of the Year by the Hibs Supporters Club at the end of the month.

There would be little complacency in the French camp before the return leg in Edinburgh. Coach Gilbert Gress, himself a former Strasbourg player, admitted that he had sweated through the final nail-biting minutes of the first game, and readily confessed that he would have been in a happier state of mind with another goal advantage to take to Scotland.

Jackie McNamara, now fully recovered from injury, and Willie Murray were Hibs' only changes from game in France; Colin Campbell and Rikki Fleming who took their place on the bench.

A magnificent, fighting team performance that earned the praise of manager Turnbull was not enough to overcome a competitive Strasbourg side that constantly enraged the Hibs support with their time-wasting, offside tactics and petty fouling, all designed to upset the rhythm of the home side. In the match, shown live on French TV, Hibs' heroic efforts were not enough to overcome Strasbourg's first-leg lead. Goalkeeper Dropsy belied his name by pulling off two incredible first-half saves to thwart a Murray effort with his legs, before diving bravely to divert a Higgins header past the post. The persistent ploy by the home side of continually hoisting high balls into the opposing penalty area both through the middle and from the wings allowed the French custodian to dominate his penalty area as his safe hands collected everything in the air, much to the exasperation of the home support.

Man of the Match Bremner was, as usual, in perpetual motion, covering every blade of grass in an attempt to urge his teammates to victory. Breaking down moves in his own penalty area one minute, he would be found in the opposing danger area the next. No one tried harder than he did to break through the blue-shirted French barrier, but unfortunately Hibs' raids carried little venom, in contrast to their fast-moving opponents, whose quick breaks and accurate passing constantly troubled the home defence.

Almost immediately after the restart Hibs were denied a penalty when Murray was brought down inside the box, but the referee waved away the appeals of the Hibs players, much to the irritation of the partisan home support who numbered less than 15,000. The Edinburgh side were still intent on relying too much on high crosses into the penalty area that were all gathered easily and eagerly by goalkeeper Dropsy and there was a distinct lack of shots on target. Late in the game, Turnbull changed tactics by switching the giant Higgins from his left-wing berth into a double spearhead role with Hutchison in the middle of the park, the change bringing an almost immediate improvement.

With 15 minutes of the match remaining, Dropsy pulled off a good save from Hutchison when to the amazement of everyone inside the stadium, including his own teammates, Piasechi became the second Frenchman on the night lucky to remain on the park after he felled MacLeod inside the box with a blatant punch that would have pleased Mohammed Ali. The incident happened right in front of referee Scheurell, leaving the official with no alternative other than to point to the spot. MacLeod himself took the kick and sent a well struck shot past Dropsy from 12 yards. Minutes earlier Strasbourg centre half Novi had also been fortunate to avoid a red card after he too had punched the Hibs inside right. Roared on by the crowd, Hibs piled on the pressure in an effort to secure the goal that would send the tie into extra time but try as they might they could not break down the stuffy resistance of the visitors, who were relieved to hear the final whistle.

FINAL SCORE: HIBERNIAN 1. STRASBOURG 0.

UEFA CUP 2ND ROUND (2ND LEG), WEDNESDAY 1 NOVEMBER 1978, EASTER ROAD.
HIBERNIAN: MCDONALD, DUNCAN, SMITH, BREMNER, STEWART, MCNAMARA, RAE, MACLEOD, HUTCHISON, MURRAY, HIGGINS.

After the game a clearly disappointed Turnbull had nothing but praise, both for his players who had given their all and the supporters who had encouraged their side magnificently throughout the entire 90 minutes. Hibs departed the European scene not only with a victory and a financial profit, but also with vital experience, particularly for the younger players, that would surely prove of enormous benefit in the future. However, as it turned out, it would be 14 long years before Hibs would again participate on the European stage.

Gordon Rae had sampled European football in his first full season with the club and anticipated that this would be the norm throughout his career. The former Whitehill Welfare player would spend 11 years at Easter Road before retiring in 1988 after a testimonial match to reward his loyalty to the club, but would never again feature in a competitive European fixture.

In the second Edinburgh derby of the season, Hibs would pay dearly for first-half blunders by MacLeod and McNamara that led to Hearts securing their first league win at Easter Road for more than ten years, and their first ever Premier League victory over their city rivals. Once again the fixture, which had kicked off an hour earlier than usual on the advice of the police, was marred by violence on the terraces. A no-go area designed to separate the rival fans proved ineffectual as troublemakers spilled over the barriers in a display of the sort of behaviour that had prompted the outspoken Hart to call for dogs to be used to control the unruly element among both sets of supporters. Ironically, the only dogs on show were those of the Royal Air Force Police Display Team that had provided pre-match and half time entertainment. The beasts on the field at least were well trained, unlike the animals who were intent on wreaking havoc on the terracing.

After a shaky start, attendances had been rising steadily since the advent of the Premier League. The format still had its critics, who were of the opinion that sides facing each other four times a season had led to a drop in the standard of entertainment in favour of a more defensive strategy. Goals had become much scarcer, and it was rare that a match would be won by more than one. It had become, in the view of Stewart Brown of the *Edinburgh Evening News* 'a platform for desperate football, with managers unsure of throwing in untried youngsters'. A challenge to the domination of Rangers and Celtic was to be welcomed, but the league had become far too tight. Before the game against Hearts, Hibs had occupied third place in the table, but after a second successive defeat, this time at Love Street, they had dropped to seventh place and into the relegation zone.

It was around this time that former Hibs player Ally MacLeod 'resigned' as manager of Scotland after the World Cup fiasco in Argentina during the summer. Jock Stein, then in the middle of what would prove an almost indecently short spell as manager of Leeds United was a front-runner for the Scotland job, as was Hibs Eddie Turnbull. One surprise candidate was young Craig Brown who had done such a marvellous job with lower league Clyde in recent months. At Easter Road Tom Hart had no objections to Turnbull taking over the Scotland job, but insisted this could only be on a part-time basis. As it turned out, Stein was appointed manager of the national side, but quick to realise the potential of Turnbull, the Hibs manager accepted the position of Stein's assistant with a remit not only to assist in the running of the full side, but also to take charge of the Under-21 set-up.

Turnbull's first task was to oversee an Under-21 side that included his own Ally MacLeod as one of the over-age players, for the European Championship match against the Norwegian Under-21s at Easter Road. Despite being on the wrong end of a 5-1 mauling, a 19-year-old Norwegian centre forward named Isak Refvik took the eye with an outstanding performance. His countryman Svein Mathisen, capped seven times at full level, was also in impressive form 24 hours later at Hampden, setting up both Norwegian goals in Scotland's eventual 3-2 victory. Refvik was originally to have been involved with the full squad at Hampden, but it was decided at the last minute to play him from the start in the Under-21 team instead, a decision that would cause Hibs untold complications during the coming months. The performance of both Refvik and Mathisen caught the eye of several other experienced observers, but as other teams dithered, Hibs took decisive action.

After a hush-hush trip to London by Hibs secretary Cecil Graham to iron out work-permit difficulties, Tom Hart and fellow director Tommy Younger travelled to Norway to sign Mathisen and Refvik, claiming to have employment permits for both in their possession. It had been hoped to include the players in the side to face Hearts at Easter Road the following Saturday, but although Mathisen agreed to sign immediately, Viking Stavanger were not keen to release Refvik until a full board meeting had taken place and Hart and Younger returned to Scotland empty-handed. A little over a week later the players arrived by ferry at Leith to sign a three-month amateur contract that could be extended if necessary. They made their debut against Morton in the League Cup quarter-final, second leg, at Easter Road on Wednesday 15 November 1978.

Refvik became an instant hero by scoring both of Hibs' goals to cancel out Morton's one-goal lead from the first leg at Cappielow, only the third Hibs player that season to score twice in one game. His speed, enthusiasm and devastating shooting power gave Hibs an edge that had been missing for some time and he quickly became a favourite of the crowd. Mathisen made a quieter first start, but he too showed enough to suggest that he would be an asset to the side in the coming months. There was a real let-off for Hibs early in the second half. With the aggregate score standing at 1-1, the usually reliable Andy Ritchie missed from the penalty spot before Refvik's second goal of the night earned his new side a meeting with Aberdeen in the semi-final.

Both imports made their home league debut in a 2-2 draw against Celtic three days later. A Refvik effort was cleared from the line by Lynch before Celtic scored what looked like being the winner, only for Callaghan to level things near the end with a spectacular 20-yard drive that was greeted by a hail of missiles from a section of the crowd.

The elation of securing the late equaliser against Celtic was short-lived; Hibs discovered that Refvik had been refused a work permit by the Home Office on the grounds that he was not a current full international and Hart appealed to the football authorities to take up the case. MP Alex Fletcher raised the subject in the House of Commons. The problem arose over a clause in Home Office regulations that required any applicant to have the ability to make a distinctive contribution in his field, Fletcher, to the amusement of his fellow politicians, requested that the Prime Minister make the trip to Pittodrie on the Saturday to judge for himself. Hopes that a satisfactory conclusion could be reached were raised when the Department of Employment agreed to investigate the matter, but after discussions Hibs were again advised that there would be no permit for the player in the foreseeable future. Somewhat ludicrously, Refvik was informed that he could play until January as an amateur on a visitor's permit, but to do so he was required to resubmit his application for clarification and approval, a ruling that would prevent the player from taking his place in the Hibs line-up against Motherwell at Fir Park.

There was no place for Mathisen as the amateur Refvik made his return against Aberdeen in the League Cup semi-final at Dens Park. In a game packed with incident and thrills, watched by a crowd of over 21,000, Aberdeen had the better of the chances, but it appeared as if neither side would break the deadlock until three minutes from the end of extra time when one moment of misjudgement by McDonald denied Hibs a place in the final and ultimately cost the player his first-team place at Easter Road. The giant keeper had earlier been in unbeatable form with several brilliant saves to deny the Dons the opportunity of winning the game in normal time, the best a block from Harper from point-blank range in the dying minutes, but he changed from hero to villain when, with the game heading for a replay, he allowed a speculative right-wing cross from Aberdeen full back Kennedy to drift over his head and into the net for the only goal of the game.

LEAGUE CUP SEMI-FINAL, WEDNESDAY 13 DECEMBER 1978, DENS PARK.
HIBERNIAN: MCDONALD, DUNCAN, KILGOUR, BREMNER, STEWART, MCNAMARA, SMITH, MACLEOD, REFVIK, CALLAGHAN, HUTCHISON. SUB: HIGGINS.

Failure to reach the League Cup Final would prove expensive in more ways than one. Just a few weeks later Bobby Smith was transferred to Leicester City for £80,000. Although attendances had been slowly rising at Easter Road in recent months, they were still well below the break-even figure, and as in previous years the board found it necessary to balance the books in the transfer market. Duncan Lambie, brother of trainer John, who had been on Hibs' books as a youngster, was signed as a replacement for Smith from German Second Division side Furth for £12,000. Turnbull had been an admirer of Lambie for some time, but with all due respect to the player, the deal was yet another example of an outgoing player being replaced by a much inferior signing.

On New Year's Day what had become a vitally important relegation clash between eighth-placed Hibs and ninth-placed Hearts at Tynecastle was cancelled due to a heavy fall of snow that made the pitch unplayable. Hibs took the opportunity to spend a few days in Mediterranean sunshine with a trip to Israel. Isak Refvik scored his third and final goal for Hibs in a 1-1 draw against a Tel Aviv XI in a hastily arranged game. Goalkeeper McDonald, whose confidence had declined since the semi-final, was rested, and after an absence of three years, Jim McArthur was reinstated to the first team. McArthur relates humorously that, far from pleased at losing his first-team place to McDonald, he complained to Turnbull that he wasn't keen on playing for the second team – a situation that was quickly remedied when the manager selected him for third-team duty, a position he would hold for almost a year.

A Scottish Cup trail that would lead all the way to Hampden began with a trip to East End Park in January. On a pitch that looked anything but playable, the players slipped and skidded to a 1-1 draw and a replay in Edinburgh. Higgins opened the scoring with a screamer from his favoured distance of two yards, but a late equaliser gave Dunfermline a deserved draw in the final stages as falling snow gave rise to real fears that the game would be abandoned. Somehow it managed to slither to the final whistle. Afterwards, Ally MacLeod described the playing surface as the worst he had ever experienced.

Since the turn of the year, Scotland had been in the grip of Arctic conditions that had decimated the fixture list. Only two of Hibs' last six league fixtures had been fulfilled and it was only the sterling work of the ground staff, aided by the old-fashioned expedient of using braziers on the pitch, that allowed the cup replay with Dunfermline to go ahead two weeks after the encounter at East End Park. Second-half goals from MacLeod and Callaghan were enough to set up an all Edinburgh clash with Meadowbank Thistle in the second round, the first ever between the clubs in a national tournament.

There was an immediate problem, however, when the police refused to allow the game to take place at Meadowbank Stadium on the grounds of safety. Hibs' offer to switch the tie to Easter Road was against the rules, and the game eventually went ahead at Tynecastle. The media lambasted this typically nonsensical ruling by the football authorities. In their wisdom, the SFA had decided that the anticipated Hibs support of over 8,000 should gain entry at the Gorgie Road end of the ground, which was serviced by only eight turnstiles, while the expected 600 Meadowbank Thistle supporters would use the McLeod Street entrances, which had 14 turnstiles available if required.

Twice postponed because of the continuing bad weather, the game went ahead five days after originally planned. Part-time Meadowbank showed stout resistance for the first 20 minutes or so, but once Hibs had taken a two-goal lead midway through the first half the result was a foregone conclusion. The Premier League side coasted to an easy 6-0 win, by far their biggest victory of the season, keeping them in the running for the sponsor's £3,000 for the top scoring side in the competition.

By that time the prolonged Isak Refvik registration farce had finally been settled. Hopes at the end of January that a work permit would soon be granted were dashed at the announcement of a new Home Office decision that from now on only one foreigner per team would be permitted. In mid-February Sven Mathisen, by then unable to command a regular start in the first team, featuring mostly as a substitute, had moved to Dutch side FC Den Haag. Twenty-four hours later, with his short-term contract now completed, countryman Refvik, who also had not figured in the side in recent weeks, decided to return to Norway. Mathisen had started only five games, failing to hit the target, while Refvik, with nine starts in all competitions, had scored three times.

At the end of February a hard-earned point against Morton at home lifted Hibs another place further from relegation and they now sat seventh in the table. Amazingly, Hibs and second-bottom Hearts were separated by eighth-placed Celtic, although the Parkhead side still had three games in hand. A Bremner strike against Dundee United at the beginning of March, Hibs' first victory at home since beating Aberdeen back in September, all but eased the relegation worries at Easter Road. That same morning forward Willie Paterson, who had featured in the first team only twice in the past three years with another six as substitute, joined Falkirk for a nominal fee.

Hearts goalkeeper John Brough, who as a boy had stood on the terracing at Easter Road supporting Hibs, had played the game of his life against Morton in the previous round to earn the Gorgie side an all Edinburgh Scottish Cup clash with Hibs at Easter Road. It would be the fifth meeting of the rivals in the competition since the war, and the first of three games between the sides in the space of 18 days. In a typically bad-tempered and foul-packed cup-tie, centre half George Stewart scored a rare goal to give Hibs a half-time lead.

Yet again the fixture was marred by trouble when fans in the Dunbar end of the ground started fighting after Gordon Rae doubled Hibs' lead. Believing the game to be won, the home side became far too casual and O'Connor pulled one back to give Hearts some hope, but despite some nervous moments Hibs managed to hold out to reach the semi-final and an opportunity to gain revenge over Aberdeen for the earlier League Cup defeat.

Seven days later, in a game vital to Hearts if they hoped to avoid relegation for the second time in three years, Colin Campbell scored his first goal for Hibs with a cute lob after 17 minutes in front of just over 13,000 fans, nearly 9,000 fewer than had watched the cup-tie the previous week. A quick equaliser by Gibson from the penalty spot ended the scoring to boost Hearts' survival prospects. In an attempt to prevent trouble between the rival factions, for the first time ever at Easter Road, the local broadcasting station Radio Forth had set up a booth to play requests before the game and at half time. Sadly the gesture proved to be largely ineffective and once again the no-go area failed to prevent frequent clashes between rival supporters.

The rescheduled New Year's Day game between the sides at Tynecastle, almost three months after originally planned and again played in a heavy snow fall, ended disastrously for the Maroons. Totally in command throughout, Hibs took the lead with a freak goal when an intended Callaghan cross deceived former Hibs player Thomson Allan in the Hearts goal to finish in the back of the net. Further strikes by MacLeod for the visitors and Gibson for Hearts before the interval ended the scoring, leaving the Gorgie side in all kinds of relegation bother five points adrift of third-bottom Partick Thistle. After 30 minutes Tony Higgins sustained a hairline fracture of the leg. Forced to leave the field, he was replaced by young Steve Brown who was making only his second competitive first-team outing.

The victory over Hearts lifted Hibs above mid-table and a third consecutive league win, this time a 2-1 win against Celtic in Edinburgh, saw them share third place with St Mirren, well in contention for Europe.

An ambitious bid to sign former Dundee striker John Duncan from Derby County on loan until the end of the season came to nothing when manager Tommy Docherty refused to sanction the deal. The £100,000 asking price for the player was well beyond Hibs' reach.

The Scottish Cup provided Hibs with yet another avenue into Europe. They faced Aberdeen in the semi-final at Hampden on a miserable, wet and windy evening in April. The supporters of both clubs had been opposed to the game taking place in Glasgow and this was reflected by the ghostly 9,837 spectators, who were all but lost in the giant stadium. Stifled in the early stages by Aberdeen's infuriating offside tactics, the Greens gradually got to grips in midfield, blotting out the dangerous probing of Gordon Strachan. Missing several opportunities to take the lead, Hibs were stunned when former Clyde player Steve Archibald opened the scoring for Aberdeen midway through the half. Rae levelled things eight minutes before the break when he swept the ball home at the far post, and MacLeod gave Hibs a deserved first-half lead from the penalty spot after Rougvie had mistimed his tackle to upend the same player inside the box.

After the break the capital side were well in control and rarely troubled except for one astonishing let-off when Joe Harper somehow managed to miss a sitter just 12 inches from goal. There were doubts if MacLeod, injured in the first-half penalty incident, could continue after the interval, but he recovered sufficiently to complete the 90 minutes and collect his £150 Man of the Match award from the sponsors as Hibs gained sweet revenge for the League Cup defeat earlier in the season. That same evening a Partick Thistle victory at Tynecastle all but condemned Hearts to relegation from the Premier League for the second time in three years.

WEDNESDAY 11 APRIL 1979, HAMPDEN PARK.

HIBERNIAN: MCARTHUR, BRAZIL, DUNCAN, BREMNER, STEWART, MCNAMARA, RAE, MACLEOD, CAMPBELL, CALLAGHAN, BROWN.

As often happens after a team reaches a Cup Final, Hibs' league form began to fluctuate. Only five points were won from the following six games as they dropped back into the bottom half of the table. An easy 4-0 win over the already relegated Motherwell was sandwiched between a 3-0 reverse at Cappielow and the worst performance by a Hibs side for many a year at Firhill. Trailing 4-0 at the interval, a weakened Hibs were lucky to escape with a 6-1 humiliating defeat by Partick Thistle at the end of the month. The small band of fans who had made their way from Edinburgh were entitled to be furious at the disastrous performance by a team that quite clearly had one eye on the Cup Final. Referee Dougie Ramsay made his own piece of history when he became the first Edinburgh official to referee a league game involving a team from the capital outside of a derby match, after the archaic rules regarding hometown referees were at last been relaxed. As a matter of interest, Edinburgh referee Eddie Pringle had previously officiated at a Hibs game, also against Partick, but although he lived in the capital when the game took place, he lived in Aberdeen at the time of the appointment.

Before the Cup Final Eddie Turnbull released his list of freed and retained players for the following season, but any supporter expecting a full-scale clearout would be disappointed. Twenty-six players were retained while just three were handed free transfers. Young Danny Aitchison, who had failed to make a first-team start, was released. He was joined by Gerry O'Brien who had made 13 first-team appearances, and Willie Temperley who had made only ten.

On Saturday 12 May 1979 cup fever once again gripped the green and white half of the city as well over a hundred buses, two special trains and a fleet of private cars ferried thousands of Hibs supporters to Hampden for the Scottish Cup Final against Rangers. Most were convinced that after a wait of 77 years this was at last to be Hibs' year. The Famous Five were back together for the first time in many years for a midweek television interview at Easter

Road and the majority of the quintet were of the opinion that their former side could overcome adversity to win the trophy. Only one of the five was openly critical of Hibs' chances, and he became the subject of considerable criticism in the Easter Road dressing room. The identity of this individual can be ascertained by a retort in a local newspaper: 'at least these players would have the distinction of appearing in a Cup Final'.

For the sixth time in eight years, including the two victorious Drybrough Cup successes, the M8 between Edinburgh and Glasgow was awash with cars and coaches, most bedecked in green and white. Bathed in brilliant summer sunshine, they made their way to the national stadium. For weeks the ticket office at Easter Road had been inundated with applications for stand tickets but at the end of the day only 50,610 paying customers were inside the ground at the kick-off, perhaps a symptom of the game being screened live on both STV and BBC.

Bobby Hutchison was a surprise inclusion in the starting line-up. Only recently recovered from a long-term injury and used mainly as a substitute since, the former Dundee man was preferred to Gordon Rae, who was on the bench. Left back Arthur Duncan was the sole survivor from Hibs' last Scottish Cup Final appearance against Celtic, in 1972.

The FA Cup Final between Arsenal and Manchester United at Wembley that same afternoon, when Arsenal required an injury-time goal to win 3-2 after leading 2-0 with only four minutes to play, has become one of the classic finals of all time – unlike the game at Hampden, which quickly developed into a dour and defensive goalless struggle. The main tactics of both sides appeared geared to cancel each other out, and although favourites Rangers had the bulk of the early pressure, at no stage did Hibs look inferior. In the final 20 minutes the Greens began to assert themselves and could well have scored on several occasions, none better than an effort from Campbell that was brilliantly saved by McCloy. With just seconds remaining, a great run into the box by Campbell seemed certain to end in the winning goal when he found himself with just the keeper to beat. Before the youngster could shoot he was blatantly upended in the box by goalkeeper McCloy. That it was a definite penalty was proved conclusively on TV, but it would take a brave man to award a penalty against either of the Old Firm teams in the last minute of a Cup Final in Glasgow and referee McGinley waved aside the furious appeals of the Hibs players to a crescendo of jeers from the Edinburgh fans gathered behind the goals.

Jackie McNamara, voted Man of the Match, had been in inspirational form, as had Bremner, who had covered every inch of grass as usual. But tellingly, most of Hibs' best performers had been in defence.

As for the penalty incident, even many years later Eddie Turnbull remained bitter, convinced that Hibs had been cheated of victory and adamant that referee McGinley was wrong not to have awarded the spot-kick that almost certainly would have given Hibs the coveted Scottish Cup after a 77-year wait.

After the game there were running battles in the Prospecthill Road area of the ground. Hardly a single coach in the designated parking areas to the east of the stadium escaped the attention of the vandals and most had their windows smashed. The Hibs Supporters Club chairman voiced his concern that the outrageous scenes would dissuade the majority of Hibs fans from attending the replay.

SCOTTISH CUP FINAL, SATURDAY 12 MAY 1979, HAMPDEN PARK.
HIBERNIAN: MCARTHUR, BRAZIL, DUNCAN, BREMNER, STEWART, MCNAMARA,
HUTCHISON, MACLEOD, CAMPBELL, CALLAGHAN, HIGGINS. SUBS: RAE, BROWN.
RANGERS: MCCLOY, JARDINE, DAWSON, JOHNSTONE, JACKSON, MCDONALD, MCLEAN,
RUSSELL, PARLANE, SMITH, COOPER. SUBS: MILLER, URQUHART.
REFEREE: B. MCGINLEY (GLASGOW).

Gordon Rae was Hibs' only change for the replay on the Wednesday replacing Hutchison who was on the bench.

The Edinburgh side had grown in confidence after Saturday's draw and with luck might have been two goals ahead in the first 20 minutes. Looking much the sharper side, they displayed the neater football and attacking intent, and only in the latter stages of normal time did the Glasgow side threaten their dominance. It was far from one-way traffic, however, and McArthur had to be at his very best when he brilliantly saved a long-range effort from Parlane in the second half. Rangers' Davie Cooper also came near when he crashed a great shot off the bar with the keeper beaten, but the best chance of the game fell to the unmarked Rae, right in front of goal deep in extra time, only for the youngster to fumble the ball and the chance was lost.

FINAL SCORE: RANGERS 0. HIBERNIAN 0. (A.E.T.)

For the first time in the 106-year history of the competition, both the final and replay, including extra time, had finished goalless. With Eddie Turnbull on Scotland duty for a home international tournament that culminated in goals by Gordon McQueen, son of former Hibs goalkeeper Tommy, and Dalglish, giving the Scots a 2-0 victory over the Auld Enemy at Wembley, the second replay was held over for 12 days. Again at Hampden, it took place on Monday 28 May 1977.

With Celtic clinching the league title the previous week and Hibs dropping to seventh place in the table, the only avenue into Europe left to the Easter Road side was winning the cup. Had second-placed Rangers finished as champions, Hibs would have qualified for the Cup Winners' Cup competition irrespective of the result in the final.

The same 11 that had started the replay lined up in front of a sparse 30,602 crowd for the third game. After 226 minutes' play, Higgins at last broke the deadlock when he opened the scoring for Hibs, but a brilliant opening 45 minutes' performance by the Edinburgh side was spoiled when Johnstone equalised for Rangers against the run of play shortly before the break. Johnstone scored again to give Rangers the lead just after half time, but Hibs were thrown a lifeline when Ally MacLeod scored from the spot after substitute Hutchison was brought down in the box with 12 minutes remaining, a somewhat soft award, and it was again on to extra time.

The 90 minutes had ended with Rangers the better side, and they resumed where they had left off. Within minutes referee Foote awarded another soft penalty, this time to Rangers, but McArthur brilliantly parried substitute Alex Miller's spot kick to keep the Greens in the game. A magnificent solo run by Ally MacLeod was well worthy of a goal but unfortunately for Hibs his final shot came back off the post. With just 11 minutes of the second period of extra time remaining, the tie was settled in dramatic fashion when Arthur Duncan, trying to clear a Cooper cross from the right, spectacularly headed the ball past the helpless McArthur to give Rangers the cup, and deny his side European competition in the coming season.

Although the Cup Final defeat was far from comical, a humorous story, perhaps apocryphal, went the rounds. A Hibs-supporting soldier stationed in Germany had made his way to Hampden for the Cup Final and decided to go AWOL for the replay. Unwilling, or unable, to stay for the second replay he had returned to barracks and detention by the time the third game took place. That evening, desperate to know the full-time score, he was eventually informed by a colleague that one of the teams had won 3-2, but he wasn't sure which one, all he knew was that a player called Arthur Duncan had scored the winning goal. The anonymous soldier's heartbreak on discovering the truth can only be imagined.

Although of little consolation for Hibs, there was an unexpected cash bonus after the game when both finalists, who had ended the cup campaign as joint top scorers, were each awarded the £3,000 prize money by sponsors Younger's instead of it being split down the middle as expected.

The extended league season was completed with a fourth consecutive game against the Light Blues, this time at Easter Road the following Thursday. Goals by Brazil and Rae gave the home side a deserved but meaningless 2-1 victory that elevated them into fifth place in the table, three points behind UEFA Cup qualifiers Dundee United.

The ever-present Ally MacLeod had again finished top scorer with 21 goals, eight of them in the league. A total of 25 players had been used in the championship run, many of them youngsters, and it was again anticipated that the experience of the past season, including the earlier European games and the two domestic cup runs, would be of immense benefit to the likes of Farmer, who had made two top-team starts during the season, and youngsters Paterson, Kilgour, Lambie, Brown, and McGlinchey, who could all expect to play a more prominent part in the coming year.

Earlier in the season Alex Edwards, a first-team regular almost since the start of the Turnbull revolution in 1971, although he had not featured in first-team action since Hibs' 1-0 victory against Ayr United at Somerset Park on 10 December the previous year, was allowed to join Arbroath. The move did not prove successful and the mercurial winger announced his retirement from the game a few weeks later without even featuring in the Angus side. In the months since his final first-team appearance for Hibs he had played only intermittently for the second team, his last appearance in a green and white jersey having been a reserve fixture against Motherwell at Easter Road in October.

19

'Best... he couldnae lace ma boots', Turnbull Resigns and Relegation

1979–80

WHAT WOULD PROVE to be a momentous season in the history of Hibernian Football Club kicked of with an Anglo-Scottish Cup match against St Mirren at Love Street. Whether or not a reluctance to participate in the competition after the disappointing experience against Bristol City two years before still remained, there was little concern at a first-round exit from what was still seen as a second-rate competition. St Mirren went through to the next round courtesy of a solitary goal at Easter Road after a thrilling 3-3 draw in Paisley. Former Hearts captain Jim Brown, a close season acquisition who had been surprisingly freed by the Tynecastle club, made a goalscoring debut in the first leg. During the summer Turnbull had travelled to Leeds to sign Anglo's David Reid and David Whyte in a double deal worth around £30,000. Derek Rodier, a former teammate of Colin Campbell, completed the close season signings when he stepped up from Edinburgh University a few days later. Unhappy at his failure to command a regular first-team place, making just 11 league starts the previous season, outside right Willie Murray had his request for a free transfer refused, but was placed on the open-to-offers list. Pat Carroll and Rikki Fleming would soon leave the club, Carroll to Raith Rovers in a £5,000 deal after five years at Easter Road, and Fleming, who had not featured in the first team since the Partick Thistle debacle the previous season, to Berwick Rangers for a similar fee.

The seemingly neverending dispute between the football authorities and the television companies regarding payment for the broadcasting of highlights had once again ended in stalemate. The offer from both the BBC and STV fell several hundred thousand pounds below what was seen as a fair figure by the SFA and the Scottish League, while the television companies were concerned at what was considered an excessive use of trackside advertising at many of the grounds around the country. With the parties unable to reach agreement, a TV blackout for the armchair fan again came into operation. Celtic chairman Desmond White complained vociferously that the television veto was seriously damaging the Parkhead club's finances. White's statement clearly infuriated Tom Hart, who accused Celtic of being oblivious to the needs of others and blinkered by self-importance. Hart also found it necessary to remind White that the ongoing negotiations were on behalf of all 38 Scottish clubs and not just Celtic. The dispute was eventually settled when the TV companies agreed to pay £2,000 for each game covered, £750 of which would go to each of the competing clubs and the rest into a common fund. The split was later reduced by the football authorities to just over £500 for each participating club, a decision that angered the Hibs chairman who felt that the teams involved on the day should benefit the most and Tom Hart again introduced his own television blackout at Easter Road until the matter was settled to his satisfaction.

As a forerunner to the season proper, a four-team 'round robin' tournament was introduced to the Edinburgh public for the first time when Hibs, Hearts, Coventry and Manchester City accepted an invitation to compete for the Skol Festival Trophy, a competition sponsored by brewing giants Ind Coope. Played in a mini-league table format, all four sides would be in action in a double-header at the same ground, with the fans able to watch both games for the same admission price. In the opening game against Hearts at Easter Road, goals from Rae and Campbell cancelled out a solitary strike by Gibson to give Hibs a 2-1 victory, Coventry later defeating Manchester City 3-1.

On the Monday evening at Tynecastle, the match between Hibs and Manchester City finished level at 1-1, but the main talking point was a horrendous collision between City's giant goalkeeper Joe Corrigan and centre forward Colin Campbell. Campbell, chasing a high ball, took the full brunt of what was thought by many to be a foolhardy challenge by the six-foot plus England goalkeeper, and only prompt action by both trainers had prevented a more serious outcome when the Hibs youngster swallowed his tongue. Campbell was rushed to hospital with severe bruising and concussion, and spent a few days in the Edinburgh Royal Infirmary. The game between Hearts and Coventry later in the evening ended all square, Hibs now having to defeat the Midlands club in their final match at Easter Road to win the trophy. Coventry City, who included Scotland caps Jim Holton, Jim Blyth, Ian Wallace and Tommy Hutchison in their line-up, took the field wearing an all chocolate coloured strip, and held on grimly against an injury weakened Hibs side in a largely unexciting match, the no-score draw good enough to see them become the first winners of the trophy.

Hibs kicked off their championship challenge with a game against holders Rangers at Easter Road. With Brazil and McNamara both suspended, the highly promising 19-year-old Craig Paterson made his league debut against one of his future clubs wearing the number six jersey, while Jim Farmer. who had come on as substitute against both Rangers and Celtic the previous season, was a surprise choice at right back in his first start for the club. A second-half strike by Gordon Rae after Cooper gave Rangers a two-goal lead at the interval briefly threatened a spirited Hibs comeback, but a third goal from Russell settled the issue.

A week later at Pittodrie Hibs had the better of the early stages and were unlucky not to be ahead after both Callaghan and Campbell saw efforts rebound from the woodwork, but 60 seconds from half time a Steve Archibald goal knocked the heart out of the visitors who eventually lost 3-0 courtesy of more defensive blunders. The result left Hibs, the only Premier League side without a point, firmly anchored at the foot of the table.

After the loss of six goals in two games, goalkeeper McDonald was recalled to the side in place of McArthur for the home game against Dundee, his first start since Christmas Eve. The highlight of the 5-2 victory was a fantastic goal by Ralph Callaghan, described in one newspaper as 'the goal of this or any other season'. Collecting a pass from Brazil more than 30 yards from goal, Callaghan proceeded to beat one opponent after another as he dribbled and tricked his way into the box, rounding the helpless keeper before tapping the ball into the corner of the net. As his delighted colleagues rushed to congratulate the goalscorer, the entire ground rose to acclaim a quite magnificent goal. Ally MacLeod, Hibs' best player on the day – and making his first start of the season after a spell in the reserves and contemplating a move from Easter Road – had celebrated his return to first-team action by scoring the opening goal.

The win was enough to lift the Easter Road side into eighth place, their highest position of the season as it would turn out, but a narrow defeat by Kilmarnock in Ayrshire saw Hibs, who had Derek Rodier making his debut, drop to ninth. Yet another defeat seven days later, this time at Parkhead, saw Hibs again plummet to the foot of the table, a position they would hold until the final game of the season. Things might have worked out differently had Latchford not saved a MacLeod penalty kick in the first half that would have doubled Hibs' one-goal advantage, but as it turned out, Celtic won easily in the end with the assistance of a penalty of their own, conceded after a McNamara blunder against his former side.

The League Cup, now sponsored by Bell's Whisky to the tune of £270,000 spread over three years, brought some welcome respite from the pressures of a so far disastrous league campaign. After a bye in the opening round, Hibs drew Second Division Montrose for the third time in five years in the same competition. In the first leg at Easter Road, a late goal by Tony Higgins, who had recently been appointed chairman of the Scottish Professional Footballers Association, was required to give his side a slender 2-1 win against hard-working and determined opponents. The victory failed to satisfy the Hibs support, who were not slow in showing show their disapproval after a particularly poor performance by the home side, the players leaving the field to resounding jeers of derision.

That same weekend, teenager Willie Jamieson became one of Eddie Turnbull's last signing for Hibs. Years later, Turnbull would recall happening to lean over the table as the player was about to put pen to paper, to see that Jamieson was wearing Rangers socks.

Several goal-line clearances and a string of brilliant saves by home keeper Moffat in the return leg of the League Cup against Montrose at Links Park ensured that a second-half goal by future Hibs striker Gary Murray would be enough to take the tie into extra time. Well on top during the final 30 minutes of normal time as the part-timers tired, only a goal by Tony Higgins five minutes into injury time prevented a repeat of the humiliating extra time defeat at the same ground five years earlier.

Appalled at the IRA slogans and obscene chants that emanated from the area of the ground containing the away support both during and after the game, Tom Hart promised that with the co-operation of the police he would banish the bigots from Easter Road, even if it meant reduced gates. The chairman had been aware of the tricolour being shown by supporters in the past and had now issued instructions to the police that they be removed. In his statement he explained:

> This is a non-sectarian club without religious or political bias, and it is a long time since we have had a connection with any of the religious feelings at one time attached to Hibs. Obviously I am aware of and dislike the modern trends which are evident throughout the country, but I am concerned only with Hibs and their supporters, most of whom are well behaved.

It was not difficult to see just where Hibs' main problem lay, and in an attempt to inject more firepower into the attack, a six-figure offer was made to Airdrie for striker Sandy Clark, an approach that was immediately rejected by the part-time player. It was reported that Clark had a good job outside football and did not relish the thought of turning full-time, but the real reason was obviously a lack of desire to sign for a struggling side. The rebuff by a player who preferred to remain in the First Division instead of joining a Premier League side concerned the Hibs supporters, who were now fully aware, if they had not known it before, of just how badly things had deteriorated at Easter Road. Clark, however, had set his sights higher than Hibs, and he would soon sign for West Ham United for a fee in the region of £120,000.

Like many others before him, Des Bremner now made it clear that he wished to try his luck in England, and in a surprise move that infuriated the supporters, in the middle of September joined Aston Villa in a £300,000 move. The official stance that the club needed the money to finance other desperately needed deals, and also that the offer was simply too good to turn down, cut no ice with fans, upset at just the latest in a series of big-money moves from Easter Road. Former Clyde centre forward Joe Ward, who had managed only a handful of first-team games for the Birmingham side since moving from Scotland nine months before, joined Hibs as an £80,000 makeweight in the deal.

Bremner had asked away during the previous season and had agreed to stay only on the understanding that Hibs would listen favourably to any offers. The player, who had made more than 300 first-team starts since joining the club from Deverondale in 1972, had refused to sign a new six-year contract at Easter Road with a testimonial thrown in as an expression of just how highly he was rated by the club. As Bremner, who would win the European Cup with Aston Villa in 1982, travelled south to link up again with former colleague Alex Cropley at Villa Park, Joe Ward prepared to make his debut against St Mirren in Edinburgh.

Ally MacLeod was making his 200th appearance for Hibs against his former club. Placed on the transfer list at his own request after completing his contract at the end of the previous season, he was now playing without an agreement of any kind. As for the game itself, there was little to celebrate as the Paisley side quickly raced to a 2-0 interval lead which turned out to be the final score, leaving the frustrated fans to vent their anger in the direction of manager Eddie Turnbull throughout most of the second half. In the opening minutes, Joe Ward might well have scored with his first touch for his new side, only a brilliant save by the keeper preventing the tall forward from opening his account.

A 2-1 defeat at Firhill at the end of the month left the Edinburgh side still seeking their first Premier League victory over Thistle in five years, and even this early the signs were ominous that Hibs were in deep trouble. Scotland goalkeeper Alan Rough was in magnificent form to deny the visitors a share of the points in the later stages of the game, but a Ward miss when he blasted over from close range with only the keeper to beat did little to ease Hibs' relegation worries.

With only two victories from the 13 games played so far, it was less than surprising when Kilmarnock ended Hibs interest in the League Cup with a 4-2 aggregate win. In the first leg at Easter Road, the visitors stunned their opponents by stealing a late victory, their first at Easter Road for 15 years, after almost incessant pressure by the home side. Before the game Turnbull demanded that his players give maximum effort and he could have had no complaints on that score, but they could not legislate for the referee allowing Kilmarnock to score the winner from a blatantly offside position after both the goalscorer and the Hibs keeper had stopped before realising that the referee had not blown the whistle.

At Rugby Park Hibs got off to a flying start when Higgins levelled the overall score after only three minutes, but keeper McDonald was badly at fault for Kilmarnock's equaliser when he failed to cut out a cross. Although not the worst, new signing Joe Ward had again failed to make an impression as part-time Killie ran Hibs ragged, scoring a second goal. The capital side had now gone eight games without a victory.

An attempt to sign former Ayr and Leeds United Goalkeeper Jim Stewart from West Bromwich Albion for £70,000 fell through, and Jim McArthur replaced McDonald for the trip to Tannadice on the Saturday. With a quarter of the season now gone, an extremely dispirited performance and a 2-0 defeat left Hibs firmly rooted at the bottom of the table and Turnbull to run a gauntlet of abuse from the Hibs fans as he made his way to the dressing rooms at the end.

In a move that was novel for the time, Easter Road staged a free open day for the fans on Sunday 14 October. Supporters of all ages took the opportunity to watch their favourites in training before a short practice match. Afterwards, there was the chance to meet the players and collect autographs. The day was generally considered a success for the fans and players alike, so much so that it was planned to make the event a regular occurrence.

In Rangers' 2-0 win at Ibrox in mid-October, Jackie McNamara was sent off after a bad tackle on Alex McDonald. The mistimed tackle, though bad, was worth no more than a booking in the view of most neutral observers, and the club were highly critical of the referee's overall performance, criticism that later brought a rebuke from the management committee. By this time the exciting young prospect Paul McGlinchey had earned a regular place on the substitutes' bench, with Stevie Brown recalled to the side for the first time since the end of the previous season.

Bobby Hutchison scored Hibs' first goal in the three games against Aberdeen that season; it appeared to be the winner until future Hibs player and later assistant manager, Andy Watson, popped up in the last minute to level the scores.

Seven days later in a game against second-bottom Dundee at Dens Park, it was imperative that Hibs take something from the vital clash and they got off to a whirlwind start when MacLeod scored from the penalty spot in the very first minute. Opportunities to increase the lead were lost when Callaghan and Ward missed easy chances. In the second half Dundee scored twice in a five-minute spell to go five points clear of the struggling bottom-placed side. Hibs' position had now moved from serious to acute.

With four months of the season gone, the already critical league position was worsening by the week. Reporter Stewart Brown proposed a radical solution. He argued that Hibs could do worse than sign the former Manchester United player George Best, then at Fulham, a suggestion that was not as far-fetched as it first appeared. Despite his genius, Best had become a long-term problem at Manchester United and had been allowed to leave, eventually ending up at Craven Cottage. The London club had given him permission to play in America during the close season although they still held his registration. The Edinburgh public thought the whole thing a publicity stunt. Within days, however, against the wishes of manager Turnbull, Hart had contacted Fulham, who gave Hibs permission to talk to the player. To the amazement of the supporters, both Best and his wife, Angie, made a surprise appearance in the Easter Road directors' box before the game against Kilmarnock. They were given a warm reception by the fans – Angie, a model, perhaps receiving an even warmer welcome than her famous husband. After watching the player in a midweek testimonial game for Ipswich manager Bobby Robson, Hibs agreed to pay Fulham the £50,000 asking-price for Best's transfer and the player agreed to sign a two-year pay-as-you-play deal rumoured to be worth an estimated £2,000 per week, a colossal sum at the time, and alleged to have been paid out of Tom Hart's own pocket. The move made front-page headlines in the national press, with Turnbull diplomatically stating his 'absolute delight' at the acquisition of a player, whom he regarded to have been, in his prime, the finest footballer he had ever seen. It would seem that Tom Hart had signed Best against the wishes of the manager, an indication that the chairman had lost faith in Turnbull and his methods.

Unfortunately for the fans, a slight injury picked up in the Robson testimonial game prevented Best from making his first appearance for Hibs in Glasgow against Celtic in what turned out to be a 3-0 defeat. Best made his debut at Paisley the following Saturday, 24 November 1979, wearing the number 11 jersey.

A crowd of 13,670, more that double what would normally have been expected for the fixture, braved a pre-match downpour to catch a glimpse of the legend in action on the rain-sodden Love Street pitch. Unfortunately, the inspiration of Best could not prevent Hibs slipping to a 2-1 defeat. Displaying that he had lost little of his skill as he directed the game from midfield with dangerous, probing passes, Best raised the cheers, and the optimism, of the large Hibs support when he scored his new side's solitary goal in the dying seconds, although too late to alter the outcome. Goalkeeper McDonald replaced McArthur for the match, his last for the first team before being freed at the end of the season.

Best made his home debut against Partick Thistle seven days later. In what would turn out to be Hibs' second victory of the season at Easter Road, his appearance drew a crowd of well over 20,000 clamouring to see the Irish wizard in action, considerably more than the 5–6,000 that might normally be expected for such a fixture. Two ahead at the interval through an own goal and a penalty by MacLeod, Partick came storming back into the match in the second half with a goal by O'Hara, but it was yet again only the magnificent form of Alan Rough late on for Thistle, who had earlier seen Jim McArthur save a penalty, that prevented Hibs from further increasing their lead.

Just before the interval, one particular piece of Best genius enthralled the fans. Shooting down the slope, Hibs were awarded a direct free kick fully 40 yards from goal. Best took the kick himself, his superb effort striking the inside of the left-hand post with Rough beaten, before being cleared to safety. The huge attendance meant that Hibs had benefited to the tune of over £18,000 before expenses, almost enough to cover Best's wages for the remainder of the season. To put the Easter Road attendance into perspective, that same afternoon the League Cup semi-final between Aberdeen and Morton at Hampden, attracted a crowd of only 12,000.

The fact that Best was being paid such a huge sum initially caused some resentment among several of the players and after training one day Tom Hart overheard Jim McArthur complaining about the gulf between Best's wages and those of the rest of the team. In the dressing room just before the Partick Thistle game on the Saturday, the chairman drew McArthur to one side and asked the goalkeeper what he could see from the small window that overlooked the pitch.

'A huge crowd, Mr Hart,' replied McArthur.

'That, son, is why George Best is being paid £2,000 a game,' McArthur was told.

Ally MacLeod had his own thoughts about the Irishman. When hearing that Best was about to sign for the club, MacLeod is famously quoted as saying, 'Best... he couldnae lace ma boots.'

With the prospect of a free Saturday because of the Bell's League Cup Final between Dundee United and Aberdeen, an attempt to fix up a friendly in Spain or Portugal against Belenenses, Porto or Valencia proved unsuccessful when a satisfactory financial agreement could not be reached. At the last minute, however, a game was arranged against Leicester City on the Monday evening in Edinburgh. Milo Nizetic, a 27-year-old goalkeeper from Hajduk Split, one of Hibs' former European adversaries, had been brought to Edinburgh for a trial period with the prospect of a £30,000 transfer if he impressed. The Under-21 cap was between the posts for the friendly against the English club, who featured former Hibs players Bobby Smith and Martin Henderson, but unfortunately a hand injury received in the game would keep the goalkeeper out of football for several weeks and he returned home before his worth could be ascertained. Bobby Robertson, an experienced goalkeeper with 12 years' service with St Johnstone, was signed for a nominal fee instead.

George Best missed the game against Morton at Cappielow on the Saturday, his absence being explained as the result of a knee injury, but the former Ireland star returned to the side to face Rangers at the end of December. Best played his part in a real team effort that resulted in an early Christmas present for the Easter Road fans when goals from Higgins and Campbell gave Hibs a well warranted and most welcome surprise victory.

It was around this time that Tom Hart was selected as the Mackinlay's Personality of the Month for his enterprise in bringing George Best to Scotland. In the boardroom after the Rangers game, he was presented with a cheque for £100 which was promptly donated to the players' Christmas fund, and a giant bottle of whisky which, presumably, he kept.

Meanwhile, Joe Ward, an £80,000 makeweight in the Bremner transfer deal, had at long last scored his first goal in Hibs colours. Unfortunately, the strike against Morton took place in a reserve match, the centre forward having been unable to secure a first-team place in recent weeks. The likeable Ward had proved to be an expensive acquisition and he would shortly leave the club after only a handful of first-team appearances without scoring a goal.

With Hearts still in the First Division, Dundee were to be Hibs' Ne'er Day visitors, but a match initially moved to the 2nd of the month because of the prohibitive policing charges for a game on New Year's Day, fell victim to winter weather. Three days later fellow strugglers Kilmarnock collected their first win for over two months when they overcame a stuffy Hibs side whose inability to score was apparent when they missed several easy chances, including a penalty. The 3-1 Rugby Park defeat earned the Edinburgh side, who were yet to win their first point on the road, the distinction of having the worst away record in the entire country.

In a sensationally unexpected move, manager Willie Ormond, who had taken Hearts to joint second top of the First Division with a game in hand, was sacked from Tynecastle on the Monday morning. Summoned to the boardroom by the chairman, he was brusquely informed that he was 'to be gone by Saturday'. The action against Ormond by what he would later describe as 'the worst board members I have ever known in all my years in football' was eventually brought before an industrial tribunal. Tom Hart immediately offered the former Hibs player a position at Easter Road, but because of the pending legal action against Hearts, he was unable to accept the proposition at that time.

It had been obvious for some time that Hibs' efforts to beat the drop would more than likely end in failure, but they were offered a tiny morsel of hope with a surprise 1-1 draw against Celtic at Easter Road. After failing to convert several easy chances to open the scoring, including a miss from the penalty spot when MacLeod smashed his shot against the bar, George Best stunned the large Glasgow support inside the ground when he gave Hibs the lead in sensational fashion. Kicking down the slope, there seemed little danger when Best collected a pass from Campbell wide on the left near the stand side touchline. Cutting inside his marker, Best suddenly unleashed a tremendous 25-yard thunderbolt that completely deceived Latchford in the Celtic goal. The home support rose as one to acclaim the brilliant goal, one that was worthy of the Irishman's five-star performance.

In the first round of the Scottish Cup Hibs were drawn against Meadowbank Thistle for a second successive year. Although Meadowbank had been drawn from the hat first, in the interests of safety the police once again refused permission for the tie to take place at Meadowbank Stadium and the game was switched to Tynecastle. At the end of a lacklustre 90 minutes, Hibs took the honours but Meadowbank the credit for a resolute and spirited performance that almost earned the lower league side a replay. Callaghan scored the only goal of a dour game in the first half, but the Bankies will still wonder how McGauran managed to miss the best chance of the match with just seconds remaining when he hit the keeper, with the goal gaping, denying his side the chance of a replay at Easter Road.

At the beginning of February, six appearances and £12,000 into his pay-as-you-play Easter Road agreement, George Best was suspended by the club before the home game against Morton after failing to turn up for training in midweek, a requirement of his contract conditions. After Best made a personal apology to Tom Hart on the Monday, the suspension was lifted. The following Sunday Ayr United were the visitors for a Scottish Cup second-round tie, a game played in brilliant winter sunshine. Full Back Duncan Lambie scored his first goal for the club with a tremendous 25-yard low drive that gave goalkeeper Rennie no chance, before MacLeod wrapped things up with another midway through the second half. Most of the conversation among the fans, however, was the latest non-appearance of Best, who had been expected to play. It was revealed after the game that the player had now been transfer listed and banned from playing for any other club. It later became public knowledge that Best had been carousing until the early hours with the French Rugby team after their game at Murrayfield the previous afternoon. For the first time Best publicly admitted that he had a drink problem, which had no doubt been exacerbated by being away from home for most of the week. With great intentions to turn up at Easter Road for light training on the Saturday, he had embarked on a drinking spree instead. Visited in his hotel room by some of the coaching staff a short time before the cup-tie, he was found in no fit state to play and was ordered by Hart, who was fast running out of patience with the wayward genius, to pack his bags and not return.

In midweek, Peter Cormack returned to Easter Road after an absence of more than ten years. Signed from Bristol City, the former Nottingham Forest and Liverpool player had turned down the opportunity to play in America with Tulsa Roughnecks to return to his native Edinburgh. With ambitions to stay in the game after his playing days were over, part of his two-year contract at Easter Road would involve coaching the youngsters in the afternoons and evenings.

Wearing the number nine jersey but dictating play from midfield, Cormack made his second Hibs debut four days later at Tannadice, but could do little to prevent yet another disappointing away defeat. It was an important win for United with seven points now separating them from bottom-placed Hibs, and although it was not mathematically impossible, it would now require a miracle to save the Greens from relegation for the first time since 1931.

Meanwhile, Willie Ormond was now free to reconsider his employment options after his legal dispute with Hearts had been settled to the satisfaction of both parties, and he returned to Easter Road for the first time since 1961 as an employee of Hibs when he accepted Tom Hart's offer to become assistant manager to Eddie Turnbull.

And still the George Best saga rumbled on. The Irishman made a return to the Hibs side to face Rangers at Ibrox after an absence of four weeks. Yet another apology to the chairman and a promise to seek medical help for his alcohol problem had led to a final chance for the player at Easter Road. Best, who had missed four of the 12 games played since first signing, was reinstated on the strict understanding that he was to play in no more testimonial games, and that he must now arrive in the city each Wednesday for training with his teammates on the Thursday and Friday. It was now revealed that the club had made several excuses to cover the player's absences during the past few months. The official line that he had missed a game against Morton because of injury was admitted to be untrue. The player had attended a midweek function in Manchester, and while he had reported to the ground in time for the game, he had been in no fit state to play.

A defeat at Ibrox, and a depressing no-score draw at Berwick in the third round of the Scottish Cup a week later, was too much for Tom Hart. He hit out publicly, accusing some players of lack of effort, furious at what he considered to be a blatant lack of professionalism in such worrying days for the club. While it was not his style to interfere in team affairs, Hart found it 'impossible to sit back and stay silent after an abysmal performance at Berwick' that was an 'insult' not only to himself but to the Hibs supporters who attended the game.

The chairman's comments made little impact, although the team managed to stutter and stumble into the semi-finals of the cup after the replay at Easter Road in midweek. As in the previous game, there appeared a distinct shortage of determination in certain quarters, and only a solitary strike by Ally MacLeod with 13 minutes remaining separated the sides. Hibs' performance again brought jeers of derision from the terraces and a barrage of abuse aimed at the manager.

With the transfer deadline looming, Tony Higgins was transferred to Partick Thistle in a deal worth £25,000, a case of second time lucky for persistent Thistle manager Bertie Auld who had attempted to sign the player earlier in the season. Striker Bobby Torrance was bought from St Mirren for a fee in the region of £30,000, joining recent acquisition Lawrence Tierney a free transfer from Hearts, both players making their debut in a 3-0 defeat at Dens Park.

Incredibly, despite remaining pointless on their travels, Hibs had not lost at home since a defeat by St Mirren in September, but this record was surrendered at the beginning of April when Dundee United won 2-0, a result that kept third-bottom United just ahead of near neighbours Dundee who were now favourites to join Hibs in the lower Division.

With relegation all but mathematically certain, it was all now or nothing in the Scottish Cup. The news that McNamara had recovered from injury to face Celtic in the semi-final at Hampden was a major boost for a side that had failed to beat the Parkhead men that season, the Edinburgh side managing only a draw in one of the four league games played.

A Lennox goal in the first half was all that Celtic had to show as Hibs played a tight defensive formation hoping to hit the Hoops on the break. Rae missed a great chance inside the six-yard box to put Hibs level just on half time, but the game was all but over just minutes into the second period when the Easter Road defence gifted their opponents a second goal. Best tried hard from midfield to repel the tide of almost relentless Celtic attacks after the interval using the ball intelligently as he attempted to create openings for his teammates, but unfortunately he was fighting a lone and losing battle, and further slack defensive play allowed Celtic to stroll to an easy 5-0 lead, and a Cup Final meeting with Rangers that they would eventually win 1-0.

FULL TIME: CELTIC 5. HIBERNIAN 0.

HIBERNIAN: MCARTHUR, BRAZIL, DUNCAN, MCNAMARA, STEWART, RAE, CALLAGHAN, TORRANCE, HUTCHISON, LAMBIE, AND BEST. SUBS: CAMPBELL, PATERSON.

After almost ten years in charge at Easter Road, on Tuesday 15 April 1980 manager Eddie Turnbull was sacked and replaced by Willie Ormond, initially on a caretaker basis. The usual banal statement that both parties had 'parted on amicable terms' ended a 26-year association at Easter Road for a man who had done more than most to further the cause of Hibernian Football Club. The news of Turnbull's sacking while dramatic, was not entirely unexpected. Under fire from a section of the support for some time, the longest-serving manager in the country at the time would not have been unaware of the mounting pressure on the chairman to make drastic changes after such a traumatic and disastrous season.

Regardless, it was a sad end for a man who had served the club faithfully as a player, trainer and ultimately manager. The scorer of the first ever European Cup goal by a British player, Turnbull, had been an integral member of the legendary Famous Five forward line, then generally regarded as the best ever Scottish attack, and had won three league titles, nine full Scottish caps and another four at inter-league level during his time with the club.

According to the man himself, things had never been quite the same for him since the Cup Winners' Cup defeat by Hadjuk Split in 1973. Then, he and a great many Hibs supporters had felt that the side was good enough to reach the final and possibly even win the competition itself.

Within a few years, however, the quality of the team had declined dramatically and they were now but a pale shadow of the side that had worked its way into Scottish football legend by their performance at the start of the decade. Admittedly there had been little money to invest, but the majority of the home grown youngsters brought in in recent years to replace the established stars had failed to realise their potential. It is rumoured that many of those young players had been terrified of a manager whose legendary temper and stubbornness had not improved over the years, a situation that was hardly conducive to the development of inexperienced youngsters.

In a letter to the newspapers, George Telfer, a former chairman of the Fifty Club, went further, stating that the decline of Hibs had come as no surprise to him:

> I must have been one of Hibs' most loyal supporters, travelling everywhere with the team both home and abroad, but I said years ago that the club needed a change of policy and I still stand by that statement. Many of my friends, like me, wanted to buy shares in the club but received no encouragement.

This was an overt dig at Tom Hart and the still fragile relationship between the chairman and the members of the private club.

Willie Ormond's first game in charge at Easter Road coincided with Hibs winning their first away point of the season in a 1-1 draw at Pittodrie. A fighting performance against the champions elect was well worthy of a share of the spoils and only a tremendous goal from 25 yards by substitute and future Hibs player and assistant manager Andy Watson had denied the visitors both points. George Best, involved in an incident in the tunnel after the game for 'adopting an aggressive attitude towards another player' – in this case, the 'shrinking violet', Willie Miller – was reported by the referee.

Now that relegation was certain, Hibs accepted an approach from North American side San José Earthquakes to sign Best on loan for the rest of the season and summer break. The cut-price deal allowed the Edinburgh side to retain Best's registration and sell the player to any one of several interested English parties on his return from the States.

Best watched Hibs go down 2-1 at home to Kilmarnock in midweek from a position in the radio commentary box, took the opportunity to thank the Hibs fans via the tannoy system for their encouragement during his time at Easter Road. At a ceremony in the Hibs Supporters Club after the game, he was presented with a gift of Edinburgh Crystal to mark his contribution to the team during the previous six months. During his time at Easter Road the Irishman had taken part in 16 competitive games, 13 in the league, scoring three goals and three in the Scottish Cup. Of the 16, four had ended in victory, three drawn and nine lost, Hibs scoring 11 goals against 28 conceded. The statistics clearly indicated that things had deteriorated so badly that it would take more than Best's declining talents to save the club from relegation.

There would be a brief return in a Hibs shirt for the player the following season when he took part in another six competitive games, four in the league and two in the League Cup, before he departed once again for America. He would later return to face his former colleagues playing for San José in a contracted friendly match in Edinburgh, making a final Easter Road appearance as a guest in Jackie McNamara's testimonial match against Newcastle United in 1984.

In later years Eddie Turnbull would claim that George Best had cost him his job, but the statistics fail to back up that claim. In the 14 league games played before Best's signing, only one had been won. In the remaining 14 before Turnbull's sacking, four had ended in victory, although admittedly Best had not featured in them all.

With an eye firmly on the future, one of the new manager's first tasks was to totally revamp the Easter Road scouting system. Former post-war player Archie Buchanan was dismissed from his role as chief scout as Ormond brought in his own men. Tom McNiven, who had left following a disagreement with Turnbull two years before, was reinstated as physiotherapist on a full-time basis, a position that had been left unfilled since his departure.

As often happens in the circumstances, the chairman pledged that money would be made available to the new manager to strengthen the side. Perhaps if money had been made available to the previous manager, the club would not have found itself in the ignominious position of having to attempt to win promotion the following season in the first place.

In the expected clearout 12 players were freed, most with first-team experience. Goalkeeper Robertson and former Leeds pair Whyte and Reid, who had both failed to make first-team impact, joined Hutchison, Campbell, Tierney, Lambie, McDonald, Kilgour and Farmer. Making up the dozen were the disappointed teenagers Leitch and Quilietti; 23 players were retained for the season ahead.

Teenage goalkeeper Dave Huggins made his first-team debut when replacing McArthur in a 1-1 draw at Cappielow. Dave Reid, signed in the summer from Leeds United, also made his debut from the substitutes' bench. A late Ralph Callaghan goal earned Hibs only their second away point of the season.

The freed Bobby Hutchison made a premature end to his Hibs career when he was helped from the field with a broken nose, sustained during a rare victory over St Mirren at Easter Road. But it was business as usual seven days later, Hibs' penultimate game in what had been a torturous season, when Aberdeen won 5-0, their first league victory at Easter Road for over five years, watched by a poor crowd of only 12,921. A gale force wind made the conditions difficult for both sides, but at no time did it threaten to prevent Aberdeen from becoming the first club outside the Old Firm to win the Premier League Championship.

A season that had promised so much after the close-run thing in the Cup Final the previous year limped feebly out with a dour and insipid, solitary goal, home defeat by Partick Thistle. Almost inevitably, it was a yet another defensive slip that led to the goal.

Few of the 1,191 supporters who watched the start of the game were still inside the ground when the referee's whistle brought a thankful end to what had been an exhausting and traumatic season. Twenty-nine players had been used in the league campaign, with Ally MacLeod again top scorer with 13 goals in all matches, a figure that tells its own story, just eight of them in the championship.

The substantial managerial experience of Ormond, who had first-hand knowledge of the First Division from his time with Hearts, would prove invaluable during the coming 12 months – a season that promised to be hazardous and trying as Hibernian attempted to resurrect the formidable reputation built up since they were last relegated in 1931. Sadly, Ormond's stay at the club would be brief. Forced to resign after only seven months in the job because of ill health, he left on November 1980. Willie Ormond died four years later, on 4 May 1984, at the age of 57.

As for Eddie Turnbull, his wealth of tactical knowledge and experience was lost to the game. He opened a bar in Easter Road which became a popular watering hole for Hibs supporters and kept the landlord close to the scene of his former glories, although his final separation from the club had been so painful that he would not enter the ground for some time thereafter. But time heals, and in recent years he was a regular attender in the boardroom at matches until his death in spring 2011.

The span of years covered in this book saw the resurgence of a club that had fallen on hard times – and what a gloriously stylish resurgence! Jock Stein's managerial inspiration and drive laid the foundations. Shankly and Macfarlane then built on Stein's legacy, before Turnbull's tactical genius harnessed and moulded some the best footballing talent Scotland has ever seen. There followed a period when reality and legend merged, giving potency to every Hibs supporter's dream that these great days will return once more to Easter Road…

Appendix 1
Hibernian FC Player and Manager History
1961–80

Players listed below played at least one league game for Hibs between 1961 and 1980. The dates given indicate when they were considered first-team players, not necessarily when they were first signed, including team signed from and joined after leaving Easter Road, if known.

Player	Signed from	Hibernian	Transferred to
Adair, Gerry	West Brom	73/74	Dunfermline
Allan, Thomson	Edina Hearts	65/66–69/70	Dundee
Auld, Bertie	Celtic	71/72	Hibs Trainer
Baines, Roy	Derby County	68/69–71/72	Morton
Baird, Sammy	Rangers	60/61–61/62	Third Lanark
Baker, Gerry	Manchester City	61/62–63/64	Ipswich
Baker, Joe	Armadale	57/58–60/61	Torino
	Sunderland	71/72–72/73	Raith Rovers
Barry, Roy	Crystal Palace	74/75–75/76	East Fife
Baxter, John	Benburb	57/58–65/66	Falkirk
Best, George	Fort Lauderdale	79/80–80/81	San José
Black, Jim	Airdrie	69/70–73/74	Airdrie
Blackley, John	Gairdoch United	67/68–77/78	Newcastle
Blair, Jim	St Mirren	70/71	St Mirren
Bogie, Malcolm	Balgreen Rovers	58/59–62/63	Grimsby
Brazil, Ally	Currie Hearts	76/77–85/86	Hamilton
Bremner, Des	Deveronvale	72/73–79/80	Aston Villa
Brown, Jim	Hearts	79/80–80/81	Dunfermline
Brown, Stevie	—	78/79–80/81	—
Brownlie, John	Pumpherston	69/70–77/78	Newcastle
Byrne, Johnny	Tranmere	62/63–63-64	Barnsley
Callaghan, Ralph	Newcastle	78/79–85/86	Morton
Cameron, Alex	St Bernards	62/63–63/64	Oldham
Campbell, Colin	Benbecula	78/79–79/80	Dundee United
Carroll, Pat	Sauchie BC	74/75–78/79	Raith Rovers
Cormack, Peter	Hearts	62/63–69/70	Notts Forest
	Bristol City	79/80–82/83	retained as coach
Cousin, Allan	Dundee	65/66–68/69	—
Cropley, Alex	Edina Hibs	68/69–74/75	Arsenal
Cuthbert, Ian	Edina Hibs	61/62	—
Davidson, Kenny	Loanhead Mayflower	70/71–73/74	Dunfermline
Davin, Joe	Drumchapel Amateurs	59/60–62/63	Ipswich
Davis, Joe	Third Lanark	64/65–69/70	Carslisle

Duncan, Arthur	Partick Thistle	69/70–83/84	Meadowbank
Duncan, Bobby	Bonnyrigg Rose	63/64–70/71	East Fife
Easton, Jim	Drumchapel	60/61–63/64	Dundee
Edwards Alec	Dunfermline	71/72–77/78	Arbroath
Falconer, Duncan	Edinburgh Norton	59/60–63/64	Apia Leichardt
Farmer, Jim	—	78/79–79/80	Stirling Albion
Fleming, Rikki	Ayr United	78/79	Berwick
Fraser, John	Edinburgh Thistle	54/55–65/66	Stenhousemuir
Frye, Johnny	Ardrossan	55/56–59/60	St Mirren
Fyfe, Graeme	Rangers	76/77	Dumbarton
Gibson, Davie	Livingston United	56/57–61/62	Leicester City
Gordon, Alan	Dundee United	71/72–74/75	Dundee
Graham, Johnny	Falkirk	69/70–70/71	Ayr United
Grant, Colin	Linlithgow Rose	65/66–69/70	Chelmsford City
Grant, John	Merchiston	54/55–63/64	Raith Rovers
Grant, Johnny	Kilwinning Rangers	63/64	Raith Rovers
Hamilton, Johnny	Cumbernauld	69/70–72/73	Rangers
Hamilton, Willie	Hearts	63/64–65/66	Aston Villa
Harper, Joe	Everton	73/74–75/76	Aberdeen
Hazel, John	Dunipace	70/71–73/74	Morton
Henderson, Martin	Rangers	77/78	Leicester City
Herriot, Jim	Birmingham	71/72–72/73	St Mirren
Higgins, Tony	Kilsyth St Pats	72/73–79/80	Partick Thistle
Hogg, Davie	Tynecastle BC	63/64–67/68	Dundee United
Huggins, Dave	Musselburgh Windsor	79/80	East Fife
Hughes, Pat	Whitburn	56/57–63/64	Forfar
Hunter, Willie	Detroit Cougars	68/69–70/71	Capetown City
Hutchison, Bobby	Dundee	77/78–79/80	Wigan
Jamieson, Willie	Tynecastle BC	80/81–84/85	Hamilton
Jones, Mervyn	Edina Hibs	66/67–70/71	Falkirk
Kilgour, Rab	Whitehill Welfare	78/79–79/80	St Johnstone
Kinloch, Bobby	Forres	60/61–62/63	Berwick
Lambie, Duncan	FC Furth	78/79–79/80	—
Leishman, Tommy	Liverpool	62/63–64/65	Linfield
Macleod, Ally	Southhampton	74/75–82/83	Dundee United
Madsen, John	Morton	66/67–68/69	Esbjerg
Marinello, Peter	Salvesen BC	67/68–69/70	Arsenal
Marjoribanks, Brian	Airth Castle Rovers	61/62	Hearts
Marshall, Gordon	Notts Forest	68/69–70/71	Celtic
Martin, Neil	Queen of the South	63/64–65/66	Sunderland
Mathisen, Sven	Start Krisiansen	78/79	Den Haag
McArthur, Jim	Cowdenbeath	72/73–82/83	Meadowbank
McBride, Joe	Celtic	68/69–71/72	Dunfermline
McClelland, Joe	Armadale	54/55–63/64	Wrexham
McCreadie, Harvey	Mossley	61/62	Altringham

McDonald, Mike	Stoke City	75/76–79/80	Berwick Rangers
McEwan, Willie	Pumpherson	69/70–72/73	Blackpool
McGee, Alec	Edinburgh Thistle	71/72–72/73	Morton
	Morton	75/76–77/78	Dundee
McGlinchey, Paul	Salvesen	79/80–80/81	Berwick Rangers
McGlynn, Tony	Edinburgh Thistle	61/62–63/64	Airdrie
McGraw, Alan	Morton	66/67–68/69	Linfield
McKay, Jim	Brora	77/78	Brora
McKenzie, Roddy	Airdrie	73/74–74/75	Clydebank
MacLeod, Ally	Blackburn	61/62–62/63	Third Lanark
McNamara, Jackie	Celtic	76/77–84/85	Morton
McNamee, John	Celtic	63/64–66/67	Newcastle United
McNeill, George	Tranent	65/66–67/68	Morton
Muir, Lindsay	—	75/76–77/78	St Johnstone
Muirhead, Willie	Arniston Rangers	59/60–61/62	Toronto City
Munro, Ian	St Mirren	73/74–75/76	Rangers
	Dundee United	84/85–85/86	—
Murphy, John	—	68/69–70/71	Morton
Murray, Willie	Salvesen BC	73/74–80/81	Cowdenbeath
Nelson, Dennis	Broxburn	71/72	Dunfermline
Nicol, Bobby	Edinburgh City	55/56–61/62	Barnsley
O'Brien, Gerry	Clydebank	78/79	—
O'Rourke, Jimmy	Edina	62/63–73/74	St Johnstone
Parke, John	Linfield	63/64–64/65	Sunderland
Paterson, Craig	Bonnyrigg Rose	77/78–81/82	Rangers
Paterson, Willie	Albion Rovers	74/76–77/80	Falkirk
Preston, Tommy	Newtongrange Star	53/54–63/64	St Mirren
Pringle, Alex	—	68/69–71/72	Dundee
Quinn, Pat	Blackpool	63/64–68/69	East Fife
Rae, Gordon	Whitehill Welfare	77/78–89/90	Partick Thistle
Refvik Isak	Viking Stavanger	78/79	Viking Stavanger
Reid, David	Leeds United	79/80	—
Reilly, Jack	Inverurie Loco	65/66–66/67	Washington Whips
Rodier, Derek	Edinburgh University	79/80–82/83	Dunfermline
Schaedler, Erich	Stirling Albion	69/70–77/78	Dundee
	Dundee	81/82–84/85	Dumbarton
Scott, Alec	Everton	67/68–68/69	Falkirk
Scott, Ally	Rangers	76/77–77/78	Morton
Scott, Jim	Bo'ness United	58/59–66/67	Newcastle United
Shevlane, Chris	Celtic	68/69–70/71	Morton
Simpson, Billy	Edina Hibs	63/64–69/70	Falkirk
Simpson, Ronnie	Newcastle	60/61–63/64	Celtic
Smith, Bobby	Musselburgh Windsor	72/73–78/79	Leicester City
	Leicester City	86/87	Dunfermline
Spalding, Derek	—	72/73–77/78	Chicago Stings

Stanton, Pat	Edina Hibs	63/64–75/76	Celtic
Stein, Colin	Armadale	65/66–68/69	Rangers
Stevens, Tom	Dunbar United	71/72–73/74	Hamilton
Stevenson, Eric	Hearts	60/61–71/72	Ayr United
Stevenson, Jimmy	Edina	64/65–66/67	Southend United
Stevenson, Morris	Motherwell	62/63	Morton
Stewart, George	Dundee	76/77–80/81	Cowdenbeath
Temperley, Willie	Celtic	78/79	Alloa
Tierney, Lawrence	Hearts	78/79	Wigan
Toner, Willie	Kilmarnock	62/63–63/64	Ayr United
Torrance, Bobby	St Mirren	79/80–80/81	Partick Thistle
Vincent, Stan	Cowdenbeath	63/64–65/66	Falkirk
Ward, Joe	Aston Villa	79/80	Dundee United
Whiteford, Derek	—	64/65–66/67	Airdrie
Whyte, David	Leeds United	—	—
Whyte, Hugh	Hurlford	74/75–75/76	Dunfermline
Wilkinson, Ian	—	68/69–69/70	Raith Rovers
Wilson, Mike	—	75/76–76/77	Dundee
Wilson, Willie	Musselburgh Windsor	59/60–68/69	Berwick Rangers
Young, John	Loanhead Mayflower	58/59–61/62	Toronto
Younger, Tommy	Hutchison Vale	48/49–55/56	Liverpool

Hibernian FC Managers 1961–80

Hugh Shaw	1948–61	First Game: 31/1/1948 v Rangers (H) 1-0
		Last Game: 4/11/1961 v Aberdeen (H) 1-1
Walter Galbraith	1961–64	First Game: 16/12/1961 v Celtic (A) 3-4
		Last Game: 28/3/1964 v Aberdeen (H) 1-3 SC
Jock Stein	1964–65	First Game: 4/4/1964 v Airdrie (H) 2-1
		Last Game: 6/3/1965 v Rangers (H) 2-1 SC
Bob Shankly	1965–69	First Game: 10/3/1965 v Motherwell (H) 2-0
		Last Game: 3/9/69 v St Mirren (H) 2-0
Willie Macfarlane	1969–70	First Game: 27/9/69 v Hearts (A) 2-0
		Last Game: 5/12/70 v Airdrie (A) 0-2
Dave Ewing	1970–71	First Game: 9/12/1970 v Liverpool (H) 0-1 Fairs Cup
		Last Game: 24/4/1971 v Clyde (H) 5-1
Eddie Turnbull	1971–80	First Game: 31/7/71 v Middlesbrough (H) Friendly
		Last Game: 12/4/1980 v Celtic (N) 0-5 SC
Willie Ormond	1980	First Game: 16/4/1980 v Aberdeen (A) 1-1
		Last Game: 15/11/1980 v Hamilton (H) 3-3

Also published by Luath Press

We Are Hibernian: The Fans' Story
Andy MacVannan
ISBN 978 1906817 99 2 PBK £14.99

We are Hibernian explores the sights, sounds and memories of fans who have taken the 'journey' to watch the team that they love. Supporters from all walks of life bare their souls with humour, emotion and sincerity.

This book celebrates the story behind that unforgettable moment when Hibernian entered the childhood of its fans' lives and why, despite their different backgrounds, these loyal fans still support a sometimes unsupportable cause together.

Is it what happens on the field of play or the binding of tradition, memories and experience that makes Hibs fans follow their team through thick and thin? Featuring interviews with many different fans, this book takes you on a journey to discover why football is more than just a game and why Hibernian is woven into the DNA of each and every one of its supporters.

My family were Irish immigrants. My father had renounced his Catholicism but had retained a blind faith in Hibs.
Lord Martin O'Neill, politician

In the early 1950s Alan, Dougie and I caught the tail end of the legendary Hibs team when they were still the best team in the world.
Bruce Findlay, music business manager

Walking away from that cup final I said 'The club will survive now'.
Charlie Reid, musician

Everyone walked out that ground like they had just seen the second coming.
Irvine Welsh, writer

Stramash: Tackling Scotland's Towns and Teams
Daniel Gray
ISBN 978 1906817 66 4 PBK £9.99

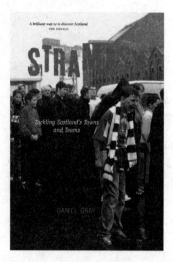

Fatigued by bloated big-time football and bored of samey big cities, Daniel Gray went in search of small town Scotland and its teams. Part travelogue, part history, and part mistakenly spilling ketchup on the face of a small child, Stramash takes an uplifting look at the country's nether regions.

Using the excuse of a match to visit places from Dumfries to Dingwall, *Stramash* accomplishes the feats of visiting Dumfries without mentioning Robert Burns, being positive about Cumbernauld and linking Elgin City to Lenin. It is ae fond look at Scotland as you've never seen it before.

There have been previous attempts by authors to explore the off-the-beaten paths of the Scottish football landscape, but Daniel Gray's volume is in another league. THE SCOTSMAN

A brilliant way to rediscover Scotland. THE HERALD

100 Favourite Scottish Football Poems
Edited by Alistair Findlay
978 1906307 03 5 PBK £7.99

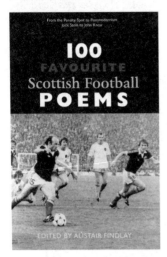

Poems to evoke the roar of the crowd. Poems to evoke the collective groans. Poems to capture the elation. Poems to capture the heartbreak. Poems by fans. Poems by critics. Poems about the highs and lows of Scottish football.

This collection captures the passion Scots feel about football, covering every aspect of the game, from World Cup heartbreak to one-on-ones with the goalie. Feel the thump of the tackle, the thrill of victory and the expectation of supporters. Become immersed in the emotion and personality of the game as these poems reflect human experience in its sheer diversity of feeling and being. The collection brings together popular culture with literature, fan with critic, and brings together subject matters as unlikely as the header and philosophy.

[this book] brings home the dramatic and emotional potential that's latent in the beautiful game. THE LIST

Luath Press Limited

committed to publishing well written books worth reading

LUATH PRESS takes its name from Robert Burns, whose little collie Luath (*Gael.*, swift or nimble) tripped up Jean Armour at a wedding and gave him the chance to speak to the woman who was to be his wife and the abiding love of his life. Burns called one of the 'Twa Dogs' Luath after Cuchullin's hunting dog in Ossian's *Fingal*. Luath Press was established in 1981 in the heart of Burns country, and is now based a few steps up the road from Burns' first lodgings on Edinburgh's Royal Mile. Luath offers you distinctive writing with a hint of unexpected pleasures.

Most bookshops in the UK, the US, Canada, Australia, New Zealand and parts of Europe, either carry our books in stock or can order them for you. To order direct from us, please send a £sterling cheque, postal order, international money order or your credit card details (number, address of cardholder and expiry date) to us at the address below. Please add post and packing as follows: UK – £1.00 per delivery address; overseas surface mail – £2.50 per delivery address; overseas airmail – £3.50 for the first book to each delivery address, plus £1.00 for each additional book by airmail to the same address. If your order is a gift, we will happily enclose your card or message at no extra charge.

Luath Press Limited
543/2 Castlehill
The Royal Mile
Edinburgh EH1 2ND
Scotland
Telephone: +44 (0)131 225 4326 (24 hours)
Fax: +44 (0)131 225 4324
email: sales@luath. co.uk
Website: www. luath.co.uk